Dance, Disability and Law

Dance, Disability and Law
InVisible Difference

Edited by Sarah Whatley, Charlotte Waelde, Shawn Harmon, Abbe Brown,
Karen Wood and Hetty Blades

intellect Bristol, UK / Chicago, USA

First published in the UK in 2018 by
Intellect, The Mill, Parnall Road, Fishponds, Bristol, BS16 3JG, UK

First published in the USA in 2018 by
Intellect, The University of Chicago Press, 1427 E. 60th Street,
Chicago, IL 60637, USA

A catalogue record for this book is available from the
British Library.

Copy-editor: MPS Technologies
Cover designer: Aleksandra Szumlas
Cover image: Pink Mist choreographed and performed
    by Claire Cunningham, photo © Eoin Carey.
Production manager: Matthew Floyd
Typesetting: Contentra Technologies

Print ISBN: 978-1-78320-868-5
ePDF ISBN: 978-1-78320-869-2
ePUB ISBN: 978-1-78320-870-8

Printed and bound by TJ International, UK

This is a peer-reviewed publication.

Contents

Blog Posts

Policy Briefs

Blog Posts from Resilience and Inclusion

Preface

Sita Popat

Dance, Disability and Law: InVisible Difference presents ground-breaking research in the field of disabled dance. It connects disciplines that are not often associated with each other, discussed by voices from across professional practice and academic study. It addresses real-world experiences and issues that are deeply rooted in cultural heritage, aesthetics, status, ownership and value. It probes beneath the surface in an area of dance that still has the tendency to attract admiring, uncritical smiles and enthusiastic cries of, 'Oh, aren't they wonderful!'

This edited volume emerged out of the InVisible Difference project, based at Coventry University's Centre for Dance Research and funded by the Arts and Humanities Research Council. The project explored how British society values dance made and performed by disabled dancers, and how those values translate into economic realities and cultural heritage preservation. Academics from dance and law joined forces with performers and choreographers to examine the particular challenges of professional work in disabled dance. The team produced important legal advice, briefings and guidance for dancers and choreographers, venue programmers and funders. As part of the innovative methodology, the project commissioned dance performances from disabled choreographers, whom the researchers followed through the process of creation, production and touring. These included Caroline Bowditch's beautiful, funny and poignant show, *Falling in Love with Frida*, which invited audiences to engage directly with disability in performance through its semi-biographical approach. *Falling in Love with Frida* was performed at Edinburgh Festival and numerous other small-scale venues, helping to develop greater comprehension and critical appreciation among audiences. At the time of writing, the research findings are being used to develop an online toolkit for disabled dance makers and the producers and programmers of their works, together with an accompanying documentary film.

The concerns of this book span the experiences of professional disabled dancers and choreographers, including reflections on personal identity, access to training and funding and cultural influence. The ways that society values disabled dance are considered through discussion of spectatorial processes and preferences, priorities in the preservation of cultural heritage and notions of aesthetics. Some chapters take the form of traditional academic essays, while other authors have chosen to write in different registers that reflect aspects of their artistic endeavours. Alongside these chapters are policy documents and briefings that illustrate how these concerns play out in practical, legal terms. Diverse in its disciplinary coverage whilst remaining tightly focused on the topic, this book is unique in its thorough investigation of a complex cultural issue. It is a rich, comprehensive and valuable resource that will influence the study and practice of disabled dance for years to come.

Introduction

Sarah Whatley, Charlotte Waelde, Shawn Harmon, Abbe Brown, Karen Wood, Kate Marsh and Mathilde Pavis

Although the arts have a long history and long-standing social significance, both the professional context and work-making processes of contemporary artists – and specifically dance artists – raise critical questions about the creative process, ownership and value of dance, which remain under-explored. When the dance is made by disabled artists, additional and often unappreciated factors complicate these questions; factors such as the social, political and legal positions of disabled persons, and the social and economic positions of disabled dance against the broader backdrop of our cultural heritage (and therapeutic interventions). These questions and factors provide the context for this book, which reflects some of the activities and outcomes of InVisible Difference: Dance, Disability and Law (InVisible Difference), an Arts and Humanities Research Council funded interdisciplinary project that ran from 2012 to 2016.[1]

At base, InVisible Difference sets out to extend thinking around the making, status, ownership and value of dance in the uncertain contemporary arts setting. It focused on dance made and performed by disabled dance artists because the unsettled performative characteristics of dance, the broad policy questions associated with disability and culture, and the general absence of serious legal analysis around dance offered a unique opportunity to apply multidisciplinary and interdisciplinary lenses to broad questions about social justice (such as the importance and utility to dance-makers of the international legal framework for the safeguarding of intangible cultural heritage and human rights), and to narrower but equally important questions about the social context of dance-making (such as the alignment of legal rules and entitlements to the reality of dance-making and the influence of different legal regimes to the lived experience of the disabled dancer).[2] At its root was a practical inquiry about whether the theoretical foundations of rights (and specifically copyright and the standards and rules it erects), and the evolving and often conflicting models of disability (e.g. the medical, the social and the affirmative models), actually serve to support the dancer and dance-maker, and more specifically the disabled dancer and dance-maker, thereby facilitating her in contributing to the cultural heritage of humanity according to her arts practice. If they do not, what other justifications, principles, models and evidence might do so?

InVisible Difference proceeded from the understanding that dancers with disabilities must overcome a variety of hurdles in order to enter and participate in mainstream professional performance practice. Some of those hurdles include:

- the ephemeral nature of the art form itself (which relies on process and often eschews fixation);

- the dominant aesthetic frameworks relied on to 'read' and 'value' dance (which typically impose a normative body and narrow sense of beauty and virtuosity frequently at odds with the diverse physicality of disabled persons);
- the dearth of robust theoretical or practical models for identifying authorship and ownership of dance's intellectual property (which means that there persists a keenly-felt but little-explored tension between the creative process and the socio-legal and economic frameworks applicable thereto); and
- the lingering of labels such as 'integrated' and 'inclusive' (which categorise disabled performers as 'other').

All of this means that disabled dancers remain relatively *invisible*, with the result that they may struggle to achieve both membership and leadership in the profession.

Given the above, InVisible Difference set out to explore how well legal mechanisms such as copyright – which protects the fixed form as opposed to the creative process – function in assigning ownership and supporting the exploitation structures necessary to develop the art form. Specific questions included:

1. What is the significance of the broad legal frames within which dance is made and preserved, and do they contribute to models of dance production that impose unhelpful or inappropriate hierarchical structures and power relationships on individuals? What are the intersections, overlaps and gaps between the relevant arts and legal perspectives, and does their operation lead to unrealistic expectations (about a range of matters, including ownership)? How do disabled dance artists participate in the construction of structures that support or determine ownership and authorship of dance?
2. How is, or should, dance be shaped by the human rights norms that notionally underpin the copyright framework, itself designed to ascribe rights in performance and thus a mechanism through which cultural expression can be preserved? How do other socially significant fields, such as medicine and healthcare, with which disabled individuals are so often associated, shape our approaches to the body, and so to dance made by disabled persons?
3. Can we conceive of new and different theoretical foundations for the protection, promotion and exploitation of dance, which respond to the diversity of dance practices and the interests of those who create and perform, including those with disabilities? In what ways are interdisciplinary investigations beneficial to scholarly thought, theory construction and to the people and communities and cultural policy-making within which the research is situated?

In considering these questions, we adopted an interdisciplinary approach that placed legal scholars from several substantive fields (intellectual property, human rights, medical law and bioethics) in conversation with both dance scholars and disability scholars, and with a range of dance practitioners, and other actors in the dance setting, the aim being to generate insights that would otherwise be beyond the reach of any single discipline acting on its own (and blinkered by its own frames, principles and processes of investigation). Within this approach, the legal scholars were not cast as the 'lead', soliciting responses from the others to generate insights into the law and to provide advice. Nor were the dance participants cast as the 'lead', developing specific works to which the rest would respond so as to assist in their development and production. Rather, the diverse partners were viewed as a ménage, a family with diverse experiences and perspectives but each of equal significance who worked together to think about questions in ways beyond the boundaries of their discipline. Adopting such an approach was considered vital because the reality of disability, and of disability in the arts, is a complex and fragmented one around which a lot of disciplines have something to contribute but none have the complete picture, and within which there are multiple pitfalls to achieving trust and participation.

Given the above approach, it was essential to craft a research strategy that encompassed a wide range of investigative and evidence-generating methods and discursive opportunities. Therefore, in addition to detailed disciplinary and comparative desk-top research, InVisible Difference relied on the following empirical activities:

- *Unstructured Engagement:* The project team spent many hours (and days and weeks) engaged in informal, unstructured and wide-ranging conversations with both the disabled dance artists formally connected with the project (e.g. Caroline Bowditch and Kate Marsh) and others more loosely associated with the project.
- *Micro-Ethnographies:* The project team undertook more formal ethnographic observations of these and other disabled dancers in the process of making dance and rehearsing pieces, both completed and in development, recording and then sharing and discussing the observations made.
- *Semi-Structured Interviews:* Multiple members of the project team undertook semi-structured qualitative interviews with eight disabled artists.[3] The interviews were, with consent, recorded. Transcripts were coded by a member of the project team and circulated for feedback, resulting in an iterative process that led to key themes and concepts being extracted from the text.
- *Observation and Text Analysis:* The project team attended works being performed publicly (some of which had been observed in development), and analysed the writing that documented and critiqued the pieces, and that circulated in academic and professional practice communities.
- *Knowledge Exchange:* The project team held a series of events so as to share performances in development by different artists, and to draw together artists, educators, researchers, lawyers, policy-makers, funders and industry representatives so they could together debate the issues that were emerging in the project. More specifically, the project team hosted: a research forum (Coventry, November 2013) to explore key issues and decision frameworks; a public research Symposium with invited speakers and artists (London, November 2014) to test evolving theses and propositions; and an open conference (Coventry, November 2015) to report on findings and solicit feedback on claims and solutions.

This multi-pronged approach led to the publication of scholarly articles, advisory papers and policy or consultation briefings (some of which we include here) that were aimed at assisting policy-makers and regulators to better understand: the contribution that artists make to our creative economy (the third largest economy in the UK); the importance of intellectual property ownership and exploitation to sustaining that economy; and the facilitating or debilitating role of different professional and legal regimes in ensuring the appropriate diversity of the creative sector. It of course also led to this book, which represents the culmination of InVisible Difference, but which should not be understood as an exhaustive summary of the research or its findings. Rather, it is a multidisciplinary conversation about a fluid setting that has not yet achieved the degree of social justice that our laws would seem to impose. We have invited contributions from other experts in the field of dance, disability and law to join this collection in order to expand the range of viewpoints and perspectives. Perhaps predictably, there is some disagreement amongst the authors, and in engaging with some questions further questions are raised. This is not a weakness but rather a reflection of its strength – it interweaves very different and sometimes productively contradictory viewpoints – performance and law – that have not before shared a space, so that they might jointly form a more holistic and coherent understanding of the challenges in disabled dance and the solutions that are both warranted and viable. Our hope is that it might encourage ongoing conversations amongst these previously estranged bedfellows so that real and enduring change can be realised.

Combined, the contributions address the legal frameworks that support, or fail to support, the work of disabled dancers, and they explore the factors that impact on the full participation and support of disabled dancers, including those related to policy, funding, artistic/professional critique and audience reception. Our own chapters reflect on our research, and draw attention to how the dancers work and the processes that shape their work. Our observations reach towards different theoretical and practical perceptions of creation, authorship, interpretation and being, and towards different perspectives on the role of law in relation to creative practice and lived experiences. We acknowledge that our own research has been situated within the United Kingdom but many of the themes we explore have wider relevance, and several contributions extend the discussion beyond a national context. The invited chapters also explore a range of theoretical frameworks to uncover what we can learn from practices or activities that have been similarly marginalised or viewed as 'other'; feminist theories, literature that focuses on the agency of the dancer, the nature of authorship, spectatorship and the individual and relational elements of creativity all feature. In each case, the invited authors have a deep interest in one or other of the topics of the book, and a curiosity with respect to the dialogue between the different themes. Our authors include established scholars and experienced practitioners, each of whom brings a particular perspective to the topic. A key aim for us was to ensure that dance practitioners represent themselves through their own writing, thereby contributing from their own direct experience to provide a counterbalance to the tendency to 'write about' the work of disabled dance artists.

The book is organised into three broad sections and explores developments up to the end of 2015, and in many cases more recent ones. The first section, 'Disability, Dance and Critical Frameworks', contains five chapters that provide the foundation or touchstones for the rest of the book; it sets out the dominant theoretical and legal frameworks relevant to (disabled) dance and the disabled dancer, and articulates how those frameworks might help or hinder the participation of disabled dance artists in mainstream performance practice. Chapter 1, 'Disabled Dance: Barriers to Proper Inclusion' by Shawn Harmon, Charlotte Waelde and Sarah Whatley introduces the challenging contemporary arts scene and offers a broad overview of the recognition of culture in different international legal regimes before looking at how realising rights within this framework is undermined by existing readings of disability and of dance. Chapter 2, 'Cultural Heritage and the Unseen Community', by Fiona Macmillan delves into the law and reality of cultural heritage in greater detail, demonstrating that law has not done a good job of mediating the relationship between cultural heritage communities and social, political and economic value. Chapter 3, 'An Analysis of Reporting and Monitoring in Relation to the United Nations Convention on the Rights of Persons with Disabilities, the Right to Participation in Cultural Life and Intellectual Property', by Catherine Easton builds on Chapter 1 by examining more closely state actions under the disability regime. Chapter 4, 'A Dance of Difference: The Tripartite Model of Disability and the Cultural Heritage of Dance', by David Bolt and Heidi Mapley offers a model of disability that is based on a distinction between 'ableism' and 'disablism'. Finally, Chapter 5, 'In a Different Light? Broadening the Bioethics Perspective through Dance', by Shawn Harmon highlights the marginalising impact of medical approaches to disability, which sees the non-normative body as 'broken', and the failure of bioethics to serve as an empowering field of practice for disabled people. It then suggests how disabled dance might be used instrumentally to change perspectives within the bioethics community, which is so influential on social characterisations of difference and disability.

The second and largest section of the book, 'Disability, Dance and the Demands of a New Aesthetic', explores some of the concepts and language that informs and occupies the broad cultural and narrower dance setting. This section provides a range of perspectives on performance practice, including the voices of performers, to offer alternatives to how we might speak about dance and disabled bodies and argue for a new aesthetic informed by the work of disabled dancers. In keeping with this section's encouragement to alter and expand the ways we view, read and understand dance, the first chapter, Chapter 6 by Luke Pell, 'A Wondering (in Three Parts)', offers a different kind of writing; it is a poetic narrative that invites the reader to experience the writing as a dance on the page. Chapter 7, 'A New Foundation: Physical Integrity, Disabled Dance and Cultural Heritage', by the InVisible Difference project team then revisits the marginalisation of disabled dance under current approaches to intangible cultural heritage. It offers an alternative organising or interpretive concept that better recognises the value and positive meanings of the non-normative body, namely that of 'integrity'; and the notion that one can achieve (physical) integrity in the absence of having an idealised body. This chapter reflects on our work with dancers with physical disabilities – 'physical integrity' is not proposed as a baseline for all disabilities (e.g. cognitive or sensory). Chapter 8, 'Disability and Dance: The Disabled Sublime or Joyful Encounters?', by Janice Richardson continues the exploration of the dance aesthetic drawing on two influential philosophers, Kant and Spinoza, and on a specific performance, *Heteronomous Male* (Turinsky 2012). This contribution demonstrates that disabled dance can be read outside the stereotypes, but that audiences need help to develop their literacy – in this way, building on both Chapters 1 and 7. Chapter 9, 'Moving Towards a New Aesthetic: Dance and Disability', by Shawn Harmon, Kate Marsh, Sarah Whatley and Karen Wood briefly highlights the current dominant dance aesthetic and its marginalising effect on disabled dance before discussing this in an interview with Dan Daw, a UK-based disabled dancer. Drawing on this conversation, it then offers a view on a new or expanded dance aesthetic. Chapter 10, 'What We Can Do with Choreography, and What Choreography Can Do with Us', by Nicola Conibere and Catherine Long also adopts a conversational format, this time exploring the potential of choreography (and the choreographer) to expand our aesthetic and social sensibilities. Chapter 11, 'Dancing Identity: The Journey from Freak to Hero and Beyond', by Eimir McGrath notes the contradictory roles of dance, and explores elements for an approach to viewing dance performances that might transform perceptions of disability. Chapter 12, 'Dance Disability and Aesthetics: A Changing Discourse', by Margaret Ames continues the exploration of a new and widened aesthetic, looking at performance in the context of cognitive disability.

The final section of the book, 'Disability, Dance and Audience Engagement', offers insights from 'inside' and 'outside' the dance to challenge the ways in which the work of disabled dance artists is received, described and celebrated (and in this way, builds on Chapter 1). It acknowledges that audience comprehension and appreciation of disabled dance is a factor in solidifying the precarious support for differently abled dance artists, and that the future of the practice is vulnerable without sufficient recognition of the work as contributing to our cultural heritage. Chapter 13, 'The (Disabled) Artist Is Present', by Claire Cunningham is an invitation by an experienced dancer to share her world and better understand her professional progression, and the qualities that she needs to hone to achieve her aesthetic aims in dance. Chapter 14, 'Disability, Disabled Dance Audiences and the Dilemma of Neuroaesthetic Approaches to Perception and Interpretation', by Bree Hadley explores in detail the phenomenon of spectatorship, suggesting that a neuroaesthetic approach has much to offer. The final chapter, 'Finding It When You Get There,' by Adam Benjamin reminds us that it is not only audiences that need improved education. Drawing on a 2014 workshop in Berlin, he explores how an embodied approach to learning can enrich our connection to the world and should serve to expand the perspective of dance education.

As will be seen, then, the content and presentational format within each section is varied, reflecting the subject matter, the diversity of the field and the situated position of the writer. To underscore the variety of approaches, the sections are marked by a number of 'interruptions' that introduce (revised) blog posts authored by the InVisible Difference team, and which link in some sense to the section themes. These short writings are offered as an alternative narrative, and they trace the development of some of the discussions that fed into and arose out of the project and the themes that inform the structure of the book. They also provide a timeline through the project, marking moments in the wider sociopolitical context. A full list of the blog posts written during the project can be found in Annex 1 in this collection.[4] The final three blog posts come from the project Resilience and Inclusion: Dancers as Agents of Change, which obtained AHRC funding to follow on from our work in InVisible Difference.[5] The intention behind including these in this collection is to indicate our ongoing work in this area, and the importance of recognising that the wider project to challenge discrimination and prejudice in the area of disability in performance is far from complete. There is much more work to be done to relieve the marginalisation and othering that people with disabilities continue to experience.

Further to the matter of linking between our projects, we have also included the text of three of the policy briefs that we compiled during the course of InVisible Difference. They are situated just before the last three Resilience and Inclusion blog posts. We wrote a number of policy briefs during the course of the project, each addressing a particular area identified during our research. A full list of the policy documents and consultation responses can be found in Annex 2, and via the InVisible Difference website. The three included in this book are: 'Policy Brief for Venues: Providing Space. Obligations and Approaches to Dancers with Different Bodies'; 'Position Brief for Dancers. Policy Brief: Asserting Copyright' (providing guidance on the legal requirements for copyright and ownership); 'Policy Brief: For Dancers' (providing guidance on the legal tools available under human rights and disability laws). We chose these three because they too have a strong link with the follow-on work carried out in Resilience and Inclusion and to policy and practical impact and engagement, which is a key goal of our work as a whole.

In summary, our primary aim and intention has been to introduce new themes that take the discussion forward in the field of dance, disability and law. This book does not and cannot cover all issues that will be of relevance to disability, to dance, to disabled dance or to the movement of the field to a more progressive or egalitarian footing. And neither does it intend to. A single collection, however diverse in its approaches and formats, could never cover so much ground in any satisfactory way. Some contributions come from a law perspective, others from dance and yet others from disability. We have contributions from single disciplines while others are interdisciplinary. We thus hope it will be of interest to a wide range of readers, including students, researchers, professional practitioners and the gatekeeper and critical friend communities across law, dance and disability. Some key matters can only be touched on, such as dance education and training, but in bringing together this multi-disciplinary collection we encourage readers to notice the frictions that we believe are productive and necessary when different experiences, expectations and theoretical frameworks collide. In so doing we believe the collection makes an important contribution not only to the dance field, but also to the fields of law, philosophical aesthetics, and disability studies, and to the emerging scholarship that considers spectatorship, or audience 'literacy', in performance.

Notes

1 Award No. AH/J006491/1. This project led to AHRC follow-on funding in the form of Resilience and Inclusion: Dancers as Agents of Change (Award No. AH/J006491/1).

2 We acknowledge the extensive and important work that already exists in relation to disability and dance, the social experience of disability and disability law, as well as to intellectual property law in the arts setting; and many chapters cite these books, chapters and other sources. However, this book is the first publication to focus on the mostly ignored and often misunderstood intersection between dance, disability and law in the quickly changing contemporary arts scene.

3 We acknowledge that this is not a lot of interviews for a qualitative research project, but it must be appreciated that the disabled dance community is a small one, and the range of other methods adopted for generating evidence and insights were viewed as sufficient to overcome any shortage in that generated by the interviews alone.

4 The full list of blog posts can also be found on the InVisible Difference website at http://www.invisibledifference.org.uk.

5 More on the project can be found at https://invisibledifferenceorguk.wordpress.com.

Section I

Disability, Dance and Critical Frameworks

Chapter 1

Disabled Dance: Barriers to Proper Inclusion within Our Cultural Milieu

Shawn Harmon, Charlotte Waelde and Sarah Whatley

Introduction

Culture has been described broadly as anything produced by humans, and not limited to tangible manifestations as exemplified by art, literature and architecture (UNESCO 1994). As we have demonstrated elsewhere (Harmon et al. 2014) dance is a part of our (or many) past and contemporary culture(s). Dance made and performed by 'differently abled' dancers, or dancers with disabilities,[1] makes both difference and diversity, and impairment and disability visible in a way that no other art-form does. (For purposes of this chapter, we use the term 'disabled dance'.) A dancer with disabilities consciously places her body on show. She encourages a response from an audience to a body that is different not only from the socially constructed norm, but also from the hegemonic body of the traditionally trained dancer. This is not only courageous,[2] it is necessary if we, as a society, wish to realise a more egalitarian, rights-based society that offers more than rhetorical support for the enjoyment of cultural and equality rights.

In this chapter, we consider both the evolving place of disabled dance in the contemporary UK arts scene, and the legal frameworks that would support inclusion within our cultural ecosystem (if they were better operationalised). First, we outline the research methodologies that support the InVisible Difference: Dance, Disability and Law project (InVisible Difference).[3] Second, we highlight the prevailing arts funding scene within which disabled dance is practiced. We argue that the failure of a critical group (i.e. gatekeepers) to positively engage with disabled dance throws power onto another arguably ancillary group: audiences. Thus, third, we consider audience comprehension and appreciation of disabled dance, drawing on empirical evidence generated by InVisible Difference. We argue that audience illiteracy threatens the recognition and future of disabled dance as a protected element of our 'cultural heritage'.[4] Fourth, we consider what the law, specifically human rights law, says about the recognition and support of disabled dance. Given the shortcomings that we expose, we conclude with some suggestions for legal and policy reform.

The InVisible Difference Project

As is noted in the introduction to this collection, InVisible Difference is an AHRC-funded empirical research project that seeks to extend thinking and alter practice around the making, status, ownership and value of work by contemporary dance choreographers and dancers, with an emphasis on the experience of 'differently abled' choreographers and dancers. InVisible Difference accepts that to critically interrogate complex social and ethical problems, it is most effective to do so at the intersection of disciplines and practices.[5] Thus, it explores questions at the nexus of dance, disability and law drawing on dance and law scholars and practitioners, with intellectual property, human rights and medical law all represented. Some of the questions being asked are:

- What is 'normal'?
- Is the disabled dancing body more exposed to public consumption than the non-disabled body, and what are the personal and professional repercussions of this?
- To what extent are the needs of the differently abled (dancer) met by different legal and regulatory frameworks?

In undertaking its work, InVisible Difference relies on multiple methodologies, including: (1) literature reviews from a range of disciplines; (2) content analysis of governing instruments and social media narratives generated in response to performances; (3) interactive workshops with a growing network of individuals who are interested in dance and disabled dance; (4) micro-ethnographies of differently abled dancers making dance in the studio and transitioning that dance to the stage; and (5) semi-structured qualitative interviews with dance artists.[6]

A Challenging Arts Scene

First, we acknowledge that support for Disability Arts *has* been growing, but that support has been and continues to be sporadic and uneven. Domestically, Scotland serves as a largely positive example (Patrick and Bowditch 2013). Beginning in 2004, the then Artistic Director of Scottish Dance Theatre, Janet Smith, embarked on a strategy to include disabled dancers in the work of that theatre. Around the same time the Scottish Arts Council (now Creative Scotland) employed an Equalities Officer who focused on arts and disability. Since then it has earmarked funds for disabled performers, created a 4-year post of Dance Agent for Change (Verrent 2010), and embedded equality into all programmes (Creative Scotland 2010-11). Scotland's leadership in this area was acknowledged in 2013 when the British Council undertook a mission to Scotland to learn more about its approaches to equality in the performing arts.

England, by contrast, serves more as a more cautionary example. Figures from the Arts Council England (ACE) show that, between 2003–04 and 2014–15, 131 awards were made to disabled dance applicants (i.e. to individuals, and to organisations with over 50% of employees identified as disabled) totalling £4,786,203. For specifics on the amounts awarded annually, see Figure 1.[7] Beyond ACE, in 2012, £3 million was made available under the Unlimited Programme,[8] a part of the Cultural Olympiad that accompanied the Paralympics 2012, with a second tranche of £1.5 million made available in 2013.[9]

Year	Number of Awards	Amount of Awards
2003–04	4	£17,878
2004–05	9	£160,364
2005–06	13	£557,044
2006–07	12	£472,737
2007–08	13	£422,215
2008–09	10	£252,958
2009–10	11	£319,620
2010–11	15	£593,203
2011–12	13	£312,268
2012–13	12	£1,123,777
2013–14	9	£313,565
2014–15	10	£240,574
Total	**131**	**£4,786,203**

Figure 1: ACE Funding of Disabled Dance.

In short, there exists a very mixed picture, which is underlined by the first UK country report under the Convention on the Rights of People with Disabilities (2006) (UK Government 2016). That report openly admits that disabled people are less likely to participate in cultural activities (UK Government 2016, para. 327), although it focuses heavily on culture consumption rather than culture-making.[10] This reflects the long-standing deficit in funding support for performance by differently abled people, who remain in a precarious position when it comes to producing and disseminating creative works. Such was acknowledged by Sir Peter Bazalgette, Director of ACE, in a December 2014 speech that he described as 'most important', and that was designed to reinforce the need to support greater diversity in the arts (Bazalgette 2014). In signalling a 'fundamental shift' in ACE's approach to diversity, Sir Bazalgette stipulated a need to recognise 'that there are substantial parts of society that are still largely invisible: disabled people […] for example' (Bazalgette 2014).[11]

This ambivalent situation is not helped by the fact that funding for the arts generally is under threat.[12] In its most recent Plan, ACE, a key gatekeeper, articulated a number of goals for the creative sector, one of which is to ensure that the arts are 'resilient and innovative' (ACE 2011a). One way to achieve that, it concludes, is through 'strengthening business models in the arts [and] helping arts organisations to diversify their income streams including through private giving' (ACE 2011a: 7).[13] Stakeholders are therefore strongly urged to diversify their dissemination and business strategies by diversifying (1) their approaches to creativity; (2) their workforce; (3) their audiences; and (4) their markets. Similar recommendations have been made in relation to dance specifically, which has been encouraged to take better advantage of commercial opportunities through better coordination and knowledge-sharing (ACE 2009a: 26).[14] Indeed, the dance pages of the ACE website state that it will:

> [...] support the development of entrepreneurial skills to ensure that companies, artists, and producers have a deeper sense of their markets and how to position themselves.
>
> (ACE n.d.)

The message from ACE is clear: artists (and art-forms) will only survive and thrive if they diversify, commercialise, and cultivate a greater sensitivity to the market.[15] One very practical consequence of this approach to culture creation is that other arts gatekeepers become critical to safeguarding the health, and securing the future, of specific art-forms.

The first are 'mediating institutions', which comprise a diverse collection of 'production organisations' (e.g. theatre and dance institutions), and 'memory repositories' (e.g. museums, galleries, libraries and archives). However, the attitudes and interest of these mediating insitutions are informed, in part, by audiences, which serve as another arguably ancillary gatekeeper. To truly benefit from the power that lies in the hands of these mediating institutions, which may reasonably be characterised as a pragmatic collection of sometimes competing institutions, artists will have to capture the imagination of audiences. This is doubly so in an arts setting that is explicitly commercialised and commodified. In such a setting, *consumer* likes will have a much greater role in dictating the success (if not the value) of an art-form. In such an environment, if audiences 'stay away in droves', the future is bleak regardless of the legal protections that might apply to the practice.

Recognising Quality in Disabled Dance

Audiences are more likely to be drawn to a practice if they have an understanding of, or a 'literacy' in, the practice, for this allows them to more effectively appreciate, assess and share it, all of which is important to the art-form's vitality (and indeed its commercial viability). As such, it is important to gather evidence relating to audience abilities to recognise and discuss the slippery idea of 'quality' (and the role of virtuosity) in disabled dance. In an effort to generate this evidence, InVisible Difference undertook investigations around lay and expert literacy, and practitioner experiences with lay and expert audiences.

We started by examining YouTube comment boards associated with video clips of differently abled dance artists attached to the project, and then expanded the sample using a snowball method. We ultimately viewed eighteen clips, with many of them visited on multiple occasions between July and November 2013.[16] We acknowledge that social media sites, including YouTube comments pages and other computer mediated communications, are not commonly associated with deep critical thinking, and that their structure imposes limitations on argumentation (Lange et al. 2008). However, the power of such online discussion forums for enhancing education and facilitating the exchange of ideas and the formation of identities is well known.[17] And this makes an examination of their content relevant and justifiable.

These data were supplemented by three discursive events. The first was a closed expert meeting (of the InVisible Difference Advisory Committee) in June 2013. The second was a by-invitation 'Intersections Forum' in November 2013. Both were attended by individuals from a range of disciplines, including those intimately connected with, or embedded in, dance. The third was an open Symposium held at Siobhan Davies Studios in London in November 2014. These resulted in detailed 'conversations' around the substantive questions posed by the project, which were then discussed collaboratively by the research team.[18]

Finally, micro-ethnographies or 'field observations' were undertaken at dance studios in Glasgow, Coventry, and Nottingham, by eight members of the project team working from a common observational template. Notes were shared within the team and the conversations and observations helped inform semi-structured interviews with three disabled dance choreographers/dancers. Indeed, each participant was interviewed multiple times, sometimes by two or more team members simultaneously, and sometimes by team members in succession. All interview notes were shared amongst the team and discussed collaboratively to identify themes, concepts and claims deserving of follow-up through other methodologies. We acknowledge the small sample size, but note that the UK-based 'disabled dance' community is very small, limiting the potential participant pool. Moreover, in resisting scientism (such as that represented by sample-size politics), Geertz teaches us that 'culture is context', and we must grasp it from the culture-creator's understandings (1973, 1980; in Shankman 1984). Geertz states:

> Believing, with Max Weber, that man is an animal suspended in webs of significance he himself has spun, I take culture to be those webs, and the analysis of it to be therefore not an experimental science in search of law but an interpretive one in search of meaning.
>
> (Geertz 1973: 5)

Our multi-pronged and multi-person collaborative approach permits a strong triangulation of evidence so that we can arrive at 'thick descriptions' and multiple-substantiated findings around the culture under review (Geertz 1973: 10).

Lay Literacy of Disabled Dance

Our lay literacy analysis relies heavily on a survey of YouTube comment boards associated with video clips, the aim being to uncover how people discuss disabled dance in public spaces. The videos exhibited wildly different levels of engagement, with some having zero comments, and others having many, most notably *The Best Dance Ever*, which had over 2.5 million views, and pages of comments. A holistic analysis of the comments, many of which were ambiguous and open to multiple interpretations, exposed five broad and overlapping typologies of responses:

1. gushing;
2. projecting/sympathising;
3. questioning;
4. resisting; and
5. critiquing.

The first and most populated typology is the 'Gushing Typology', which was dominated by representations about being inspired or amazed, and which resonates strongly with the image of the 'supercrip' discussed in Disability Studies. The following comments are representative:

> That's amazing that their [sic] continuing to dance despite their disabilities. Very inspirational :)

> Majestic display of the human spirit! Bravo!

> This is the most inspiring thing ever too me.

> You can never say I can't do it because these two incredible dancers dance while missing an arm or leg…..since they are determined to do their dreams then so can you!

These comments are ambiguous in that while they *might* refer to the dance itself, they more probably refer to the courage of the dancer for applying effort and achieving something (i.e. for managing to do *anything* in the face of their physical difference). In this way, they are almost certainly examples of the 'heroic' discourse from which disabled people (and dancers) generally wish to move away (Hardin and Hardin 2004). And the sentiment expressed seems closely allied to the observed reality of people too often purchasing tickets to see disabled dance to watch the disability rather than the dance (O'Smith 2005).

Not far removed from this typology is the 'Sympathising Typology', which is characterised by statements such as: 'I feel sad for them' and 'I feel bad but it was wonderful'. Again, this could be a response to multiple things, but the suggestion (if we discard the possibility that the second commentator was actually feeling unwell) is that they are regretful for the dancer's physiological and/or social situation, but impressed by what they have seen. However, their sympathy seems to overpower any critical view they might take about the dance itself. For example, in response to 'dislikes' clicks, one commentator said:

> OK … who are those 'dislikes'?!? but seriously WHO R THOSE 138 DISLIKES THATS JUST RUDE!!!!!

The suggestion here is that one could not possibly dislike the dance on its merits; because the dancers are disabled, it is rude to dislike it, an assumption supported by the commentator's neglect to engage with the dislikes on a critical level. In many ways this typology straddles the 'Gushing Typology' and the 'Questioning Typology'.

Symptomatic of the 'Questioning Typology' are the many comments to the effect that, 'I don't get it'. While it would be wrong to read too much into such bland responses, they could nonetheless be full of meaning and significance: they could be a reference to not understanding the narrative, or the overall aesthetic; they could be a questioning of the very presence of a disabled dancer; they could be the benign statements of individuals seeking further instruction. Alternatively, they could be grounded in an absence of language with which to evaluate or discuss the dance (i.e. ignorance). In any event, they seem most aligned with the 'baroque stare' theorised by Garland Thomson: 'Unconcerned with rationality, mastery, or coherence, baroque staring blatantly announces the states of being wonderstruck and confounded. It is gaping-mouthed, unapologetic staring' (2009: 50). This is a typology populated by those who could, potentially, be supporters of disabled dance if they had the observational and linguistic skills (i.e. literacy) to engage with it.

The fourth typology, and the one that generated the most interactive and visceral discussions, was the 'Resisting Typology', which contained an arc of comments ranging from the dismissive to the marginalising. With respect to the latter, comments with no apparent value other than to show disdain were relatively common:

Why crying? About people who don't realize they will never ever be great dancers? I have a problem accepting people who cannot accept their own facts. I find it macabre to display people with bodily issues in such ways. I can't help, but it feels like visiting a zoo …

F**k this s**t.

The man must save a lot of money on shoes. Half price I say!

This was really stupid. I admire their passion, but it isn't anything to get worked up about. I've seen retards dancing by themselves in public that inspired me more.

These comments disclose a lamentable level of compassion and solidarity, and they sparked corrective responses, some understated (e.g. comments like, 'classy') and others exorcised:

You don't know s**t about dance.

go rot in hell.

What the hell is wrong with you? These are people with hope, trust, beliefs and love! Dancing is all about those facts! You don't even know what you're talking about! Seriously, don't write shit like that.

Ultimately, the 'Resisting Typology' largely disregarded the dance in favour of a discriminatory discourse around the propriety of the dancers to claim to be 'dancers' at all, or to participate in dance.

The last typology is the 'Critiquing Typology', which was by far the least populated. Here, commentators offered an assessment of the aesthetic or mechanics of the dance and the feelings or imagery it evoked. While the assessments were presumably reasoned, they were equally likely to have been purely emoted, but they are generally considered to be a valid and defensible response to an art-form. Comments included 'sensual', 'luminous', 'intense', 'aesthetically beautiful', 'I could feel myself move …', 'so wonderful and looks so easy and full of light' and 'great performance, looks so sensual'. However, within this typology there was a strong normalising steam. Comments like this were not uncommon:

This is beautiful. I feel like she has both arms because she puts her all into each movement and it extends to the other arm as well even though it's not there.

This suggests that the dancer's energy creates an illusion of being 'whole', and that there is something essentially beautiful in 'wholeness'. If the body is impaired, then the dance needs to make up for that loss; there is a responsibility for the dance/dancer to provide an illusion of wholeness, which equates to normalness.

Ultimately, there were precious few comments that engaged with the dance itself (i.e. that intellectually or emotionally analysed the dance or explored the meaning of the dance as a story, or focused on the body as an expressive medium of communication in its own terms).[19] This is almost certainly contrary to what the dancers would have wished; unlike the baroque stare, it is widely accepted that dancers would prefer to create the 'engaged stare': a stare that draws the looker in and towards the object, drawing its intensity from a need to know or make sense, and which is often associated with some control on the part of the staree (Garland Thomson 2006). Here there was little evidence of the engaged stare; the dancers' impairments were central to most comments, positive or negative, and there was a strong narrative of 'overcoming' their disability rather than understanding and interpreting what they were trying to convey.

Critic Literacy of Disabled Dance

In our second line of investigation, we examined another representative of audiences, namely the critic, who holds a privileged place in relation to audiences and their development of audience literacy. Criticism (as undertaken by the critic) is:

[…] a gesture that carries the dance beyond its curtain time, extending it to readers near and far, present and future. Criticism transfigures dance into a much larger, discursive existence.

(Daly 2002: xv)

The role of the dance critic, and the natural or inevitable consequences of her observations, is to advance the careers of choreographers and dancers,[20] and to stimulate debate amongst, and develop, audiences.[21] But even critics can be challenged when looking for ways to talk about disabled dance.

Bowditch and Pell (2012) examined newspaper articles and online reviews of dance companies featuring disabled dancers from the early 1990s to 2011. We updated that review, looking at reviews from 2012 to 2015.[22] Bowditch and Pell note:

> Critics predominantly discussed the morphological differences between disabled dancers and their non-disabled peers (or indeed peers whose disabilities are less visible). With disabled dancers observed as specimens and alluded to as victims, medical model perceptions of disability were embedded throughout.
>
> (2012: 148)

In other words, there was an absence of focus on the dance: instead, and in parallel with the social media comments, attention was most often placed on the 'otherness' of the disabled body by comparison with the able bodied, with the 'Gushing' and 'Sympathising' Typologies most prevalent, together with an emphasis on the medical model of disability. Albright, who studied reviews of David Toole, a man with no legs who dances on his hands, concluded:

> Toole's abilities as a dancer are remarkable and are often the subject of extended discussions within reviews and preview articles about Candoco. Adjectives such as 'amazing', 'incredible', 'stupefying', are liberally sprinkled throughout descriptions of his dancing. This language of astonishment reflects both an evangelistic awakening (yes, a disabled man can swagger!) and traces of freak show voyeurism (see the amazing feats of the man with no legs!).
>
> (1997: 79)

This strain is further exemplified in de Marigny's observations of another Toole performance:

> David Toole is a man with no legs who possesses more grace and presence than most dancers can even dream of […]. Toole commands the stage with an athleticism that borders on the miraculous.
>
> (1993: 45)

Toole's dancing has also been subject to excoriating criticism, strongly reminiscent of the 'Resisting Typology':

> There is a horrific, Satyricon quality to Candoco that heaves up in the chest – nausea at the moral rudderlessness of a world where we would pay money to watch a man whose body terminates at his ribcage, moving about the stage on his hands.
>
> (Scott in Smith 2005: 80)

The responses of critic Arlene Croce, who characterised a range of dances as 'victim art' and 'undiscussable' are in a similar vein.[23] Similarly, in a critique of Candoco's *I Hastened through My Death Scene to Catch Your Last Act* (de Frutos 2000), the reviewer based his judgement of beauty on, and compared the dancers to, a classical aesthetic, characterising the disabled state as one of abject negativity.[24]

Thankfully, not all reviews follow this pattern. Mary Brennan, a Scottish art critic writing for, among others, the *Herald Scotland*, had this to say of a pre-premier performance of *Falling in Love with Frida* (2014) choreographed by Caroline Bowditch and performed by Bowditch, Welly O'Brien and Yvonne Strain in Glasgow in March 2014:

> *Falling in Love with Frida* is one to watch, savour and then reflect on at length. At first, the bold criss-crossing between movement, text, music and performative actions, registers like a massive crush on the Mexican painter Frida Kahlo (1907–1954). [...] But gradually what emerges, not least in a deliciously wry, humorously conversational – and disarmingly frank – monologue is a statement of Bowditch's own life experiences as a disabled woman, and an artist. There is, however, a profound and thought-provoking undercurrent to the mood of sensuality, sexual discoveries, and self-fulfilment and that is to do with how other people perceive, or remember us. What, if anything, is legacy? Frida never knew that 50 years after her death, Bowditch would lovingly celebrate her in a performance that is, in itself, full of memorable vitality.
>
> (Brennan 2014)

This review both celebrates the story on which the dance is based, and makes reference to, and questions, the notion at the heart of the work, namely that of legacy. While Bowditch's disability is mentioned, it is placed within the context of the work, and not used as the focus of the work or as a means to contrast her bodily differences with her co-performers.

The Brennan critique is therefore in line with the last and most constructive typology, the 'Critiquing Typology'. Similarly, Kelly Apter's 2012 review of Claire Cunningham's *Ménage à Trois* (2012), and Judith Mackrell's 2014 critique of Jérôme Bel's *The Show Must Go On* (2004), fall in this category, hint at a perceptible shift. Apter states:

> Cunningham's recent production, *Ménage à Trois*, in which she explored her relationship with her crutches, is one of the finest dance shows I've seen this year. Yes, it was thought-provoking and moving, for reasons inextricably linked with her disability. But above and beyond that, it was just a great piece of theatre, fusing choreography and video design in ways few others have managed.
>
> (Apter 2015)

In the Mackrell review, bodily difference is highlighted but not central. She states:

> In *The Show Must Go On*, which has been restaged for the disabled and able-bodied dancers of Candoco, plus additional guests, Bel creates that world from a playlist of

classic hits. The 21 performers line up to the Beatles' Come Together, and as they stare out at us, we look back at them: the slender, bearded man with his elegant tattoos; the one-legged woman on crutches; the delicate blonde using a wheelchair; the guy with the cosy beer belly. [...] For each performer, the choreography is a different physical challenge: for some, it's an obvious struggle, but their differences are swept aside in the collective uplift of emotion and association these deeply familiar songs inspire. Having seen this work before, I was unsure how it would move me a second time. But the chemistry of the Candoco cast and the unerring wit and humanity of Bel's direction are irresistible. When the stage darkens for John Lennon's Imagine and the audience gradually join in a soft, spontaneous singalong, it's one of the most potent moments of theatre I've known.

(Mackrell 2014)

These more recent reviews represent a step forward in response to the call for aesthetic criteria that can respond to dance by disabled dancers and serve the interests of those artists by speaking to the quality of the work (Smith 2005: 83). We would argue that a great deal more similarly informed critical engagement with disabled dance is needed to start building the audience literacy that might underwrite disabled dance's survival in the new arts environment and secure its position in our cultural heritage (Todd 2014).

Participant Experiences of Literacy

Finally, we inquired of our participant dancers both their objectives for their dances and their experiences of audience (lay and critic) understanding and appreciation. On the former, they reported thinking and re-thinking about what their work is about, and the relationship of their work to disability. One of them stated that while disability is present in her work, the work is not *about* disability. Rather, she aims to ask audiences: 'What do you see?' Another participant acknowledged performing to take control over how she is viewed by her audiences – reminding us of the 'engaged stare' (Garland Thomson 2009). In short, a lot of intellectual and emotional (as well as physical) labour goes into the production process and is, it is hoped, eventually acknowledged and appreciated by audiences.

With respect to the latter, audience literacy, our participants reported having thought about their interactions and relationships. There was a strongly held view that audiences have little or no frame of reference when watching dance by disabled dancers, and each of them had experienced reactions to their work that would fit into all five of our typologies, although, again, the 'Critiquing Typology' was under-represented. One participant stated, tongue in cheek, that if she set up a dance company she would call it 'Ain't They Marvellous', a reflection of the sometimes dominant audience reaction to her work, which is of the 'Gushing Typology'. Another described a rehearsal undertaken in a public gallery wherein she was twice interrupted by onlookers: first by an elderly lady who asked if she needed help; and second, by a woman who, without word, intervened to physically move her from her backward-bending dance position to an upright position. Both interventions might fall under the 'Questioning Typology' above. Our participants have also been subject to more visceral comments typical of the 'Resisting Typology', with one describing an audience member in Scotland who made a comment not dissimilar in tone to that contained in the Scott review of David Toole.

Focusing on critics, one participant suggested that times have changed with regard to the review of shows; whereas unmoved reviewers of disabled dance would simply ignore the work, they now more often write *something*, and *some* are beginning to focus on the work rather than the disability (as evidenced above). It may be notable that this performance took place in Scotland for our participants indicated that it is much more likely that a performance by a differently abled artist will be critiqued (and critiqued insightfully) in Scotland where there is a growing interest in a disabled dance ethic and aesthetic.[25] Reviews in England, by contrast, are rarer; an absence of critical interest founded on, it is postulated, the absence of investment as compared to the strategic investment provided under Creative Scotland's recent strategy.

Analysis of the Evidence = Misaligned Expectations and Understandings

The evidence comprises three distinct strands but tells a single and consistent story: there is a significant mismatch between the ways in which our participants think about themselves, their work and the place of disability in that work on the one hand, and their lived experiences in professional dance on the other. While they think deeply about movement, meanings, concepts, presentation, etc., espousing notions of variation, transformation, and equalisation, audiences and critics are much less likely to engage with these critical aspects of the art-form, focusing rather on binary concepts of bodily difference and deviations from the 'normal' dancing body. The dancers might like to control or at least profoundly shape the 'stare' to which they are subject, highlighting the fluidity and multiplicity of identity, the connectivity of people to their environment, technologies and others, and the ability of both dancer and audience to feel different and so become different from what they were before the shared encounter of the dance, but doing so requires building relationships with audiences, a process which has proved challenging.

Currently, as demonstrated by our YouTube and critic surveys, and our interviews, audiences do not have the language to discuss the work. They do not know, or understand, how to respond to dance by differently abled dancers, and this is at least in part due to the deeply entrenched idea of disability being an individual physiological condition (i.e. the medical model of disability), and of bodies characterised by difference or variation being a transgression from the 'norm'. These overpowering and largely negative ideas too often blind audiences to the deeper (although sometimes obvious) narratives meant to be conveyed, and to the quality of the movements that are on display. While critics *could* play an important role in tutoring audiences, they have found it difficult to find the language that moves us beyond the dominant discourses that underpin the disabled body and the traditionally understood dance aesthetic that marginalises that body. Fundamental to this shortcoming is the absence of an appreciation of the 'viewing strategies' facilitative of understanding and so better appreciating disabled dance.[26]

Arts practitioners and gatekeepers (mediating institutions and audiences) need to find ways to disarm the preconceptions and expectations that audiences currently bring to performances, encouraging a 'viewing position' wherein disability becomes ordinary; just another source of possibility within the performance. They need to provide audiences with the tools for informed criticism. Our participants are working towards this through 'visual activism' (Garland Thomson 2009: 193), which generally consists of three stages: look; think; and act. The 'look at me' and 'think about me' stages are designed to cause changes in the 'act' stage whereby the starer behaves differently, such as by viewing and building the world differently (Garland Thomson 2009: 193). Our participants occupy the 'look at me' stage, but collaborative actions are needed to help audiences (starers) move into the 'think about me' stage and the 'act stage', becoming catalysts for greater appreciation of disabled dance (and social change).

We will address this issue later, but now turn to the question of how the law might be used to redress the situation and support the development of audience literacy so that disabled dance can be better assured of its rightful place within our contemporary (and future) cultural heritage.

Legal Frameworks and Disabled Dance

The most promising potential avenue to address the above-noted cultural deficit is through the use of human rights. International human rights instruments support general rights to culture and cultural rights, as well as specific cultural rights in relation to disability. We have argued elsewhere that disabled dance falls within the definition of cultural heritage for the purposes of protection by these instruments (Harmon et al. 2014). The question remains: What substantive provisions within these instruments might support disabled dance generally and a programme of audience literacy in particular?

Cultural Rights and the Right to Culture in General Instruments

Cultural rights in general human rights instruments focus on respect for, and protection of, cultural diversity and integrity, and those rights are both broadly and narrowly based: broad in the sense of referring to general notions of cultural identity and diversity; narrow in the sense of prescribing specific culture-related rights (Eide 2001). The idea that culture is central to identity is a foundational tenet of the Universal Declaration of Human Rights 1948 (UDHR).[27] The International Covenant on Civil and Political Rights 1966 (ICCPR),[28] develops and concretises cultural rights by erecting the right to seek, receive and impart information and ideas in any media of choice,[29] and the right of minorities to enjoy culture.[30] Other cultural rights that add to the richness of framework include the right to enjoy the arts; conservation, development and diffusion of culture; freedom of assembly and association and the principle of non-discrimination. In articulating the important elements that contribute to the realisation of cultural rights it has been said that they are:

> A category of human rights that puts enhanced emphasis on moral rights, collective cultural identity, cultural integrity, cultural cooperation, cross cultural communications, and intercultural exchange.
>
> (Coombe 2009)

The right to culture is another important element of the human rights cultural framework. Articles 27.1 and 27.2 of the UDHR refer to the right of cultural participation and the right to protection of the products of culture, saying that everyone has:

- the right freely to participate in the cultural life of the community, to enjoy the arts and to share in scientific advancement and its benefits; and
- the right to the protection of the moral and material interests resulting from any scientific, literary or artistic production of which he is the author.[31]

This idea of the right to participate in culture and the right to enjoy cultural artefacts and practices is expanded on in the International Covenant on Economic, Social and Cultural Rights 1966 (ICESCR),[32] which stipulates that States must ensure that everyone has the right to: (a) take part in cultural life; (b) enjoy the benefits of scientific progress and its applications; and (c) benefit from the protection of the moral and material interests resulting from any scientific, literary or artistic production of which he is the author.[33]

Cultural Rights in Culture-Specific Instruments

Culture and cultural identity are also addressed in more culture-specific instruments, many of which emanate from UNESCO. They refer variously to 'culture', 'cultural heritage', 'cultural property' and the 'common heritage of mankind' (terms that are not necessarily interchangeable). While commentators have argued that it is challenging to capture the concept of intangible cultural heritage because it 'is not an object, nor a performance, nor a site; it may be embodied or given material form in any of these, but basically, it is an enactment of meanings embedded in collective memory' (Arizpe 2007: 362), two of UNESCO's most recent conventions focus squarely on the intangible elements of our cultural heritage.

The Convention for the Safeguarding of Intangible Cultural Heritage 2003 (2003 Convention)[34] defines 'intangible cultural heritage' as the practices, representations, expressions, knowledge, skills – as well as the instruments, objects, artefacts and cultural spaces associated therewith – that communities, groups and, in some cases, individuals recognise as part of their cultural heritage.[35] Article 2.1 goes on to state that this intangible cultural heritage is transmitted from generation to generation, is constantly recreated by communities and groups in response to their environment, their interaction with nature and their history, and provides them with a sense of identity and continuity, thus promoting respect for cultural diversity and human creativity.

More pertinent perhaps is the Convention on the Protection and Promotion of the Diversity of Cultural Expressions 2005 (2005 Convention).[36] Article 1 refers not to 'cultural heritage', but to the 'cultural heritage of humanity', which it seeks to protect by recognising cultural diversity expressed, augmented and transmitted through a variety of cultural expressions and modes of artistic creation, production, dissemination, distribution and enjoyment, whatever the means and technologies used. As with the 2003 Convention, the 2005 Convention contains a strong use of human rights language in reference to cultural values, and stress is laid on the importance of cultural identities.[37] However, and importantly, it also protects *current* artistic creativity and values, partly encompassed within definitions of cultural expressions,[38] cultural content[39] and cultural activities.[40]

Cultural Human Rights and Disability

It is not just UNESCO's cultural instruments that are relevant to the right to culture and cultural rights. Human rights instruments applicable to disability are also important. Developed via a participative and inclusive process, the UN Convention on the Rights of Persons with Disabilities 2006 (CRPD)[41] has been described as one of the most successful international treaty negotiations (Arbour 2006),[42] followed by one of the speediest ratifications.[43] More importantly, it was conceived of as 'an unprecedented opportunity for domestic law, policy reform, and genesis on behalf of the globe's "largest minority"' (Lord and Stein 2008: 451), with significant transformative potential.[44] The CRPD directs States to ensure that people with disabilities have access on equal terms to cultural materials and places of cultural performances and services.[45] It also requires States to ensure that persons with disabilities can take part on an equal basis in recreational, leisure and sporting activities, and have access to services provided by organisations in these areas.[46]

Nothing is said in the CRPD about participation in cultural performance.[47] While this *could* be problematic, two arguments suggest that such is not the case. First, analogies can be drawn with the reasoning of the Human Rights Committee in General Comment 21, where the Committee noted that there are three interrelated parts to the right to participate in cultural life; one of these is contribution to cultural life.[48] Contribution to cultural life 'refers to the right of everyone to be involved in creating the spiritual, material, intellectual and emotional expressions of the community' (CESCR 2009).[49] Given the reference to *participation* in the title of Article 30, CRPD, it can be argued that the Article is apt to cover the right to participate in cultural performance.

Second, the right to participation *for all* is embedded in the human rights framework.[50] For example, a non-binding Resolution in relation to the ICESCR and ICCP was adopted in 1993, which acknowledges the 'strong moral and political commitment of Governments to take action to attain equalisation of opportunities for persons with disabilities'.[51] It directs States to ensure that persons with disabilities can utilise their artistic potential for their own benefit and for the benefit of the community,[52] and that places and works of culture should be accessible to those with disabilities.[53] In 1994, the UN Committee on Economic, Social and Cultural Rights issued a General Comment on persons with disabilities that made reference to the 1993 Resolution.[54] It states that, although there is no specific reference to disability in the ICESCR, the position of persons with disabilities is within the human rights framework, and the position of persons with disabilities should be protected and promoted through general and specific instruments and actions.[55] It also stresses the right to full participation, stating that it should be made clear that persons with disabilities have equal rights to access cultural venues, and that communication barriers in particular should be eliminated.[56]

Analysis of the Legal Frameworks = Law is an Ineffective Cul-de-sac

The above demonstrates that the 'human rights framework'[57] is strong and directly applicable to the disabled dance context, giving differently abled performers rights to both participate in, and produce, culture. However, while the rights framework(s) place obligations on States to ensure that individuals can exercise and benefit from their rights, they are exceedingly difficult for individuals to enforce, either against the State or others who might erect barriers (Brown 2012).

One *might* argue that disabled dancers could claim preferential treatment in funding decisions through 'special measures'; a 2009 General Comment requires States to take a range of steps to facilitate participation in cultural life,[58] and indicates that States could adopt special measures to 'attenuate or suppress conditions which perpetuate discrimination' provided they are reasonable, objective and proportionate and, exceptionally, permanent.[59] The long-standing and persistent deficit in funding support for performance by disabled people continues to restrict opportunities, and could serve as grounds to trigger this provision. However, a difficulty arises from the fact that States enjoy a wide 'margin of appreciation'. Operation of this legal principle recognises the competing obligations and priorities which States bear, and ensures that States retain effective discretion within which to exercise their power and determine policy objectives.

All told, while an argument might be made for preferential treatment, it is unlikely to succeed. Thus, the more practical power of identifying, facilitating and safeguarding cultural practices that are deemed to be valuable falls to the gatekeepers we have identified above, but who are not all bound by the frameworks in the same way as States (which has resulted in the unequal reality that we've empirically demonstrated above). Given that the tantalising (legal) promise of inclusion and support has been largely unrealised, we must think more creatively and meaningfully about this question:

What does the CRPD right to take part in cultural life actually mean?

It is a question with which the UK Government failed to engage in its *Initial Report* to the monitoring committee under the CRPD.[60] Given that so little attention has been paid to it,[61] the opportunity exists to forge an understanding explicitly informed by the values contained in the CRPD. If such an approach were adopted by the key actors, the CRPD's norms could be encouraged to permeate society and inform the practices of States, mediating institutions, and practitioners.

Forging an Inclusive Arts Environment

It is our position that the operationalisation of the right to take part in cultural life will be improved by re-inventing the arts environment so that it is inclusive and welcoming. Only by doing this can we move away from 'negative social constructions' towards 'rights-aligned perspectives' such that disabled dance and its performers can *thrive*. Given that the State has largely failed in its obligations to respect, protect and fulfil its human rights duties in relation to the inclusion of those with disabilities in our cultural life,[62] we need to design multi-pronged (non-litigious[63]) strategies that achieve the aim of fashioning an inclusive arts environment within which disabled practitioners (and specifically dancers) can flourish.

Government Action

There is much that can be done by the State to lay firm foundation stones on which other stakeholders can build. Our empirical encounters have uncovered two persistent recommendations, one relating to inclusive schooling from the earliest age, and one relating to the independent living fund (ILF), which assists disabled people to live in their communities rather than in residential care.[64]

On the former, there is an extensive international legal and policy framework that supports inclusive education,[65] and there are a range of measures, mostly grounded in human rights norms, that would support and facilitate inclusive schooling from the earliest age and from which many success stories emerge (Black-Hawkins et al. 2007). While it is acknowledged that there is a long way to go in the education system before it could be regarded as truly inclusive (Rouse 2008), emerging research tends to suggest that inclusive education leads to more inclusive societies.[66] Young people who have had the privilege of an inclusive education system would be unlikely to find it as challenging as some of those responding to the YouTube videos to understand and to find the vocabulary to describe the dance.

On the ILF, there is grave concern. After the Court of Appeal ruled that the Government had failed to fulfil its duty to promote equality when it made the decision to shut the fund,[67] it was thought that the fund might survive. However, following a new equality impact assessment, the Government pressed ahead with closure which happened in 2015.[68] While the relevance of the ILF for its beneficiaries was much greater than participation in the arts, our evidence suggests that its demise will have a significant impact on the ability to participate in the cultural milieu. Our participant practitioners are uncertain of how, practically, they will be able to continue their work, and our Symposium participants constantly referred to those who were and will be excluded from participation in these events due to its withdrawal. Many dancers work on a project basis and so move from contract to contract, or are independent artists, leading their own projects and companies. Sustaining a career as an independent artist is only possible with Government support, which facilitates dancers with disabilities having an equal stake in the dance workforce through support for travel, fair access, etc. The reinstatement of the ILF would be one small step to supporting cultural participation.[69]

In addition to these policy changes, law reform might also be considered. First, both the Human Rights Act 1998 and the Equality Act 2010 could be amended to better reflect the CRPD and its retreat from the medical model of disability, which places the onus on individual bearers of difference. It has been argued that this would be the 'single most progressive change that could be made in UK human rights law' (Scottish Human rights Committee 2015: 6). Additionally, while much is said in the Equality Act 2010 about accessibility to certain places, and while discrimination on the grounds of disability is prohibited (in employment practices, for example), nothing is said about culture and the right to participate in culture. Though culture might be an elusive concept to concretise in legislation, an attempt would at least ensure that cultural rights are foregrounded (rather than 'Cinderella'ed') as policy-makers develop strategies.[70]

Scotland attempted to do just this with the introduction of the Culture (Scotland) Bill 2006, which contained a provision for 'local cultural entitlements'.[71] This would have required local authorities to consult with the public on the types of cultural activities or services wanted within the area, which the local authority would then seek to make available. Many of those who responded to the consultation, while generally finding the idea of cultural entitlements an interesting idea, opined that such a policy would be impossible to implement without significant additional funding.[72] Ultimately, the Bill was not passed into law.[73]

Gatekeeper Action: Funders

Funders could adopt measures to nurture not only the art-form but also its comprehension and appreciation. In a context where, despite its role being unclear (Helfer and Austin 2011), the market is being advocated as a pillar for the development of artistic work (ACE 2011), funders should facilitate fair market responses by addressing directly the audience literacy 'problem'. If receptiveness is to be nurtured (as stipulated by the CRPD) and performers are to be given the chance to succeed, then a programme for audience (including critic) literacy is necessary. Audiences are important communities who could facilitate greater visibility for disabled dance and its acceptance, thereby fostering the potential to reach *wider* audiences. One can see the reinforcing cycle that this creates, embedding disabled dance ever deeper in our culture, and so achieving a true social transformation in respect of dance made and performed by people with disabilities.

There are already a number of innovative research projects that seek to understand audience engagement with dance. Watching Dance: Kinesthetic Empathy,[74] an AHRC-funded project that concluded in 2011, used audience-targeted research and neuroscience to explore how spectators respond to and identify with dance. Culturehive,[75] supported by the National Lottery and ACE, provides a resource to discover and share best practice in cultural marketing, publishing a report on audiences for contemporary dance in 2010. Respond,[76] funded by Nesta, ACE and the AHRC, uses digital technologies to enable audiences and enthusiasts to 'have their say' as two dance artists make new work. Audiences have been identified by Nesta as a stakeholder group that should be investigated using public research and development funding, arguing that the trialling of new uses of technologies can help organisations to engage with audiences in new ways.[77] The example cited in the report involves the use of an app to sell unsold tickets for classical music events.

We can find no publicly funded project that specifically addresses audiences for dance made and performed by differently abled dancers. If funder gatekeepers, who receive their budgets at least in part from the State, are to take their responsibilities under Article 30, CRPD, seriously, they should rectify this lacuna.[78]

Gatekeeper Action: Repositories

It is not just funders who could respond proactively. A frustration consistently expressed by participants at our November 2014 Symposium was that the same questions and issues within the area of disability dance have been raised for the last 10+ years. These concern matters of quality, of virtuosity, of difference and of otherness. How can matters be moved on? One suggestion, and one that we have raised elsewhere (Harmon et al. 2014), is that this is in part due to disabled dance being almost entirely absent from our memory Institutions. While there are some examples of engagement, they are lamentably few, and records appear to be woefully incomplete. For example, while the Victoria and Albert Museum has some records of a very small number of dancers with disabilities at various times in history, these dancers are rarely named and tend to be referred to by their disability (e.g. 'the dancer with one hand').[79] This particular shortcoming is likely part of a wider phenomenon in UK heritage circles in which museums are seeking ways to think about and to include intangible cultural heritage within our heritage,[80] but that reality makes it more, rather than less, pressing to develop the mechanisms necessary to instigate inclusiveness and visibility. A proactive programme to incorporate the best examples of disabled dance within our national repositories so that they are available for ensuing generations to enjoy and to re-work would ensure that disabled dance and the issues associated with it are not forgotten.

Ancillary Gatekeeper Action: Participants

Despite (or because of) all of the challenges, participants within the disabled dance sector are determined that they and their art-form will be seen. While, as noted above, concerns abound about the persistence of issues around exclusion within the dance sector, some of our participants believed that we (finally) could (really) be at a 'tipping point': a point at which it *may* be possible to say that the differently abled dancer does not need to aspire to the same aesthetic as the non-disabled dancer, and that the disabled dancer can work with the non-disabled dancer without being universally seen as lacking, or as 'less than'. This is in large part attributable to those engaged in the practice, whom must be characterised as activists.

Indeed, there were some excellent performances of in-development dance works at InVisible Difference's November 2014 Symposium: Dan Daw performed *Beast* (2015); Welly O'Brien and Kate Marsh performed *Famuli* (2015); and Kimberley Harvey, Robert Hesp, and Kitty Fedorec performed *Moments Revisited* (2014). These were powerful, playful and joyous respectively, and were described by the audience as 'rare', 'humorous', 'mesmerising', 'thought-provoking' and 'passionate'. Set within the context of the Symposium, each work furthered the debate about the poetics of disability in dance without being illustrative of a specific aesthetic, and each work dealt quite differently with the relationship between performer and audience. Daw's solo work presented a 'nearly naked' body that drew on his involuntary spasms and the conventions of the framing of performance to question the audience's tendency to stare at difference. Marsh and O'Brien confronted gaze through a mannered, gestural essay on self-consciousness, whilst Harvey's triadic exploration invited us to notice how differently abled dancers approach space, time and gesture from a unique sense of embodiment.

Together the dancers demonstrated that their own experience of disability is a rich source for their choreography, and whilst not overtly political, their individual and collective offerings show that their work should be taken seriously through 'intelligent critique'. While this Symposium was open (and so the 'audience' came from a range of backgrounds), it was the case that, almost without exception, participants had prior experience of disabled dance. If the art-form is to thrive, audiences with diverse backgrounds must understand how to engage in this 'intelligent critique', and so we revert to our recommendation under Funders above. Another avenue of action is for practitioners to think about the setting in which their work is shown, for setting can help highlight the difference between a 'community event' and a work of art that an audience will pay to see.

Conclusions

The broad disability setting demonstrates that we still struggle to understand and to give meaning to human rights. We remain unaware of, and/or insensitive to, different ways of being, particularly those ways exemplified by vulnerable groups (i.e. people made vulnerable by how individuals, architectures, policies and law impact disproportionately on them), who are, ironically, the very people that rights frameworks are meant to assist most directly or immediately. The rights frameworks relating to cultural heritage and disability combine to impose on States the obligation to give these rights practical effect through the formulation of programmes and the provision of mechanisms opening up participation in, and creation of, culture. While these rights may be enforceable against the State, however, it would be naïve to think that they erect funding entitlements in individuals: programmes and mechanisms in pursuit of these rights will always need to be balanced alongside other pressing obligations. In short, despite these frameworks, the law will not always be the most profitable/effective course of action.

Other relevant stakeholders include gatekeepers like funders, mediating institutions, and audiences. In resource-limited contexts such as the present, artists will have to heed the instruction of funders to diversify and commercialise their activities. Of course, the commercial success of disabled dance, like any art-form, will depend on public responses to it. Our research suggests that publics have low levels of understanding both in relation to disability generally and disabled dance more specifically. Combined, this has resulted in very low levels of critical literacy, such that disabled dance is still measured against an inappropriate aesthetic using unhelpful language. This lack of capacity to discuss disabled dance intelligently hampers the formation (and appreciation) of an aesthetic appropriate to disabled dance (i.e. a more diverse and sometimes challenging aesthetic that does not rely on the balletic form and motion).

Building an appreciation of disabled dance through the development of a critical literacy is therefore of the utmost importance to the future of the art-form. Developing this critical literacy will enable audiences to move away from the first four response typologies that our research uncovered (e.g. the gushing, projecting/sympathising, questioning and resisting typologies) and towards the more positive and desirable Critiquing Typology. In short, enhanced critical literacy will facilitate meaningful and informed discussions over what is good versus what is mediocre (disabled) dance, a development that differently abled dancers crave and deserve. This, in turn, will help push production organisations (e.g. theatres and repertory dance companies) to make space for disabled dancers and productions of disabled dance, and memory institutions (e.g. museums and galleries) better able and more willing to vet and curate records of disabled dance performances.

The UK and similarly situated jurisdictions need to show moral and practical leadership. While this might mean amending domestic laws as we have articulated, it more practically demands that policy-makers take an appropriate (and expected) lead in *operationalising* human rights. This can be done at the policy and programme level, and we have offered a number of recommendations that would move the United Kingdom in the right (just) direction.

References

Aboelala, S., Larson, E., Bakken, S., Carrasquillo, Olveen, Formicola, A. Glied, S., Haas, J. and Gebbie, K. (2007), 'Defining interdisciplinary research: Conclusions from a critical review of the literature', *Health Services Research*, 42, pp. 329–46.

Albright, A. C. (1997), *Choreographing Difference: The Body and Identity in Contemporary Dance*, Hanover: Wesleyan University Press.

Apter, K. (2012), 'How much have attitudes towards disability really changed?', *The Scotsman*, 10 October.

Arbour, L. (2006), *UN High Commissioner for Human Rights, General Assembly Ad Hoc Committee, 8th Session*, New York, 5 December.

Arizpe, L. (2007), 'The cultural politics of intangible cultural heritage', *Art Equity and Law*, 12, pp. 361–82.

Arts Council England (ACE) (n.d.), http://www.artscouncil.org.uk/what-we-do/supporting-artforms/dance/. Accessed 6 May 2016.

—— (2009a), *Joining up the Dots: Dance Agencies – Thoughts on Future Direction*, London: ACE.

—— (2009b), *Dance Mapping: A Window on Dance 2004–2008*, London: ACE.

—— (2011a), *Arts Council Plan 2011–2015*, London: ACE.

—— (2011b), *The Role of Diversity in Building Adaptive Resilience*, London: ACE.

Bazalgette, P. (2014), 'Arts council and the creative case for diversity', http://www.artscouncil.org.uk/media/uploads/Sir-Peter-Bazalgette_Creative-Case-speech_8-Dec-2014.pdf. Accessed 6 May 2016.

Beckett, A. (2009), "Challenging disabling attitudes, building an inclusive society": Considering the role of education in encouraging non-disabled children to develop positive attitudes towards disabled people', *British Journal of Sociology of Education*, 30:3, pp. 317–29.

Bel, J. (2004), *The Show Must Go On*, Kaaitheater, Brussels, premiere 14 October.

Black-Hawkins, K., Florian, L. and Rouse, M. (2007), *Achievement and Inclusion in Schools*, London: Routledge.

Bowditch, C. (2014), *Falling in Love with Frida*, Dance 4, Nottingham, premiere 29 May.

Bowditch. C. and Pell, L. (2012), 'Below the waterline', in L. Keidan and C. J. Mitchell (eds), *Access All Areas: Live Art and Disability*, London: Live Art Development Agency, pp. 148–51.

Boyd, K. (2001), 'Disability', *Journal of Medical Ethics*, 27:6, pp. 361–62.

Brennan, M. (2014), 'Review of *Falling in Love with Frida*', *Herald Scotland*, 10 March.

Briggs, H., Kolb, A. and Miyahara, M. (2012), 'Able as anything: Integrated dance performance in New Zealand', *Brolga 37*, http://ausdance.org.au/articles/details/able-as-anything-integrated-dance-in-new-zealand. Accessed 6 May 2016.

Brown, A. (2012), *Intellectual Property, Human Rights and Competition: Access to Essential Innovation and Technology*, Cheltenham: Edward Elgar.

Brown, A. and Waelde, C. (2014), 'Human rights, persons with disabilities and copyright', in C. Geiger (ed.), *Research Handbook on Human Rights and Intellectual Property*, Cheltenham: Edward Elgar, pp. 577–602.

Burri, M. (2013), 'The UNESCO convention on cultural diversity: An appraisal five years after its entry into force', NCCR trade regulation working paper no. 2013/1, http://papers.ssrn.com/sol3/papers.cfm?abstract_id=2223922. Accessed 6 May 2016.

Cameron, C. (2014), 'Developing an affirmative model of disability and impairment', in J. Swain (ed.), *Disabling Barriers – Enabling Environments*, 3rd ed., London: Sage, pp. 24–30.

Canguilhem, G. (1990), *On the Normal and the Pathological*, Holland; USA and UK: D. Reidel.

Cantor, J. (2008), 'Defining disabled: Exporting the ADA to Europe and the social model of disability', *Connecticut Journal of International Law*, 24, pp. 399–434.

Chan, P. (2013), 'The role of the contemporary critic', *Huffpost Arts and Culture*, http://www.huffingtonpost.com/phil-chan/the-role-of-the-contempor_b_2610965.html. Accessed 6 May 2016.

Coombe, R. (2009), 'The expanding purview of cultural properties and their politics', *Annual Review of Law and Social Science*, 5, pp. 393–412.

Creative Scotland (2010–11), *Annual Report and Financial Statements 2010–1*, Edinburgh: Creative Scotland.

Cunningham, C. (2012), *Menage a Trois*, Tramway, Glasgow, premiere 24 August.

Daly, A. (2002), *Critical Gestures: Writings on Dance and Culture*, Hanover: Wesleyan University Press.

Davis, L. (1995), *Enforcing Normalcy: Disability, Deafness and the Body*, London and New York: Verso.

Daw, D. (2015), *Beast*, The Borough Hall, London, premiere 6 November.

de Marigny, C. (1993), 'A little world of its own', *Ballet International*, 16, p. 45.

Eide, A. (2001), 'Cultural rights as individual human rights', in A. Eide, C. Krause and A. Rosas (eds), *Economic, Social and Cultural Rights*, 2nd ed., Netherlands: M. Nijhoff Publishers.

de Frutos, J. (2000), *I Hastened through My Death Scene to Catch Your Last Act*, Candoco.

Garland Thomson, R. (1997), 'Feminist theory, the body and the disabled figure', in L. Davis (ed.), *The Disabilities Studies Reader*, New York and London: Routledge. pp. 279–306.

—— (2006), 'Ways of staring', *Journal of Visual Culture*, 5:2, pp. 173–92.

—— (2009), *Staring: How We Look*, Oxford: Oxford University Press.

Geertz, C. (1973), *The Interpretation of Cultures*, New York: Basic Books.

—— (1980), 'Blurred genres: The refiguration of social thought', *The American Scholar*, 49:2, pp. 165–79.

Guernsey, K., Nicoli, M. and Ninio, A. (2007), *Convention on the Rights of Persons with Disabilities: Its Implementation and Relevance for the World Bank*, SP discussion paper 0712, http://siteresources.worldbank.org/SOCIALPROTECTION/Resources/SP-Discussion-papers/Disability-DP/0712.pdf. Accessed 6 May 2016.

Hardin, M. and Hardin, B. (2004), 'The "Supercrip" in sport media: Wheelchair athletes discuss hegemony's disabled hero', *Sociology of Sport Online*, 7:1, pp. 1–16.

Harmon, S., Donaldson, H., Brown, A., Marsh, K., Pavis, M., Waelde, C., Whatley, S. and Wood, K. (2015), 'Disability and the Dancing Body: A Symposium on Ownership, Identity and Difference in Dance', *SCRIPT-ed*, 21:1, pp. 59–69.

Harmon, S., Waelde, C. and Whatley, S. (2014), 'Disabled dance: Grounding the practice in the law of "Cultural Heritage"', *Web Journal Current Legal Issues*, 20:3, p. 370.

Harvey, K. (2014), *Moments Revisited*, New Diorama Theatre, London, premiere 16 November.

Helfer, L. and Austin, G. (2011), *Human Rights and Intellectual Property: Mapping the Global Interface*, Cambridge: Cambridge University Press.

Howard, P. and Parks, M. (2012), 'Social media and political change: Capacity, constraint, and consequence', *Journal of Communication*, 62:2, pp. 359–62.

Jays, D. (2015), 'No pity party: Moving beyond victim art', *The Guardian*, 8 January.

Kietzmann, J., Hermkenslan, K., McCarthy, P., Silvestre, B. (2011), 'Social media? Get serious! Understanding the functional building blocks of social media', *Business Horizons*, 54:3 pp. 241–21.

Lange, C., Bojars, U., Groza, T., Breslin, J. and Handschuh, S. (2008), 'Expressing argumentative discussions in social media sites', in A. P., Sheth, S., Staab, M., Paolucci, D., Maynard, T. Finin and K. Thirunarayan (eds), *The Semantic Web – ISWC 2008*, Berlin: Springer-Verlag Berlin Heidelberg.

Lord, J. and Stein, M. (2008), 'The domestic incorporation of human rights law and the United Nations Convention on the rights of persons with disabilities', *Washington Law Review*, 83, pp. 449–79.

Macaulay, A. (1996), '"Victim Art" put through its paces', *Financial Times*, 24 June.

Mackrell, J. (2015), 'The show must go on review – Jérôme Bel conjures stage magic with Candoco', *The Guardian*, 23 March, http://www.theguardian.com/stage/2015/mar/23/candoco-jerome-bell-the-show-must-go-on-review. Accessed 15 April 2016.

Marsh, K. and O'Brien, W. (2015), *Famuli*, Southbank Centre, London, premiere 16 March.

Martin, J. (1967), *Reflections of John Joseph Martin*, Los Angeles: University of California.

Nelson, J. (2000), 'The media role in building the disability community', *Journal of Mass Media Ethics*, 15:3, pp. 180–93.

Pak, C. (2006), 'Multidisciplinarity, interdisciplinarity and transdisciplinarity in health research, services, education and policy: Definitions, objectives, and evidence of effectiveness', *Clinical & Investigative Medicine*, 29:6, pp. 351–64.

Patrick, H. and Bowditch, C. (2013), 'Developing professional equality: An analysis of a social movement in the Scottish dance industry', *Scottish Journal of Performance*, 1:1, pp. 75–97.

Plomer, A. (2013), 'The human rights paradox: Intellectual property rights and rights of access to science', *Human Rights Quarterly*, 35:1, pp. 124–75.

Quinlan, M. and Bates, B. (2008), 'Dances and discourses of (dis)ability: Heather Mills' embodiment of disability on *Dancing with the Stars*', *Text & Performance Quarterly*, 28:1–2, pp. 64–80.

Rouse, M. (2008), 'Developing inclusive practice: A role for teachers and teacher education?', *Education in the North*, 16:1, pp. 6–13.

Saadé, R. and Huang, Q. (2009), 'Meaningful learning in discussion forums: Towards discourse analysis', *Issues Informing Science & IT*, 6:1, pp. 87–98.

Samaha, A. (2007), 'What good is the social model of disability?', *University of Chicago Law Review*, 74, pp. 1251–308.

Scottish Human Rights Committee (2015), *Human Rights for All – Forwards or Back?*, Edinburgh: SHRC.

Sganga, A. (2015), 'Right to culture and copyright: Participation and access', in C. Geiger (ed.), *Research Handbook on Human Rights and Intellectual Property*, Cheltenham and Nottingham: Edward Elgar, pp. 560–76.

Shankman, P. (1984), 'The thick and the thin: On the interpretive theoretical program of Clifford Geertz', *Current Anthropology*, 25, pp. 261–80.

Shaver, L. and Sganga, C. (2009), 'The right to take part in cultural life: Copyright and human rights', *Faculty Scholarship Series*, 23, http://digitalcommons.law.yale.edu/fss_papers/23. Accessed 6 May 2016.

Silva, C. and Howe, P. (2012), 'The (in)validity of supercrip representation of Paralympian athletes', *Journal of Sport & Social Issues*, 36:2, pp. 174–94.

Smith, A. (1776), *The Wealth of the Nations*, vol. 1, London: Methuen & Co.

Smith, L. and Waterton, E. (2009), '"The envy of the world" intangible heritage in England', in L. Smith and N. Akagawa (eds), *Intangible Heritage*, Abingdon: Routledge, pp. 289–91.

Smith, O. (2005), 'Shifting Apollo's frame – Challenging the body aesthetic in theater dance', in C. Sandahl and P. Auslander (eds), *Bodies in Commotion: Disability and Performance*, Michigan: University of Michigan Press, pp. 73–85.

Swain, J. and French, S. (2000), 'Towards an affirmation model', *Disability & Society*, 15:4, pp. 569–82.

Tay, M. (2000), 'In the company of able(d) dancers', *The Flying Inkpot Theatre Reviews*, 2 October, http://www.inkpot.com/theatre/00reviews/00revcanddanccomp.html. Accessed 6 May 2016.

Todd, A. (2014), 'Critical engagement please!', *Arts Professional*, 24 April, http://www.artsprofessional.co.uk/magazine/273/article/critical-engagement-please. Accessed 6 May 2016.

UK Government (2012), *UK Initial Report on the UN Convention on the Rights of Persons with Disabilities*, CRPD/C/GBR/1.

UNESCO (1994), *Report on the Expert Meeting on Routes as a Part of our Cultural Heritage*, WHC-94/CONF.003/INF.1.

Verrent, J. (2010), *Dance Agent for Change – Impact Report*, http://issuu.com/scottishdancetheatre/docs/dance_agent_for_change_impact_report?e=1806484/4041706. Accessed 6 May 2016.

Whatley, S. (2007), 'Dance and disability: The dancer, the viewer and the presumption of difference', *Research in Dance Education*, 8, pp. 5–25.

Notes

1 There are (contested) differences between 'impairment', 'disability' and 'differently-abled'. 'Impairment' refers to physiological conditions, which cause one's physical, sensory,

cognitive or emotional capabilities to stray from that which is classed as 'normal'. 'Disability' is manufactured by the combination of physiological variation and social forces and architectures, which cause that variation to have some belittling, limiting or foreclosing consequences; it emerges from the complex interrelationship between the physiological and the social. 'Differently-abled', originating from the affirmative model of disability, refers to a more positive construction of variation, and an affirmation of new ways of being situated in society. For more, see Canguilhem (1990), Davis (1995), Garland Thomson (1997), Boyd (2001), Samaha (2007) and Cameron (2014).

2 We do not wish to perpetuate the narratives of courage that often get assigned to disabled people who break into previously inaccessible fields. Rather, we simply acknowledge that it often takes individual fortitude, and exacts a personal price, to render explicit difference, and to challenge shared notions or norms.

3 See http://www.invisibledifference.org.uk/. Accessed 7 May 2016.

4 Given the funding environment, disabled dance will become increasingly dependent on how it is received by audiences, which, in turn, depends on venues programming disabled dance performances. On the 'chicken-and-egg' issue of which must come first, popularity or programming, see L. Gardner (2014), 'Learning disabled theatre: Where is the UK's answer to back to back?', *The Guardian*, 17 October, http://www.theguardian.com/stage/theatreblog/2014/oct/17/learning-disabled-theatre-creative-minds-diverse-futures?commentpage=1. Accessed 6 May 2016.

5 See Pak (2006); Aboelala (2007).

6 For more on its findings and outputs, see http://www.invisibledifference.org.uk/research/overview/. Accessed 6 May 2016.

7 Figures obtained under a Freedom of Information request and supplied on 19 January 2015. In terms of total spend, and as an example, in 2014–15 ACE invested £851.8 million of Grant-in-aid and Lottery funding.

8 http://www.paralympic.org/news/london-2012-launches-programme-celebrating-arts-people-disability. Accessed 6 May 2016.

9 http://weareunlimited.org.uk/ready-steady-launch/. Accessed 6 May 2016. Funding came from London 2012, ACE, Creative Scotland, the Arts Councils of Wales and Northern Ireland and the British Council.

10 Though, it does mention ACE funding for promotion and participation in the arts by disabled people, the support of the Big Lottery Fund for a 'number' of projects involving engagement with the arts, and the Unlimited Programme: UK Government 2016, paras. 328–330.

11 He also noted that a further £1.8 million will be invested in Unlimited, although the time-frame was not mentioned.

12 In 2010–11, public funding to ACE stood at £450 million. That amount dropped by 14% in 2011–12, 7.5% in 2012–13 and 3% in 2013–14, and it is set to drop to £343 in 2014–15. The National Lottery also gives significant funds to ACE; total funding, including lottery funding, in 2010–11 was £601 million. In 2014–15 it is expected to be £605 million. See https://www.gov.uk/government/policies/supporting-vibrant-and-sustainable-arts-and-culture. Accessed 6 May 2016.

13 And see Arts Council England (2011b), *The Role of Diversity in Building Adaptive Resilience*, London: ACE.

14 See also Arts Council England (2009b), *Dance Mapping: A Window on Dance 2004–2008*, London: ACE.

15 The economic contribution of performers has long been questioned. As early as 1776 Adam Smith described performances as the epitome of unproductive labour: 'players, buffoons, musicians, opera-singers, opera-dancers' whose work 'perishes in the instant of its production'.

16 *The Best Dance Ever* (Artist: Unknown; Posted: 10 January 2009); *The Prefect Human/Still* (Artist: Candoco; Posted: 20 January 2009); *Promotional Video* (Artist: Candoco; Posted: 27 January 2009); *How To Dance Without Legs* (Artist: David Toole; Posted: 10 October 2009); *Extraordinary (Dis)ability* (Artist: David Toole; Posted: 22 June 2010); *Candoco Dance Company 2005–2010* (Artist: Candoco; Posted: 11 August 2010); *AXIS Dance Company Demo 2010* (Artist: Axis Dance Co.; Posted: 14 December 2010); *Evolution* (Artist: Claire Cunningham; Posted: 20 June 2011); *AXIS on SYTYCD* (Artist: Axis Dance Co.; Posted: 10 November 2011); *Dancing Without Limits* (Artist: Claire Cunningham; Posted: 11 November 2011); *The Impending Storm* (Artist: David Toole; Posted: 29 August 2012); *Birdy – Bird Gerhl (Anthony and the Johnsons Cover)* (Artist: David Toole; Posted: 2 September 2012); *Olympics Closing Ceremony* (Artist: Candoco; Posted: 6 September 2012); *Unlimited Commissions* (Artist: Candoco; Posted: 23 August 2012); *Elevation* (Artist: Caroline Bowditch; Posted: 19 September 2013); *She Was A Knife Thrower's Assistant* (Artist: Caroline Bowditch; Posted: 19 September 2013); *Three Acts of Play* (Artist: Candoco; Posted: 25 January 2013); and *The Cost of Living – David Toole* (Artist: David Toole; Posted: Unknown).

17 See Saadé and Huang (2009); Kietzmann et al. (2011); Howard and Parks (2012).

18 For more, see Harmon et al. (2015).

19 We would disambiguate the role of, and response to, Heather Mills on *Dancing with the Stars*; neither her performance nor her role as a 'dancer', nor indeed the reactions to her performance are representative of, or generalisable to, disability dance (Quinlan and Bates 2008).

20 For example, John Martin, considered a great dance critic, greatly influenced the career of Martha Graham through his writings.

21 With respect to the former, it has been said that: 'A good review should promote discussion and persuade the reader to engage in the art, good or bad. A strong criticism should cause the reader to think for themselves' (Chan 2013). With respect to the latter, some critics explicitly acknowledge that the one of the purposes of their work is to develop an audience: 'Once I became intrigued by the modern dance I was all for it […]. I thought it was a great art manifestation, and I felt that it was my business […] to build an audience for this art' (Martin 1967: 86).

22 From 12–14 April 2015, we reviewed *The Times, The Guardian, The Telegraph, The Daily Telegraph, The Sunday Telegraph, The Daily Mail, The Scotsman, The Herald Glasgow, The Gloucestershire Echo, The Penarth Times* and conducted a Google search of blog reviews, identifying fourteen examples.

23 As discussed by Jays (2015), who, in interviewing Stine Nilson, Candoco, reported that critiques will still list the dancers' disabilities.

24 See Tay (2000) and the discussion in Briggs et al. (2012).

25 On this point, see Patrick and Bowditch (2013). While we make the argument that intelligent critique is one way in which audiences can learn to appreciate the dance, this takes time.

26 On this point, see Whatley (2007).

27 At http://www.un.org/en/documents/udhr/. Accessed 6 May 2016.

28 At http://www.ohchr.org/en/professionalinterest/pages/ccpr.aspx. Accessed 6 May 2016.

29 Article 19, ICCPR.

30 Article 27, ICCPR.

31 For a discussion on the drafting history of Article 27 and its juxtaposition with IP, see Plomer (2013).

32 At http://www.ohchr.org/EN/ProfessionalInterest/Pages/CESCR.aspx. Accessed 6 May 2016.

33 Article 15.1, ICESCR.

34 At http://portal.unesco.org/en/ev.php-URL_ID=17716&URL_DO=DO_TOPIC&URL_SECTION=201.html. Accessed 6 May 2016.

35 Article 2.1, 2003 Convention.

36 At http://portal.unesco.org/en/ev.php-URL_ID=31038&URL_DO=DO_TOPIC&URL_SECTION=201.html. Accessed 6 May 2016. For more on this convention, see Burri (2013).

37 Articles 2 and 4, 2005 Convention.

38 'Cultural expressions' are defined as those expressions that result from the creativity of individuals, groups and societies, and that have cultural content: Article 4.3, 2005 Convention.

39 'Cultural content' refers to the symbolic meaning, artistic dimension and cultural values that originate from or express cultural identities: Article 4.2, 2005 Convention.

40 'Cultural activities, goods and services' refers to those activities, goods and services, which at the time they are considered as a specific attribute, use or purpose, embody or convey cultural expressions, irrespective of the commercial value they may have: Article 4.4, 2005 Convention. Moreover, cultural activities may be an end in themselves, or they may contribute to the production of cultural goods and services: Preamble, 2005 Convention.

41 At http://www.un.org/disabilities/convention/conventionfull.shtml. Accessed 6 May 2016.

42 For a discussion on the CRPD's development, see Guernsey et al. (2007).

43 It is the second most rapidly ratified Treaty: UN Human Rights Council (2009), *Annual Report of the United Nations High Commissioner for Human Rights and Reports of the Office of the High Commissioner and the Secretary General*, UN Doc A/HRC/10/48, 26 January, para 4, http://www.un.org/disabilities/documents/reports/ohchr/A.HRC.10.48AEV.pdf. Accessed 6 May 2016.

44 Those drafting the CRPD sought to inculcate a transformative vision that would move beyond current human rights practice: UN Secretary-General (2006), *Official Statement: Secretary-General Hails Adoption of Landmark Convention on Rights of People with Disabilities*, UN Doc SG/SM/10797, 13 December.

45 Articles 1 and 30, CRPD.

46 Articles 1 and 30, CRPD.
47 We have argued elsewhere that this raises complex questions (Brown and Waelde 2014).
48 Committee on Economic, Social and Cultural Rights, 43rd Session, 2–20 November 2009, General Comment No. 21, para. 15.
49 Committee on Economic, Social and Cultural Rights, 43rd Session, 2–20 November 2009, General Comment No. 21, para. 15 (c).
50 The ICESCR contains the right to take part in cultural life (Article 15.1a), and the ICCPR contains the right to receive and impart information Article 19, both of which are required to be delivered without discrimination as to race, colour, sex or 'other status' (Article 2.2, ICESCR, and Article 2.1, ICCPR) the latter of which was expected to encompass disability.
51 Recital 14, Resolution on The Standard Rules on the Equalization of Opportunities for Persons with Disabilities, 48/96, Annex, 20 December 1993, adopted by UN General Assembly, Forty-Eighth Session.
52 Rule 10.1, 1993 Resolution.
53 Rule 10.2, 1993 Resolution.
54 General Comment No. 5 (1994): Persons with Disabilities, E/1995/22(SUPP), 1 January 1995.
55 Paras 5 and 6, General Comment No. 5.
56 Paras 37, 38 and 39, General Comment No. 5.
57 Which, regarding disability, also includes the Resolution on The Standard Rules on the Equalization of Opportunities for Persons with Disabilities, 48/96, Annex, 20 December 1993, adopted by UN General Assembly, Forty-Eighth Session, General Comment No. 5 (1994): Persons with Disabilities, E/1995/22(SUPP), 1 January 1995, and General Comment No. 21: Right of Everyone to Take Part in Cultural Life, E/C.12/GC/21, 21 December 2009.
58 Paras 48 and 52(d), General Comment No. 21: Right of Everyone to Take Part in Cultural Life, E/C.12/GC/21, 21 December 2009.
59 Para 23, 2009 General Comment. The EU Charter can support similar arguments under Articles 21.1 and 26.
60 UK Government (2012). The narrative in relation to participation in cultural life opens by admitting that disabled people are less likely to participate in cultural activities, and responds by stating that the United Kingdom is committed to addressing this, building on progress already achieved, and 'providing disabled people with equal opportunities to participate in culture, recreation, leisure and sport' (para. 327). However, the UK focused on the consumption of culture rather than its production and performance (with a slight caveat for paras. 328–30). Contrary to the transformative vision suggested for and by the CRPD, this seems woefully unambitious: InVisible Difference (2014), *Policy Brief: The UN Convention on the Rights of Persons with Disabilities (CRPD). Thoughts on the UK Initial Report CRPD/C/GBR/1*, http://www.invisibledifference.org.uk/media/papers/Policy_Brief_CRPD_2.pdf. Accessed 6 May 2016. When the InVisible Difference team challenged the Government's response to the UN Committee responsible for overseeing the implementation of the CRPD, arguing that not nearly enough was being done to fulfil its obligations, the Ministerial Correspondence Team pointed us to: the government's disability strategy, *Fulfilling Potential – Making it Happen*; ACE support of artistic and cultural experiences,

including works choreographed and/or performed by disabled people; the ACE goal relating to diversity and skills, ensuring that the leadership and workforce of the arts and cultural sector reflects the diversity of the country; and the website of the Intellectual Property Office for information on copyright: Department of Work & Pensions (2014), Letter, TO/14/15646, 29 September, http://www.invisibledifference.org.uk/research/publications/. Accessed 6 May 2016. This was a typically political response that did little to address the richness of the potential in the CRPD. It also illustrates the practical shortcomings of the human rights framework.

61 Brown and Waelde (2014). Some, albeit limited, attention has been paid as to the meaning of the right to take part in cultural life in other Instruments: UN Committee on Economic, Social and Cultural Rights (2009), *General Comment No. 21: Right of Everyone to Take Part in Cultural Life (art. 15, para. 1a of the Covenant on Economic, Social and Cultural Rights)*, 21 December, E/C.12/GC/21, http://www.refworld.org/docid/4ed35bae2.html. Accessed 6 May 2016; Shaver and Sganga (2009) http://digitalcommons.law.yale.edu/fss_papers/23. Accessed 6 May 2016.

62 See the text accompanying notes 10 and 11. Sir Peter Bazalgette has taken arts stakeholders to task for paying lip service to inclusion, saying, 'The plain fact is that despite many valuable, well-intentioned policies over the past decade, when it comes to diversity, we have not achieved what we intended'. Similarly, pointing to data collected by the relevant Sector Skills Councils, the Warwick Commission's *Report on the Future of Cultural Value* (2015: 35), states: 'The diversity of the creative workforce in Britain has progressively contracted over the past five years in relation to gender, ethnicity and disability [...]'. The report goes on to state that, 'the stark reality is that the possibility to express oneself artistically and creatively at a professional level is curtailed by social background and personal characteristics to an unacceptable degree [...]', asserting that this raises questions about the extent to which the cultural and creative sector fulfils its obligations under the *Equality Act 2010*.

63 Lord and Stein (2008: 474) highlight the importance of non-legal mechanisms in achieving social change.

64 See https://www.gov.uk/government/organisations/independent-living-fund. Accessed 6 May 2016.

65 See the UN's 'Education for All' initiative, the UNESCO framework, the European Agency for the Development of Special Needs Education, and various national initiatives such as the provisions in the *Education Act 1996* (ss. 316 and 316A, Schedule 27).

66 See Beckett (2009), and http://www.unesco.org/new/en/education/themes/strengthening-education-systems/inclusive-education/10-questions-on-inclusive-quality-education/. Accessed 6 May 2016.

67 See *Bracking et al. v Secretary of State for Work and Pensions* (2013) EWCA Civ 1345 (CA).

68 See http://www.communitycare.co.uk/2014/03/06/government-renews-bid-shut-independent-living-fund/#.UyAOsRZTPkw. Accessed 6 May 2016.

69 And its importance was also noted by the Warwick Commission on Cultural Value (2015: 35). https://warwick.ac.uk/research/warwickcommission/futureculture/finalreport. Accessed 8 May 2016.

70 Sganga (2015).

71　See Scottish Education Department (2006), *Draft Culture (Scotland) Bill: Consultation Document*, Edinburgh: Scottish Executive, which contains the draft bill, http://www.moray.gov.uk/downloads/file70857.pdf. Accessed 15 April 2016.

72　Responses to the consultation can be found at http://www.gov.scot/Publications/2007/05/11154331/0. Accessed 6 May 2016.

73　England, by contrast, relies on a series of government – imposed and – led thematic initiatives. Those initiatives introduced in 2008 were *children and young people, community, economy, delivery,* and *Olympics*: United Kingdom of Great Britain and Northern Ireland, *Implementation of the International Covenant on Economic, Social and Cultural Rights. Fifth Periodic Report submitted by State Parties under Articles 16 and 17 of the Covenant.* E/C.12/GBR/5. While the priorities will undoubtedly have moved on, the approach endures.

74　http://www.watchingdance.org. Accessed 6 May 2016.

75　http://culturehive.co.uk. Accessed 6 May 2016.

76　http://www.respondto.org. Accessed 6 May 2016.

77　Nesta (2014), *The New Art of Finance: Making Money Work Harder for the Arts*, http://www.nesta.org.uk. Accessed 6 May 2016.

78　There are signs that ACE is starting to take this seriously, as suggested by Sir Peter Bazalgette, ACE Chair, who wants arts organisations to make more progress with audience, programme and workforce diversity, or risk having their funding axed: http://www.theguardian.com/uk-news/2014/dec/08/arts-council-england-make-progress-diversity-funding-axed-bazalgette?CMP=share_btn_fb. Accessed 6 May 2016.

79　Jane Pritchard, Curator of Dance at the Victoria and Albert Museum, London, discussed the concept of disability and dance as being part of the 'invisible material' that exists during her talk at the InVisible Difference Symposium, Siobhan Davies Studios, London on 26 November 2014. Jane highlighted an event some years prior where a 'mystery dancer' in *Come Dance with Me* was identified following an assessment of a donation to the Museum. A remark was made in the materials dismissing a dancer who was referred to as a 'girl had a wooden hand'. The author was however informed that 'an excellent glove was preserved for her special use'. Jane Pritchard's talk can be viewed from 1:04:30, https://www.youtube.com/watch?v=5cRMvs91kRU. Accessed 6 May 2016.

80　Smith and Waterton (2009) quote an extract from an interview with a representative from English heritage as follows: 'INTERVIEWEE: The UK has not said that it will ratify [the 2003 Convention] and I think it will be quite a long time before it does. INTERVIEWER: What are the reasons for that? INTERVIEWEE: It is just difficult to see how you could apply a convention of that sort in the UK context … it is not relevant … it just does not fit with the UK approach … I think it would be very difficult to bring in a convention that says we are actually going to list this sort of stuff and protect it. What are the obvious examples you come up with? Morris Dancing? As intangible heritage and so on? The UK has no intangible heritage.' (Interview 1, English Heritage, 4 July 2005) at 297.

Chapter 2

Cultural Heritage and the Unseen Community

Fiona Macmillan

Around me were a million human beings who had been alive all this time whose existence had never concerned me. They were alive. I was thousands of kilometres from home. I could not understand their language. They walked quickly, all of them. And as they overtook and passed me, they cut themselves off from me. I felt lost.

(Camus 1970: 40–41)

These days it is not always possible to say with any assurance whether these identities are intranational, infranational, or transnational; whether they are 'cultural', 'religious', 'ethnic', or 'historical'; whether they are legitimate or not – not to mention the question about which law would provide such legitimation; whether they are real, mythical or imaginary; whether they are independent or 'instrumentalized' by other groups who wield political, economic, and ideological power [...]

(Nancy 2000: xii–xiii)

Introduction

The idea that cultural heritage belongs to communities is one that seems, not only widely accepted, but also much like a statement of the proverbially obvious. In a moment, however, one sees that to make any sense this claim must involve some understanding of both the concepts of 'belonging' and 'community'. Locating such a search for meaning in a legal context immediately complicates the task. Occidental legal systems have concepts of 'belonging' that tend to revolve around the notions of ownership and property, which might not be quite the same thing as something belonging to a community in a cultural heritage sense. And then there is this problematic concept of community. In international law, which is where discussions about the legal protection of cultural heritage tend to lead us, community is a much contested concept. There are, at least, two reasons for this. First, because the strong statist tendency of international law may result in community being understood as essentially constitutive of nation, which is in turn constitutive of the state, itself understood both as constituting and constituted by international law. Secondly, and approaching the question from the opposite end of the spectrum, it is sometimes suggested that law is somehow constitutive of community.

In this chapter, which seeks to investigate how a cultural heritage community is formed and recognised, both of these contested concepts of community require some further analysis. The second part of the chapter focuses on the way in which international law, and specifically the international law governing the protection of cultural heritage, understands the relationship between community, nation and state. Part three investigates how community is constituted and the role of law, including relevant international legal instruments, in this process. This then forms the basis of the consideration in part four of the specific case of the disabled dance community as a cultural heritage community that is, at least relatively, unseen, although not absent. Continuing this focus on the disabled dance community, the final part of the chapter returns to the *pas de deux* between belonging and community, with which this chapter opened, in order to critique the way in which the law mediates the relationship between cultural heritage communities and social, political and economic value.

'Community' in International Cultural Heritage Law

The exact nature of relationship between the nation state and the constitution of international law is a matter of debate. At one pole of this debate is the claim that international law is dependent on the nation state (Carty 1997) and, specifically, on the passing 'upwards' of national sovereignty. Bearing in mind, however, that international law also creates a system to which sovereign states must conform in order to be recognised as such, the more convincing view is that the relationship between the nation state and international law is mutually constitutive (e.g. Fitzpatrick 2006). Whatever position is taken in this theoretical debate, we end up with the proposition that the juridical actors of international law are the states themselves and the supranational, international and intergovernmental organisations created through the mutually interdependent process of international law-making. Communities, despite being recognised in political theory as constituting the common political identity that forms the basis of the nation (Anderson 2006), and perhaps also the common cultural identity that precedes a common political identity, have traditionally received little formal attention in international law precisely because their identity has been submerged into that of the nation-state.

This concept of international law and of international law-making is clearly exclusionary. One of its consequences is that in the post-colonial context Indigenous Peoples, not constituting a state in international law, have found themselves without a voice at the international law-making table. A late and limited acknowledgement of the particular injustice of this state of affairs has recently made some inroads into the language of international law. As a result, the word 'community' has started to creep into international legal instruments. The Convention for the Safeguarding of the Intangible Cultural Heritage of 2003, for example, recognises in its sixth recital 'that communities, in particular indigenous communities, groups and, in some cases individuals, play an important role in the production, safeguarding maintenance and recreation of the intangible cultural heritage'. Despite the contextual association with the position of Indigenous Peoples the operative provisions of the Convention make it clear that the concept of community in this Convention is, however, not to be read as limited to such communities. Particularly important in this respect is the Convention's definition of intangible cultural heritage. According to Article 2.1 of the Convention, 'intangible cultural heritage' means:

> [...] the practices, representations, expressions, knowledge, skills – as well as the instruments, objects, artefacts and cultural spaces associated therewith – that communities, groups and in some cases, individuals recognise as part of their cultural heritage. This intangible cultural heritage, transmitted from generation to generation, is constantly recreated by communities and groups in response to their environment, their interaction with nature and their history, and provides them with a sense of identity and continuity, thus promoting respect for cultural diversity and human creativity.

The Convention does not seek to define the concept of community. Nor does it attempt to indicate expressly how a community might be recognised by the law, although as is argued below the reflexive relationship between community and cultural heritage in this provision gives some indication of a possible approach to this issue.

The Constitution of Community

Community comes before the law, which is to say that it cannot be regarded as constituted by law. Nor can community be contained in legal accounts of its existence or life (Christodoulidis 1998: 145–48). That community interacts with such accounts does not change the fundamental proposition that, as Christodoulidis argues, community can converge 'around a political/ethical understanding both capable of upholding a commitment, and dynamic, always potentially disruptable internally; and with no measure of authority, force, persuasion and violence capable of upholding it externally' (Christodoulidis 1998: 237, citing Cover 1983).

Legal accounts of community, of course, exist. Despite the paucity (both quantitative and qualitative) of references to the concept of community in international law instruments, it is clear there is a substantial engagement with this concept in national legal systems. Given the reflexive relationship between community and cultural heritage, which is acknowledged in the Convention for the Safeguarding of the Intangible Cultural Heritage and will be further explored below, it is not surprising to discover that this engagement sometimes takes place in the cultural heritage context. For example, particularly in states having an Indigenous population that predates the establishment of the state, the Indigenous population is recognised as a community enjoying, at least, a distinct identity and, often, also particular rights. The same is also true in relation to states in which ethnic or linguistic minorities live. To some extent, these types of rights reflect obligations (actual or hortatory) in international law even though their origins might not be directly attributable to such obligations. However, there are also other well-known examples in national law of the recognition of community and associated community rights, where community is less than the public at large. It is common, for example, for legal systems to recognise community rights in property based on customary use (Clarke 2015). An interesting variation on this is the recognition, nationally and internationally, of certain rights associated with the marking of products made in a certain geographical location (Aylwin and Coombe 2013).

The pivotal question here is not whether we can find a basis in law for delineating a community, which might then lay claim to certain community rights. It has already been argued that we cannot regard law as constitutive of community. However, at the same time, we may be able to find some indicia in existing legal accounts around which to build a concept of community that might then be the carrier of certain cultural heritage rights and obligations in law. The types of (overlapping) indicia that seem to be important in national systems as they relate to communities that form less than population of the state as a whole are: common political identity; common ethnic identity; common language; common religious identity; common geographical location; common sustenance practices; and common history. As will be evident, with the possible exception of common language (Anderson 2006: 196; Hobsbawm 2013: 147) and common religion (Hobsbawm 2013: 147), these are all also indicia of the type of communities that constitute nation states in international law. All these rather specific 'legal' indicia of community in fact draw on certain foundational concepts that are generally identified as being essential to the formation of community in any context, whether directly mediated by law or not. It is, arguably, these foundational concepts to which we should return in a quest to identify communities that should be regarded as enjoying cultural heritage rights or claims.

It seems that the central foundational concepts around which all these more specific indicia of community rotate are identification and memory, which are reflexively linked to one another. For Anderson, communities (with the possible exception of 'primordial villages of face-to-face contact' [Anderson 2006: 6]) are always imagined. By this he means not that they are fake or false, but rather that they are created by the imagination, that is by being imagined. Accordingly, he observes that '[c]ommunities are to be distinguished not by their falsity/genuineness, but by the style in which they are imagined' (Anderson 2006: 6). Anderson's classic account of community is focused on the way in which community produces nation, and with it nationalism. Nevertheless, his observations on the formation of community also seem pertinent in the context of communities forming less than the nation-state as a whole. These observations do much to enrich the foundational relation of identification and memory. There are three, in particular, that go to the heart of how community is imagined. First, Anderson notes the 'deep horizontal comradeship' (Anderson 2006: 7) that characterizes the imagined community – something that might also be referred to as solidarity. Secondly, he places emphasis on the temporal aspect of community, 'this sense of parallelism or simultaneity' (Anderson 2006: 188). The temporal dimensions here are both horizontal and vertical. Horizontal because comradeship and solidarity carry with them some notion of a shared temporal space. Vertical because if memory is critical to the imagined community then this implies a shared concept of the community's history and its temporal progression. Following on from this, the third aspect of Anderson's study that has particular resonance is exactly this question of how a community imagines its relationship with its own past. Thus, we arrive at the critical question of the reflexive relationship between community and memory.

How a community imagines, or remembers, its past is an important question in the cultural heritage context because it goes directly to the troubling question of the difference between history and heritage. Not only is 'history' a contested concept, but it is also the case that the concept of cultural heritage is strangely difficult to define in overarching terms (Macmillan 2015). The approach of Article 2.1 of the Intangible Cultural Convention, if recast at a more general level (i.e. removed from the specific context of intangible cultural heritage) might be taken to provide a possible approach to a broad(er) definition of cultural heritage. Based on this provision, such a definition might be something to the effect that cultural heritage is what is transmitted from generation to generation by communities and groups in response to their environment, their interaction with nature and their history, thus providing them with a sense of identity and continuity. This tends to reflect suggestions by commentators (including me) who have proposed an overarching concept of cultural heritage as being expressions of creativity (moveable and immoveable, tangible and intangible) that a community or people considers worth handing on to the future (Blake 2000; Macmillan 2015). There is, of course, an obvious political element in identifying and selecting what is considered to be worth handing on to the future and this carries with it a degree of malleability and slipperiness. In other words, from a cultural heritage perspective how the past is remembered is part and parcel of the question of how it is forgotten, or what part of it is forgotten. This very same mixture of remembering and forgetting lies at the heart of the discourse of the imagined community (Anderson 2006: ch. 11; Hobsbawm 2013: 150–51). As Anderson says: 'All profound changes in consciousness, by their very nature, bring with them characteristic amnesias. Out of such oblivions, in specific historical circumstances, spring narratives' (2006: 204).

Taking all this forward in the context of an enquiry into the existence and life of the disabled dance community leaves us with a few questions at which an attempt at resolution is necessary. The most obvious ones (to me at least) are: Is community always and only a subjective phenomenon? Or do there have to be externally perceptible signs of community? Is the existence of community essential to a cultural heritage claim? In order to make life easier, this chapter proceeds on the basis that the existence of a relevant community, in some way, is essential to a cultural heritage claim. Unless we accept the proposition that all the types of things that we understand as cultural heritage are simply and only the cultural heritage of all humankind, without any more particular association, then some type of concept of community seems to be necessary in order to hold up any given cultural heritage claim. In fact, even the proposition that cultural heritage is simply and only the heritage of all humankind probably entails a claim that humankind *en masse* is a community of sorts.

Assuming, however, that communities can be formed by less than everyone and, more importantly, less than the public at large in any given nation-state, the question of their subjectivity is an important one. When we talk about the reflexive relationship between identification and memory in the context of community formation, whose identification are we talking about? Whose memory? In particular, if the narrative of community built on collective memory is also about forgetting, who is remembering and who is forgetting? It is in relation to questions of this sort that Anderson's insight that communities are imagined is particularly useful. This is because it is clear from his focus on comradeship-solidarity, and his focus on common perceptions of time and history, that the communities he is talking about are imagined *from the inside out*. This suggests, of course, that not only is community a subjective concept, but also that the identification of oneself as a member of a community is subjective both for the individual and the community. The complication here is that a community may, and often does, impose objective requirements for community membership. These types of requirements are evident in the examples given above of circumstances where law has recognised community. These examples, however, are more than a happy and coincidental illustration of a claim about community membership. They are highly relevant to law's difficulty in recognising community outside easily identifiable constellations such as the nation state. If community is a subjective concept, employing objective criteria as part of that subjectivity, then law's problem with it will always be that it will see the objective criteria, but not necessarily their subjugation to the subjective identification of community.

Must we insist on the importance of subjectivity in forming community? The sort of history that we might prefer to forget, but would do so at our obvious peril, is full of examples of what we might call forced identification and membership of a community from outside that community (i.e. *from the outside in*). Sometimes this has been an effect achieved by law, but not always. The more significant point about it is that it has, it seems, always spelt trouble for the community and its members (whether they considered themselves members or not). The inverse of this is that the subjective identification of a community and its members is nearly always made in order to make some sort of positive claim. This seems to be the case with respect to cultural heritage claims made by a community. The fact that some cultural heritage may be burdensome (e.g. certain ritual practices that are not considered acceptable in human rights terms in the twenty-first century) is not necessarily a problem for the community because the whole point about cultural heritage, as its proposed definition above suggests, is that it is reflexive and so changes with community practice (Fitzpatrick and Joyce 2007). But the fact that community should always be a subjective concept, grounding certain claims (including claims with respect to cultural heritage), does not mean of course that community is not also grounded in mutual obligation and duty. This is a point to which this chapter will return after considering the specific question of the existence and life of the disabled dance community.

Disabled Dance as a Cultural Heritage Community

Concepts of cultural heritage are strongly associated with the creative arts (Hobsbawm 2013). This is reflected in Article 2.2 of the Convention on Intangible Cultural Heritage, in which specific instances of the sort of stuff that falls within the general definition in Article 2.1, reproduced above, is listed inclusively as follows:

(a) oral traditions and expressions, including language as the vehicle of the intangible cultural heritage;
(b) performing arts;
(c) social practices, rituals and festive events;
(d) knowledge and practices concerning nature and the universe; and
(e) traditional craftsmanship.

One of the markers of the social acceptance of a practice as part of the creative arts in occidental society seems also to be the fact that that practice then came to be protected as a copyright work (Bently and Sherman 2009). Accordingly, the fact that dance is a protected art form under copyright law is a consequence of its social acceptance as a creative form. In the light of the foregoing discussion of community it seems feasible to talk about a community cohering around dance as an art form. That is, a community that is constituted in the reflexive relation between identification and memory, in its sense of solidarity, and in its horizontal and vertical temporal dimensions. The dance community is also formed in relation to law in a very particular way. Even though the legal recognition of dance as a creative form occurred through copyright law, and despite the mutually constitutive nature of the relationship between art forms and their recognition in copyright law, historically the dance community has operated and regulated itself outside the formal architecture of copyright law (Yeoh 2012). This is because the technical formalities of copyright law serve its interests poorly. The point here is not, as I have already argued above, that law is constitutive of community. Rather, it is that the very unusual relation of the dance community with (copyright) law is part of its own narrative of community. And perhaps we could say is part of the way that it is recognised externally as a community. But how much does external recognition matter in the formation of community? I have already argued above that community cannot, and should not, be regarded as being formed from the outside. But does it need to be visible from the outside in order to have some claim to being a cultural heritage bearing community?

This is the point where I can no longer put off the question hanging over this chapter and which is prefigured in its title. The question is not, and I think cannot be, whether those involved in the production of dance by disabled artists constitute a community inside, or perhaps beside, the dance community. Everything that I have written above must surely lead to the conclusion that the strong identity of this community, reflexively engaging with its environment (including not only the creative practice of dance, but also international legal instruments that make reference to disabled persons, not to mention research projects such as that which generated the book in which this chapter appears), has produced and imagined a discourse of community that cannot be easily denied. That the formation of such a community may involve contestation, subjective identification and the use of certain (subjectively) objective criteria makes it no different to other communities and, indeed, tends to reinforce its nature as a community imagined *from the inside out*. So rather than a question about the existence of the disabled dance community, the burning question is how do we deal in cultural heritage terms with a community that is to some extent unseen *from the outside*? To ask this question, and to base it on the premise that the disabled dance community in some respects conforms to this description, leads us to a consideration of the relationship between the disabled dance community and the dance community at large.

It is clear that the type of identity that constitutes community can occur at multiple levels producing individuals who are simultaneously part of multiple communities. In this sense, there is nothing problematic about the idea that a person may be part of the dance community and the disabled dance community at the same time, or about the idea that the disabled dance community exists within the dance community. The problem here, if there is one, relates to the fact that while community membership depends upon one's identity, it also depends upon the community accepting that such a self-identification conforms to the community's narrative. This is what I described above as the relationship between subjective identity and objective criteria. The question of whether the dance community accepts disabled dance as part of its art form, and disabled dancers as members of its community, is not one I will try to answer here. The same goes for the related question of whether the disabled dance community exists inside the dance community or beside it. Answering these questions depends exactly on the way each of these communities imagines itself in its reflexive engagement between identity and memory (and forgetting). Whatever the nature of the relationship between the disabled dance community and the dance community more generally, there is a question of the extent to which the somewhat invisible disabled dance community might find a way to achieve greater visibility as a cultural heritage community through the particular type of engagement with law that characterises the dance community as a whole. The next section considers the nature of that engagement in the cultural heritage context.

Law, Value and the Cultural Heritage Community

As has already been noted, in terms of its identity as a creative arts community, the dance community has two very particular engagements with law that impact on its character as a community. One of these depends on the character of dance as a form of cultural heritage and the other on its character as a form of copyright. The question of the relationship between cultural heritage and intellectual property is a particularly fraught one (Macmillan 2013, 2014a, 2014b, 2015). The central tension rests on the fact that while cultural heritage is something that 'belongs' to a community, intellectual property including copyright is a rivalrous form of private property. Consequently, these two systems involve two very different ways of expressing value.

In the neo-liberal period there is a tendency for everything to be subjected to what has been described as 'total market thinking' (Christodoulidis 2013, citing Supiot 2010). Seeing the world through the spectacles of the neo-liberal framework leads to the conclusion that value can only be expressed through the market, which means that it can only be expressed in the form of a commodity. When we talk about the commodification of artistic works, such as dance, then the relevant instrument of commodification is almost always copyright because it is copyright that turns the creative forms of dance into private property. This raises the question of the relationship between commodification through copyright and the identification of something as cultural heritage. Specifically, it raises the question of whether it is commodity value that makes something cultural heritage. Answering this question positively would involve, however, the failure to distinguish between the fundamentally different concepts of not only copyright and cultural heritage, but also of the market and the community. Copyright and cultural heritage express and control the meaning of value in different ways. The same distinction can be made between market and community. While copyright as a private property right locates all relationships in the context of the market, the context of cultural heritage relationships is the community, of which the market forms a part but does not (or should not) control the whole.

In the world of total market thinking formal systems of private property rights such as copyright enjoy particular prestige. The more valuable the right in the market place the greater the prestige. In terms of the relationship between intellectual property and cultural property/heritage, it seems clear that cultural property/heritage has suffered from the ensuing prestige deficit, with a consequent impact on the way it is protected under international law (Slaughter 2011; Macmillan 2013, 2015). However, if we want to have cultural practices that resist this reduction of everything to its value in the market, then we also need to find a device that resists the commodification, or creeping propertisation, of everything and proposes an alternative basis for expressing and controlling value. At the moment, the best bet we have for this form of resistance is a more fully articulated concept of cultural heritage, which expresses and controls value according to the norms and identity of a community and not according to the market value of private property rights (Macmillan 2013, 2015).

None of this is to say that copyright is not valuable to individuals working in all areas of creative production. Copyright not only allows individuals to gain an economic benefit over their creative labour, it also confers control – although that control is considerably diminished if copyright does not remain in the hands of the original creator. However, private property rights like copyright are not a route to building a community of cultural and creative value. Such a community needs to be built by a bottom-up commitment to the value of the artistic practice, which then communicates that value to increasingly wider communities. The fact, as noted above, that the dance community tends to operate outside the formal architecture of copyright law means that it has successful experience in building and controlling value outside the system of private property rights imposed through copyright law. As a result, it is reasonable to conclude that the cultural heritage of the dance community, rather than the private rights of copyright holders, still dominates its cultural practice.

What are the implications of this for the disabled dance community? The answer to this question is closely linked to the fact that the cultural heritage of a community is a way of expressing its identity. This gives it a particular importance, both inside the community and with respect to its relations with the outside. Cultural heritage not only addresses the question of how a community is comprised and according to what values, it also functions as a way of telling those outside the community about the community and why it might deserve to be valued. For a community that is largely unseen, as I have suggested is the case for the disabled dance community, the role of cultural heritage in expressing its identity outside the community is particularly important.

The fact that a community is to some extent unseen from the outside does not mean that it is non-existent. What it may mean, however, is that the community has greater difficulty in accessing the benefits, collective and individual, that may flow from the external expression of its identity. And perhaps there is also a reflexive relationship between the internal solidarity of the community and its external expression that is mutually reinforcing. In the light of these observations, there are a number of questions that must be considered by the disabled dance community if it is to find a way of effectively using its cultural heritage as a means of expressing its identity. These questions include:

- How, bearing in mind our multiple identities and communities, the disabled dance community locates itself in relation to the community of dance in general? As has already been suggested, this is a complex question that depends upon the imagined discourse of both communities, but it does not seem unreasonable to suggest that the identities of these communities interact with each other.
- How can the disabled dance community use the heritage of the wider dance community, in particular the way in which it has built value outside the system of private property relations, to create a discourse of cultural heritage that reinforces community and resists the subjugation of that discourse to the system of total market thinking?
- And how can the disabled dance community build value for individual choreographers and dancers that is also capable of accessing the benefits of the property rights conferred by copyright without undermining the rights that other members of the community have in their shared cultural heritage?

If the disabled dance community can find good answers to these questions then market thinking ceases to be total and becomes only one artefact of the ties that bind that community together. What is particularly important to emphasise here is that the private property relations of copyright, which are produced by the law, do not and cannot be regarded as constituting community or controlling all aspects of the relationships within it. As has been argued above, community is produced by a reflexive relationship between identity and memory. It imports, however, a concept of solidarity, of mutual obligation. It is not that property relations cannot have a place in community, but rather that they should be subject to the mutual obligations of community, which are always present whether we can see them from the outside or not. The proper role of the law here is to give community the means to express its identity and the collective claims that flow from that identity, having reference always to the multiple and overlapping communities that form and give substance to human existence. International cultural heritage law shows some signs of recognising this role, but the intensely state-based nature of international law creates difficulties in recognising communities forming less than the public as a whole (Macmillan 2015). At the same time, the current transcendence of total market thinking has prioritised private property rights over community relations (Macmillan 2015). The political battle to change this state of affairs, including the laws through which it has been realised, is something that should matter to everyone who considers that the claims of community should provide the framework for a system of property rights that holds up community rather than attempting to pull it down (see further Keenan 2014).

References

Anderson, B. ([1983] 2006), *Imagined Communities: Reflections on the Origin and Spread of Nationalism*, London and New York: Verso.

Aylwin, N. and Coombe, R. (2013), 'Marks indicating conditions of origin in rights-based sustainable development', in R. Buchanan and P. Zumbansen (eds), *Human Rights, Development and Restorative Justice: An Osgoode Reader*, Oxford: Hart.

Bently, L. and Sherman, B. (2009), *Intellectual Property Law*, 3rd ed., Oxford: Oxford University Press.

Blake, J. (2000), 'On defining cultural heritage', *International & Comparative Law Quarterly*, 49, pp. 61–85.

Camus, A. (1970), 'Death in the soul', in E. Thody (ed.), *Albert Camus: Lyrical and Critical Essays* (trans. E. Conroy Kennedy), New York: Vintage, pp. 40–51.

Carty, A. (1997), 'Myths of international legal order: Past and present', *Cambridge Review of International Affairs*, 10, pp. 3–22.

Christodoulidis, E. (1998), *Law and Reflexive Politics*, Dordrecht: Kluwer.

—— (2013), 'The European Court of Justice and "total market thinking"', *German Law Journal*, 14:10, pp. 2005–20.

Clarke, A. (2015), 'Property, human rights and communities', in T. Xu and J. Allain (eds), *Property and Human Rights in a Global Context*, Oxford and Portland: Hart, pp. 19–39.

Cover, R. (1983), 'Nomos and the narrative', *Harvard Law Review*, 97, pp. 4–68.

Fitzpatrick, P. (2006), '"The new constitutionalism": The global, the postcolonial and the constitution of nations', *Law, Democracy and Development*, 10:2, pp. 1–20.

Fitzpatrick, P. and Joyce, R. (2007), 'Copying right: Cultural property and the limits of (occidental) law', in F. Macmillan (ed.), *New Directions in Copyright Law*, vol. 4, Cheltenham: Edward Elgar, pp. 169–90.

Hobsbawm, E. (2013), *Fractured Times: Culture and Society in the Twentieth Century*, London: Little, Brown.

Keenan, S. (2014), *Subversive Property: Law and the Production of Spaces of Belonging*, Abingdon: Routledge.

Macmillan, F. (2013), 'The protection of cultural heritage: Common heritage of humankind, national cultural "patrimony" or private property?', *Northern Ireland Legal Quarterly*, 64, pp. 351–64.

———— (2014a), 'Arts festivals as cultural heritage in a copyright saturated world', in H. Porsdam (ed.), *Copyrighting Creativity: Creative Values, Cultural Heritage Institutions and Systems of Intellectual Property*, Farnham: Ashgate, pp. 95–115.

———— (2014b), 'Arts festivals: Property, heritage or more?', in K. Bowrey and M. Handler (eds), *Law & Creativity in the Age of the Entertainment Franchise*, Cambridge: Cambridge University Press, pp. 197–215.

———— (2015), 'Cultural property and community rights to cultural heritage', in T. Xu and J. Allain (eds), *Property and Human Rights in a Global Context*, Oxford and Portland: Hart, pp. 41–62.

Nancy, J.-L. (2000), *Being Singular Plural* (trans. R. D Richardson and A. E. O'Byrne), Stanford: Stanford University Press.

Slaughter, J. R. (2011), 'Form & informality: An unliterary look at world literature', in R. Warhol (ed.), *The Work of Genre: Selected Essays from the English Institute*, Cambridge, MA: English Institute in Collaboration with the American Council of Learned Societies, pp. 177–240.

Supiot, A. (2010), *L'esprit de Philadelphie. La justice sociale face au marché total*, Paris: Seuil.

UNESCO Convention for the Safeguarding of the Intangible Cultural Heritage of 2003 (2003), http://portal.unesco.org/en/ev.php-URL_ID=17716&URL_DO=DO_TOPIC&URL_SECTION=201.html.

Yeoh, F. (2012), 'Copyright does not adequately accommodate the artform of dance', Ph.D. thesis, London: Birkbeck, University of London.

Chapter 3

An Analysis of Reporting and Monitoring in Relation to the United
Nations Convention on the Rights of Persons with Disabilities, the
Right to Participation in Cultural Life and Intellectual Property

Catherine Easton

Introduction

The United Nations Convention on the Rights of Persons with Disabilities (UNCRPD, 2008) is an international treaty that aims to shape law and policy to achieve equality for disabled people. It contains innovative bridging provisions that seek to support States Parties, the countries and organisations who have agreed to its provisions, in the implementation of its measures. These can be found in Article 33, which outlines the need to 'designate one or more focal points within government for matters relating to the implementation of the present Convention'. Furthermore, there is an overarching obligation on States Parties 'to promote, protect and monitor implementation of the present Convention' (Art 33.1). The UNCRPD itself was drafted in a unique, collaborative manner that facilitated and financed the participation of disabled people throughout all negotiations (Justesen and Justesen 2007). The Convention enshrines this approach in its Article 33.3), which requires that States Parties ensure that disabled people are involved in the development of national implementation measures.

Writing in 2014, the InVisible Difference team concluded that in relation to the Convention's Article 30 Participation in Cultural life, the UK's implementation of the Convention 'did little to address the richness of the potential in the CRPD' (Harmon et al. 2014). This chapter examines the approach taken to the Convention's Article 30 by analysing States Parties' Reports to the oversight Committee (OHCHR 2015a) and tracking its responses. The research undertaken for this chapter took place in August 2015. The aim will be to highlight examples of good practice and to provide further recommendations as to how the reporting and monitoring process could be revised in order to bring about tangible change and improve participation in disabled dance.

The Right to Participation in Cultural Life

The Universal Declaration of Human Rights (1948) in its Article 27.1 enshrines The Right to Participate in Cultural Life stating: 'everyone has the right freely to participate in the cultural life of the community'. This right has subsequently been referenced in international instruments (ICEAFRD 1963; CEDAW 1979). In relation to disability rights, the gap in disability-specific provisions was initially addressed by The Standard Rules on the Equalization of Opportunities for Persons with Disabilities, adopted in 1993. This non-binding, policy-shaping instrument in its Rule 10 upholds culture as a target area for equal participation and calls upon States to ensure that disabled people are given the opportunity to achieve their 'creative, artistic and intellectual potential'. This equality is deemed not only to be of benefit to disabled people but to the wider community as a whole, and dance is specifically given as an example of a relevant activity alongside 'music, literature, theatre, plastic arts, painting and sculpture'. These targets were crucial in the shaping of many national provisions and provided a starting point for the negotiations that ultimately led to the drafting of the UNCRPD (ENABLE 2015). While the Rules separated 'Culture' from 'Recreation and Sport', the Convention enshrines in its Article 30 a right to equal participation in cultural life, recreation, leisure and sport. In its paragraph 2 it creates a duty on States Parties to:

> [...] take appropriate measures to enable persons with disabilities to have the opportunity to develop and utilize their creative, artistic and intellectual potential, not only for their own benefit, but also for the enrichment of society.

Shaver and Sganga (2009) believe that the use in international provisions of the term 'cultural life' represents a desire not just to encompass existing, traditional culture but all manner of human creative expression. In this way it will be able to evolve to apply to new cultural manifestations, such as those developed with or enhanced by new technologies. Harmon et al. (2014) strongly highlight the importance of dance, and particularly disabled dance, within cultural life. However, they identify a gap, in that guidance and information does not exist in the area of intellectual property issues in relation to disabled creation and ownership of dance. In this way, Article 30's scope has been diminished by a failure to provide required supportive and regulatory measures.

In general, the approach taken to intellectual property issues and disability usually relates strongly to the accessing of cultural works rather than post-creation protection. For example, intellectual property and access for disabled people have been given recent international legal prominence through the development of the Marrakesh Treaty (2013), which focuses on providing access to published works. This builds upon Article 30.3 of the UNCRPD:

> States Parties shall take all appropriate steps, in accordance with international law, to ensure that laws protecting intellectual property rights do not constitute an unreasonable or discriminatory barrier to access by persons with disabilities to cultural materials.

The Marrakesh Treaty has heralded a new shift in the approach of the international copyright regime towards redressing key power imbalances between rights holders and society. However, these developments will only have their desired impact if supported with political commitment backed up by tangible action and strategy (Harpur and Suzor 2013). This chapter seeks to examine the role of dance as part of Article 30's right to cultural life, building upon the following observations of the InVisible Difference team:

It is disappointing to note [...] that the initial report of the United Kingdom submitted in 2013 did not engage adequately with participation and elite participation by artists with different bodies.

(Brown and Waelde 2015: 581)

Furthermore, attention will be paid to the Article 33 provision relating to implementation and monitoring:

33(3) Civil society, in particular persons with disabilities and their representative organizations, shall be involved and participate fully in the monitoring process.

This research has been carried out in order to probe ways in which the Convention could be implemented to give more weight to the voice of disabled people in, for example, addressing the position of dance in cultural heritage. It is accepted that the research undertaken in this chapter will merely provide a snapshot of ongoing reporting and monitoring, but key trends can be identified, which could shed light on how the Convention's implementation can be improved to move towards greater equality. There is a need to translate this legal framework into tangible measures that lead to support for disabled dance at all levels. These need to be adequately funded and can include strategies such as promoting and marketing disabled and integrated dance initiatives; funding workshops, events and conferences on disabled and integrated dance; facilitating networking; providing supported qualifications in integrated dance; and establishing national training programmes and mentoring.

Reporting, Monitoring and the Convention on the Rights of Persons with Disabilities

Under Article 35, States Parties are required to submit a 'comprehensive' report to the Convention's Committee within two years of it coming into force in the relevant jurisdiction. This is followed by reports submitted every four years, or more frequently if the Committee requests, and these, expressly, need not repeat information already contained in the initial report. It is open to States Parties to highlight any reasons for impeded progress in the achievement of the Convention's obligations. Importantly, this reporting Article also references Article 4.3, which calls for the need for the involvement and consultation of disabled people and groups of disabled people in the implementation of the Convention and related decision-making processes.

The Committee has the power to make suggestions and general recommendations, with the States Parties being given the opportunity to respond with further information (Art 36.1). Transparency is a key factor, with the UN Secretary-General tasked with making the reports available to all States Parties (Art 36.3), and the States Parties themselves called upon to disseminate them as widely as possible (Art 36.4). The reports are made available on the website of the Office of the High Commissioner for Human Rights (OHCHR 2015a), as are the List of Issues raised by the Committee (OHCHR 2015b) and the Committee's Concluding Observations (OHCHR 2015c). These are the resources that have been analysed in order to shed light upon the position of disabled dance within the States Parties' implementation measures and the extent to which disabled people have been consulted and given the opportunity to be heard within the implementation and reporting process.

States Parties Reports (Table 1)

There are 84 reports of States Parties available on the website and they were published from 2010 to 2015. Of these, eight[1] could not be fully accessed due to technical issues or the need for further translation. The reports were analysed to determine the approach taken to the Article 30 right to cultural life, the Article 33.3 relating to civil society participation and the approach, if any, taken to intellectual property. These results are summarised in Table 1.

The notion of 'cultural life' is a wide one and, as highlighted earlier, the Convention's drafters chose to align this with recreation, leisure and sport. There is potentially a risk that the reports will prioritise sport at the expense of culture, so a decision was made to note the frequency of references to sport. Reference to access to cultural performances and venues was recorded separately from the facilitation of participation in cultural performances. Furthermore, specific references to dance were recorded. In relation to intellectual property, references to measures to facilitate access to works were recorded separately from those relating to ownership of intellectual property by disabled people.

Finally, the inclusion of measures to address the Article 33.3 involvement of disabled people in policy-making was recorded. This was approached on a wide basis, as there are a number of ways of facilitating participation; where there were no acceptable measures but work was being undertaken to put these in place a 'P' for pending was included in this column.

List of Issues (Table 2)

Analysis was made of the 38 available Lists of Issues raised by the Committee in response to the reports. References to the need to address access to and participation in sports were recorded, as was reference to the need to increase access to and participation in cultural activities, as broadly defined. Any comment related to intellectual property was recorded, as was any specific reference to the need to improve civil society participation as held in Article 33.3.

Concluding Comments (Table 3)

The 33 available Concluding Comments reports were analysed. Record was made of any reference to Article 30 and the specific point made was recorded in the table. Any reference

Table 1: References to specific spheres in States Parties' reports.

State Party	Access to sports venues and participation	Access to cultural performances/venues	Participation in cultural performances	Specific reference to dance	Ref to IP-Access	Ref to IP-Creation	Involvement of groups of disabled people in decision-making
Algeria	X	X	X				X
Argentina	X						X
Armenia	X	X	X				
Australia	X	X					X
Austria	X	X	X	X	X		X
Azerbaijan			X				
Belgium	X	X					
Bolivia	X						
Bosnia & Herzegovina	X	X					X
Brazil	X	X	X				X
Bulgaria	X	X	X		X		X
Canada	X	X					X
Chile	X	X					X
China	X	X	X	X	X		
China: Hong Kong	X	X	X	X	X		
China: Macau	X	X	X				
Columbia	X	X	X				X
Costa Rica	X	X	X				X
Cook Islands	X						X
Croatia	X	X	X				X
Cuba	X	X	X	X			X
Cyprus		X	X	X			X
Czech Republic	X	X	X	X			P
Denmark	X	X					X
Dominican Republic			X				P
Ecuador	X	X	X	X		X	X
El Salvador	X	X	X	X			X
Ethiopia	X						X
European Union	X	X	X				X
Gabon	X		X		X		P
Germany	X	X	X				X
Greece	X	X	X				P
Guatemala	X						
Haiti	X	X	X				X

	Col 1	Col 2	Col 3	Col 4	Col 5	Col 6	Col 7
Honduras	X	X	X				X
Hungary	X	X	X		X		P
Iran	X	X	X				X
Italy	X	X			X		X
Kenya							
Korea (Rep. of)	X		X	X	X		X
Latvia			X				X
Lithuania	X	X	X				X
Luxembourg	X	X	X				X
Macedonia (FYR)	X	X		X			X
Malta	X					X	X
Mauritius	X		X	X			X
Moldova		X	X				
Mongolia	X	X	X	X	X		
Montenegro	X	X	X	X	X		X
Nepal	X	X	X				X
New Zealand	X	X	X		X		X
Norway	X						X
Panama	X						
Paraguay	X						
Peru	X	X	X	X			
Philippines	X	X	X	X	X		
Poland	X	X	X		X		
Portugal	X						
Qatar	X	X					
Rwanda	X		X				X
Senegal			X				X
Serbia	X		X				
Seychelles	X				X		
Slovakia	X	X	X				X
Slovenia	X	X	X				X
South Africa	X	X					X
Spain	X	X	X		X		X
Sweden	X	X	X	X			X
Thailand		X					X
Tunisia	X	X					
Turkmenistan	X	X	X	X	X		X
UK	X	X	X	X	X		X
Ukraine						X	X
Uganda	X	X					
Uruguay	X						X

Table 2: References made in the Committee's List of Issues.

State Party	Access/ participation sports	Access/ participation culture	IP-related comment: Marrakesh Treaty	Civil society participation 33.3
Argentina				X
Austria				
Australia				X
Azerbaijan				X
Belgium				
Brazil		X		
China (HK& Macau)				X
Cook Islands		X	X	X
Costa Rica				X
Croatia		X	X	X
Czech Republic		X	X	
Denmark				X
Dominican Republic		X	X	
Ecuador		X		
European Union		X	X	X
Gabon	X			
Germany				
Hungary				
Kenya				
Korea (Rep. of)				X
Lithuania				
Mauritius		X		X
Mexico		X	X	
Mongolia		X	X	X
New Zealand		X	X	
Paraguay	X	X		X
Peru				X
Portugal		X	X	X
Qatar		X		
Serbia				
Slovakia				
Spain				
Sweden				X
Thailand				
Tunisia				
Turkmenistan		X	X	
Uganda	X	X		X
Ukraine				X

Table 3: References made in the Committee's Concluding Comments.

State Parties	Art 30	Ref to the Marrakesh Treaty	Art 33.3 specific concern
Argentina			
Australia			X
Austria			
Azerbaijan		X	
Belgium		X	
Brazil	Need for accessible libraries and tourism	X	
China (inc HK/Macao)			X
Cook Islands	Need for accessible travel and tourism	X	X
Costa Rica		X	
Croatia	Need to establish arts festivals	X	X
Czech Republic		X	
Denmark		X	
Dominican Republic	Access to tourist/artistic/ cultural sites and promote participation	X	
Ecuador	Access to sports centres and cultural venues	X	X
El Salvador	Access to sports centres and cultural venues		
European Union		X	
Gabon		X	
Germany		X	
Hungary			X
Kenya		X	X
Korea (Rep. of)		X	
Mauritius	Accessible tourism needed	X	X
Mexico		X	
Mongolia			X
New Zealand	Increase audio-described TV	X	
Paraguay			
Peru			
Qatar		X	X
Spain			
Sweden		X	
Tunisia			X
Turkmenistan		X	
Ukraine		X	X

for the need to accede to or implement the Marrakesh Treaty was recorded. Finally, any specific mention to the need to increase the participation of disabled people as enshrined in Article 33.3 was recorded. Those highlighted in the table are the relevant specific comments as the following general comment is included in each report:

> The Committee strongly encourages the State party to involve civil society organizations, in particular disabled persons' organizations, in the preparation of its second periodic report.

Results

This research aimed to evaluate the extent to which the UNCRPD reporting process can support disabled dance, including at an elite level. It is accepted that in relation to dance the term 'elite' is contested. While it can be used as a substitute for 'professional', the use of the term in this chapter is wider in scope and encompasses Privette's (1981) characteristics of peak performers: high level performance; clear focus; spontaneity; expression of self; and a fascination with the task. The aims of the research were achieved through an examination of the position of dance in the reports alongside an analysis of the approach taken to the protection of intellectual property.

Dance and Article 30

The comprehensive initial reports of the States Parties tend to approach the reporting process on an Article by Article basis. The decision to include 'recreation, leisure and sport' alongside cultural life in Article 30 immediately was seen to have an impact on reporting as, often, much, if not all, of the content reported has a focus on sporting activities. This was an ongoing theme, with seven of the reports giving extensive information on access to sport and leisure while failing even to address culture. Conversely, there were a number of reports that only outlined issues relating to cultural life without covering sport, but this was often in the context of a very brief treatment of the Article as a whole. This could be a reflection of the in-depth expansion given on participation in recreational, leisure and sporting activities provided in paragraph 5 of the article. Indeed, on inspection, the reports tend to mirror the format of the articles and give more in-depth information in relation to the components of the Article for which greater detail is provided.

Another striking issue is the wide range of activities and services that can fall into the category of 'cultural life'. This includes, as expanded upon in the article itself, access to books and libraries, audio-described television, access to tourist sites and museums, and access to and participation in theatre, music and the visual arts. This leads to a situation in which dance, even at a basic level, is competing with a wide range of activities that fall under this very widely drafted Article.

In 20 of the 76 reports there is a specific reference to dance. Of these, the following outline initiatives that are aimed solely at children and young people: Mongolia's 'Child World' event, the Czech Republic's 'Programme for the Support of Non-Professional Artistic Initiatives', which has events and activities aimed at encouraging participation in 'all types of dancing from folklore up to stage and modern dance', Peru's Marinera dance performances in Lima, the Cyprus Youth Organisation's 'Youth in Action' free dance workshops, Montenegro's two workshops including modern dance sessions for children, and Latvia's youth dance collective. In a similar manner, the approach of Argentina and Spain to dance is to refer to it in relation to educational programmes. These initiatives are all positive developments as they support the experience of dance at a young age and, in this way, could nurture talent and lead to a lifelong interest and potential careers in dance. However, there is the risk that these States Parties could see their duty to support dance as discharged when a person leaves childhood. This approach does not facilitate a transition to elite participation and ownership in dance for adults. This can become particularly problematic when the transition to elite for disabled artists does not mirror provisions to support such transition for non-disabled artists.

In a similar manner, some States Parties' reference to dance link it back to its health and therapeutic benefits, rather than its position as art. This can be seen in Cuba's provision of dance therapy and the Philippines 'care giving services' with dance-based modules. The benefits of dance therapy for some groups of disabled people have been proven (Sandahl and Auslander 2008: 6) and these initiatives are positive. However, these States Parties have taken an approach that deems dance a part of treatment rather than an art form in its own right.

In relation to initiatives to support dance as an art form that goes beyond childhood, there was a number of differing approaches. These included: India's Mahatma Gandhi Institute which provides resources free of charge to NGOs to deliver dance training, a folkdance performance in Ecuador which included the participation of 20 disabled people, and Macedonia's training of dance groups.

A small number of references were made to adult, potentially elite, dance. The report from China holds that:

There are already 195 performing art troupes of persons with disabilities, who are supported by government departments in their cultural visits and exchanges in many countries. Some artists with disabilities have become household names in China.

More clarity would be needed to determine whether or not this is a segregated approach that separates disabled and able-bodied performers but the language used appears to indicate a segregated approach. In South Africa, the African Sinakho Arts Group is a touring company that comprises more than 300 disabled performers alongside able-bodied performers. The language used in the report from Sweden is succinct and demonstrates a high level of elite integration:

It is becoming increasingly common for professional theatre and dance groups to include actors and dancers both with and without disabilities.

However, it is the approach taken by New Zealand that stands out with its strategy created by Dance Aotearoa New Zealand (2010) entitled: 'Would you like this dance?' This is a comprehensive, strategic approach with themes and actions to be taken as part of a wide-ranging plan to promote what it terms 'integrated dance'. Aim 2.1, for example, is to achieve a position in which '[i]ntegrated dance is a career option within the dance and recreation industry' and this is followed by clearly defined objectives such as improving access to qualification schemes and developing networks to support elite disabled dance. The strategy demonstrates a strong commitment to long-term development of disabled dance at all levels. The creation of artistic works is addressed within the section on resources with its aim 5.4 to 'Develop a wider range of funding for disabled people to develop their own dance DVDs, books and dance material'. However, even in this detailed approach to disabled dance, as so often in dance practices, the issue of ownership and intellectual property is not tackled.

Within the Committee's List of Issues and Concluding Comments there are no express references to dance. Perhaps due to many of the States Parties' in-depth treatment of access to and participation in sport, there were many more issues raised in relation to cultural access and participation (sixteen) than to those relating to sports (three). Within the final Concluding Comments eight of the 33 reports refer to the need to address measures relating to Article 30. Of these, six highlight the need to increase access and two relate to the need to increase cultural participation.

Intellectual Property

As outlined above, the UNCRPD in Article 30.3 addresses intellectual property rights in terms of the elimination of unreasonable or discriminatory barriers in relation to access to cultural materials. There is no reference to the need to support ownership of artistic creation. On examining the reports, only eighteen of the 76 specifically reference measures taken to use intellectual property law to facilitate access to cultural materials for disabled people. This is despite it being an express provision in Article 30. The majority of the reports highlight existing domestic legal provisions that either already enable access to cultural works for disabled people, or outline steps taken to amend existing legislation. Examples of this include Hungary's Copyright Law, which states that 'people living with disabilities can have free access to all copyright contents' and an amendment to the Intellectual Property Code of the Philippines to allow exemptions for 'reproduction or distribution of published articles or materials in a specialized format exclusively for the use of the blind, visually and reading impaired persons'. The European Union's response outlines the nature of the Copyright Directive's (2001/29/EC) exceptions allowing access for disabled people and highlights its role and negotiations in relation to the drafting of the Marrakesh Treaty. In a similar manner, the United Kingdom outlines its role in a pre-Marrakesh dialogue with the World Intellectual Property Organisation to improve access to artistic works for blind and visually impaired people. An interesting example of the Convention being used to shape legislative change can be found in the Cook Islands' response which acknowledges that it did not, at the time of reporting, have an intellectual property law framework at all but, following Article 33.3, states that it will involve disabled people in the consultation process to develop one.

Only three of the 76 reports include any reporting that may be seen to outline an approach that addresses ownership of intellectual property by disabled people. In statements without further detail or an outline of implementation measures, Ecuador and Mauritius' reports hold that creator and authorship rights are to be given to all people, regardless of disability. The relevant section in the Ukraine's report merely restates Article 54 of its Constitution, which enshrines that all citizens have a right to intellectual property protection. It does not go further to address issues specific to ownership and disabled people and, in this way, may just be a simple restatement of the relevant domestic law without any tailoring to the nature of the Convention. None of the States Parties, therefore, have adequately outlined any existing regulatory or legal changes relating to the unique position of disabled people and copyright ownership.

Within the List of Issues, ten of the 38 reports refer to intellectual property, but all of these focus solely on the Marrakesh Treaty and the need either to accede, ratify or implement its measures. This trend is followed in the Concluding Comments with 22 of the 33 reports specifically referencing the Marrakesh Treaty with no other mention of intellectual property.

Civil Society Monitoring

The Convention requires disabled people and groups of organisations to be involved in the ongoing monitoring of its implementation. This is crucial, as failing to address the voice of disabled people can give rise to a paternalistic approach which leads to further discrimination. In the States Parties' reports, 46 demonstrate a level of engagement with civil society at differing levels. These range from liaison with representative groups on an ad hoc basis to the establishment and funding of committees, such as Brazil's National Council for the Protection of the Rights of People with Disabilities (CONADE), which liaises with law and policy-makers on an ongoing basis.

Four States Parties acknowledge the lack of civil society monitoring but indicate that measures will be implemented to address this as, for example, Gabon's report states:

A national committee for the integration of persons with disabilities shall be established, comprising the relevant ministerial departments, non-governmental organizations and associations of persons with disabilities.

In the List of Issues and Concluding Comments a number of States Parties are singled out by the Committee to address the strategies relating to civil society monitoring. These responses range from clarification of the nature of the monitoring or of the composition of named groups, through to the blunt statement directed at the Cook Islands:

> The Committee is concerned at the absence of an independent monitoring framework and the lack of civil society involvement.

A number of the reports refer to civil society involvement in the creation of a shadow or alternative report, drafted by civil society. These are not available directly alongside the list of official reports but, as part of the Convention monitoring process are submitted as 'Information from Other Sources'. A good example is the European Disability Forum's Alternative Report (2015), which takes an in-depth and comprehensive approach to each Article, although it does not address ownership of intellectual property.

An innovative approach was taken in the Austrian formal report, which expressly incorporates the civil society shadow commentary. This allows for a voice that directly contradicts with the official response with, for example, the statement in relation to Article 30 that:

> For civil society organisations, the services offered in this field are not satisfactory. They consider that a lack of funding and a lack of awareness are responsible for this situation.

This response also raises the issues that:

> Civil society organisations have pointed out what they view as an unsatisfactory situation regarding the implementation and monitoring of the Convention in the Länder [States of Austria] as well as a general lack of information. They also criticise the fact that the national monitoring committee has too little funding and that its work is carried out in a purely honorary (non-remunerative) capacity.

This approach is to be lauded and adds further weight to the implementation of Article 33.3. A fully amalgamated official report into which the civil society voice has been incorporated through negotiation may give less emphasis to the voice of disabled people, whereas the civil society input into the Austrian submission is independent and strong, highlighting the need for change.

Analysis

The States Parties' reports outline a range of legal measures and provisions to meet duties under the Article 30 Right to Participate in Cultural Life. There is a wide disparity in the level of engagement with this provision with some reports providing no information and others giving extensive, detailed reviews of on-going strategies backed up by funding. In general, the approach to reporting on the Article is one which, firstly, deals with the sport, leisure and recreation aspects before addressing others. As outlined above, this may be due to the greater detail given to the areas of sports and recreation in paragraph 5 or it may be due to the potentially wide notion of 'cultural life'. Furthermore, there is a great emphasis on access to culture rather than actual participation and again, this may be due to paragraph 1's emphasis on access to specific aspects of cultural life.

In 2009, General Comment 21 of the UN Economic and Social Council provided further detail on article 15.1a of the International Covenant on Economic, Social and Cultural Rights, the Right of everyone to take part in cultural life. In its paragraph 15 it defines participation as comprising three interrelated components: participation, access and, crucially, contribution. Contribution includes a right to be 'involved in creating the spiritual, material, intellectual and emotional expressions of the community'. Harmon et al. (2014) highlight that this, in turn, leads to the UNCRPD Article 30 enshrining a 'right to participate in cultural performance'. Inspection of the State Parties reports and Committee responses highlights that measures to ensure this are, in the main, missing from the reporting and monitoring procedures, with the predominant focus being given to access.

While there are still wide-ranging improvements that need to be made to enable access, real emancipatory equality will only be achieved when participation is achieved on an equal basis. There is an argument that States Parties need to enable access as a baseline before developing further, but if the Committee's responses do not emphasise improvements to be made in participation then progress in this area will be slow or overlooked completely. The Committee needs to provide more nuanced responses, which indicate how change can be achieved that reaches further than addressing minimum standards of access.

In a reflection of the situation relating to non-disabled dance, the need to shape intellectual property law to encourage creation and ownership of elite disabled dance is, sadly, missing in both the Convention's reporting and the monitoring processes. The sole reference in the Convention itself to intellectual property relates to access and none of the reports outline any specific measures relating to authorship. Even New Zealand's wide-ranging strategy fails to tackle this issue; this is particularly surprising in the light of the well-developed approach to intellectual property and cultural heritage in this jurisdiction (Frankel and Drahos 2012).

The Committee's responses only reference intellectual property in relation to the Marrakesh Treaty. This treaty was signed in June 2013 and as of February 2016, fourteen of the 82 signatories had ratified the instrument, falling short of the twenty ratifications it needs to come into effect. The Treaty aims to increase the amount and range of books that are made openly accessible to visually impaired and print disabled people. This will be achieved through the use of new technology and agreements made in relation to the position of rights holders. Harpur and Suzor (2013) see the Marrakesh Treaty as heralding a fundamental shift in copyright law, as it goes against opposition to the imposition of maximum standards of protection and creates what they see as a 'ceiling' to the strength of intellectual property protections. Crucially, they see the inter-operation of the UNCRPD with this Treaty as fundamental to its impact and the 'paradigm inversion' it has created.

The Marrakesh Treaty has a specific focus on increasing access to literary works and is a positive development, although it will need a high level of monitoring for it to have the widest possible reach and to ensure that domestic regulators and rights holders comply with the new duties. On examining the UNCRPD Committee's responses, all the statements provided, which related to the need to address intellectual property, refer to the Marrakesh Treaty. In this way, there is a danger that the Marrakesh Treaty could be seen to fulfil all required intellectual property revisions and regulations needed to ensure the equality of disabled people. Legal measures that go beyond charitably providing access to works and actually empower disabled people to have control and power over the artistic works they create need to be a further focus of States Parties' reporting and the Committee's responses.

While the Marrakesh Treaty is narrow in its focus, it has the potential to provide a framework for those wishing to press for global intellectual property law reform relating to disabled people's ownership of works. Its existence has given the UNCRPD Committee's an easily recognisable international set of rights and duties that can be given strength by the monitoring provisions of the Charter. It is accepted that the Marrakesh Treaty was the culmination of years of negotiation and international collaboration but, further measures need to be taken in order to avoid a situation where it becomes the only normative instrument in the shaping of the Charter's intellectual property law provisions. The Committee on the Rights of Persons with Disabilities has, to date, made two General Comments under Article 39 (OHCHR 2015d); these relate to equal recognition before the law and to accessibility. A comment on women with disabilities is currently being drafted (OHCHR 2015e). A recommended move for the Committee would be to work towards a general comment on Article 30. This would address much needed issues of clarity in relation to further definition of the importance of cultural life, in the face of States Parties' emphasis on sports and recreation. It could also highlight the need to ensure that the article is used to shape States Parties' law and regulation to facilitate and support participation, creation and ownership of cultural performance.

Throughout the reports there are varying degrees to which the Article 33.3 duty to involve civil society is tackled. These often relate to the establishment, and sometimes the funding, of a liaison body that works with a group or groups of disabled people. However, despite the reports holding forth a variety of measures to increase participation, the voice of disabled people does not come across as central to the Convention's implementation. Furthermore, in relation to the Committee itself, Quinn highlights that, although innovation was recommended in civil society monitoring, in relation to the Committee 'they in fact reverted to a very traditional model' (Quinn 2009: 252). An example of good practice is to be found in Austria's approach, which directly incorporated a civil society response in its formal report that often runs contrary to the official State position. In turn, the Committee could introduce some innovation into its reporting by directly addressing the points raised by civil society in its concluding comments. This approach, with practical suggestions from civil society to bridge the gap between the law and the realities of experience, could mitigate the 'typically political response' identified in the UK Government's answer to charges (Harmon et al. 2014) that it was not deemed to fulfil Convention obligations in relation to participation in cultural performance.

The Convention itself was negotiated and drafted using a ground-breaking participatory model, as Justesen and Justesen (2007: 43–44) write:

> This process required a level of transparency, cooperation, self-restraint, and consensus unmatched in human rights treaty drafting and allowed civil society to monitor, participate in, and influence all decision-making discussions.

This initial transformative zeal appears to have been lost in the more mundane realities of ongoing monitoring and reporting. It needs to be rejuvenated through a more engaged dialogue with civil society in order for the Convention to achieve not only minimum standards of access but true equality in relation to equal participation and, in turn, ownership of cultural creation.

Conclusion

Through an examination of the States Parties' reports it can be seen that while some measures are in place to support dance, there are still many areas in which progress needs to be made. At a basic level, dance is lost within the wide reach of Article 30, with just over a quarter of the reports (as outlined in Table 1) referring to it specifically. This gives scope for reports to go into great detail in relation to certain areas, with sport and recreation being prominent, while overlooking others. A recommendation in relation to this would be to require, perhaps through a template, the reports to address each sphere of participation in cultural life independently. This would provide more transparency in relation to what is lacking, as an empty space or column would reveal a failure to implement measures in key areas. It would also make it easier for the Committee and other interested parties to analyse the reports themselves. In turn, if such an approach were taken to the Committee's List of Issues and Concluding Comments then key sectors would not be overlooked.

The analysis of the reports demonstrates a worrying approach to intellectual property rights. The introductory text of the Convention strongly highlights that it heralds a move away from charity and medical models that treat disabled people as passive, towards a more rights-based framework through which disabled people are treated as 'active members of society'. However, in relation to intellectual property issues, Table 1 shows that while the majority of States Parties referenced the Marrakesh Treaty on access to works, only three reference intellectual property in relation to creation. This may be due to the existence of the Marrakesh Treaty, a specific legal instrument against which to measure progress but it also shows a passive approach of 'allowing access' for disabled people rather than providing support to be active, creative and assertive of rights of ownership. As outlined above, a General Comment from the Committee on the area of intellectual property could provide a much-needed wider focus here.

Finally, given the wider emancipatory aims of the Convention, civil society participation is crucial and, while there are some initiatives to include disabled people in the monitoring process, these often do not go far enough to place the voice of disabled people at its heart. The development of civil society shadow commentary reports does draw attention to certain issues not raised by the States Parties but, by its very nature, this split approach can be marginalising. While it might take more time and effort on the part of States Parties, there is a need to include direct input from civil society groups in all official reports. This should be supported by a strong requirement from the Committee to the extent that the reports are only valid if they include direct participation.

The InVisible Difference team (Brown and Waelde 2015) has highlighted a number of areas for improvement in relation to the development of and ownership of disabled dance. The UNCRPD provides a framework to facilitate these changes but, as demonstrated from an analysis of the reporting procedures, dance and intellectual property ownership have been side-lined. Intrinsically linked is the piecemeal nature in which measures to ensure civil society participation are addressed. Given the need to empower and achieve a true rights-based approach, there is a need for the Committee, and in turn States Parties, to engage with disabled dancers, record their concerns formally and implement tangible measures to achieve equality.

References

Brown, A. and Waelde, C. (2015), 'Human rights, persons with disabilities and copyright', in C. Geiger (ed.), *Research Handbook on Human Rights and Intellectual Property*, Cheltenham: Edward Elgar.

CEDAW (1979), 'Convention on the elimination of all forms of discrimination against women', http://www.un.org/womenwatch/daw/cedaw/. Accessed 18 September 2015.

Dance Aotearoa New Zealand (2010), 'Would you like this dance?', http://danz.org.nz/uploads/sites/danz/files/PDFs/NZ%20Dance%20and%20Disability%20Strategy%20-%20Would%20You%20Like%20This%20Dance.pdf. Accessed 1 October 2015.

Directive 2001/29/EC of the European Parliament and of the Council of 22 May 2001 on the harmonisation of certain aspects of copyright and related rights in the information society (2001), Official Journal L 167, 22/06/2001 P. 0010–0019.

European Disability Forum (2015), 'Alternative report on the implementation of the UN Convention on the Rights of Persons with disabilities in Europe', http://www.edf-feph.org/Page_Generale.asp?DocID=13855&thebloc=34249. Accessed 23 September 2015.

Frankel, S. and Drahos, P. (2012), 'Indigenous Peoples innovation: Intellectual property pathways to development (ANU epress)', http://press.anu.edu.au/titles/indigenous-peoples-innovation-ip-pathways-to-development/pdf-download/. Accessed 24 February 2016.

General Comment (2009), 'No. 21: Right of everyone to take part in cultural life', E/C.12/GC/21, UN Economic and Social Council, 21 December.

Harmon, S., Waelde, C. and Whatley, S. (2014), 'Disabled dance: Grounding the practice in the law of cultural heritage', *European Journal of Current Legal Issues*, 20:3, http://webjcli.org/article/view/370/472. Accessed 2 October 2015.

Harpur, P. and Suzor, N. (2013), 'Copyright protections and disability rights: Turning the page to a new international paradigm', *University of New South Wales Law Journal*, 36, p. 745.

ICEAFRD (1963), 'International convention on the elimination of all forms of racial discrimination', http://www.ohchr.org/EN/ProfessionalInterest/Pages/CERD.aspx. Accessed 17 September 2015.

Justesen, T. and Justesen, T. R. (2007), 'An analysis of the development and adoption of the United Nations Convention recognizing the rights of individuals with disabilities: Why the United States refuses to sign this UN Convention', *Human Rights Brief*, 14:2, pp. 36–47.

Marrakesh Treaty to Facilitate Access to Published Works for Persons Who Are Blind, Visually Impaired or Otherwise Print Disabled (2013), http://www.wipo.int/treaties/en/ip/marrakesh/. Accessed 2 October 2015.

Office of the High Commissioner for Human Rights (OHCHR) (2015a), 'CRPD states parties reports', http://tbinternet.ohchr.org/_layouts/treatybodyexternal/TBSearch.aspx?Lang=en&TreatyID=4&DocTypeID=29. Accessed 25 September 2015.

—— (2015b), 'CRPD lists of issues', http://tbinternet.ohchr.org/_layouts/treatybodyexternal/TBSearch.aspx?Lang=en&TreatyID=4&DocTypeID=18. Accessed 25 September 2015.

—— (2015c), 'CRPD concluding remarks', http://tbinternet.ohchr.org/_layouts/treatybodyexternal/TBSearch.aspx?Lang=en&TreatyID=4&DocTypeID=5. Accessed 25 September 2015.

—— (2015d), 'CRPD general comments', http://www.edf-feph.org/Page_Generale.asp?DocID=13855&thebloc=34249. Accessed 25 September 2015.

—— (2015e), 'CRPD draft general comment on women with disabilities', http://www.ohchr.org/EN/HRBodies/CRPD/Pages/GCWomen.aspx. Accessed 25 September 2015.

Privette, G. (1981), 'The phenomenology of peak performance in sports', *International Journal of Sport Psychology*, 12, pp. 36–42.

Quinn, G. (2009), 'Resisting the temptation of elegance', in O. M. Arnardóttir, and G. Quinn (eds), *The UN Convention on the Rights of Persons with Disabilities*, Leiden: Martinus Nijhoff, pp. 215–55.

Sandahl, C. and Auslander, P. (2008) (eds), *Bodies in Commotion: Disability and Performance*, Michigan: The University of Michigan Press.

Shaver, L. and Sganga, C. (2009), 'The right to take part in cultural life: Copyright and human rights', *Faculty Scholarship Series*, 23, http://digitalcommons.law.yale.edu/fss_papers/23. Accessed 25 September 2015.

UN ENABLE (1993), 'Standard rules on the equalization of opportunities for persons with disabilities', http://www.un.org/esa/socdev/enable/dissre00.htm. Accessed 28 September 2015.

—— (2015), 'Chapter two: The Convention in detail', http://www.un.org/disabilities/default.asp?id=222. Accessed 8 September 2015.

United Nations Convention on the Rights of Persons with Disabilities (UNCPRD) (2008), http://www.un.org/disabilities/default.asp?id=150. Accessed 15 September 2015.

United Nations International Convention on Civil and Political Rights (1966), http://www.ohchr.org/EN/ProfessionalInterest/Pages/CCPR.aspx. Accessed 8 September 2015.

Universal Declaration of Human Rights (1948), http://www.un.org/en/documents/udhr/#atop. Accessed 14 September 2015.

Note

1 Jordan, Morocco, Oman, Mexico, Morocco, Russia, Saudi Arabia and Sudan.

Chapter 4

A Dance of Difference: The Tripartite Model of Disability and the Cultural Heritage of Dance

David Bolt and Heidi Mapley

Cultural heritage is widely discussed in the dance community. One of the main observations is that dance, as a fluid entity, cannot be contained in the tangible way that cultural heritage requires (Waelde 2015). It is argued that, by its very nature, dance cannot be captured, that its essence exists in an embodied moment that cannot be accurately recorded. Farooq Chaudhry, a choreographer and former dancer, is concerned that, because normative ideas of beauty are so dominant, if cultural heritage is pursued then the classics of the past will remain valued at the expense of current work (Waelde 2015). The desire to hold on to normative dance experiences that prioritise traditional aesthetics can be deemed problematic for all dancers and is particularly detrimental to the advancement of what is sometimes termed disability dance. Recognition of how 'alternative embodiments' (Mitchell and Snyder 2015: 6) can shape an understanding of dance – and, by extension, contribute to the cultural heritage of dance – is necessary if we are to move forward. It is our hope that this chapter will contribute to an understanding of the 'cultural heritage of dance' (InVisible Difference 2014), one that appreciates the value and beauty of 'alternative lives' (Mitchell and Snyder 2015: 6).

Our proposition is that understandings of the role of dance in cultural heritage can be enhanced by consideration of the tripartite model of disability that is based on a conceptual distinction between ableism and disablism. While there is no uniformly accepted term for discrimination against people who identify or are labelled as disabled (Harpur 2012), a form of prejudice referred to as the nameless apartheid (Goggin and Newell 2003), Anglophone terms have emerged in the form of 'ableism' and 'disablism'. 'Ableism' is more widely used globally and 'disablism' is favoured in the United Kingdom (Ashby 2010), which reflects the distinction between person-first and British social model language (Harpur 2012).[1] Thus, although in both cases the terminology denotes discriminatory or abusive (e.g. disability hate crime) conduct towards people based on physical or cognitive abilities (Harpur 2009, 2012), we follow work that appreciates the respective merits of the two terms (Campbell 2008, 2009; Harpur 2012; Bolt 2014). From this perspective, 'ableism' and 'disablism' render different understandings of disability: the former is associated with the idea of ableness, the perfect or perfectible body; and the latter relates to the production of – disability, in accordance with a social constructionist understanding (Campbell 2008). That is to say, ableism renders nondisabled people supreme over disabled people and disablism is a combination of attitudes and actions against said individuals.

The premise of the tripartite model is that ableism and disablism can be understood as normative positivisms and non-normative negativisms respectively, both of which should be explored, but that consideration must also be given to what have been elsewhere designated non-normative positivisms (Coole and Frost 2011; Mitchell and Snyder 2015). Based on experience and theory, this model recognises passive and active prejudice in the forms of Otherness and victimisation, but not at the expense of positive things about disability, like the appreciation of diversity, culture, innovation and so on. As such, the model is manifestly pertinent to the subject of dance. How does dance privilege certain minds and bodies? How does it problematise other minds and bodies? How does it promote an appreciation of the minds and bodies that come under the rubric of disability? These are the questions around which the chapter is structured as we apply the tripartite model of disability in the quest for a meaningful, profound and indeed intangible cultural heritage of dance.

Normative Positivisms: How Dance Privileges Certain Minds and Bodies

The first part of the tripartite model of disability pertains to the ongoing affirmation of socially accepted standards – that is, normative positivisms that are marked by ableism. Ableism has been defined as a political term that calls attention to assumptions about normalcy (Davis 1995); it has been traced back to 'handicapism', a term coined nearly four decades ago to denote not only assumptions but also practices that promoted the unequal treatment of people because of apparent or assumed physical, mental and/or behavioural differences (Bogdan and Biklen 1998; Ashby 2010). The concept of ableism, however, has been societally entrenched, deeply and subliminally embedded in culture, and rampant throughout history; it has been widely used by various social groups to justify their elevated rights and status in relation to other groups (Campbell 2008; Wolbring 2008). Whatever and however we term it, ableism is an age-old concept that equates with normative positivisms.

Recent cultural history has provided a clear example of normative positivisms in the form of two *Top of the Pop's* dance troupes. In the late 1960s, the 1970s and the early 1980s, Pan's People and Legs and Co were the most successful dance acts in the United Kingdom. In both troupes the same embodiment was dominant, for all of the dancers were slim, long-legged and young (under 22 years of age when they first joined). Their body shape was emphasised by the troupe name 'Legs and Co', which was chosen via a viewer's competition (Panspeople. com 2011) and as such exemplified the way in which the dancers were viewed by the public. Evidently, these dance troupes were founded on an exclusionist view that selected dancers according to their ability to fit physical and aesthetic ideals. The prevailing image endorsed by this exclusionist approach was that of the dancer as 'white, female, thin, long-limbed, flexible' and 'able bodied' (Albright 1997: 58). That is to say, these two dance troupes were defined by ableist ideology.

This implicit ideology has historical resonance that dates back to the bleak era of Nazi Germany, for the profession of dance indirectly endorsed the principles of the Third Reich. The Nazis recognised that the arts could be utilised as an ideological weapon via which political propaganda could be disseminated. Dance, as a component of the arts, supplied 'the political movement with a thought structure'; while some dancers, along with other artists, 'realised their own aesthetic principles' by aligning themselves with the political framework of the Nazi party (Karina and Kant 2004; Kant 2008: 8). Nazi legislation, moreover, was put into practice by Rudolf von Laban and Mary Wigman, representatives of modern dance, whose influential dance groups and dance schools are believed to have used the Re-Establishment of the Professional Civil Service to their own advantage.[2] In order to cleanse their profession (in a eugenic sense), and ensure that the physical and aesthetic principles of dance remained intact, some dancers and choreographers conveniently labelled and subsequently ostracised certain colleagues as '"Jews" or "degenerate" or both' (Karina and Kant 2004; Kant 2008: 10). This public denouncement aided the establishment of Nazism and further entrenched the hegemonic desire for so-called perfection, values that become all the more disturbing when we remember the hundreds of thousands of disabled people who lost their lives as a result of the Nazi's programme.

What we have learned from this history is a moot point, but many variants of ableism certainly remain in culture and society. For instance, cognitive ableism is a bias in favour of the interests of people who actually or potentially have certain cognitive abilities, as in neurotypicality over autism (Carlson 2001); lexism is an array of normative practices, assumptions and attitudes about literacy, which result in, among other things, dyslexia (Collinson 2014); sanism is the privileging of people who do not have so-called mental health issues, meaning that those given diagnostic labels like schizophrenia or depression are disadvantaged (Prendergast 2014); audism pertains to the normative landscape in which everyone perceives by auditory means and the deaf community are thus ignored (Bauman and Murray 2009); and ocularcentrism is the dominance of visual perception that leaves no scope for other means of sensory engagement (Jay 1994). The list could go on and on, for many normative positivisms are embedded in culture and informed by ableism.

A thing to remember is that when we endeavour to occupy the subject position of ableism, we buy into a myriad of normative assumptions but often do so without premeditation or intent. While many 'progressive intellectuals' decry racism, sexism and class bias, it does not occur to most of us that the very foundations on which our information systems are built, our very practices of 'reading and writing, seeing, thinking, and moving are themselves laden with assumptions about hearing, deafness, blindness, normalcy, paraplegia, and ability and disability in general' (Davis 1995: 4–5). Ableism is a deeply rooted, far-reaching network of beliefs, processes and practices that produces a corporeal standard, a particular type of mind and body, which is projected as the perfect human (Campbell 2001). This network of notions about health, productivity, beauty and the value of human life, represented and perpetuated by public and private media, renders abilities such as productivity and competitiveness far more important than, say, empathy, compassion and kindness (Rauscher and McClintock 1997; Wolbring 2008). Indeed, so pervasive is this network that we are likely to pick up detailed knowledge of ableism via the gradual absorption of ideas that results from continual exposure to culture. Ableism can therefore become part of us with or without intent.

Irrespective of intent, the widespread endorsement of ableism has dire consequences for society. Many bodies and minds are constructed and positioned as Other, meaning that many people fall outside the dominant norms of bodily appearance and/or performance and thus face social and material exclusion (Ashby 2010; Hodge and Runswick-Cole 2013). From this perspective, impairments are necessarily negative: they must be improved, cured or else eliminated altogether (Campbell 2008). In effect, ableism becomes a combination of discrimination, power and prejudice that is related to the cultural privileging of non-disabled people; it oppresses those who have so-called mental health problems, learning difficulties, physical impairments, sensory impairments, cognitive impairments and chronic pain (Rauscher and McClintock 1997; Eisenhauer 2007). In other words, the normative positivisms of ableism indirectly result in the social exclusion, victimisation and stigmatisation of people who identify or are labelled as disabled.

Despite its dramatic effects, ableism has been referred to as a nebulous concept that evades both identification and definition (Hodge and Runswick-Cole 2013). What is more, the term has been deemed limited in content and scope on the basis that it should not allude exclusively to disability, but should be used as an umbrella term (Wolbring 2008), a call for terminological specificity that is answered to some extent by the term to which we now turn: *disablism*. After all, although ableism itself is often obscured, the value it places on certain abilities leads to disablism (Wolbring 2008; Hodge and Runswick-Cole 2013). In accordance with the tripartite model, therefore, the normative positivisms of ableism result in the non-normative negativisms of disablism.

Non-Normative Negativisms: How Dance Problematises Some Minds and Bodies

The second part of the tripartite model of disability pertains to problematised deviations from socially accepted standards – that is, non-normative negativisms that are marked by disablism. The term 'disablism' is derived from the social model of disability, whereby the everyday practices of society perpetuate oppressive structures on people who have biological impairments (Madriaga 2007). Discriminatory, oppressive and/or abusive behaviour arises from the belief that said people are somehow inferior to counterparts who do not have impairments (Miller et al. 2004), meaning that so-called less able people are discriminated against and different abilities become defined as disabilities (Thomas 2004; Wolbring 2008). Disablism, then, involves not only the social imposition of restrictions of activity but also the socially engendered undermining of psycho-emotional well-being (Thomas 2007). Physical barriers to access become internalised by disabled people and thus function on a profoundly personal level. Disablism is arguably a deeper and more specific development of ableism.

This specificity notwithstanding, disablism is not necessarily explicit. The term *aversive disablism* denotes subtle forms of prejudice (Deal 2007). Aversive disablism is often unintentional, so aversive disablists may recognise the problems of disablism without recognising their own prejudice (Deal 2007). For example, the AXIS Dance Company has a 'distinguished 25-year history as one of America's leading mixed ability dance troops'; it has included dancers who 'use wheelchairs, crutches, prosthetic limbs, and other mobility aids, and access for physically disabled audiences has always been a priority' (Kleege 2014: 13). However, as has been documented, audience members who have visual impairments are often excluded: 'The only reason I knew what was going on was that I had discussed the composition at length with the choreographer' (Kleege 2014: 13). While this scenario illustrates aversive disablism, we return to the AXIS Dance Company on a far more positive note later in the chapter.

Aversive disablism is sometimes premised on altruism. Disabled individuals may face various barriers to participation – such as a lack of opportunities to progress, inaccessible performance and recreational areas, financial and geographical constraints, and so on – but one of the most significant barriers, particularly when starting out, is the altruistic protective nature of family, teachers, peers, professionals and carers who fail to perceive dance 'as a viable or appropriate activity (never mind career) for people with disabilities' (Aujla and Redding 2013: 81). Claire Cunningham, an aerial dancer who was diagnosed with osteoporosis as a young child, observed how throughout her life doctors continuously focused on what her body could not do. In one instance, deterring Claire from her passion for dance, medical staff made the assumption that an accident she had while training was as a result of her disability, because 'a person on crutches shouldn't be doing things like that' (Fisher 2007). Defying this medical advice, Claire continued to dance and as a result grew 3cm taller and her bone density increased by 5 per cent (Fisher 2007). In other words, medical professionals aimed to protect Claire from a career choice that improved her lifestyle in ways that they themselves would surely have to recognise.

Of course not all forms of disablism are subtle or well-intentioned. A recent interview illustrates how certain political practices are by their very nature disabling and thus illustrative of non-normative negativisms. In this interview Claire highlights how an assessment for Disability Living Allowance seeks only to assess limitations, no consideration is given to the complexity of embodiment (Pollock 2015). This testing is compulsory if someone wishes to claim the financial support to which he or she is entitled. Claire makes the point that, for disabled dancers who spend their professional careers demonstrating what they can achieve, such an experience can be particularly difficult. Having to prove one's supposed failings on command can be emotionally and psychologically damaging, something that Claire resists by utilising performance as a means of creatively and affirmatively displaying her body's limitations (Pollock 2015). She talks about how the crutches she uses to negotiate everyday life and her dance routines are highly relevant to her embodied state: 'My relationship with them changed as I began to accept them more as an extension of my body, and their movement became more organic as well' (Cunningham, cited in Pollock 2015).[3] Indeed, as a dancer, Claire embodies an, 'enhancement of abilities created by disability' and epitomises how 'perceived limitations can become a skill or unique talent' (Cunningham, cited in

Fisher 2007). This complex perception of hybrid embodiment and how it can alter the body and mind clearly points us in the direction of non-normative positivisms.

This bringing together of body/mind and technology[4] can nonetheless fall prey to the oppressive behaviour that typifies non-normative negativisms. Disablist views that pertain to this hybrid form of embodiment are likely to render the disabled person in two ways: first, as lacking independence, due to her or his reliance on assistive technologies; and second, as subject to a kind of 'normate reductionism', whereby the disability symbolism of the technology obscures not only its purpose but also its user (Garland Thomson 1997; Bolt 2012: 292). The reality is that, when considering the examples of computers and cars, technology enhances humanity on a daily basis. As Haraway (1991: 150) points out, 'we are all chimeras, theorized and fabricated hybrids of machine and organism; in short, we are all cyborgs'. That is to say, the cyborg defies the myth of independence by accentuating the reality of interdependent relationships.

This being so, normate reductionism is challenged, given that we, as interdependent beings, may all find that our qualities and successes can be reduced in some way to influencing factors. Hybrid embodiment enables us all to confront limitations and consider possibilities, for it highlights how 'we gradually re-evaluate our own bodily boundaries in terms of the technology we are using' (Marks 1999: 15). In view of this complex relationship that humanity shares with various forms of technology, a disabled dancer should not be solely defined by the technology he or she utilises. Assistive technology, even when considered in terms of hybrid embodiment, cannot be assumed to displace autonomy. The performance very much belongs to the dancer, who should retain control of how and when to make use of her or his choice of technology (Quinlan and Bates 2014). Hybrid embodiment, then, troubles the normate subject position from which so many reductive assumptions are made.

Hybrid embodiment certainly went unacknowledged in relation to Heather Mills's appearance on the reality show *Dancing with the Stars*. Mills's experience introduced a highly pervasive form of disablism that illustrated normate reductionism insofar as some viewers, who found it difficult to connect disability and dance, focused solely on her impairment. An analysis of 'journalistic and blogger comments' highlights three themes that support the reductionism attached to Mills's performances, these are 'supercrip', 'taking advantage of the sick role',[5] and the 'sexualised disabled body' (Quinlan and Bates 2010: 64). Following Heather's performance, it was argued that if Heather was fit enough to dance then she did not require her blue badge; and that the (assumed) disadvantage could actually have been an advantage that gained her a sympathy vote from the judges (Quinlan and Bates 2010). This scrutiny of Heather's participation in dance can be viewed as a form of psycho-emotional disablism, whereby the disabled person is always open to the scrutiny of the gaze. Psycho-emotional disablism has many ramifications, as it may instigate psychological barriers that can prove to be as insurmountable as any environmental barriers.

Disabled dancers, aware of the scrutiny to which they are exposed, may, in accordance with the Foucauldian concept of bio-power (Nadesan 2011), self-regulate by adapting their behaviour to satisfy authoritative beliefs. Psychological disruption of this kind may lead to the dancer not accessing the services to which he or she is entitled or not requesting reasonable adjustments that enable full participation (Quinlan and Bates 2010). As a result, already established barriers such as access and financial constraints may be left unchallenged, while services and entitlements may be underused and put at risk of removal, all of which could create further difficulties for disabled dancers who wish to enter the profession. Similarly, if dancers manage to overcome each of these barriers but are then left feeling as though their success is not their own, they may be less likely to progress and succeed. This disruption has repercussions for dance more broadly. After all, how can we facilitate a cultural heritage of dance that is appreciative of the value of all people if there is a hierarchical contention that attributes all successes to those who are deemed superior?

Non-Normative Positivisms: How Dance Promotes an Appreciation of the Minds and Bodies That Come Under the Rubric of Disability

The third part of the tripartite model of disability pertains to affirmed deviations from socially accepted standards – that is, non-normative positivisms that depart from ableism and disablism. It is not enough to recognise disability along a continuum of difference that defines human variation; it is important to consider how the ideology of neoliberal inclusiveness profits from the instability of previously fixed identities (Jordan 2013). Disability is now more apparent than ever, a state of affairs that, in part, has resulted from so-called tolerance, or inclusionism (Mitchell and Snyder 2015). However, there is a need for non-normative positivisms because the fight for equality is both limited and limiting in its very scope, while empowering and progressive potential is offered by the profound appreciation of Othered experience (Mitchell and Snyder 2015). That is to say, inclusion may well be paramount in culture and society but can become transformative and more comprehensively productive when disability is recognised as a site for alternative values.

The continuum of normative positivisms and non-normative negativisms, then, can be disrupted productively by the recognition of non-normative positivisms, which is why the tripartite model is tee-shaped in its conceptual form. This development draws on recent approaches that encompass individual, collective and cultural positivisms, whereby it is emphasised that people who identify as disabled can lead full, satisfying and even exemplary lives (Swain and French 2000; Kuppers 2009; Mitchell and Snyder 2015). To assert a positive identity around impairment is to repudiate the dominant value of normality, so the affirmative model offers more than a transformation of consciousness about disability, it facilitates an assertion of the value and validity of the lives of people who have impairments (Swain and French 2000). These approaches resonate with the performance artist Aaron Williamson's reframing of the common conception of hearing loss as Deaf Gain (Bauman and Murray 2009), a conceptualisation that has been applied to disability more generally (Garland Thomson 2013).

Recent cultural history provided an example of non-normative positivisms when familial experience of disability and dance led Alessi to co-organise 'a "contact improvisation" workshop' that was open to everyone, regardless of dis/abilities (Alessi and Zolbrod 2008: 330). This workshop proved highly successful. On a quantitative level, approximately 100 people gathered together to dance. However, it was on a qualitative level that true success was witnessed. The year was 1987, just after the time of the *Top of the Pop's* dance troupes, yet members of the community present at the workshop included a blind mother with her young daughter, young men injured in various accidents, professional dancers, contact improvisers and so on (Alessi and Zolbrod 2008).[6] What Alessi and his co-organiser, Karen Nelson, thereby demonstrated was the intrinsic value of *all* people to the culture of dance. In accordance with the 'tongue dancing' performed at the Society for Disability Societies (SDS) Annual Convention (Garland Thomson 2007: 121), Alessi and Nelson broadened the definition of dance to include a movement of eyes or a 'left pinky finger' (Alessi and Zolbrod 2008: 329). Through this definition, they emphasised a respect for the humanness of everyone, a realisation of interdependency that recognised each person present had something valuable and unique to offer the group. When the dance environment is so open to the fact that 'all kinds of bodies and minds are beautiful, are wonderful, are delightful' (Brashear, 2013), benefits can be observed across the board. It becomes much easier to 'open up and explore new movement possibilities' when occupying a space that is open to your presence (Alessi and Zolbrod 2008: 330). Furthermore, the more diverse ways of moving and thinking that people encounter the more they can step outside of their fixed identities and explore 'other aspects of their own hybridity' (Wiesel et al. 2013: 2394).

Non-normative positivisms, then, can be realised when consideration is given to 'body awareness' and 'spatial awareness', which have been defined as fundamental to 'dance ability' (Kauffman cited in Zitomer and Reid 2011: 138). Of course these two constructs do not exclude disabled people from dance. In fact, the opposite is true, as Cunningham discovered when choreographers commented on the interesting ways in which she managed her body in order to ease the pressure on her legs (Fisher 2007). After all, the disabled body may perform 'a series of touches, leans and counterbalances', with or without 'human or technical supports', on a daily basis, as disability requires a 'real negotiation of space and the body' (Davies 2010: 56). In this instance, non-normative positivisms result from a 'complex embodiment' that involves 'the reciprocal transformation between the body and its environment' (Siebers 2014: 3). Hence, the disabled dancer can be appreciated for a use of knowledge acquired by non-normative embodiment.

This use of knowledge is illustrated by the international breakdance crew, 'ILL-Abilities', which features five dancers who consider themselves to be 'differently abled'. Each dancer stresses the disruptive nature of non-normative positivisms by accentuating how disability can be considered in terms of strength and advantage, not just limitation. Their dance routines are utilised as a means to redefine societal views of disability and to promote the fact that disability does not have to equal restriction, that it can actually be viewed in terms of fresh and exciting possibilities. Workshops designed by ILL-Abilities are underpinned by these beliefs; they are inclusive to all people, regardless of age, ability and skill level, as dance is explored as a universal experience (ILL-Abilities 2013). Indeed, the very name 'ILL-Abilities' incorporates this philosophy. In hip-hop culture it is common to take something with negative connotations and recreate it positively. Using this form of appropriation, the word *ill* comes to mean 'incredible, amazing, intricate, or super talented' (ILL-Abilities 2013). Thus, ILL-Abilities take ownership of a term that is, as a result of medicalisation, often used in reference to disability and limitation, and reconfigure it in order to illustrate the positive capabilities of alternative corporealities.

The potential offered by an appreciation of alternative corporealities can be further illustrated if we return to the example of the AXIS Dance Company that commissioned choreographer Victoria Marks's *What If Would You*, which premiered in Oakland, California, 2013.[7] The premise was that 'access is both more effective and more aesthetic if it is in the artist's mind from the outset, rather than something tacked on in post-production, and delegated to access specialists who may be several removes from the artist's thinking' (Kleege 2014: 11). As a result, Marks composed a dance that was meant to be experienced by haptic means:

> The dancers came into the audience and asked, 'Would you like to join me in this dance?' The dancers then led the audience members into the performance space, and stood back-to-back with them. When all the couples were positioned around the space, at some prearranged signal, the dancers performed a sequence of small gestural movements while in contact or close proximity to their partners from the audience. These included light touches to the partner's shoulders, leaning the crown of the head into the partner's back, walking around the partner while touching his or her shoulder or arm, taking the partner's hand, and walking him or her to a new location. After this sequence was performed, the dancer left the first partner and moved to the next person in the space. Then the sequence of movements was repeated.
>
> (Kleege 2014: 11)

This aspect of the AXIS Dance Company's version of the composition was met with much enthusiasm: the onstage participants 'described feeling included in the dance, transcending the barrier between performer and spectator' (Kleege 2014: 13). The point we want to stress here is that Marks's 'complete engagement with the question about how dance is experienced opens up possibilities for new ways of thinking about blind access, and coincidentally for the art form in general' (Kleege 2014: 13). In other words, it was the endeavour to address non-normative negativisms that led to a realisation of non-normative positivisms.

Conclusion: Culture and Community

In this chapter, it is apparent that community plays a significant role in the recognition and fostering of non-normative positivisms; and that non-normative positivisms ensure the cohesiveness of the community. Interestingly, Fiona Macmillan highlights that it is the community that decides what should be conserved as cultural heritage. She suggests that while disabled dance may form a community in itself, it must also form a valuable part of the wider dance community. This value is necessary to ensure advancement towards a meaningful, profound and intangible cultural heritage of dance (InVisible Difference 2014). Dance companies such as Axis, Candoco, Stop Gap and ILL-Abilities, among others, are at the forefront of this advancement, as they recognise the reciprocal relationship between community and non-normative positivisms.

The disruptive power of non-normative positivisms emphasises that the cultural heritage of dance should not aspire to ableist expectations of normalcy. Indeed, disabled dancers are central to the creativity of dance, as they provide an original and exciting perspective founded on the knowledge they gain from complex embodiment. In order to make relevant the significance of non-normative positivisms to an intangible cultural heritage of dance, communities must realise the connection between interdependence and embodiment. All dancers and choreographers need to reflect not only on their strengths and advantages but also on their constraints and vulnerability, so that each can be utilised in a creative and innovative manner. Only then can we facilitate a cultural heritage of dance that moves away from the dominant aesthetic discourse and towards a recognition of the value, beauty and humanness of all participants.

References

Albright, A. C. (1997), *Choreographing Difference: The Body and Identity in Contemporary Dance*, Middletown: Wesleyan University Press.

Alessi, A. and Zolbrod, S. (2008), 'Dance and disability', in N. M. Jackson and T. Shapiro-Phim (eds) *Dance, Human Rights, and Social Justice: Dignity in Motion*, Lanham: The Scarecrow Press Inc, pp. 329–32.

Ashby, C. (2010), 'The trouble with normal: The struggle for meaningful access for middle school students with developmental disability labels', *Disability & Society*, 25:3 pp. 345–58.

Aujla, I. J. and Redding, E. (2013), 'Barriers to dance training for young people with disabilities', *British Journal of Special Education*, 40:2, pp. 80–85.

Bauman, H-D. and Murray, J. M. (2009), 'Reframing: From hearing loss to deaf gain', *Deaf Studies Digital Journal*, 1, pp. 1–10.

Bogdan, R. and Biklen, S. K. (1998), *Qualitative Research for Education: An Introduction to Theory and Method*, Boston: Allyn & Bacon.

Bolt, D. (2012), 'Social encounters, cultural representation and critical avoidance', in N. Watson, A. Roulstone and C. Thomas (eds), *Routledge Handbook of Disability Studies*, Abingdon: Routledge, pp. 287–97.

—— (2014), *Changing Social Attitudes Toward Disability: Perspectives from Historical, Cultural, and Educational Studies*, Abingdon: Routledge.

Brashear, R. (2013), *Fixed: The Science/Fiction of Human Enhancement*, Making Change Media.

Campbell, F. A. K. (2001), 'Inciting legal fictions: Disability's date with ontology and the ableist body of the law', *Griffith Law Review*, 10, pp. 42–62.

—— (2008), 'Exploring internalized ableism using critical race theory', *Disability & Society*, 23:2, pp. 151–62.

—— (2009), *Frontiers of Ableism*, Australia: Palgrave Macmillan.

Carlson, L. (2001), 'Cognitive ableism and disability studies: Feminist reflections on the history of mental retardation', *Hypatia*, 16:4, pp. 124–46.

Collinson, C. (2014), '"Lexism" and the temporal problem of defining "dyslexia"', in D. Bolt (ed.), *Changing Social Attitudes Toward Disability: Perspectives from Historical, Cultural, and Educational Studies*, Abingdon: Routledge, pp. 153–61.

Coole, D. and Frost, S. (eds) (2011), *The New Materialism: Ontology, Agency, and Politics*, Durham: Duke University Press.

Davies, T. (2010), 'Mobility: Axis dancers push the boundaries of access', in B. Henderson and N. Ostrander (eds) *Understanding Disability Studies and Performance Studies*, Abingdon: Routledge, pp. 43–63.

Davis, L. J. (1995), *Enforcing Normalcy: Disability, Deafness and the Body*, London: Verso Books.

Deal, M. (2007), 'Aversive disablism: Subtle prejudice toward disabled people', *Disability & Society*, 22:1, pp. 93–107.

Eisenhauer, J. (2007), 'Just looking and staring back: Challenging ableism through disability performance art', *Studies in Art Education: A Journal of Issues and Research*, 49:1, pp. 7–22.

Fisher, M. (2007), 'She turned a disability into dance revolution', *The Sunday Times*, 23 September, Boston, MA: Cengage Learning, Inc. Accessed 10 July 2015.

Garland Thomson, R. (1997), *Extraordinary Bodies: Figuring Physical Disability in American Culture and Literature*, New York: Columbia University Press.

—— (2007), 'Shape structures story: Fresh and feisty stories about disability narrative', *Narrative*, 15:1, pp. 113–23.

—— (2013), 'Disability gain', *Avoidance in/and the Academy: The International Conference on Disability, Culture, and Education*, Liverpool Hope University, Liverpool, 11 September.

Goggin, G. and Newell, C. (2003), *Disability in Australia: Exposing a Social Apartheid*, Sydney: University of New South Wales Press.

Haraway, D. (1991), *Simians, Cyborgs, and Women: The Reinvention of Nature*, London: Free Association Books.

Harpur, P. (2009), 'Sexism and racism, why not ableism?: Calling for a cultural shift in the approach to disability discrimination', *Alternative Law Journal*, 35:3, pp. 163–67.

—— (2012), 'From disability to ability: Changing the phrasing of the debate', *Disability & Society*, 27:3, pp. 325–37.

Hodge, N. and Runswick-Cole, K. (2013), '"They never pass me the ball": Exposing ableism through the leisure experiences of disabled children, young people and their families', *Children's Geographies*, 11:3, pp. 311–25.

ILL-Abilities (2013), 'About', http://illabilities.com/about/. Accessed 12 August 2015.

InVisible Difference (2014), 'Opening of the day and the first panel – Disability dance and cultural heritage', https://www.youtube.com/watch?v=5cRMvs91kRU. Accessed 23 August 2015.

Jay, M. (1994), *Downcast Eyes: The Denigration of Vision in Twentieth-Century French Thought*, Berkeley and London: University of California Press.

Jordan, T. (2013), 'Disability, able-bodiedness, and the biopolitical imagination', *Review of Disability Studies*, 9:1, pp. 26–38.

Kant, M. (2008), 'Practical imperative: German dance, dancers, and Nazi politics', in N. Jackson and T. Shapiro-Phim (eds), *Dance, Human Rights, and Social Justice: Dignity in Motion*, Lanham: The Scarecrow Press, pp. 5–19.

Karina, L. and Kant, M. (2004), *Hitler's Dancers: German Modern Dance and the Third Reich*, Oxford: Berghahn Books.

Kleege, G. (2014), 'What does dance do, and who says so? Some thoughts on blind access to dance performance', *British Journal of Visual Impairment*, 32:1, pp. 7–13.

Kuppers, P. (2009), 'Toward a rhizomatic model of disability: Poetry, performance, and touch', *Journal of Literary and Cultural Disability Studies*, 3:3, pp. 221–40.

Madriaga, M. (2007), 'Enduring disablism: Students with dyslexia and their pathways into UK higher education and beyond', *Disability & Society*, 22:4, pp. 399–412.

Marks, D. (1999), *Disability: Controversial Debates and Psychosocial Perspectives*, Abingdon: Routledge.

Marks, V. (2013), *What If Would You*, Malonga Casquelourd Center for the Arts, Oakland, premiere 12 April.

Miller, P., Parker, S. and Gillinson, S. (2004), *Disablism: How to Tackle the Last Prejudice*, London: Demos.

Mitchell, D. T. and Snyder, S. L. (2015), *The Biopolitics of Disability: Neoliberalism, Ablenationalism, and Peripheral Embodiment*, Ann Arbor: University of Michigan Press.

Nadesan, M. H. (2011), *Governmentality, Biopower, and Everyday Life*, Abingdon: Routledge.

Panspeople.com (2011), 'History', http://www.panspeople.com/?q=history. Accessed 10 July 2015.

Parsons, T. (1951), *The Social System*, New York: Free Press.

Pollock, D. (2015), 'Claire Cunningham on staying creative in a climate of fear', http://www.wow247.co.uk/2015/08/11/claire-cunningham-on-staying-creative-in-a-climate-of-fear/. Accessed 12 August 2015.

Prendergast, C. (2014), 'Mental disability and rhetoricity retold: The memoir on drugs', in D. Bolt (ed.) *Changing Social Attitudes Toward Disability: Perspectives from Historical, Cultural, and Educational Studies*, Abingdon: Routledge, pp. 60–68.

Quinlan, M. and Bates, B. R. (2010), 'Dances and discourses of (dis)Ability: Heather Mills's embodiment of disability on dancing with the stars', in B. Henderson and N. Ostrander (eds), *Understanding Disability Studies and Performance Studies*, Abingdon: Routledge, pp. 64–80.

—————— (2014), 'Unsmoothing the cyborg: Technology and the body in integrated dance', *Disability Studies Quarterly*, 34:4. http://dsq-sds.org/article/view/3783/3792. Accessed 24 October 2017.

Rauscher, L. and McClintock, M. (1997), 'Ableism curriculum design', in M. Adams, L. A. Bell and P. Griffin (eds), *Teaching for Diversity and Social Justice: A Sourcebook*, Abingdon: Routledge, pp. 198–230.

Siebers, T. (2014), 'Returning the social to the social model', *The Society for Disability Studies in Minneapolis, MN*, https://nonnormativepositivisms.wordpress.com/. Accessed 1 July 2015.

Swain, J. and French, S. (2000), 'Towards an affirmation model of disability', *Disability & Society*, 15:4, pp. 569–82.

Thomas, C. (2004), 'Developing the social relational in the social model of disability: A theoretical agenda', in C. Barnes and G. Mercer (eds), *Implementing the Social Model of Disability: Theory and Research*, Leeds: The Disability Press, pp. 32–47.

—— (2007), *Sociologies of Disability, 'Impairment', and Chronic Illness: Ideas in Disability Studies and Medical Sociology*, London: Palgrave Macmillan.

Waelde, C. (2015), 'Dance and cultural heritage', *InVisible Difference*, http://www.invisible difference.org.uk/blog/. Accessed 12 July 2015.

Wiesel, I., Bigby, C. and Carling-Jenkins, R. (2013), '"Do you think I'm stupid?': Urban encounters between people with and without intellectual disability', *Urban Studies*, 50:12, pp. 2391–406.

Wolbring, G. (2008), 'The politics of ableism', *Development*, 51, pp. 252–58.

Zitomer, M. R. and Reid, G. (2011), 'To be or not to be – Able to dance: Integrated dance and children's perceptions of dance ability and disability', *Research in Dance Education*, 12:2, pp. 137–56.

Notes

1 *Ableism* designates the ideology against which a focus on personhood rather than disability is asserted, while *disablism* resonates with the contention that people with biological impairments become disabled because of social barriers.

2 The Re-Establishment of the Professional Civil Service was on 7 April 1933.

3 See also Herr (Brashear, 2013), who asserts, 'My artificial limbs are part of my body [...] they are part of my identity now'.

4 By technology we mean all assistive equipment and life forms.

5 The sick role is a concept developed by Parsons (1951), who believes that individuals who qualify are granted certain societal privileges, which can extend into an exemption from particular duties.

6 Several non-disabled people attended with an assumption that they would be supporting and helping disabled people, a misconception that was swiftly addressed once the session began.

7 The work was a development of Marks's contribution to an arts and accessibility workshop that Georgina Kleege helped to organise at the University of California, Irvine, 2012.

Chapter 5

In a Different Light? Broadening the Bioethics Perspective through Dance

Shawn Harmon

Introduction

A chapter on ethics, and more specifically on bioethics, might seem like a bit of an outlier when considered against the broader thrust and content of this book, which, like the InVisible Difference project itself, is more about extending thinking and altering practice around the making, status, ownership and value of work by contemporary disabled dance choreographers. It may seem even less directly pertinent when one considers that we have not been concerned within the project with rehabilitative or community dance, which is most closely associated with the medical encounter and healthcare machinery. However, despite the apparent remoteness of questions associated with the functioning of bioethics, the chapter is not so much of an outlier as one might imagine. The matter of bioethics arose within our empirical encounters when it became clear that, while many of our participant dancers did not consider the medical framework to be particularly relevant to their work, they *did* have negative experiences within the medical architecture, and, in some cases, that experience coloured the creative process and the stories they told. This proximity of the medical to the creative makes a consideration of the bioethical not only relevant, but positively critical if we are to offer a more holistic view of the experience of disabled dancers and of the solutions that might be pursued to improve their overall existence. So let us begin.

It has been argued that we must, in both ethics and the humanities, strive to cast acts in such a way as to allow them to be viewed 'in a different light' (Keane 2014). By doing so we can better consider them, understand them, critique them, position ourselves and others in association with them, and, ultimately, shift social practice. One of the fundamental questions that is asked within the field of ethics is this:

How should we live?

This question must also be central to medical ethics, or 'bioethics'; if the field fails to engage with this question, then it is not worthy of the name. Assigning this question a central role in bioethics (or any other field) necessitates its interrogation within every act, every encounter and every technological deployment that is assessed, and of course, we should always strive to view those acts, encounters and deployments in a different light. However, we in bioethics seem to believe that we have answered the question of how we should live, and, I would argue, we have too often settled into a comfortable application of that answer across a range of clinical circumstances and technological deployments.

Given the above, in this chapter, I articulate how I believe we have answered the above question, and the mechanisms we rely on to realise that existence. Second, I offer a suggestion as to why we have come to this answer, articulating some of the consequences of the narrow view that we have adopted in bioethics. Third, I argue that a broader view and greater attention to empirical evidence should help us become more critical in our approach to ethical questions, re-introducing this particular substantive question to our deliberations. Once this has been done, we might better acknowledge that there are many movement vocabularies and ways of being that we ought to value, but that we currently undervalue or do not value at all.

How Should We Live?

'How should we live?' Theorists from the philosophers of antiquity (e.g. Socrates, Plato, Aristotle), to the early-modern and modern philosophers (e.g. Kant and Bentham), to the current legal and human rights philosophers (e.g. Rousseau, Dworkin, Donnelly), have been concerned with this question to varying degrees (Striker 1987), and often, the answer can be distilled, quite simply, to the following answer, 'With dignity'. But of course, this glib response begs further questions, especially given that the specifics of that notion will vary across time and theory; indeed, in the contemporary setting, the difficulties associated with the elasticity of the notion of dignity have been noted (Heard 1997; Macklin 2003; Häry and Takala 2005; Pinker 2008).

Be that as it may, if pressed to elaborate, our stock answer, or starting point, in the field of bioethics might be summed up as follows:

We should live independently and autonomously, without coercion or interference, with few imposed duties, free to avoid risk and to vigorously protect our physical and emotional integrity against state organs, private entities, and individuals.

Such is the consequence of our blending of moral theory with more pragmatic and instrumental human rights thought and mechanisms, and of the rise, both in the West and more generally, of individualism.[1]

Of course, the above statement (moral position?) is an oversimplification, and it will not bear out in full in every bioethical assessment, but the great majority of substantive bioethical assessments that one can find will either explicitly state or implicitly begin from a foundational proposition not far removed from this statement. It is the state of being that we value the most and strive to preserve – physical integrity or 'wholeness' and autonomous individuality (Stirrat and Gill 2005). While I do not reject this premise or the state of being associated with it – I actually think many important philosophical, ideological and legal battles have been fought to get governments and other authorities to invest in it (Wexler and Winick 1992; O'Neill 2002; McWhirter 2012), often in the wake of egregious misconduct (i.e. the research atrocities of the Second World War, the Tuskegee scandal in the United States, the organ retention scandal in the United Kingdom, etc.) – the lack of depth in our ethical reflexivity, such that we do not often drill down to question the premise, is disheartening. It is particularly disconcerting when one considers that an ethical assessment must surely be one of the most suitable places to problematise the uncritical pursuit of wholeness and autonomous individuality.

How have we embedded this premise so deeply that we proceed from it in almost every medical, research and bioethical encounter, and indeed in most social constructions of the good life and of normality? I believe the law, or rather the convergence of law and ethics, has been a driving factor.

Convergence and Its Consequences

While there was once two primary currents in bioethics – one focusing on individual rights and choice, and the other on the social and cultural meanings of biomedical developments – the former has come to dominate (Callahan 1999). Moreover, its associated regulatory and clinical bioethics – both highly instrumental servitors to the vast biomedical architecture that exists – form the bulk of bioethics inquiry and scholarship. For example, Wendell (1989: 104–24) argued that the vast majority of ethical literature that considered disability was concerned with two questions: (1) Under what conditions is it morally permissible/right to kill/let die a disabled person? (2) How potentially disabled does a foetus have to be before it is permissible/right to prevent its being born? Writing a decade later, Callahan (1999: 281–82) noted that one will search in vain for bioethics literature connecting questions of meaning to questions of ethics.

In short, bioethics has evolved into an interdisciplinary field that is increasingly distant from moral philosophy and broader questions of being, and that is increasingly entangled with legal principles and rules, specifically those derived from human rights law.[2] In the result, legal instruments that view ethics within the human rights paradigm have become the key shapers of ethical thought and practice. Consider the highly influential Convention on Human Rights and Biomedicine 1997 (Biomedicine Convention), which states, in Article 1:

> Parties to this Convention shall protect the dignity and identity of all human beings and guarantee everyone, without discrimination, respect for their integrity and other rights and fundamental freedoms with regard to the application of biology and medicine.

Articles 5, 6, 7, 9, 61, 17, 19 and 20 of the Biomedicine Convention erect consent as the mechanism to do this, and Article 10 addresses confidentiality and privacy.

Consider also the UNESCO Universal Declaration on Bioethics and Human Rights 2005 (Bioethics Declaration), which, in the Preamble, identifies UNESCO's role as identifying:

> [...] universal principles based on shared ethical values to guide scientific and technological development and social transformation in order to identify emerging

challenges in science and technology [...] and that questions of bioethics [...] should be treated as a whole, drawing on the principles already stated in the Universal Declaration on the Human Genome and Human Rights and the International Declaration on Human Genetic Data and taking account not only of the current scientific context but also of future developments.

Article 2 of the Bioethics Declaration states that its aims are, inter alia, to:

- provide a universal framework of principles and procedures to guide States in the formulation of their legislation, policies or other instruments in the field of bioethics;
- promote respect for human dignity and protect human rights, by ensuring respect for the life of human beings, and fundamental freedoms, consistent with international human rights law;
- recognise the importance of freedom of scientific research and the benefits derived from scientific and technological developments, while stressing the need for such research and developments to occur within the framework of ethical principles and fundamental freedoms; and
- foster multidisciplinary and pluralistic dialogue about bioethical issues between all stakeholders and within society.

And these are only some of the legal instruments that bear heavily on bioethics.[3] The point is that, while generally positive and useful, they and the principles and rules they advocate have the potential to diminish dramatically the *scope* of the bioethics inquiry and imagination.

The consequences of this legalistic turn are manifold, implicating both the practice of bioethics and the range of outcomes that it can tolerate. One of the more fundamental consequences, foreshadowed above, is a narrowing of the bioethics view; certain possibilities and deliberations are off the table because the *law*, which largely adopts the 'medical model of disability', and which is increasingly integrated into bioethical thought, will not contemplate them.[4] Under the medical model of disability, physiological variation and disability are constructed as personal medical issues/problems (with connotations of blame), as deviance from the (mythologised and barely plausible normative and non-disabled body), and as individually tragic (and sympathy- or disdain-evoking).[5] And because the law is informed by a particular foundation – one that is autonomy-based and highly individualised – other moral positions that *might* lead to alternative answers (e.g. communitarianism or solidarity) are not deeply considered in modern bioethics. Ultimately, bioethics suffers from a value narrowness to which it remains mostly blind (Koch 2006; Amundson and Tresky 2008).

Another practical consequence of this convergence is that bioethics has increasingly concerned itself with instrumental issues relating to treatment delivery, focusing on individual capacity, modes of consent and techno-grounded questions around the allocation of responsibilities with respect to medical resources such as cadavers, organs and tissue, under what circumstances control can be exercised, and to what ends (Martensen 2001), all of which are matters heavily coloured by legal reasoning, legal principles and legal structures. This has led to allegations that bioethical issues are too often reduced to questions of moral agency and the propriety of actions in a world of limited resources (Lash 1996), and that they are too often culturally decontextualized and divorced from the lived experience of patients (MacDonald 1999). In other words, the key inquiries are often restricted to whether the individual can exercise, and has expressed his or her agency, or autonomy (i.e. consented), and whether the limits that existing resources allow permit that decision to be honoured; and the resource issue itself closes down any detailed examination of the individual's personal context, thereby limiting the richness and nuance of the investigation.

Related to this decontextualisation, a third consequence is that bioethics has separated from the person as an intentional, value-holding, moral agent (Leder 1990), and in doing so has applied increasingly 'depersonalised' norms and principles, which serve to disembody that person (Campbell 2009). Both the lived experience, noted above, and, just as importantly, the particularities of individual bodies have been rendered invisible. This invisibility can have particularly profound impacts on differently abled people, because it permits them to be viewed as 'others' based on the form and functionality of their physiology (Finger 1990; Wendell 1996; Linton 2006). Indeed, the medical model of disability, which, as indicated above, erects difference as personal loss or shortcoming centred in the individual (i.e. in his or her genetic or physiological deviation from the norm), has led to the construction of a rather narrow understanding of what a normal, desirable, acceptable or passably healthy body is.

In short, the medical framework is a powerful social organiser, informing general sensibilities about health, healthiness, fitness, etc., and it imposes a particular 'gaze' on (disabled) people. This gaze has given rise to, or at least implicitly encouraged, a social repugnance towards the different or divergent body (i.e. it has served as a marginalising social force), and this has created space for misunderstandings such as the notion that different or divergent bodies are necessarily weak, painful, homogenous, non-sexual and lesser than (Begum 1992; Smith 2003).

The Benefits of a Wider View

The bioethics undertaking would benefit from a wider view permitting deeper deliberations about health and illness in their broader and experiential contexts. This wider view can be encouraged by the injection of more empirical evidence from interested communities (Molewijk et al. 2004), including the disabled community.[6] Calls for empiricism in ethics, which are not new, are grounded on the convictions that morality is not a coherent system of beliefs but rather an interlocking collage of values and practices, and that empirical research improves our understanding of people's preferences, thereby giving greater context to the environment about which decisions are made (MacIntyre 1981; Timmons 1999; Musschenga 2005). They assume that experience is a useful source of moral wisdom (Molewijk et al. 2004); that the embodied experiences of stakeholders can aid reflection, analysis, and the development and implementation of normative guidelines applicable to given practices (Widdershoven et al. 2009).[7]

Happily, there *is* a growing number of empirical studies that investigate different clinical and research settings, and these *can* be used to improve practices (Dierckx de Casterlé et al. 2004). The InVisible Difference project, to which we turn now, is not such a study (i.e. it is not aimed at improving the medical encounter, but rather seeks to extend thinking and alter practice around the making, status, ownership and value of work by contemporary disabled dance choreographers).[8] Again, while questions associated with the functioning of bioethics might seem remote, the assumptions and actions of physicians and the wider healthcare architecture, and so of bioethics, arose when it became clear that many of the dancers with whom we interacted had suffered negative experiences in this setting. In short, a bioethics perspective was not viewed as a positive discourse-widener by our participants.

The evidence derived from the InVisible Difference project confirms the above assertion of invisibility. Our respondents reported learning how to speak to doctors using the 'medical language and view' so as to facilitate the clinical interaction (i.e. they reported conforming to, and complying with, the medical paradigm in pursuit of treatment). They reported 'being put on display' from an early age, with doctors and interns parading through their space, the latter quizzed on what they observed in 'the patient'.[9] One respondent wondered whether differently abled people were not 'conditioned to perform'. And they explicitly confirmed that medical agents never truly engaged with their lived experience. One reported:

They never quite appreciated the experience of my bones, and those bones and my condition informs my dance in many ways.

We can therefore confirm conclusions reached elsewhere that medicine too often reduces the person to the biological, not sufficiently acknowledging everything that is salient to health or well-being (Canguilhem 1990; Davis 1995; Garland Thomson 1997).

The InVisible Difference project also offers some lessons about the disabled body itself, the most important of which is that the disabled, or divergent, or 'diseased' body can be remarkably robust, and not as 'other' as typically constructed, both medically and socially.[10] On the former, it is often argued that the medical gaze strips differently abled bodies down, and, with advanced imaging technologies, increasingly opens them up. This disempowers patients, who report feelings of shame, vulnerability and invalidation during medical encounters that focus on the ways in which they are deviant or deficient (Reeve 2002). The social gaze to which differently abled people are often subjected is one whereby they are *objects* of care, sympathy, or worse, pity, requiring social protection, or *objects* of disdain or derision, consuming social resources (Hendriks 2007). Their non-normative bodies are constructed as uncivilised bodies with unusual boundaries and uncanny characteristics, and the result is isolation, concealment and prosthetic masking (Snyder and Mitchell 2001).[11]

By exposing themselves through dance, our respondents affirm themselves as *subjects* entitled to respect and the full enjoyment of rights and opportunities, and as uniquely abled individuals with particular and valuable talents. They report that dance is 'safe' for them, and valued because they can present themselves in ways that the medical gaze has been incapable of capturing, and the social gaze has been unwilling to acknowledge. They are in charge of their bodily exposure. It is also 'safe' for *us* as the audience because we have been 'invited' to share a space with them, on their terms. We are not interlopers sneaking glances at strange bodies, but rather viewers welcomed to look in a sustained way and to form a communion – a participatory experience – with them. Thus, dance can introduce us to the (radical?) idea that disabled bodies are not inevitably 'broken bodies' as they are commonly constructed, but rather richly diverse embodiments of humanity that offer a unique and useful voice through which individuals can speak.

Importantly, attention to disabled dance can demonstrate to the medical practitioner, the ethicist, and to various publics alike that disabled bodies can be robust, and supple, and fragile in turns, and can be used to tell compelling stories that may or may not be about disability. Moreover, dance opens up the possibility that the audience will experience 'kinesthetic empathy' despite their profound physiological differences from the dancer. Kinesthetic empathy has been described by Foster (2008: 49) as:

The inherent contagion of bodily movement, which makes the onlooker feel sympathetically in his own musculature the exertions he sees in someone else's musculature.

It is an awakening of something physical in the viewer, though the exact form of this awakening varies and is influenced by prior experience, expectations and taste (Reason and Reynolds 2010). The discovery of kinesthetic empathy with a body that one might view as (profoundly) 'other' is an important conceptual movement that could lead to the celebration of the so-called divergent body. And this celebration rightfully undermines the medical framework's subtle (and perhaps unintentional) message, namely that the disabled person's underlying physiological and medically labelled condition is something that, acting beneficently, we *should* wish to eradicate, or to cure, or to manage, and that therefore what you get from a disabled body is something that is produced from a position of deficiency, or deviance, or un-wholeness (i.e. from a position other than that of physical integrity), and so cannot be expected to be as good or as valuable as something from a non-disabled body. In the dance context, the consequence of this message is to suggest that we need not trouble ourselves to articulate measures for excellence and debate that is specifically appropriate for disabled dance and dancers; to do so may be counteractive to our (read, 'the medical') corrective programme.

Observation of dance and the experience of kinesthetic empathy offers a sense of what differently abled individuals experience and how their body is both like and unlike the normative body as it has been constructed. It reaffirms that we need to give special moral value to all bodies and the common and unique experiences to which they give rise. The implications for bioethics are that we might then be able to:

- loosen our conceptual grip on the idea of the 'broken body';
- more accurately and sensitively locate individuals in their diverse physiological and social contexts, and grasp the idea of the differently abled body that is robust and beautiful; and
- refine the core values on which bioethics relies when constructing human well-being and social equity (by giving greater weight to, for example, solidarity), and thereby think more critically about what constitutes 'good lives' worth supporting and celebrating.

This movement will allow bioethics to better engage with human diversity and human rights, to more confidently set trajectories for biomedical innovations and medical interventions, and to collaboratively design more sensitive and effective care practices *and language* within the medical architecture.

Conclusions

I am not suggesting that the relationship of mainstream bioethics to law is entirely incorrect or unhelpful. Indeed, the opposite is true, but law – or rather specific legal concepts and elements, such as autonomy and the legally normative body – can be particularly colonising. It is incumbent on bioethics (as an intellectual practice) to resist subversion by those elements of the law that would narrow its scope and imagination. Additionally, I am not arguing that adopting a more empirically informed perspective will always change outcomes in medical or technological interventions that are subject to ethical review. Indeed, it might rarely do so. But the process through which those reviews are undertaken could be more inclusive and more informed, and the analyses potentially more nuanced (and so more broadly moral). Rather, I am suggesting that we need to be more rigorous when considering bioethical questions, ensuring that we turn them over and over, and view them 'in a different light'. We need to more often and more fully engage with the following questions:

How should we live?

How can we properly acknowledge that humans have different ways of (normal) living?

How can we value the diversity that exists in ways of being and ways of moving?

If we foreground our analyses with a deeper appreciation of these questions, then we might expand the possibilities that we entertain in relation to questions about how the doctor/patient relationship should unfold, whether we should fund/support certain research or certain interventions, what it means to equitably support disabled citizens within the context of care programmes, etc.

Related to the above, I contend that bioethics should serve as a site of social collaboration on both broad and narrow questions. Our experience within the InVisible Difference project supports the claim that more systematised connections between stakeholders will facilitate this; more frequent and more engaging interactions as between physicians, nurses, technicians and ethicists, on the one hand, and disabled individuals, on the other, would be salutary. And those interactions should occur on a more equal basis. In other words, it would benefit everyone – bioethics and bioethicists, and patients, including, particularly, disabled patients – if we recognise (and we are starting to) that a single class on disability each year in medical school is insufficient to educate practitioners about the realities and roots of disability, and that the 'performance' of a notionally sensitive interview between doctor and disabled patient, conducted at the front of a lecture theatre, is hardly going to encourage an appreciation in our future carers of the social or affirmative models of disability.

Ultimately, in addition to having disabled people better represented on bioethics committees, we need more meaningful encounters between our ethics practitioners and disabled individuals. I would suggest that encounters with *disabled dancers* would be especially valuable to those tasked with undertaking bioethical analyses, and for a variety of reasons:

- because they would view the disabled individual in a space where that frequently disempowered individual is the centre of authority;
- because they would see the disabled individual undertake an activity that can be beautiful, challenging and physically demanding; and
- because they would be invited to really look at the physicality and to really ponder the experience of the disabled individual.

And none of these experiences are likely to be achieved within the context of the medical classroom, the hospital ward, the local surgery, or the clinical or research ethics committee room. In short, more meaningful encounters with disabled individuals (here read dancers) will better enable bioethics practitioners to view people and issues in a different light.

References

Amundson, R. and Tresky, S. (2008), 'Bioethics and disability rights: Conflicting values and perspectives', *Bioethical Inquiry*, 5, pp. 111–23.

Areheart, B. (2008), 'When disability isn't "just right": The entrenchment of the medical model of disability and the goldilocks dilemma', *Indiana Law Journal*, 83, pp. 181–232.

Ashcroft, R. E. (2010), 'Could human rights supersede bioethics?', *Human Rights Law Review*, 10, pp. 639–60.

Begum, N. (1992), 'Disabled women and the feminist agenda', *Feminist Review*, 40, pp. 70–84.

Beyleveld, D. and Brownsword, R. (2001), *Human Dignity in Bioethics and Biolaw*, Oxford: Oxford University Press.

Boyle, R. and Haynes, R. (2009), *Power Play: Sport, the Media and Popular Culture*, Edinburgh: Edinburgh University Press.

Callahan, D. (1999), 'The social sciences and the task of bioethics', *Daedalus*, 128, pp. 275–94.

Campbell, A. (2009), *The Body in Bioethics*, London: Routledge.

Canguilhem, G. (1990), *On the Normal and the Pathological*, New York: Zone Books.

Davis, L. J. (1995), *Enforcing Normalcy: Disability, Deafness and the Body*, London: Verso.

Dierckx de Casterlé, B., Grypdonck, M., Cannaerts, N. and Seeman, E. (2004), 'Empirical ethics in action: Lessons from two empirical studies in nursing ethics', *Medicine Health Care and Philosophy*, 4, pp. 31–39.

Finger, A. (1990), *Past Due: A Story of Disability, Pregnancy and Birth*, Seattle: Seal Press.

Foster, S. L. (2008), 'Movement's contagion: The kinesthetic impact of performance', in T. C. Davis (ed.), *The Cambridge Companion to Performance Studies*, Cambridge: Cambridge University Press, pp. 46–59.

Francioni, F. (ed.) (2007), *Biotechnologies and International Human Rights*, Oxford: Hart.

French, S. and Swain, J. (1997), 'It's time to take up the offensive', *Therapy Weekly*, 23, p. 7.

Garland Thomson, R. (1997), 'Feminist theory, the body and the disabled figure', in L. J. Davis (ed.), *The Disabilities Studies Reader*, New York: Routledge, pp. 279–306.

Häry, M. and Takala, T. (2005), 'Human dignity, bioethics and human rights', *Developing World Bioethics*, 5, pp. 225–33.

Heard, A. (1997), 'Human rights: Chimeras in sheep's clothing?', http://www.sfu.ca/~aheard/intro.html. Accessed 1 April 2016.

Hendriks, A. (2007), 'UN Convention on the rights of persons with disabilities', *European Journal of Health Law*, 14, pp. 273–98.

Keane, W. (2014), 'Affordances and reflexivity in ethical life: An ethnographic stance', *Munro Lecture Series*, University of Edinburgh, Edinburgh, UK, 27 March.

Koch, T. (2006), 'Bioethics as ideology: Conditional and unconditional values', *Journal of Medicine and Philosophy*, 31, pp. 251–67.

Kuczewski, M. G. (2001), 'Disability: An agenda for bioethics', *American Journal of Bioethics*, 1, pp. 36–44.

Lash, S. (1996), 'Introduction to the ethics and difference debate', *Theory, Culture & Society*, 13, pp. 75–77.

Leder, D. (1990), *The Absent Body*, Chicago: Chicago University Press.

Linton, S. (2006), *My Body Politic*, Ann Arbor: University of Michigan Press.

MacDonald, M. (1999), 'Health, health care and culture: Diverse meanings, shared agendas', in H. Coward and P. Ratanakul (eds), *A Cross-Cultural Dialogue on Health Care Ethics*, Waterloo: Wilfred Laurier Press, pp. 92–112.

MacIntyre, A. (1981), *After Virtue: A Study in Moral Theory*, Notre Dame: University of Notre Dame Press.

Macklin, R. (2003), 'Dignity is a useless concept', *British Medical Journal*, 327, pp. 1419–20.

Martensen, R. (2001), 'The history of bioethics: An essay review', *Journal of the History of Medicine and Allied Sciences*, 56, pp. 168–75.

McWhirter, R. E. (2012), 'The history of bioethics: Implications for current debates in health research', *Medicine and Health*, 55, pp. 329–38.

Molewijk, B., Stiggelbout, A. M., Otten, W., Dupuis, H. M. and Kievit, J. (2004), 'Empirical data and moral theory: A plea for integrated empirical ethics', *Medicine Health Care and Philosophy*, 7, pp. 55–69.

Murphy, T. (ed.) (2009), *New Technologies and Human Rights*, Oxford: Oxford University Press.

Musschenga, A. W. (2005), 'Empirical ethics, context-sensitivity, and contextualisation', *Journal of Medicine and Philosophy*, 30, pp. 467–90.

Oliver, M. (1996), *Understanding Disability: From Theory to Practice*, Basingstoke: Macmillan.

O'Neill, O. (2002), *Autonomy and Trust in Bioethics*, Cambridge: Cambridge University Press.

Phillips, M. J. (1990), 'Damaged goods: Oral narratives of the experience of disability in American culture', *Social Science and Medicine*, 30, pp. 849–57.

Pinker, S. (2008), 'The stupidity of dignity', *New Republic*, 28, pp. 28–31.

Plomer, A. (2005), *The Law and Ethics of Medical Research: International Bioethics and Human Rights*, London: Cavendish.

Priestly, M. (1999), *Disability Politics and Community Care*, London: Jessica Kingsley.

Reason, M. and Reynolds, D. (2010), 'Kinesthesia, empathy, and related pleasures: An inquiry into audience experiences of watching dance', *Dance Research Journal*, 42, pp. 49–75.

Reeve, D. (2002), 'Negotiating psycho-emotional dimensions of disability and their influence on identity constructions', *Disability & Society*, 17, pp. 493–508.

Rothman, D. J. and Rothman, S. M. (2006), *Trust Is Not Enough: Bringing Human Rights to Medicine*, New York: New York Review of Books.

Siebers, T. (2001), 'Disability in theory: From social constructionism to the new realism of the body', *American Literary History*, 13, pp. 737–54.

Smith, A. (2003), 'Persons with disabilities as a social and economic underclass', *Kansas Journal of Law & Public Policy*, 12, pp. 13–68.

Snyder, S. and Mitchell, D. (1997), *Vital Signs: Crip Culture Talks Back*, USA: Brace Yourself Productions.

——— (2001), 'Re-engaging the body: Disability studies and the resistance to embodiment', *Public Culture*, 13, pp. 367–89.

Stirrat, G. and Gill, R. (2005), 'Autonomy in medical ethics after O'Neill', *The Journal of Medical Ethics*, 31, pp. 127–30.

Striker, G. (1987), 'Greek ethics and moral theory', *The Tanner Lectures on Human Values*, 9, pp. 183–202.

Swain, J. and French, S. (2000), 'Towards an affirmation model of disability', *Disability & Society*, 15, pp. 569–82.

Timmons, M. (1999), *Morality Without Foundations: A Defense of Ethical Contextualisation*, Oxford: Oxford University Press.

Wendell, S. (1989), 'Toward a feminist theory of medical ethics', *Hypatia*, 4, pp. 104–24.

——— (1996), *The Rejected Body: Feminist Philosophical Reflections on Disability*, New York: Routledge.

Wexler, D. B. and Winick, B. J. (eds) (1992), *Essays in Therapeutic Jurisprudence*, Durham: Carolina Academic Press.

Widdershoven, G., Abma, T. and Molewijk, B. (2009), 'Empirical ethics and dialogical practice', *Bioethics*, 23, pp. 236–48.

Notes

1   And for an example of this broad notion in action, one might refer to the otherwise complex legislative regime that applies to healthcare and medical research, which, in the United Kingdom, includes the Human Fertilisation and Embryology Act 1990, as amended, the Human Tissue Act 2004, the Mental Capacity Act 2005, the Care Act 2014 and many, many, many more.

2   And there is much literature on their relationship: Beyleveld and Brownsword (2001); Plomer (2005); Rothman and Rothman (2006); Francioni (2007); Murphy (2009); Ashcroft (2010).

3   Others include the UNESCO Universal Declaration of the Human Genome and Human Rights (1997), the WMA's Declaration of Helsinki (2000), the CIOMS International Ethical Guidelines for Biomedical Research Involving Human Subjects of the (2002), the OECD Genetic Databases Guidelines (2009), the OECD Clinical Trials Recommendation (2012) and more.

4   For an example of this, see the UK's Disability Discrimination Act 1995, which, though it acknowledges the social model of disability in several respects, relies heavily on the medical model of disability.

5   For more on this model and its negative consequences, see Oliver (1996); French and Swain (1997); Priestly (1999); Swain and French (2000); Areheart (2008); and more.

6   The rich cache of evidence in relation to disability that has been generated by the disabled community in the context of disability studies has been little noticed in bioethics (Kuczewski 2001).

7   The idea of 'embodiment' here is a recognition that we must pay due attention to our physical self; that it is interacting with, and a part of, nature, and that the Cartesian mind-body dichotomy is not entirely helpful insofar as it encourages us to dismiss our (more messy) physicalness as merely a vessel.

8   And in doing so, it relies on several methodologies, including (1) multidisciplinary literature reviews; (2) content analysis of governing instruments/texts and social media narratives generated in response to videos of performances; (3) micro-ethnographies of differently abled dancers making dance; and (4) semi-structured qualitative interviews with differently abled dancers.

9   This echoes the experiences reported in Snyder and Mitchell (1997).

10 For more on the social construction of disability and the body, see Wendell (1996) and Siebers (2001), and for representations in popular culture and the media, see Phillips (1990) and Boyle and Haynes (2009).

11 That is not to say that disabling physiological conditions cannot benefit from medical interventions and support. They certainly can. However, this intervention, and the personal encounters that form a part of it, need not 'other' these bodies, thereby marginalising or devaluing them and the things they can accomplish.

Interruption 1

Dance, Medicine and Marginalisation: The Limits of Law and a Shift to Values

11 November 2015

Shawn Harmon

*A*t our third *In Visible Difference Symposium*, '*Beyond the Tipping Point? Dance Disability and Law*' (6–7 November 2015, in Coventry), a number of questions were raised in relation to the operation of law in the dance, and more specifically, the disabled dance setting. While some areas of law are much more pertinent to the practice of dance and the actions that dancers might take to protect their rights and income streams, the significance of the medical framework, it seems, should not be dismissed. It might be conceded that this framework – which includes medical education, medical law, and the vast medical architecture – is not so relevant as a legal standard-setter in dance (i.e. it does not directly influence participation in the creative process, ownership of dance, or the 'mainstreaming' of disabled dance), but it does sit stoutly if not resoundingly in the background.

The medical framework, which is informed by the medical model of disability, is a powerful social organiser, informing general sensibilities about health, healthiness, fitness, etc. In short, it imposes a particular 'gaze' on (disabled) people and so serves as a marginalising social force. Through its so-called objective (scientific) standards/measures, it identifies species-typical functioning, and so helps define the 'normal body'. Thus, it characterises the different body as something that is 'broken' – as something in need of repair, or special management – and so not to be highly valued. To put the worst possible spin on it, in a very strong and *authoritative* voice, this framework says, perhaps subtly:

> What you get from a disabled dancer is something that is produced from a position of weakness or un-wholeness, and so cannot be expected to be as good as something from a non-disabled dancer – it is therapeutic, not expert, and because the dancer's underlying physiological and medically-labelled condition is something we would wish, acting beneficently, to eradicate, or to cure, or to manage, we need not trouble ourselves to articulate measures for excellence and debate that is specifically appropriate for these dancers; to do so may be counteractive to our corrective programme.

This message, even if unintentional, influences perspectives and outcomes in cultural practice, cultural acceptance, and cultural memory.

Of course, while disabling conditions can *benefit* from medical interventions and support, it is not a given that we need to 'other' these bodies, which has the effect of marginalising or devaluing them and the things they can accomplish. Indeed, while many of those dancers with whom we interacted did not consider the medical framework to be particularly relevant to their work, they *did* have negative experiences within the medical architecture, and that, in some *cases, coloured the creative process, the stories told, etc. One of the messages coming from the Symposium was that more could be done in medical, ethical, and legal education to change the view taken of variance and variety in the human body, and to encourage a less potentially disempowering gaze within the context of the medical encounter.*

In support of this, the importance of human rights was noted. Interestingly, both medical law and bioethics are informed by the human rights framework (and some might even suggest that they are sub-categories of this framework). Indeed, medical law has come a long way in the last 20 years to move medical practice away from old-style paternalism toward a more dignity-centred, patient-centred, autonomy-grounded approach. And we are now seeing the very beginnings of that approach being bolstered in some respects by an equally dignity-based solidarity approach – an approach to decision-making that isn't just about empowering patients and patient families, but is also about viewing decisions within the context of a wider caring society within which we all acknowledge that we owe duties in addition to holding rights. It would be useful to think about how we can further encourage and operationalise this solidarity approach, and what that might mean for the acceptance, and indeed the celebration of difference within society and within cultural practices (like dance).

This suggestion highlights something that it is critically important to recognise, namely that there is 'politics' in what we're doing, and there are limits to what the law can accomplish. Indeed, in addition to the project team, multiple participants in the project and at the Symposium noted that fact. And if the law is not really getting us where we want to be because of the model it endorses (i.e. as in the medical law), or the limitations placed on who can make claims and against whom (i.e. as in human rights law), then we need to devise some complimentary non-legal strategies. Bearing that in mind, there are two things that stakeholders might do.

First, public debate. Human rights discourses could be used more often and more explicitly within dance, bioethics, and beyond to help shift perspectives on the value of difference/variance. In undertaking these discourses, there is value in thinking at a level higher than rights – we might move away from discussions about standards and think more about the values that inform standards, and how we can better operationalise those values to make a more equitable society in which disabled dance, for example, is better understood, better supported, better heralded, etc. UNESCO encouraged this with its Universal Declaration of the Human Genome and Human Rights (1997), and its Universal Declaration of Bioethics and Human Rights (2005), both of which are meant to inform domestic discourses. As practitioners of law, dance, medicine, and more we should explicitly draw on these instruments whenever we can, transporting them beyond the legal setting.

Second, we might think very seriously about reorienting medical education. While physiological approaches and scientific measures of the 'normal' are inevitable and valuable, medical training should be altered such that those experts who emerge at the end of the process to become part of the powerful framework that is the medical architecture have a broader and more holistic perspective, with a new and less marginalising language, for this language and perspective clearly shapes society's perspective on normality and of the value attached to different ways of being. Encouragingly, we heard some stories at the Symposium of medical schools trying new approaches to educating their students about disability, such as getting med students to partner with disabled dancers for a semester to better understand the different ways of being. Programmes like this echo the recommendations previously made (Harmon 2015).

References

Harmon, S. (2015), 'The invisibility of disability: Using dance to shake from bioethics the idea of "broken bodies"', *Bioethics*, 29, pp. 488–98.

Universal Declaration of Bioethics and Human Rights (2005), http://portal.unesco.org/en/ev.php-URL_ID=31058&URL_DO=DO_TOPIC&URL_SECTION=201.html.

Universal Declaration of the Human Genome and Human Rights (1997), http://portal.unesco.org/en/ev.php-URL_ID=13177&URL_DO=DO_TOPIC&URL_SECTION=201.html.

Interruption 2

Language

27 October 2014

Kate Marsh

*T*he language used to describe, discuss and represent disability has a history of dividing opinion. The etymology of key words and phrases associated with impairment gives an insight into shifting perceptions of disability over periods of history. The term 'Handicapped', widely rejected in current UK discourse, holds negative connotations and has been rejected, in particular, by individuals and organisations championing the rights of people with disabilities. A brief inspection of the history of this term indicates that it is synonymous with themes of burden or carrying extra 'weight'. There is one school of thought suggesting that handicapped is derived from 'hand in cap' a description of 'cripples' begging. Another theory relates to the term handicapped as disadvantaged in some way, take the golfing metaphor for example. Whatever the definition it is not a term promoting positivity and equality.

As a research team, we have talked about language surrounding disability and as a person with a disability these discussions have brought my attention to my own preferences and interpretations of words and phrases employed to discuss or describe disability. There is something about labelling with language that is prominent in my own personal feelings on this matter, as a teenager I strongly rebelled against the term disabled or any kind of title with my 'one handedness' at its core, I did not want to be perceived as 'different' from my non-disabled peers.

As an adult, with more experience and frankly greater exposure to other people with disabilities, I started to feel proud of this 'label'. History and habit still means that the word handicapped provokes a negative reaction in me, but I am generally happy and indeed pleased to describe myself as disabled/a person with a disability or a person with an impairment. There is also much debate around these terms, and this debate is important, the unpacking of terminology and its associated meaning and interpretation has been and continues to be central to the rights and voices of people with a disability or impairment. There is a valid discussion to be had around disabled versus impaired. Professor Mike Oliver offers a useful definition of 'impairment' as 'individual limitation' and disability as 'socially imposed restriction' (1993: 17). Even within these definitions there seems to be a potential further discussion around the terms 'limitation' and 'restriction', my point here is that the debate is key. Historically individuals with impairment were relatively passive in the language used to talk about their own bodies and terminology originated from medical definitions of impairment. I welcome discussion – and argument over terminology, critical discourse from a range of communities, disabled and non-disabled, activists and policy makers, can only draw greater focus on the voices of people with disabilities.

I feel about the term disabled rather the same way as I feel about my maiden name, I have associated myself with the word for quite some time, and truthfully it has defined me, and provided me with many opportunities. I do not wish to be reduced to my disability alone. I do find, however, that the term gives me sense of belonging in a wider community, which is empowering in many ways.

What is particularly interesting as we progress with our team research is that the discussion is actually happening. I have experienced situations where a fear of saying the 'wrong' word leads people to say nothing. To me this is far more damaging than any conversation or debate about which term is best. I have found that the most effective means for progression and shifting perceptions is to communicate about disability. For example I do not like the term handicapped, equally I am no fan of 'differently abled'. I have no wish to impose my preferences on others, however, expressing my view of these terms is key to maintaining a debate and without debate The fear of 'getting it wrong' could halt progression and lead to assumption and polite skirting around issues.

I have learnt through my practice in dance and in particular the dance and disability sector, that communication, verbal and non-verbal, is central to examining ways of working and training. I have experienced or seen many scenarios whereby a dancer with an impairment is left to find his or her own adaptations in a class or workshop, maybe because the language used to talk about impaired bodies feels like such a controversial area. The body in this instance just isn't referred to at all. We need to talk about each individual body in dance, there is no 'one size fits all' this might mean we get it 'wrong' or will be corrected by someone, but the most valuable thing is to keep the debate going, in doing this we are questioning assumption and acknowledging the essential choice of the individual to decide the language of her own body and her experiences.

Reference

Oliver, M. (1993), 'Introduction' *Disabling Barriers – Enabling Environments*, London: Sage publications.

Interruption 3

Difference?

21 November 2013

The InVisible Difference Team

'*Difference*': this is a word that has come up many times during the first months of our *InVisible Difference* project. But what does the word mean to us both individually and collectively as it relates to what we are striving to do within and for the disabled dance community, and in respect of the legal structures that surround and support the dancers and their work? We have shared some thoughts and will be having a debate at our team meeting and Intersections Forum on 25 and 26 November.

Our initial thinking has focused on two strands: the first relates to difference and the physicality of the dancers; the second to the difference that we want to make through our project. In relation to the first strand these are some of the responses: '*Difference is the recognition of something that asks for greater equality, but equality that accommodates difference as a positive part of human experience and which sharpens our perceptions and our articulations of excellence and quality*'; '*Difference can have overtones of there being a normal, from which one might be marginalised and different*'; '*Difference can be a means of othering*'; '*There is a continuum – we are all different and no one 'difference' is better than another*'; '*Difference is to be celebrated – who wants to conform to the norm?*'

In relation to the second strand – the difference we want to make through our project, we asked this question in three ways: for whom are we trying to make a difference; what sort of difference are we trying to make; what steps do we need to take in order to make that difference? Our ideas range from making a difference for the dancers; for the audiences; and to the way in which society in general thinks about dance made and performed by dancers with disabilities. The sort of difference we are trying to make includes developing audience perception of dance performed by dancers with disabilities; to deepening our understanding the creation process; to identifying gaps in the legal frameworks supporting this genre. Some of the steps that we have identified that we need to take include strengthening networks; developing debate using different media; not being afraid to confront difficult issues head on (not sugar-coating our messages); playing devil's advocate to bring tough issues to the surface.

Our challenge is to shape thinking around difference in such a way that difference in relation to dancers and their dance becomes one with the difference that we want to make through our project – they become mutually reinforcing. In so doing we need to find a vocabulary that we can use to talk about dance made and performed by disabled dancers that not only does justice to their work and their physicality, but which also enables us to identify and appreciate the virtuosic while having the confidence to speak about what we find mediocre.

We do know that we have to focus our efforts and pick our battles. Developing a plan of engagement is one of the things that we will be doing at our team meeting and Intersections Forum. If our readers have any views and ideas, we would love to hear them. There will be an update on our progress on this blog in the New Year.

Section II

Disability, Dance and the Demands of a New Aesthetic

Chapter 6

A Wondering (in Three Parts)

Luke Pell

A Remembering

Today, I remember,
Memory is a live *act*
a choreography, of connection.
We, re-remember.

Today, *I remember* that Ophelia said
Rosemary is for remembrance. Pansies are for thoughts.

I have so many. Thoughts and words
For forgotten bodies. Magic that did not go

Still, here. Transformed.
Terra incognita.

I remember they said
Here, be dragons and, witches to burn.

I remember they said
To write with left is wrong.

I remember they said
Don't ever wipe tears without gloves.

What atrocities arise, from fear of some unknown

I remember that 'truths' change.

Today, my hands will be wet and muddied,
as I tend to what might grow.

Today,
tomorrow, *I* will remember those we won't yet know.

A Wondering

We lived in times where academics, anthropologists, artists, activists and other such folks sought to shed light and understanding on other ways of being in the world. By telling stories, making models, inventing theories to wonder about the universe.

At the heart of this particular wondering beat thinking that informed a Social Model of Disability.

A model that became a catalyst for change in these islands

Attempting to address an inequality in living for disabled people.

Distinguishing disability from physical impairment, medical condition and different ways of learning.

Proposing that disability was not located in the individual but, in the world around us

Constructed by society, in attitudes, built environments, precious precarious towers.

Spiraling steps to castles preventing people who use wheelchairs from gaining access to these teetering towers, because the only way in or out is up, a hundred crumbling, narrow steps.

It is not whatever physical impairment, temporary or enduring ailment, that might require a person to use a wheelchair that disables them. It is that the castle does not have a ramp, Rapunzel or any other means of access.

And so, decrees were passed in the land that required reasonable adjustments be made that all people could fully participate in society and have an equality of life.

Yet discussion of disability politics, legal frameworks and fairy tales are not my sole purpose upon this page.

What I seek to do is share how this notion – the principles of a Social Model of Disability – might extend to dance and performance, theatres and galleries, to village halls and taxicabs and other places of magic in each of our day-to-day lives.

Since discovering the Social Model of Disability, it has become a golden thread through my work as a maker of dances, and in the way I perceive and understand the world around me.

I have spent many moons in theatres along with other theatre folk, and over time I have come to believe that these spaces, places for gathering, sharing utterings and gestures of what it is to live (and die) on land and sea, are built upon values from days of yore.

Although we can now list spaces that have taken measures to make reasonable adjustments so that people might access them, as artists and audiences, I have come to believe that these buildings, these manmade structures, these ways of seeing and sensing, still rely upon values drawn from just one way of being in the world.

A tradition of castles and theatres, dwellings and outhouses, built for a hierarchy of courts and classes.

A tradition of castles and theatres built and made with one way of seeing in mind.

A tradition of castles and theatres, built for looking up or looking down.

Grand balconies, best boxes, top turrets proposing

One better way of seeing
One better way of perceiving
One better way of making meaning
One better of way of appreciating

And although our traditions may be evolving, although there may be new dances in theatres and choreographies in great halls, on farms, lochs and mountains, that interrupt, disrupt, disturb, question these ways of

Sensing
Knowing
Valuing
Sharing

Our efforts, our endorsements, our measures of worth, still look up and down towards these buildings.

These enchanted spaces are inaccessible.

Not just to disabled people

But to people

We continue to structure our buildings with hierarchical ideologies.

Looking up to gods and down upon those in the cheap seats.

Looking up to elaborate, formal gestures, of assailing, rising.

Looking up to a mastery of one tongue taken from many.

Turning away from people falling, writhing, rolling, leaking, weeping, seeping, weathering, shrinking, stumbling, dripping, beautiful messings. Away, from the wet stuff that lets us know we are alive.

Beasts and beings, a world moving

Instead we keep arranging chess-set staff in buildings, looking up to Kings and Queens and down on the ground, workers, demons, goblins

No-man is an island.

We force fabricated structures upon ecology by looking up to gods, only occasionally encountering, the fleeting folks living in the land, crossing waters.

Fixed upon a vertical ascent, increased accumulation.

When we could, look out, around, behind, beyond beneath

We could listen, lean back, laydown and dig

Squirm and squeeze and shake. Reach, rollout, embrace, breathe out, in and go

A Wandering

Pouring milk into a cup of coffee,

Wait

for

what

islands

might come

to eye or to tongue.

Take yourself

out

of here

to there.

Find

a

W I D E

E X P A N S E

A Wondering (in Three Parts)

How is the air

                                                                    Scent

                                     Light

Noise

                      a
                      hum

Take yourself   towards

                      that

        What's behind?

                            a reach

     grasp

                      let   go

smudge

          How wet

                                  is what is

            in   between

Chapter 7

A New Foundation: Physical Integrity, Disabled Dance and Cultural Heritage

Abbe Brown, Shawn Harmon, Kate Marsh, Mathilde Pavis, Charlotte Waelde, Sarah Whatley and Karen Wood

Introduction

Leading dance commentators have argued that 'disability remains a marginalised and under-theorised area in dance studies', notwithstanding advances in the growth of mixed ability dance companies, and the expansion of critical scholarship around dance and disability (Albright and Brandstetter 2015: 3, 5). We agree that 'disabled dance' is under-theorised; in the light of this we have chosen to continue to use the term 'disabled dance'; but we stress that we do not claim that disabled dance should be seen as a distinct art-form, and certainly not a distinct genre, but as a unique and important integrated element of the dance community that deserves its place alongside any other sector within that community.[1] Further, for as long as this is so and disabled dance lacks a philosophy to deepen understanding and knowledge of the dance and its philosophy, disabled dance will continue to evolve in fits and starts, and to be persistently at the margins of dance.

Dance has been argued to pose unique philosophical questions relating to inter alia the importance of the human body, the dynamics of agency, the collaborative nature of dance and the individuality of the body, and the meaning generated in different dance activities (Bunker et al. 2013). But disabled dance (bearing in mind the point made above) raises much deeper enquiries. Accordingly, in this chapter, we have two primary aims. Firstly regarding marginalisation, to argue that disabled dance, already an important component of the rich mosaic that comprises our cultural heritage, meets the criteria demanded for protection and promotion under the law pertaining to intangible cultural heritage (ICH); as such, practitioners and other communities of interest must do more to make disabled dance and its agents more visible. Secondly, and to assist in delivering the first aim, this chapter will offer a theory – or at least an interdisciplinary grounded and principled foundation – around which disabled dance might coalesce and through which it might be examined. This foundation could ultimately facilitate disabled dance in becoming a more visible, acknowledged and safeguarded part of ICH. Through these dual aims, our overall purpose in this chapter is to help disabled dance thrive and take its rightful place in the cultural milieu more generally.

We seek to do this from an interdisciplinary perspective. The InVisible Difference project was of course an interdisciplinary effort, bringing together academics in law (intellectual property, human rights and medical law) and dance, and dance practitioners.[2] This chapter was written, not only because of the particular contribution that we wanted to make to developing a philosophy of disabled dance, but also because we wanted to write a true inter-disciplinary piece so that we could show how far our thinking had come during the course of the project. To that end we met in early 2015 to conduct an 'article sprint'.[3] While generally the aim of a book sprint is to finish a book in 3–5 days, we did not quite manage that with our chapter, and as is often the way with these initiatives, other priorities took over once our meeting was finished. However, we persevered, and sequentially, rather than concurrently, we completed this chapter which we think makes a unique contribution to the literature and indeed to the final output of the InVisible Difference project.

The Fight Against Marginalisation and the Intangible Cultural Heritage Perspective

A strong theme through this collection is the existence, value and quality of disabled dance. 'Pioneering' integrated dance companies of the 1980s and 1990s set a path to show that the work of disabled dance artists should be taken seriously.[4] Contemporary disabled dance artists tend to continue in this pioneering mode, as autodidacts and self-resourced. Communities of artists grow up in locations that are most supportive of the work, still sometimes remote from the dance 'mainstream', however well the work may be received. There is plenty of evidence of the quality of this work. We witnessed it during our observations of rehearsals and work in performance,[5] and our own project events featured performances to draw attention to the need for the work to be witnessed, documented and transmitted more widely.

While a rich and feted cultural practice might persist in the shadows for a while, it cannot thrive indefinitely away from widespread critical review, lay audiences, and major funding sources. This is especially the case when the practice is pursued by members of society who have traditionally been side-lined and discriminated against (such as disabled individuals). Some assistance can come from international law and resulting practices and opportunities pertaining to intangible cultural heritage (ICH).

ICH has its present roots in the United Nations Educational, Scientific and Cultural Organisation (UNESCO), established in 1945 in the belief that peace should rest on the basis of humanity's intellectual and moral stability. UNESCO seeks to build intercultural understanding through the protection of heritage and support for cultural diversity (UNESCO n.d.). Further, the Universal Declaration of Human Rights 1948 (UDHR), the starting point of 'modern' international human rights regime which is part of the same package of international activities which followed the atrocities of the two world wars, states:

> [...] the advent of a world in which human beings shall enjoy freedom of speech and belief and freedom from fear and want has been proclaimed as the highest aspiration of the common people [...] All human beings are born free and equal in dignity and rights.
> (Article 1)

Within this framework, UNESCO long focussed on tangible cultural heritage – heritage that can be touched such as monuments, buildings and paintings. However, 2003 saw the UNESCO Convention for the Safeguarding of Intangible Cultural Heritage 2003 (ICHC) which refers, in its first recital, to international human rights instruments. The ICHC defines intangible cultural heritage as the practices, representations, expressions, knowledge, skills – as well as the instruments, objects, artefacts and cultural spaces associated therewith – that communities, groups and, in some cases, individuals recognise as part of their cultural heritage (ICHC, Article 2.1). It goes on to state that this ICH is:

- transmitted from generation to generation;
- constantly recreated by communities and groups in response to their environment, their interaction with nature and their history; and
- provides them with a sense of identity and continuity, thus promoting respect for cultural diversity and human creativity.

The ICHC then enumerates oral traditions and expressions, including language, performing arts, social practices, rituals and festive events, knowledge and practices concerning nature and the universe, and traditional craftsmanship as examples of ICH – insofar as they are compatible with human rights (ICHC, Article 2.1 and 2.2). The ICHC also stipulates that 'safeguarding' entails ensuring the viability of the intangible cultural heritage, including the identification, documentation, research, preservation, protection, promotion, enhancement, transmission, and revitalisation of various aspects of such heritage (ICHC, Article 2.3). ICH is, in other words, living heritage - a term that resonates strongly when one considers disabled dance.

One can of course argue that disabled dance is part of ICH whatever a treaty says. Yet the recognition of something as forming a part of cultural heritage under the ICHC has important legal, social, political and economic consequences. The importance placed on ICH can be understood when considering that, as of February 2016, 166 States out of a possible 195 were parties to the ICHC – although sadly not yet the United Kingdom that has been the focus of much, although not all, of the work of the InVisible Difference project. The ICHC is thus likely to become the standard-setting instrument for safeguarding living cultural heritage for years to come.

From an instrumental perspective, the ICHC means that a web of formal and informal legal mechanisms becomes available to facilitate protection and promotion. As noted, states must safeguard ICH (ICHC, Article 1a, 11a) and other obligations are imposed to help ensure the continuity, transmission and development of the relevant ICH, and to foster continuity between past, present and future generations (ICHC, Article 1, 2.1, 11). From a socio-cultural perspective, ICH affirms and enhances a sense of identity and belonging within the community that generates the ICH. Members of the community whose ICH is to be safeguarded are to be full partners in its identification and management (ICHC,

Article 15). In describing this as 'an extraordinary bottom-up, grass roots participatory provision', Kurin (2007: 14) noted that:

> [...] it is not the songs sung in any recreated or imitative form – no matter how well meaning or how literally correct – by scholars, or performers, or members of some other community. It is the singing of the songs by the members of the very community who regard those songs as theirs, and indicative of their identity as a cultural group. It is the singing by the people who nurtured the traditions and who will, in all probability, transmit those songs to the next generation.

Others have argued that the focus on community means that the values held by groups, and the individuals that make up those communities, should form a part of what is valued in ICH, including what makes individuals human. ICH is thus 'composed of deeper, underlying values such as teamwork and generosity, as well as significance that stems from senses of belonging and pride', and 'elements such as emotions, values and memories should also be placed within the concept of the intangible' (Stefano 2012: 19). Looking more broadly, this breadth of perspective enhances cultural enrichment for communities and society as a whole. The ICHC is instrumental in encouraging openness towards different cultures and respect for cultural diversity, and in maximising the creative potential and evolution of cultural memory and the opportunity to inspire new cultural initiatives (Nafziger and Telesetsky 2014; Vadi and Schneider 2014).

This final perspective is a reminder of the multi-faceted nature of recognising and safeguarding ICH. ICH is part of the living heritage of its 'own' community and this community will have a role in managing it; this is in marked contrast to the universal focus of tangible cultural heritage. Further, this community is unlikely to equate to all the citizens of one country and may cross borders, yet the obligations under the ICH are imposed upon states. Finally, notwithstanding its local (non-universal) element, ICH is also part of the wider cultural space and experience of other communities and of global society, including as part of the universal nature of the human rights framework (Blake 2000: 61–85; Lenzerini 2011).

The creation of this framework is a valuable step forward for ICH in general, and we consider it to be essential, in order to avoid further marginalisation, that disabled dance is recognised as a part of it.

Making Dance Part of Intangible Cultural Heritage

Historically, the way in which something became an 'authorised' part of cultural heritage was by it entering the records of (mostly public) institutions charged with the task of recording, curating and preserving our past. Disabled dance is conspicuous by its absence from these records, and records that do exist appear to be woefully incomplete. For example, while the Victoria and Albert Museum (V&A) has some records of a very small number of dancers with disabilities at various times in history, these dancers are rarely named and tend to be referred to by their disability (e.g. 'dancer with one hand');[6] an approach that underscores our trepidation about using the term 'disabled dance'.

However, the focus in the ICHC on living heritage should mark a radical change in thinking towards disabled dance; an emphasis on living heritage means that an historical absence from archives and museums is no legitimate bar to recognition of something as a proper, important and valued component of living heritage. In other words, under the modern regime, historical marginalisation is not a bar to recognition of disabled dance as part of our ICH; the key issue is for disabled dance to satisfy the definition. Thus, while disabled dance is obviously an intangible art form, we must inquire whether it meets the other necessary criteria within the ICHC: transmitted across generations, constantly recreated by communities, and, at its heart and as discussed above, providing a sense of identity and continuity for 'the individual groups and communities that embody, practise and transmit' the ICH (ICHC, Article 15).[7] Other works in this project, and the points made at the start of this chapter, suggest that there is at least some transmission across generations, and that disabled dance is constantly being recreated (Harmon et al. 2015). The focus of this chapter then is the need for a sense of identity in those who practice the customs and traditions in question, and which shifts as cultural practices are reworked by communities. This sense of identity is also essential to the grounding of individual dignity, the facilitation of self-confidence and the formation of community – each of which are deeply entrenched ideas in the human rights system within which ICHC exists (InVisible Difference Symposium 2014; ICHC, Article 15). We contend that the disabled dance community *is* a community with an identity for the purposes of ICHC.

To support this assertion, we develop the second aim of this chapter – articulating a foundational concept, around which disabled dance can coalesce. This would also help to fill that gap referred to in the quote at the outset: 'disability remains [...] [an] under-theorised area in dance studies' (Albright and Brandstetter 2015: 5). An example of the link between a foundational concept and a community can be seen from what might seem to be a related field: Disability Arts. Disability Arts is in fact a quite distinct community and has an identity because of the philosophy that underpins it, and which has been adopted by this group.

Disability Arts Distinguished from Disabled Dance

Disability Arts is a movement that formed in the mid-1970s. Sutherland (1989: 159) describes Disability Art as 'art made by disabled people which reflects the experience of disability'. He also suggests that disability politics was central to its emergence, and that without disability politics, Disability Art may not be what it is now:

I don't think Disability Arts would have happened without disability politics coming first [...] Our politics teach us that we are oppressed, not inferior [...] Our politics have given us self-esteem. They have taught us, not simply to value ourselves, but to value ourselves as disabled people.

(Sutherland 1989: 159)

Something of the political flavour of the movement can be gleaned from Bragg's 2007 blog post describing the debate held at the Tate Modern in relation to a motion that disability and deaf arts ought to be dead and buried (i.e. that we are all in the mainstream now). Bragg (2007) noted the passion elicited in favour of Disability Arts, going so far as to quote the view of one speaker that Disability Arts could be seen as 'the last remaining avant-garde movement' comparable to the early days of feminism and black arts. More recently, Dadafest, as part of its 2014 Congress, held a debate around the motion that '[t]his congress proposes that Disability Arts is a form of human rights activism and as such only disabled people should be its leaders'. The motion was ultimately carried by 31 votes to 26. In keeping with the politicised nature of the movement, Darke (2003: 130) argues that:

Disability art philosophy is based upon legitimising the experience of disabled people as equal within art and all other cultural practices [...] it is part of a process of re-presenting a more accurate picture of society, life, disability and impairment and art itself. Disability Art is a challenge to, an undermining of (as a minimum), traditional aesthetic and social values.

Brisenden (1990) has authored a moving account of what it means to be part of the movement:

The culture of disability is the web that binds us together on the basis of what is common but leaves us room to move and grow. It is built upon appreciating and valuing many things, including things that may have been patronised or ignored in the past. For instance, an important element of our culture is our history. We should not wait for the academics to decide this is important, but we must begin charting it ourselves by listening to and recording the reminiscences of older people with disabilities. Their stories are our lost history, a central element of the culture we belong to. But a disability culture must also celebrate the present and the future. [...] Disability culture is about expressing ourselves in whatever way comes naturally, and about realising that these expressions are valuable. It is not a question of shutting ourselves off from society, as some people seem to think. On the contrary we must take our place in society fortified and empowered by the knowledge that we do not need to discard our cultural identity as the price of integration.

Importantly for our purposes, this philosophical tradition engenders a sense of belonging for the community. When one sits within a particular philosophical tradition, it can act both as a guiding principle for one's actions, and as an enabler for outsiders to better understand what drives and shapes one's actions: an artist working within the Disability Arts movement follows an established tradition – a community with which to identify – while at the same time her audience has an intellectual framework to better understand the work.[8] As Boyce (2013: 265) has noted; there is a mutual dependence between the artistic and philosophical attainment of a work:

> [...] it is in virtue of what the work achieves as art that it achieves something philosophically important. It is in virtue of what it achieves philosophically that the work succeeds as art.

There is no doubt that the Disability Arts movement has a powerful identity, and no doubt that a community has coalesced around its philosophy – a community which holds strong values and traditions that are passed on to others. The physical manifestations of their movement – the artworks, the paintings, the books, the sculptures, the dances, the performances – are the subject of public and private efforts to capture, so that the history and the tangible manifestations of the movement can be available to others (National Disability Art Collection and Archive). The Disability Arts movement and its manifestations, in other words, are in the course of becoming a curated part of our cultural heritage. Some elements of this are tangible and some intangible, but at the heart of which is the intangible nature of the movement; its underlying values, its politics, the sense of belonging and pride that it inculcates, the emotions it generates, the memories that it leaves – and these are continuously reworked by the community over time.

Conversations with our disabled dance collaborators make clear that while they have respect for the Disability Arts movement and its politics, these disabled dancers do not form a part of the Disability Arts movement; these dancers are rather fundamentally apolitical. Further, and as we have argued extensively elsewhere,[9] while disabled dance challenges traditional aesthetic values, it is difficult to claim that it also seeks to undermine these values in the sense of making traditional aesthetics less powerful or less likely to succeed on their own terms – a strong claim made by the Disability Arts movement. In short, the philosophy underlying Disability Art does not serve as a foundation through which the disabled dancers who have formed part of this project can identify as a community for purposes of 'qualifying' for ICHC protection.

Towards Intangible Heritage Status: A Foundation to Facilitate Community and Critique

The key question, then, is:

> What theoretical notion should ground the disabled dance community so that disabled dance can better become an explicit part of our cultural heritage?

The next section will explore the theoretical component of this question with consideration given to 'who' compromises the community (noting that our focus in the InVisible Difference project was in the United Kingdom, but the same conditions may apply to disabled dance across national boundaries or in other countries), and what constitutes a 'foundation' to which members of the community might implicitly align from a sense of belonging and pride (Stefano 2012: 19), or in the absence of the growth of an alternative, or splinter movement.

A starting point in the search for theory or foundation might seem to be the concept of 'embodiment'. This has been relied on in different discursive contexts, including that associated with the description of dance, where it has entered common parlance. Embodiment is, however, a protean concept, particularly within the confines of dance and may be insufficient as a foundation.

With respect to the individual dancer, embodiment as a term has been used to: include the body embodying choreographic intention (McFee 2011: 131–35, 181–84); reflect incorporeal exchanges between the choreographer, dancer, audience and the conscious-world and the self-other (Carr 2013: 63, 64); regard the body as having a double nature – being a subject and a thing (2013: 64); highlight an intrinsic intertwining of body and mind as both are fully given over to the dance experience (Ness 2001: 72–73, 75, 77–78; Williamson 2004); and describe the shared habits of dancers, who have a high level sensitivity to bodily sensations produced by their movements (Hunter et al. 2015: 10). In contrast, the work of philosopher Merleau-Ponty (2002: 84) on the body as subject suggests that the idea of embodiment may be tied up with traditional notions of the objectified dancer, which have been challenged in late twentieth century developments in the art-form. Probing more deeply, embodiment has often been used to highlight the notion that one is deeply invested in the dance. To 'fully give ourselves over' to a dance experience is to be fully 'in our body', and this somehow relates to the sincerity or virtue of the dance. This understanding is exemplified by the following:

> Unlike the actor's, the dancer's body inevitably resists being given away. The more fully a dancer throws themselves into dancing a part, the more they come across physically as completely themselves. It is a paradox, not just of dance, but of our own existence, that often when physical being is at full tilt, the human essence seems most visible. When a dancer is giving it all they've got, what we see is no illusion, even if they are performing a 'role': the animating spirit cannot be borrowed or faked, it is the dancer's own.
>
> (Williamson 2004)

Thinking about embodiment in dance (as distinct from the dancer) does not alleviate the difficulty. At base, and this may not be without controversy, it may refer to a physical and emotional phenomenon located in the individual, sometimes in cooperation or synchronicity with other individuals. However, when categorised into a framework of words so as to develop a shared understanding of this experience, it becomes evasive. It is a highly personal and transitional practice; even when we are 'copying' someone else's movement, we cannot help but translate and interpret this through the fibres, sinews, and cells of our own bodies, the memory and physical consequences of our own experiences, and the emphases, prejudices, and foibles of our own understandings. Moreover, our bodies, always central to dance, are ever changing, minute-by-minute, day-by-day, year-by-year. In the light of this, can embodiment be applied more specifically to disabled dance?

There has been some consideration of unusual and mutable bodies from the perspective of deconstructing dance (Bixler 1999: 242–45; Dodds 1999: 218–20). There have also been some critiques of binary approaches to disability/non-disability and the focus in dance on one particular type of thin, non-disabled, beautiful, balletic body, rather than on how different bodies with different legacies dance within their own abilities (Dils and Albright 2001: 236; Burt 2001: 44). The relationship of the disabled dancer to the notion of embodiment (and the further fragmentary effect it has on that notion) has, however, hardly been considered. We contend that the lived experience of disability has the potential to make a person 'better' at embodiment in part because those with a disability are familiar with scrutiny:

> If born disabled our very 'difference' makes us interesting we are either being scrutinised for potential 'normalisation' or scrutinised for ways in which we might benefit from changed perceptions. We (our bodies) are central to the debate.

> The experience of impairment insists that we think about our bodies frequently, impaired bodies in a normative world are constantly adjusting and negotiating as part of the experience of being in the world; from public transport and visiting restaurants to everyday tasks essentially designed for a 'fully functioning' body.

> (Marsh 2015)

Yet so far there has been limited consideration of how physical difference can radically transform the transmission of embodied knowledge.

Further, a focus on lived 'embodied' experiences raises interesting questions of disability models. As we and others have explored elsewhere (UPIAS 1976: 14; Campbell 2009; Swain and French 2000: 569–82; Brown and Waelde 2015: 578), there are strong views that the medical model of disability, which sees disability as a problem to be cured, is unacceptable to disabled dancers; and that a social model (which sees disability as arising from the subjective structures which society imposes) or an affirmative model (that the focus should be on what people can do, rather than what they cannot) are preferable approaches. Embodiment is deeply intertwined with the medical model. A disabled person cannot live ignorant of her body when there are constant reminders such as medical interventions, physical access, and the perpetuation of the 'normal' or 'perfect' body in the media. So it could be argued that the disabled body is constantly embodying, and through this a disabled person becomes highly effective at capturing and utilising unique body knowledge. This problematic base could argue against embodiment being a unifying concept.[10]

As seen, however, there are other objections to arguing for a foundational role for embodiment. The 'dance understanding' of embodiment is multiple, varied, and poorly differentiated and articulated, and the 'disability understanding' of embodiment is negative or loaded. Further the law (not just ICH law) does not directly engage with the notion except tangentially through law's concept of 'performance'. In the (non-legal) definition of 'performance' offered by the New Oxford Dictionary, the link between the notions of performance and embodiment is clearly stated: performances are the embodiment on stage of creative works (literary, musical, choreographic works) (Pearsall and Hanks 1999: 602). Through its regulation of the production and dissemination of performances, the law arguably indirectly engages with the question of embodiment in dance.

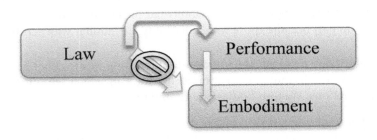

Law does not, however, articulate a place for a more or less embodied performer or performance, or any question of degree or quality of embodiment because performances are not understood as adding any particular value to a work during the creative process. Performances are seen as a neutral, though sometimes necessary, step in the communication of a work to the audience, but never one that impacts the substance, quality or authority of the underlying work. To the extent that it respects the integrity of the work it conveys, a performance is not expected to evidence artistic quality or 'integrity' since it is limited to its function of transmission. In this logic, performing bodies merely function as a canvas for the communication of the underlying work.

This idea of performance as being meaningless is a by-product of two independent but interlinked phenomena of the law in relation to creative works (i.e. of intellectual property law). First, the existing framework seems to over-estimate the authority of both the authors and the works performers interpret – for our purposes, the choreographers and the choreographic works. In essence, the choreographic work is seen as transcending the performing body to reach the audience. Such limited understanding of the performing process transpires in the writing of the English judge Justice Park when he describes the creative collaboration between composers and performing musicians as follows:

A composer can 'hear' the sound of his composition in his mind before he ever hears it played. [...] When Mr Kemp was devising his songs the sound which he had in his musical consciousness must surely have been the sound they would have when performed by Spandau Ballet, not the sound they would have when sung by Mr Kemp alone to the accompaniment just of his own guitar.[11]

Second, and within this, the law considers the performer to be an inter-changeable performing template whose peculiarities would or should be rubbed off to let the choreographic work stand by itself. This approach to the performing body was the crux of the *Garcia v Google* case in the United States,[12] in which Cindy Garcia, an actress, had put forward a claim for the co-ownership and authorship of a video clip on the basis of her performance. Her contention was rejected on the grounds that performing was nothing more than acting as the mouthpiece for the author of a script:

> Garcia did not write the script; she followed it. Garcia did not add words or thoughts to the film. She lent her voice to the words and her body to the scene.[13]

In effect, this view limits performers' role to being the authors' puppets (Diderot 1883: 62; Pavis 2014: 12).[14] In doing so, the law assimilates the dancing body to that of a sophisticated pasteboard whose skills reside in the ability to interpret the work without modifying it content, meaning or quality (Diderot 1883: 62). Failing to do so would lead to unwanted variations, one might say distortions, of the performed version of the choreographic work. This approach thus presumes that dancers with similar bodies and equivalent skill levels should perform an almost identical rendering of the same choreographic work.

Couched in such terms, the act of performing becomes a process of *disembodiment* of the dancing body for it is expected to strip itself from its own physical, intellectual or emotional particularities to adopt those of the work. The relationship between the choreographic work and the performance of the choreographic work thus conceptualised offers no room for 'embodiment' as a meaningful notion. This leads us to conclude that performance – which is the only conceptual platform available to understand the idea of embodiment in law – is 'disembodied', leaving us with a strange theoretical paradox of 'disembodied embodiment'.

From the dance perspective, therefore, embodiment has not done much to facilitate inclusiveness in dance, and indeed may be a barrier to inclusiveness insofar as it has failed to facilitate understandings of disabled dance, or the disabled experience. The legal contribution is also limited. Ultimately, then, the notion of embodiment is slippery and contested, and does not offer the unifying theoretical foundation that we seek for disabled dance and around which the necessary community can coalesce for the purposes of ICH. We therefore suggest that another organising concept, one that is perhaps more readily comprehensible, and, additionally, presently more relevant and familiar to existing legal frameworks, might be more useful in capturing the diversity of being and moving that characterises disabled dance. This starts with the human rights imbued concept of 'integrity'.

A Better Foundation: Integrity

We consider that integrity can help us to achieve a new and necessary respect for the human body and the place of the disabled or differently abled body in dance than was seen to be so in respect of embodiment. Further, as will be explored, integrity has important links with the field of cultural heritage, and, like heritage, it has human rights foundations.

Integrity is closely linked to dignity, which refers inter alia to the unity and wellbeing of the person (Foster 2011; UDHR and UNESCO Universal Declaration on Bioethics). As such, the constitution of human integrity, both physical and emotional, has been argued to be dependent on the experience of 'intersubjective recognition' (i.e. it depends on receiving approval and respect from others) (Honneth 1992: 187–201). This idea of intersubjectivity founds several theories of recognition (Hegel 1978), which generally hold that individuation is a process in which the individual expresses an identity to the extent permitted by those with whom she is in communication and partnership; we construct our identity in large part by learning from, and drawing on, the perspectives of others toward our qualities and abilities – an idea that is closely linked to the meaning of community within the ICHC. Identity construction has been termed a process which is 'fragmentary, complex, multi-faceted and changeable' (Briginshaw 2001: 119) – again identity is central to the ICHC.

This social entanglement by its very nature renders us vulnerable to 'disrespect', which, depending on the form it takes, can upset one's relationship to self. It has been argued that there are three gradations of disrespect which, importantly, can derogate from one's integrity. The first, and arguably least damaging, is that which has negative consequences for one's social value, either individually or as a group. It entails a social devaluing that erodes both one's own self-perception as worthy of esteem, and others' perception that one is deserving of esteem (Speier 1952; Berger 1970: 338–47). This can occur when one's qualities and abilities are measured, through that communicative and externally influenced process, against a standard or norm informed by the majority. Foucault, in his discussion of 'normalisation', noted those modes of 'which work by setting up standards or "norms" against which individuals continually measure, judge, and "discipline" and "correct" their behaviour and presentation of self' (Bordo 1993: 199). In short, one can have one's identity and integrity eroded or disregarded through social normalisation such as of physique, movement, acumen, and one can thereby be marginalised.

The second, and arguably more damaging form of disrespect is that which is structured. The exclusion of individuals or groups from certain rights that members of a given society expect within that society undermines more than just esteem. This form of disrespect has been described as follows:

> For the individual, having socially valid legal rights withheld from him or her signifies a violation of the person's intersubjective expectation that he or she will be recognized as a subject capable of reaching moral judgments. To this extent, the experience of being denied rights is typically coupled with a loss of self-respect, of the ability to relate to

oneself as a partner to interaction in possession of equal rights on a par with all other individuals.

(Honneth 1992: 191)

Denial of rights and social ostracism lead to a downgrading of the form of living exemplified by the target group, and therefore to 'social death'; and, on an individual basis, it unravels the identity that is (often painstakingly) constructed (or attempted to be constructed) through ongoing socialisation.

Again, the process of normalisation is critical, and the historical exclusion of difference is exemplified by how lepers led to the recognition of 'madman', both of whom were ridiculed for their differentness. Foucault (1965: 11) explains the lepers' and madmen's care by external society but exclusion from internal society as an admission that 'what was formerly a visible fortress of order has now become the castle of our conscience'.[15] So, as a society, we are often ill-equipped to engage with someone who, historically (though often wrongly), has never been taken seriously, or who has been excluded. Instead, society has withheld its benefits from them and thereby eroded their integrity. Disability has often been a basis of this form of disrespect, and systematic denials of rights have signalled that the disabled person is not deemed worthy of the moral accountability shown to others (Feinberg 1980: 143–58).

The third and often most disastrous form of disrespect is that whereby the individual is forcibly deprived of physical integrity (i.e. of her power to make decisions with respect to her own body). Attempts to 'seize control' over another's body typically impose physical pain and defenceless-ness, they destroy the victim's confidence that she can govern her body autonomously. On this form of disrespect the following has been said:

[…] one of the consequences, wedded to a type of social shame, is the loss of self-confidence and trust in the world, and this adversely affects all practical interaction with other subjects, even at a physical level. Through the experience […] the person is deprived of that form of recognition that is expressed in unconditional respect for autonomous control over his own body, a form of respect acquired just through experiencing emotional attachment in the socialization process. The successful integration of physical and emotional qualities of behaviour is thus shattered post facto from without, crippling the most fundamental form of the practical relationship to self, namely, confidence in oneself.

(Honneth 1992: 190)

This extreme disrespect interrupts positive self-image even at the corporeal level; studies have found, for example, that torture and rape can result in 'psychological death' (Honneth 1992; Elsass 1997).

The above demonstrates strong arguments for the theoretical bases for integrity to have a moral and readily definable meaning. Our research in the InVisible Difference project supports the validity of this meaning and also demonstrated that our participating dance artists have been the subject of all three levels of disrespect. In relation to the first level of disrespect – that of social devaluation when their work is judged by social norms – our YouTube analysis has shown how the qualities of disabled dance are judged by the audience according to the standard expected of the dancing body by the majority of society. In relation to the second level of disrespect – the structured and systemic nature of exclusion from society – the general discrimination against and exclusion of those with a disability from our cultural milieu is indicative of a denial of rights and erosion of integrity. In relation to the third level of disrespect – where an individual is forcibly deprived of physical integrity – the ongoing prominence given to the medical model of disability within society and the subjection of persons with disabilities to the outcomes of its teachings illustrates this form of disrespect in action.

Our understanding of integrity also has strong traction within the law. In the human rights context of which cultural heritage has been seen to form part, two interrelated moral interests have been argued to underlie all true claims to rights – autonomy and physical integrity (Allam 2011: 24). These two interests are argued to speak to our welfare, to reflect what we innately value in humanity, and to apply to all people equally. At an instrumental level, Article 8 of the European Convention on Human Rights, which protects the right to private life (UK Human Rights Act 1998, Sections 3 and 6), has been held by a court to encompass moral and physical integrity and to extend to situations of deprivation of liberty.[16] Integrity becomes even more important when one is not in a position to exercise autonomy. For example, the UK's Mental Capacity Act 2005 articulates the idea of 'best interests' (Section 1); when decision-makers take decisions on someone's behalf, they must do so in that person's best interest as understood from the perspective of that person, and where a decision is taken that interferes with the person's physical integrity, the option that represents the least restrictive means must be adopted.[17]

Integrity has also informed an important category of human rights which aim at protecting individuals and groups from arbitrary physical harm at the hands of governments and other official organs (Humana 1992; Walsh and Piazza 2010: 551–77). These rights, enumerated in multiple instruments, direct authorities to refrain from committing such acts as extrajudicial murder, disappearance, torture and political imprisonment by authorities, and declare illegal all such actions (Cingranelli and Richards 1999: 407–17). Integrity is also explicitly protected under the Convention on the Rights of Persons with Disabilities 2006 (CRPD), to which the UK is a party, and which stipulates that every person with disabilities has a right to respect for his or her physical and mental integrity on an equal basis with others (CRPD, Article 17).

The notion of integrity can also be found, perhaps more indirectly, in the cultural human rights treaties (to which the United Kingdom is again a party) where those rights are aimed at preserving and making accessible cultural phenomena such as language, ethnic history and artistic productions and interpretations of heritage.[18] These are outward looking rights aiming to open avenues for the individual to engage in the cultural milieu. And once again, the CRPD also speaks to this right, requiring States to ensure that persons with disabilities enjoy access to cultural materials and venues, and have the opportunity to develop and use their creative artistic and intellectual potential for the enrichment of society (CRPD, Article 30).

Accordingly, the law has placed, sometimes explicitly and sometimes implicitly, the notion of integrity at the centre of principles and mechanisms that seek to address integrity-eroding conduct such as that discussed above. Integrity appears, therefore, to be a possible foundation for disabled dance, which acknowledges the wholeness or undividedness of the (disabled) body.

This discussion so far has led to the premise that the values encompassed by integrity are a fine starting point for an organising philosophy facilitative of identity – and community-formation for disabled dance; but we wish to shape it further, to reflect the core of disabled dance through the concept of physical integrity.

Physical Integrity: A Foundation for Disabled Dance

The conjunction of 'physical' with any other term suggests a prioritising of the corporeal and the somatic over the mental or spiritual, which may suggest a separation of mind from body. Our conjunction of them is not meant to do so; dancers and dance theorists have rejected such dualism, asserting the importance of the 'minded body' (Fraleigh 1987: 9; Brown and Waelde 2015: 580–82), and the intelligent body of the dancer, and we are minded of this scholarship. Rather, through its close connection to dignity, and to a sense of personal wholeness, we view physical integrity as reflective of Spinoza's position that the mind and the body are one thing, expressed in two different ways (Lord 2015: 2–3, 8; Williams 2015: 17; Mack 2015: 28, 29).[19]

Put positively, physical integrity is concerned with the flourishing of the individual and it signals, through its concern with the relationship to self, that integrity can be achieved in the absence of conformity to the social norm. And the absence of conformity to the social norm is exactly where disabled dancers have been shown to be situated. Alternatively, claiming (or re-claiming) integrity is a way to emphasise that though the dancer may not have the taken-for-granted or normative 'physical integrity', she is nonetheless not 'compromised'. Whatever the configuration of the dancer's body, and whether or not the dancer performs with a prosthetic or some other aid, the dancer performs her own individual identity, and exemplifies her own unique and valuable physical integrity. The dancer's body may be fragile, or it may be circumscribed, extended or scattered; but all bodies are fragile and in some ways broken or breaking, and the dancer in all cases exercises her agency, finding integrity in her performing body (her physicality), whether a 'whole' or 'repaired/enhanced' body.[20] Further, whatever prostheses the dancer may use cannot be said to erode her integrity; for some, the prosthesis will 'complete' the dancer and integrate seamlessly into the dance, whereas for others, the prosthesis is but an aid, purely functional, used to get her where she needs to be.[21] Either way, the prosthesis is no bar to achieving or exemplifying integrity.

Physical integrity reflects, therefore, practices and perspectives in disabled dance: it can be a foundational theory around which a community could coalesce such that disabled dance, either generally or in a particular locality, could be accepted as ICH and be safeguarded by its community and by the relevant state.

Importantly, physical integrity could help to signal to audiences that the disabled dancer is not broken or un-whole; she has physical integrity unique to her being, and that integrity is manifested in the dance, whatever form it takes.[22] Physical integrity could be explored in audience tools and pre-performance publicity material. Gaining experience of how to attend to a performance, of how to look, witness and read a performance is built over time and any reading is always contingent on the position of the viewer. By starting from a physical integrity base, the viewer may be in a more open position to engage seriously with the dance, its subject matter and be active in ensuring that the dance is judged openly and fairly.[23]

Conclusion

This chapter has sought to bring about greater theorisation of disabled dance and to challenge its marginalisation from an interdisciplinary perspective. It has done so by exploring the benefits (for all, and for disabled dance and its immediate supporters) which can arise from disabled dance being part of ICH – an international legal framework of support with strong roots in human rights. We have developed an underpinning foundation or theory – physical integrity – for a disabled dance community (whichever or wherever that may be) which can be used as a base for engagement with the relevant authorities within a state to show why disabled dance should be considered a part of ICH. As part of ICH, the safeguarding responsibilities imposed on states, and the opportunities these would bring for community involvement, could be a fluid and effective means of influencing new activities on the part of states and others to ensure wider respect for, and delivery of, relevant cultural human rights for the disabled dance community. Future questions are how to develop this theory; so that it can effectively create a clear base for leveraging a more visible and central place for disabled dance within local and universal cultural life and scholarship.

References

Albright, A. C. and Brandstetter, G. (2015), 'The politics of a prefix', *Choreographic Practices*, 6:3, pp. 3–8.

Allam, P. (2011), 'A conception of rights', *UCL Jurisprudence Review*, 17, pp. 19–33.

Berger, P. (1970), 'On the obsolescence of the concept of honor', *European Journal of Sociology*, 11:2, pp. 338–47.

Bixler, L. (1999), 'Zebra talk: The absurd world of Philippe Decouflé', in J. Adshead-Lansdale (ed.), *Dancing Texts: Intertextuality in Interpre*tation, London: Dance Books, pp. 231–52.

Blake, J. (2000), 'On defining the cultural heritage', *International and Comparative Law Quarterly*, 49:1, pp. 61–85.

BookSprints (n.d.), 'What is a book sprint?', http://www.booksprints.net/about/. Accessed 28 April 2016.

Bordo, S. (1993), 'Feminism, Foucault and the politics of the body', in C. Ramazanoglu (ed.), *Up Against Foucault*, London: Routledge, pp. 179–202.

Boyce, K. (2013), 'The thinking body: Philosophy, dance and modernism', in J. Bunker, A. Pakes and B. Rowell (eds), *Thinking through Dance: The Philosophy of Dance Performance and Practices*, Hampshire: Dance Books.

Bragg, M. (2007), 'The last remaining avant-garde movement', *Society Guardian*, http://www.theguardian.com/society/2007/dec/11/disability.arts. Accessed 27 April 2016.

Briginshaw, V. (2001), *Dance, Space and Subjectivity*, Basingstoke: Palgrave Macmillan.

Brisenden, S. (1990), 'Disability culture', *Adults Learning (England)*, 2:1, pp. 13–14.

Brown, A. and Waelde, C. (2015), 'Human rights, persons with disabilities and copyright', in C. Geiger (ed.), *Research Handbook on Human Rights and Intellectual Property*, Cheltenham: Edward Elgar Publishing.

Bunker, J., Pakes, A. and Rowell, B. (eds) (2013) *Thinking Through Dance: The Philosophy of Dance Performance and Practices*, Hampshire, Dance Books.

Burt, R. (2001), 'The trouble with the male dancer', in A. Dils and A. C. Albright (eds), *Moving History/Dancing Cultures: A Dance History Reader*, Middletown, CT: Wesleyan University Press, pp. 44–55.

Calder, S. (2015), 'George Eliot, Spinoza and the ethics of literature', in B. Lord (ed.), *Spinoza Beyond Philosophy*, Edinburgh: Edinburgh University Press, pp. 168–87.

Campbell, A. (2009), *The Body in Bioethics*, Abingdon: Routledge.

Carr, J. (2013), 'Embodiment and dance: Puzzles of consciousness and agency', in J. Bunker, A. Pakes and B. Rowell (eds), *Thinking Through Dance: The Philosophy of Dance Performance and Practices*, Hampshire: Dance Books, pp. 63–81.

Cimini, A. (2015), 'The secret history of the musical Spinozism', in B. Lord (ed.), *Spinoza Beyond Philosophy*, Edinburgh: Edinburgh University Press, pp. 87–107.

Cingranelli D. and Richards, D. (1999), 'Measuring the level, pattern and sequence of government respect for physical integrity rights', *International Studies Quarterly*, 43, pp. 407–17.

Copeland, R. (2004), *Merce Cunningham: The Modernizing of Modern Dance*, London: Routledge.

Darke, P. A. (2003), 'Now I know why disability art is drowning in the river lethe (with thanks to Pierre Bourdieu)', in S. Riddell and N. Watson (eds), *Disability, Culture and Identity*, Essex: Pearson Education Ltd., pp. 130–42.

Diderot, D. ([1883] 2007), *The Paradox of Acting* (trans. W. Pollock), London: Kessinger Publishing.

Dils, A. and Albright, A. C. (2001), 'Historical moments: Rethinking the past', in A. Dils and A. C. Albright (eds), *Moving History/Dancing Cultures: A Dance History Reader*, Middletown: Wesleyan University Press, pp. 232–37.

Dodds, S. (1999), '"Streetwise, urban chic": Popular culture and intertextuality in the work of Lea Anderson', in J. Adshead-Lansdale (ed.), *Dancing Texts: Intertextuality in Interpretation*, London: Dance Books, pp. 208–30.

Eliot, G. (2015), 'Spinoza and the ethics of literature', in B. Lord (ed.), *Spinoza Beyond Philosophy*, Edinburgh: Edinburgh University Press.

Elsass, P. (1997), *Treating Victims of Torture and Violence*, New York: New York University Press.

Feinberg, J. (1980), 'The nature and value of rights', in J. Feinberg (ed.), *Rights, Justice and the Bounds of Liberty: Essays in Social Philosophy*, New Jersey: Princeton University Press, pp. 143–58.

Foster, C. (2011), *Human Dignity in Bioethics and Law*, Oxford: Hart.

Foucault, M. (1965), *Madness and Civilization*, New York: Pantheon Books.

Fraleigh, S. (1987), *Dance and the Lived Body*, Pittsburgh: University of Pittsburgh Press.

Harmon, S., Donaldson, H., Brown, A., Waelde, C., Whatley, S. and Wood, K. (2015), 'Disability and the dancing body: A symposium on ownership, identity and difference in dance', *SCRIPT-ed*, 12:1, pp. 59–69.

Hegel, G. (1978), *Hegel's Philosophy of Subjective Spirit* (trans. M. Petry), Dordrecht: Reidel

Honneth, A. (1992), 'Integrity and disrespect: Principles of a conception of morality on the theory of recognition', *Political Theory*, 20, pp. 187–201.

Humana, C. (1992), *World Human Rights Guide*, New York: Oxford University Press.

Hunter, L., Smith, W. and Emerald, E. (2015), *Pierre Bourdieu and Physical Culture*, Abingdon: Routledge.

International Covenant on Economic, Social and Cultural Right, adopted and opened for signature, ratification and accession by General Assembly resolution 2200A (XXI) of 16 December 1966 (1966).

InVisible Difference (2014), *InVisible Difference Symposium*, 26 November, https://www.youtube.com/watch?v=5cRMvs91kRU. Accessed 27 April 2016.

Keck, M. and Sikkink, K. (1998), *Activists Beyond Borders: Advocacy Networks in International Politics*, New York: Cornell University Press.

Kurin, R. (2007), 'Safeguarding intangible cultural heritage: Key factors in implementing the 2003 Convention', *International Journal of Intangible Heritage*, 2, pp. 9–20.

Lenzerini, F. (2011), 'Intangible cultural heritage: The living culture of peoples', *European Journal of International Law*, 22:1, pp. 101–20.

Lord, B. (ed.) (2015), *Spinoza Beyond Philosophy*, Edinburgh: Edinburgh University Press.

Mack, M. (2015), 'Spinoza's non-humanist humanism', in B. Lord (ed.), *Spinoza Beyond Philosophy*, Edinburgh: Edinburgh University Press, pp. 28–47.

Marsh, K. (2015), *Examining Embodiment*, unpublished.

McFee, G. (2011), *The Philosophical Aesthetics of Dance: Identity, Performance and Understanding*, Hampshire: Dance Books.

Merleau-Ponty, M. (2002), *Phenomenology of Perception*, London and New York: Routledge.

Nafziger, J. A. R. and Telesetsky, A. (2014). 'Toward a broader concept of the intangible cultural heritage', *Transnational Dispute Management*, 11:2, www.transnational-dispute-management.com/article.asp?key=2094.

National Disability Arts Collection and Archive (n.d.), http://www.ndaca.org.uk/. Accessed 27 April 2016.

Ness, S. A. (2001), 'Dancing in the field: Notes from memory', in A. Dils and A. C. Albright (eds), *Moving History/Dancing Cultures: A Dance History Reader*, Middeltown: Wesleyan University Press, pp. 67–86.

OHCHR (n.d.), 'Cultural rights', http://www.ohchr.org/EN/Issues/CulturalRights/Pages/SRCulturalRightsIndex.aspx. Accessed 27 April 2016.

Pavis, M. (2014), 'Is there any-body on stage? A legal (mis)understanding of performances', *Platform: Journal of Theatre and Performing Arts*, 8:2, pp. 12–41.

Pearsall, J. and Hanks, P. (eds) (1999), *The New Oxford Dictionary*, Oxford: Oxford University Press.

Roudinesco, Elisabeth, Canguilhem, Georges and Postel, Jacques (1992), *Penser la folie, Essais sur Michel Foucault*, Paris: Galilée.

Speier, H. (1952), *Social Order and the Risks of War: Papers in Political Sociology*, Cambridge, MIT Press.

Stefano, M. (2012), 'Reconfiguring the framework: Adopting an ecomuseological approach for safeguarding intangible cultural heritage', in M. Stefano, P. Davis and G. Corsane (eds), *Safeguarding Intangible Cultural Heritage*, Newcastle: Newcastle University, Boydell Press, pp. 223–38.

Still, A. and Velody, I. (eds) (1992), *Rewriting the History of Madness: Studies in Foucault's Histoire de La Folie*, London and New York: Routledge.

Sutherland, A. (1989), 'Disability arts, disability politics', *DAIL Magazine*, September. Rpt. in A. Pointon and C. Davies (eds), *Framed: Interrogating Disability in the Media*, London: BFI, p.159.

Swain, J. and French, S. (2000), 'Towards an affirmation model', *Disability and Society*, 15:4, pp. 569–82.

——— (2008), 'Conclusions: Some reflections on key questions', in J. Swain and S. French (eds), *Disability on Equal Terms*, London: Sage.

Torrey, E. F. and Miller, J. (2001), *The Invisible Plague: The Rise of Mental Illness from 1750 to the Present*, New Brunswick, New Jersey and London: Rutgers University Press.

UN General Assembly, Convention on the Rights of Persons with Disabilities, 13 December 2006, A/RES/61/106, Annex I (2006), http://www.refworld.org/docid/4680cd212.html. Accessed 29 April 2016.

UN General Assembly, Universal Declaration of Human Rights (1948), 10 December , Paris: Palais de Chaillot.

UNESCO (n.d.), *Introducing UNESCO*, http://en.unesco.org/about-us/introducing-unesco. Accessed 27 April 2016.

UNESCO General Conference, Convention for the Safeguarding of the Intangible Cultural Heritage, 17 October 2003, 32nd session, Paris.

UNESCO Universal Declaration on Bioethics and Human Rights (2005), http://portal.unesco.org/en/ev.php-URL_ID=31058&URL_DO=DO_TOPIC&URL_SECTION=201.html. Accessed 27 April 2015.

United Nations (2015), *Report of the Special Rapporteur on the Rights of Persons with Disabilities*, UN General Assembly, Human Rights Council, 28th session, A/HRC/28/58, www.ohchr.org/EN/HRBodies/HRC/.../A_HRC_28_58_E.doc. Accessed 27 April 2016.

UPIAS (1976), *Fundamental Principles of Disability*, London: London Union of the Physically Impaired, London. Rpt. in M. Oliver, *Understanding Disability: From Theory to Practice*, Basingstoke: Palgrave Macmillan, pp. 19–29.

Vadi, V. S. and Schneider, H. (2014), 'The new frontiers of cultural law: Intangible heritage disputes', *Transnational Dispute Management*, 11:2, www.transnational-dispute-management. com/article.asp?key=2093.

Waelde, C., Harmon, S. and Brown, A. (2015), 'SCRIPT: A legacy of vitality', *SCRIPT-ed*, 12:1, pp. 51–58.

Walsh, J. and Piazza, J. (2010), 'Why respecting physical integrity rights reduces terrorism', *Comparative Political Studies*, 43, pp. 551–77.

Williams, C. (2015), 'Subjectivity without the subject: Thinking beyond the subject with/through Spinoza', in B. Lord (ed.), *Spinoza Beyond Philosophy*, Edinburgh: Edinburgh University Press, pp. 11–27.

Williamson, J. (2004), 'An act of embodiment', *The Guardian*, 22 April, http://www.theguardian. com/culture/2004/apr/22/guesteditors. Accessed 27 April 2016.

Notes

1 Our research has been informed by our work with dancers with disabilities during the InVisible Difference: Disability, Dance and Law project and more generally. Neither we, nor those dancers, see disability dance as a separate art-form or genre from dance. Dancers with disabilities wish to be viewed and evaluated as dance artists equal to other professional dance artists – a point to which we will return in the chapter. Use of the term 'disability' *can* permit discounting of the work because the dancer is seen as 'other' than the non-disabled performer; when placed within the frame of disability, neither the dance, nor the dancer tends to be taken as seriously as dance by the non-disabled. The outcome is that the dancer (and the dance) disappears.

2 We authored, both separately and together, over 50 publications in a variety of outlets. For a detail lists of our publications please visit the project's official website at http://www. invisibledifference.org.uk. Accessed 28 April 2016.

3 For more on the notion of 'book sprint' see BookSprints (n.d.), *What is a Book Sprint?*, http://www.booksprints.net/about/. Accessed 28 April 2016.

4 For example, Cleveland Ballet Dancing Wheels (Dancing Wheels) in the United States in 1980 and Candoco in the United Kingdom in 1991.

5 Including Dan Daw's *BEAST*, Chisato Minamimura's App, Bowditch's *Falling in Love with Frida* and Claire Cunningham's *Guide Gods* – both winners of the Herald Angel Award at the Edinburgh Fringe Festivals.

6 Jane Pritchard, Curator of Dance at the V&A (Victoria and Albert Museum), London, has discussed the concept of disability and dance as being part of the 'invisible material' that exists (InVisible Difference Symposium 2014). Pritchard highlighted an event some years prior where a 'mystery dancer' in Come Dance with Me was identified following an assessment of a donation to the Museum. A remark was made in the materials dismissing a

dancer who was referred to as a 'girl had a wooden hand'. The author was however informed that 'an excellent glove was preserved for her special use'.

7   ICHC, Article 15 reads: 'Within the framework of its safeguarding activities of the intangible cultural heritage, each State Party shall endeavor to ensure the widest possible participation of communities, groups and, where appropriate, individuals that create, maintain and transmit such heritage, and to involve them actively in its management'.

8   A quest for a philosophy should not, however, be a sop for an intellectual inferiority complex, reminiscent of the fears of Duchamp who, Copeland (2004: 226) reports, 'seemed to suffer from an intellectual inferiority complex – or at least a fear that the visual arts were perceived as less "mentally demanding" than the verbal arts. In a remarkable burst of candor, he once admitted, "The painter was considered stupid, but the poet and writer were intelligent. I wanted to be intelligent"'.

9   See for example the contribution to this collection *Disabled Dance: Barriers to Proper Inclusion within our Cultural Milieu.*

10   We have noted elsewhere the risk that overly focussing on models could lead to potentially practical useful initiatives being discounted. See Brown and Waelde 2015: 580, 596–98, 602.

11   *Hadley v Kemp* (1999) All ER (D) 450, para. N5.

12   The *Garcia v Google* case is a dispute tried before the ninth circuit court of appeal of the United States. Unlike *Hadley v Kemp*, it is not a case ruled under UK law and as such is not a binding precedent for judges applying it. However, the *Garcia* dispute remains relevant to our conversation insomuch as it reveals the conceptualisation of performances afforded by a legal system neighbour to that of the United Kingdom, with which it shares a common historical and cultural background as well as the same international influences in intellectual property law. See, *Hadley v Kemp* (1999) All ER (D) 450.

13   *Garcia v Google Inc*, 743 F. 3d 1258 (9th Cir 2014) 1274. Those comments were made as part of Justice Smith's dissent in the first instance decision, dissent which became the majority decision when the 2014 Garcia decision was overturned in appeal. See, *Garcia v Google Inc, 786 F. 3d 733* (9th Cirt 2015).

14   This analogy between the role of performers and the input of puppets was first articulated in 1883 by the French philosopher Denis Diderot (1883) with respect to acting.

15   Foucault noted that leprosy was both a manifestation of God's anger and mercy; the leper has been 'afflicted', but, through God, he can be healed (a theme picked up by Cunningham in Guide Gods, a performance exploring power, punishment and how world faiths view deafness and disability). It may be worth noting that Foucault's work in *Madness and Civilization* knows as many supporters as it has detractors. Indeed, his work on mental illness and disability has been the subject of great controversies for many considered that his thesis, though compelling, suffered from many historical inaccuracies (Still and Velody 1992; Roudinesco et al. 1992; Torrey and Miller 2001: 303).

16   *Husayn v Poland* (2015) 60 EHRR 16 (ECtHR). See also *Dickson v UK* (2008) 46 EHRR 41 (Grand Chamber).

17   It must impose on them in a limited way and the idea of proportionality is important. Section 4 of the Act outlines the multiple elements of the best interests test, and an examination of

the jurisprudence in this area underlines the importance of physical integrity when applying this test. On this see *A Local Authority v K* (2013) EWCOP 242 (Fam), *Aintree University Hospital NHS Foundation Trust v James* (2013) 3 WLR 1299 (SC), and *Mental Health Trust and others v DD* (2015) EWCOP 4 (Fam).

18 Article 15(a) of the ICESCR imposes on states a right for individuals to take part in cultural life; whilst Article 15.2 also requires that they implement measures to develop and diffuse culture. See also the appointment and activities of United Nations Special Rapporteur in the field of cultural rights: OHCHR (n.d.); and the report of the Special Rapporteur on the rights of persons with disabilities: United Nations, Devandas-Aguilar (2015).

19 The argument that Spinoza saw little place for the visual arts from the perspective of developing truth, as he considered them to be overly focussed on the mind and words is challenged from the perspective of experiential art (Cimini 2015; Calder 2015).

20 During the course of our ethnographic observations, Caroline Bowditch asked all present, including the researchers, to write a letter to our bodies. It was a powerful and emotional exercise, and we all clearly felt that we had some broken aspects of our body. This undermines the normative and the whole/broken dichotomy. Feeling whole is more about having a feeling of physical integrity, which encompasses a sense that one is able to 'flourish and find identity as an individual'.

21 For example, Caroline Bowditch, one of our dance collaborators, reported that she feels 'whole' without the mechanized chair that she uses to get around. Similarly, Welly, another collaborator, reported using her leg for purely functional purposes, setting it aside when she danced.

22 It is also about broadening the general understanding of 'dance'. For some the word 'dance' signals a ballet aesthetic. Acknowledging and honouring the difference in bodies and that each have physical integrity. An emphasis on integrity, and the foregrounding of the dancer's physical integrity, will encourage this shift in attitude and environment. The artists that we worked with already embrace the idea of physical integrity, dismissing disability as something that 'simply exists', not hidden or accentuated.

23 Funders should also encourage the adoption of such steps. There are already a number of innovative research projects in the United Kingdom that seek to understand audience engagement with dance: http://www.watchingdance.org. Accessed 27 April 2016. http://culturehive.co.uk. Accessed 27 April 2016. http://www.respondto.org. Accessed 25 July 2014. There are signs that the Arts Council is starting to take this seriously as was made clear by Peter Bazalgette, chairman on the Arts Council England who wants arts organisation to make more progress with audience, programme and workforce diversity or risk having their funding axed. See http://www.theguardian.com/uk-news/2014/dec/08/arts-council-england-make-progress-diversity-funding-axed-bazalgette?CMP=share_btn_fb. Accessed 27 April 2016.

Chapter 8

Disability and Dance: The Disabled Sublime or Joyful Encounters?

Janice Richardson

Introduction

In this chapter, I draw from two different philosophers, Kant and Spinoza, to think about how conceptual frameworks from the philosophy of aesthetics can inform how we think about disabled dance. Additionally, I consider what new concepts can emerge (and how existing philosophical frameworks can be challenged) when this area of aesthetics – which is also closely associated with politics – is brought into view. In doing so, I consider in detail a performance called *Heteronomous Male* (2012) choreographed and performed by Michael Turinsky at the Integrart Symposium, 'Dance' and 'Normality',[1] in 2015. My aim is to demonstrate that disabled dance can be read outside the normal stereotypes and in nuanced and challenging ways, and that this reading can be facilitated or hampered by the approach adopted. Audiences therefore need much more help in developing their literacy so that they can more fruitfully read disabled dance.

The Analytical Approach

In undertaking the above analysis, I consider the extent to which some aspects of feminist and critical race theory can be employed to help think about disabled dance. In doing so, I am sensitive to the fact that it is necessary to avoid the trap of assuming that different areas of oppression and subordination can be unconditionally subsumed into each other (i.e. that all mechanisms of oppression work in the same way; that women, black persons or persons with disabilities can be assumed to stand in for 'otherness', always set against a norm of white, able-bodied men). However, an example of the way that feminist and critical race philosophy can contribute is in problematising conceptions of what it is to be human. In particular, how we think about aspects of humanity: bodies, imagination and reason. A brief example of how they can unsettle common perceptions is warranted here.

In aesthetics, there have been debates about 'the naked and the nude'. Feminists have highlighted a mainstream concern that the portrayal of men as 'nude' in art may be threatened by depictions of women as merely 'naked'. The argument is that men in art can appear as dignified within their own skin, without the need for clothes (Nead 1990). In contrast, unclothed women, as shown in paintings, risk being perceived as 'naked'; as abject rather than self-possessed. Feminists detected a mainstream worry that the portrayal of naked women would 'contaminate' the appreciation of the male nude by forcing viewers to see all human beings as naked and vulnerable rather than as nude and clothed within their own skin.

A second example is available in relation to race. In 'The whiteness of privacy: Race, media, law' Osucha (2009) analyses Warren and Brandeis' 1890 *Harvard Law Review* article on privacy. They famously argued for the development of the common law to protect privacy, but Osucha argues that their privacy concerns need to be understood within the context of racism in the United States at that time. Whereas, in the history of portraiture, upper class white families were depicted in flattering terms and as 'self-possessed', black persons were shown in a demeaning way; the images of black persons in the US press of the nineteenth century represented the antithesis of the upper class white tradition of the portrait within the stately home. Osucha argues that Warren and Brandeis, who were white and upper class, were worried that when images of their families appeared in the press (after the invention of the Kodak camera) their own white images would take on a demeaning character, by association with the public portrayal of black persons. Like the case of the male nude and female nakedness, the perception of the public portrayal of the white body was viewed as precarious: as subject to contamination, by the way in which images of black persons had been produced.

Does the same move apply in the case of disabled dance? If so, some of the power of disabled dance, at this point in time, may derive from the depiction of the disabled body as threatening to society's conception of the meaning of the 'able body'. For those who view dance as illustrating the flexibility and strength of the human body to achieve certain moves, as a sort of gymnastics, disabled dance may remind the audience of the limitations of *all* human bodies and of their vulnerability; that the human body is not simply a machine that seamlessly reproduces choreographed dance. The ability to 'read' disabled dance in more than one way – to go beyond the interpretation of disabled dance evoked by its challenge to stereotypes – opens up wider experiences. Carrie Sandahl describes overcoming this hurdle,

> Many audiences often do not recognise or understand the complexity of Disability Art because the disability condition is widely presumed to be a state of incompetence. Incompetency and creativity are paradoxical. If disabled people are fundamentally incompetent then how can they be creative? Because both being incompetent and creative is paradoxical, many audiences encountering Disability Art become, for want of a better word, 'stuck' and as they are stuck puzzling through this paradox they regrettably miss a good deal of the work's content.
>
> (Sandahl, quoted in Wheatley 2015)

While some contemporary audiences may already experience disabled dance in nuanced and diverse ways, this is not the norm. For many, disabled dance can only be understood as challenging the appreciation of the human body and the place of the disabled body. While the fact that disabled dance challenges stereotypes of disability is important today, it is not the singular role of all disabled dance, and disabled dance must not be limited in this way.

Kant, Heteronomy and the Sublime in a Disabled Dance Performance

In this section, I consider Turinsky's *Heteronomous Male*, performed in 2015. In doing so, I apply the aesthetic frameworks of Kant and Spinoza, starting with Kant's ideas from the *Critique of Judgement* (1987). The link with Kant is obvious in that the title of the work refers to 'heteronomy', the opposite of autonomy, a central Kantian concept. However, Kant's description of the experience of the sublime is also relevant; Kant describes audiences' appreciation of the sublime in art as beginning with a feeling of discomfort. I think that it is useful to theorise this feeling, while recognising the diversity of disabled dance. Turinsky's dance is particularly useful as its theme is the lack of autonomy experienced by those with disabilities. By considering what is really involved in Kant's idea of autonomy, it is clear that heteronomy is a condition that is shared by all of us. I will argue that by moving on to replace Kant's framework with that of Spinoza, disabled dancers can be seen to both increase their own freedom and that of their audiences.

When watching Turinsky's dance, I initially felt discomfort at the sight of someone with severe physical disabilities being wheeled on stage and then having his wheelchair overturned by his carer. This was a portrayal of an act of cruelty, even though its staging meant that the audience did not feel any responsibility to intervene; that no actual cruelty was really involved but was merely depicted. The dance consisted of Turinsky's slow struggle to get onto his feet and then move around. It was accompanied by grunts, indicating the extent of his struggle to move his limbs, and by some dialogue, which, among other things, indicated the difficulty he had with speech. When he had succeeded in standing up, he moved around the stage again, illustrating how he controlled his limbs only with great difficulty. While this appears to be the opposite of the Kantian sublime, I want to map my reaction onto Kant's analysis from the *Critique of Judgement* and to re-work the sublime in keeping with Kant's main arguments.

Kant (1987) explains the dynamic sublime as a two-stage process. The first is associated with art in which nature is depicted as threatening to us. This lies in contrast to pictures of the beautiful in which nature is envisaged as if it were made for us; as charming and unthreatening. In his pre-critical work (Kant 1991), he associated beauty with women and the sublime with the male warrior. In the *Critique of Judgement*, the art object illustrates the might of nature and its ability to evoke terror. As examples, Kant suggests lightning and thunder claps, volcanoes, hurricanes (Kant 1987: 120).

The depiction of nature as 'mighty' and dangerous to us creates a discomfort in the viewer. However, this tension is overcome in the second stage of the sublime experience. Viewers,[2] who are able to appreciate the sublime, are aware that they could face up to the might of nature by virtue of having the ability to reason. Even when nature threatens their lives, they would be able use their ability to reason in order to behave morally under pressure, rather than giving in to fear. Even though they are part of the natural world, their ability to use reason gives them the resources to also divide themselves off from nature. This gives viewers the thrill of the sublime experience, which reminds them of their vocation as moral rational beings. In other words, the experience affirms our belief that, as creatures of reason, we could obey moral rules even in the face of danger.[3] As creatures of reason, we can 'stand up' to the threat posed by the natural world:

> Though the irresistibility of nature's might makes us, considered as natural beings, recognize our physical impotence, it reveals in us at the same time an ability to judge ourselves independent of nature, and reveals in us a superiority over nature that is the basis of a self-preservation quite different in kind from the one that can be assailed and endangered by nature outside us. This keeps the humanity in our person from being degraded, even though a human being would have to succumb to that dominance [of nature].
>
> (Kant 1987: 121)

The fact that we are not actually in danger as we look at an artwork (that evokes the sublime experience within us) does not detract from our experience because the experience still serves as a reminder of our ability to reason. Anyone who felt only terror could not experience the sublime. Kant based his aesthetic analysis upon a conceptual framework in which the viewer is envisaged as having innate faculties. The sublime experience arises as a result of the interaction of the viewers' own mental faculties of imagination and reason that are prompted to interact in a particular way upon viewing certain types of art object. There are a number of problems with this way of envisioning ourselves (and also our relationship to nature and to what is considered as outside of us, as I will discuss further below. However, what made me think about the sublime experience is that it appeared to map onto my own reactions, albeit that I would view them as arising from historical cultural misunderstandings of disability rather than innate faculties of the mind.

Upon seeing Turinsky thrown to the floor and struggling to get up, finding it difficult to gain control of his limbs and moaning with the effort, I felt discomfort, which – like the discomfort in the first stage of the sublime – was then overcome in ways that align with Kant's view of reason. My tension was released as Turinsky was eventually able to get up and to move around, albeit with painful slowness. In other words, I both witnessed and experienced nature as threatening to Turinsky followed by a release from the threat that can be characterised in Kantian terms. In this case, the threat of nature was not that of the thunderstorm but of the problem posed by gravity and of a human body as struggling against this basic element of nature in order to literally stand up.

From the perspective of the viewer who witnesses Turinsky's struggle to get off the floor, his dance is, in some ways, a reversal of the Kantian sublime. This reversal brings my analysis closer to Kant's pre-critical work because it is the art 'object' (Turinsky himself) who could be described as sublime. This lies in contrast to Kant's later *Critique of Judgement*, applied above, in which *the viewer* experiences the sublime as a result of an interaction between the viewer's own faculties of imagination and reason. The artwork merely evokes rather than illustrates this interaction of the faculties of the viewer. In the dance, it is Turinsky who is threatened by being overturned onto the floor and then enacts the recovery. Hence, it could be argued that viewers merely watch rather than enact the experience of the sublime themselves. Yet the viewer *does* experience the initial feeling discomfort and then resolution through a different act of reason than that described by Kant: that of recognising *another person*, who is able to withstand a threat by setting and enacting his own goal through the use of his own reason. Turinsky is recognised as a person whose dance prompts us to consider all persons' abilities to overcome a natural threat (which is here depicted as the vulnerability of the human body itself and the impact of gravity); a person's ability literally to stand up in the face of a natural difficulty. The Kantian framework, in this reworking, again prompts an interpretation of an individual act of will over the recalcitrant body that fits with the second aspect of the sublime: the emphasis upon reason as triumphing against nature.

Interestingly, immediately after the performance, there was a comment from the organiser that Turinsky had other ambitions prior to his disability but that now he was a dancer. This picked up a comment within the dance in which Turinsky states, 'When I was a child I dreamed of becoming a football coach. Now instead...'. It could be regret, demonstrated by his struggle against gravity. However, the organiser characterises Turinsky's comment positively. This added to the sense that – irrespective of an earlier threat of nature, which in this case had already occurred thereby reducing Turinsky's ability to move – he was able to recover; to set goals and to enrich the lives of others through dance; that the ability to dance was part of this recuperation. In other words, the dance was both a depiction of a struggle to get off the floor but also to achieve broader success as a dancer, a success which he was enacting as he danced.

The Feminist Correction of Kant's White Male Perspective

When read through Kant's philosophy of aesthetics, Turinsky's struggle appears to be that of an individual's successful fulfilment of his goals, set against the initial insult of being thrown to the floor by his carer (as well as the difficulty of defeating nature in the form of gravity in order to rise). However, feminist insights may improve on the Kant's framework for conceptualising disability and dance, or at least may highlight the problems with Kant that Spinoza may resolve.

As Held (1987) has pointed out, the position of carers is a political issue that often fades into the background. Like all of us, the ability to achieve goals involves others who may either block, or facilitate our ambitions. Again, others are brought to mind when we consider that Turinsky's ambition is not simply one of getting up but also self-expression and the power to challenge his audience.

Battersby (1998) details the way that the Kantian sublime relies upon an opposition between the individual and nature. The second part of the sublime in which the viewer is released from the tension – that is initially produced by the perception of nature as threatening – envisages the viewer as able to oppose nature. Kant, she argues, envisages viewers in terms of a split from their outside; from the otherness of nature. As Battersby (1998) illustrates, Kant argues that western women could *but should not* appreciate the sublime because they may be pregnant and should not consider standing up to the might of nature. In addition, for Kant, some men – defined in terms of race – are unable to avoid being afraid of nature as threatening in order to experience the sublime in art (Battersby 2007).

In contrast to Kant's description of the person as split off from nature, both women and persons with disabilities have been viewed as having 'leaky boundaries' (Shildrick 1997). Battersby argues against a phenomenological assumption that we view our bodies as bounded against the outside. She argues that, if women's historical experiences were to be viewed as the norm, then selfhood would not be viewed in terms of 'what we are not' or 'what is outside of us'. Instead, selfhood would be conceptualised as emerging gradually through interactions with others, which provides a better model for everyone. Turinsky's *Heteronomous Male* is a work of art that highlights the problem of autonomy for those with disabilities. As Battersby's work implies, Turinsky's dance may be diminished by simply interpreting it through a Kantian framework that positions his dance as another repetition of the familiar tale of an isolated male hero, cut off from nature.[4]

We can conclude from the above that the initial framing of the dance in terms of Kantian sublime is flawed insofar as it relies on the idea of an individual who is threatened and recovers by splitting himself off from nature, or from 'otherness'. In short, then, the Kantian framework does not really offer enough resources for thinking about disability and dance; that is, the Kantian reading falls short in its image of what it is to be human. However, we might turn to Spinoza for a better way of thinking about disability and dance.

Spinoza, the Body, Imagination and Reason – Connected to Nature

In order to rethink how the disability movement challenges the meaning of selfhood through the practice of dance today, I want to employ the work of a seventeenth-century philosopher, Spinoza. This may initially appear to be a strange claim given the arguments that Spinoza does not have a philosophy of aesthetics (Morrison 1989).[5] However, as a major figure of the Radical Enlightenment, Spinoza provides a conceptual framework through which to think about disabled dance in ways that prompt different understandings of the body, imagination and reason than those of Kant. It is also one in which communication is of central importance. I want to consider each of these areas in turn.

I will start with the body. For Spinoza, there is no mind/body split. Both mind and body are viewed as aspects of the same human being, conceived in different ways: 'The mind and the body are one and the same individual, which is conceived now under the attribute of thought, now under the attribute of extension' (*Ethics:* II.P21S).

Additionally, there is no 'ideal form' or 'exemplar' attributed to the human body. What it is to be human is not defined in terms of specific abilities or in comparison to a template.

Spinoza's characterisation of the relationship between our selves and nature differs starkly from that described in the Kantian sublime. Recall that the Kantian sublime relies upon a split between the individual and external nature that arises as the individual is threatened by nature but then overcomes the threat (by recognising he is a creature of reason). In contrast, Spinoza stresses that human beings are part of nature and not a 'kingdom within a kingdom' (*Ethics*: III.Preface).[6]

Similarly, there is no image of the self as split from its outside, which includes, not only nature, but also other persons and things. Spinoza envisages what Balibar (1997) refers to as a 'trans-individual', a unique way of conceptualising the relationship between individual and society. We are made up of parts that are also individuals, such as bacteria in our guts, but we are also parts of other entities. For Spinoza, we can be classed as part of a singular thing when we act together to have an effect upon other things, both human and non-human.[7] So, at times a human being as an individual can be viewed as a singular thing but at other times (and in contrast with the individualism within liberalism) we are part of a greater whole that is itself a singular thing. For example, we act as one singular thing when we join our 'powers of acting' to pull on a rope together, pooling the powers of our bodies to have an effect on the world. Similarly, we combine our 'powers of understanding' when we communicate in order to tackle an intellectual problem, thereby becoming a singular thing.

The use of wheelchairs or wider use of technology to increase bodily ability provides an important example. We can all form such a singular thing by employing technology, irrespective of whether the initial individual is viewed as 'abled-bodied' or not. This raises questions about how technology is viewed. At the Symposium where Turinsky performed, US representatives argued that the use of wheelchairs as props in a dance should be avoided because they viewed the wheelchair as part of their own body and therefore part of their identity. They felt uncomfortable, as if it were a threat to that identity, to have these 'parts of themselves' used as props. This was not a concern shared by European dancers with disabilities. It may be that those European dancers (who do not share the US dancers' phenomenology) experience their wheelchair as part of themselves, but are not worried about any parts of themselves being treated as props. Alternatively, they may not experience the wheelchair as parts of their identities in the same way. In fact, the dancers associated with the InVisible Difference project, it is reported, indicated that their wheelchairs, crutches and prosthetics were much more instrumental as opposed to identity-forming.

This is a matter of phenomenology, although it is interesting that the implications of this experience go beyond that of a psychology in relation to disability. The initial experience seems to be that we take time to adapt to new technologies to which we are intimately related but that, when we do so, we view the technology as part of ourselves. This can be conceptualised in Spinozist terms. Spinoza's conceptual framework is not based upon the assumption that the mind will have a static notion of what the body is or can do. It is the idea of the body and changes as the body changes, registering its increase and decrease of power that occur as the body forms associations with other people and things, such as a wheelchair. I will explain this further by extending my discussion of Spinoza. The mind does not have perfect knowledge of the body – a point that is made famous by Gilles Deleuze (1988: 17; 1990: chap. XIV) who has emphasised Spinoza's comment:

[…] no one has yet determined what the body can do, that is, experience has not yet taught anyone what the body can do from the laws of Nature alone, insofar as Nature is only considered to be corporeal.

(Spinoza *Ethics:* II.P2S)

Of course, nature can also be considered through the attribute of thought as well as the body. Whereas Descartes viewed mind and body as two different substances, for Spinoza there is only one substance. Everything that exists is part of this one substance, which he calls God, or Nature, meaning that the two are synonymous. It is useful to think of this as equivalent to 'the whole of everything that exists'. Thought (minds) and Extension (bodies) are attributes of nature of which we are a part. A human individual simply is both mind and body as different aspects of the same thing. There is no split, as discussed above. The mind is the idea of the body, just as the body is the embodiment of the mind – i.e. different ways of perceiving the same thing. When either our minds or bodies change, they are not envisaged as somehow changing the other aspect of our selves in a causal relation. It is simply that we change. It is this change that is central to our ability to thrive and survive.

This framework can further inform our understanding of the US disabled dancers' concerns about the use of wheelchairs or crutches as a prop. Given that the mind is the idea of the body, it will also form ideas of bodily changes, particularly something such as a crutch or wheelchair that the body will start to use automatically. In parallel, the body itself adapts to the use of technology. This development can also be seen in artists who employ technology in ways that challenge our conception of 'able bodies', such as Stelarc who had an extra ear attached to his arm. Spinoza's conception of the body is useful in envisaging the human body (along with the mind) as having the capacity to form 'singular things' with other things as well as other human beings. This can increase our powers of acting in ways that challenge the idea of there being an exemplar of the human body.

Spinoza also provides a way of thinking about the relationship of imagination and reason. To illustrate this, it is again useful to compare Spinoza's framework with that of Kant. Kantian aesthetics is based upon the idea that our perception of a beautiful artwork involves the free play of different faculties: imagination and understanding, which produces a sense of harmony. In contrast, the sublime, as discussed above, is experienced when there is a clash between the faculties of imagination and reason. Our imagination allows us to envisage nature as threatening to us, but then is 'elevated' (Kant 1987: 121) when we become aware of our ability to use reason, such that we can withstand such a threat. This is the main move within the dynamic sublime, which I discussed in the context of disabled dance above. The mathematical sublime also illustrates the way that Kant envisages the interaction of imagination and reason, with reason given the more important role. The experience of the mathematical sublime is also a two-stage process. Again, it starts with the discomfort of the viewer at an art object (such as the Alps or the ocean) that prompts the imagination to try to envisage the enormity of nature; to try to capture that vastness within one image and to fail. The discomfort is overcome when we realise that this feat of the imagination was attempted because we are creatures of reason. Such impossible attempts made by the faculty of imagination to picture the infinitely large give us a sense of those 'ideas of reason' that go beyond the 'concepts of the understanding' about things in the world. Kant, unlike Spinoza, distinguishes between our ability to *understand* mundane concepts and our ability to use *reason* to think of ideas that are beyond the world (that remind us of our 'super-sensible vocation') such as morality, God and freedom.

There is no super-sensible realm in Spinoza's analysis of ethics, God or freedom, nor does he distinguish between understanding and reason. To live a life that is virtuous or free involves understanding our encounters with other things that exist. I will explain this point and its relevance to understanding disabled dance by focusing upon Spinoza's conceptions of imagination and reason, as sources of knowledge. Knowledge of our encounters changes us and so is more related to ontology (who we are and the lives that we can lead) than epistemology (what we can know).

When we (as human beings) encounter other bodies and other minds (ideas) we may have feelings of sadness or joy, which accompany our image of the thing that we have encountered. As discussed, it is only through our encounters with others that we learn something about ourselves and about the other body or ideas that we have encountered. At this first stage of knowledge, associated with our imagination and emotions we register whether something has increased or decreased our powers by whether we experience joy or sadness. When the power of either our mind or body is increased then we, as a whole, have our powers increased.

For example, at the first stage of knowledge, that of 'inadequate knowledge', we have an image of another body that we have encountered, say a snake, that is associated with the emotion of fear. This knowledge is inadequate because we do not understand fully our reaction of fear. Sad passions, such as fear, may perpetuate our ignorance because they can lead to superstition. As we do not really understand the actual cause of our distress, we label the snake as evil and assume that this allows us to fully understand what has happened in the encounter. To move to the second stage of knowledge, that of 'adequate knowledge', we need to work out what it is about the snake's body that disagrees with our own body, how it can diminish our powers of acting. This involves recognising that a snake can poison us. Similarly, food can increase our powers of acting and hence is associated with joyful passions, leading us to label food as good. With adequate knowledge, we come to understand the biology involved and move from the partial knowledge provided by the imagination (accompanied by emotions) to the fuller knowledge gained by understanding the encounter. The same applies to ideas, some of which can also act as 'poison' in that they diminish us. Again, we are tempted to label such ideas (or those who communicate them) as evil rather than understanding why they act so as to create sad passions (that indicate that they are diminishing us).

In a society that cruelly segregated persons with disabilities, the image of the disabled body can come as a shock and produce sadness. However, disabled dance can have the radical effect of communicating more than initial sad passions, and can help us to gain adequate knowledge. It has the potential to increase our understanding of our encounters with those bodies classified as disabled, along with the accompanying idea of those bodies.

Spinoza points out that, in society, we imitate each other's emotions and can spread both sad and joyful passions, which are accompanied by images that give us 'inadequate' or only partial knowledge. Spinoza views organised religions as an example of a collection of ideas that can perpetuate the sad passion of fear of damnation, for example. We are able to change ourselves and live freer, active and virtuous lives when we are able to understand our encounters with other bodies and other minds. While we communicate emotions, we are also useful to each other in spreading adequate knowledge (i.e. understanding of our encounters) that goes beyond our initial emotions and images. We never lose these emotions or these initial images but our knowledge of the encounter can be improved.

Our ability to move to an adequate understanding of our encounters is therefore central to Spinoza's ethics. When we communicate, and help each other to form such adequate understandings of the world, we do more to increase our powers of acting and understanding than is possible in a one-off joyful encounter, such as eating a meal. We also open ourselves up to more varied encounters that further enrich our lives. We are able to boot-strap our understanding by pursuing more varied encounters and selecting encounters that increase our powers. This makes communication, including – I will argue, the communication that can arise through disability and dance – central to Spinoza's thought. Hence Balibar (1998: 99) has described Spinoza as a 'philosopher of communication'.

Turinsky's Dance Through Spinoza's Lens

How is my earlier analysis of Turinsky's dance altered when Kant's conceptual framework is replaced by Spinoza's? There is no longer an image of an individual hero who 'stands up' to nature. Applying Spinoza' framework to disabled dance cannot rely upon a sense that someone overcomes threatening nature because, for Spinoza, we are a part of nature. The encounter can again be viewed as taking place in two stages, which also involve both our imagination, at first, followed by the use of reason in the second stage. However, this time what is meant by imagination and reason differs, as does the image of the individual dancer and his (and our) freedom.

At the start of the dance, from a Spinozist position, the image of a carer seen overturning a disabled person's wheelchair again evokes sad passions because we mimic others' emotions. We view this as a sad encounter between dancer and carer that diminishes the dancer's powers of acting. Some of the audience may also associate what is still an unusual sight (that of a severely disabled person on stage) as disturbing because the experience is associated with a threat to our own perception of our bodies, a reminder of our vulnerability. As a result of the mimicry of emotions, we are later relieved by Turinsky's successful struggle to get off the floor, to dance and, more broadly, to realise his ambition to become a dancer and to affect audiences.

However, disabled dance is also viewed through the lens of the political historical subordination of those with disability. The image of the disabled body, and the political oppression associated with it, has a history that prompts the audience to feel pity but not necessarily respect. Pity is a sad passion, which Spinoza criticises: 'Pity is a sadness, accompanied by the idea of an evil which has happened to another whom we imagine to be like us' (*Ethics*: III.DefAff.XVIII).

For Spinoza, wise people help others, not out of pity, but out of a recognition that living in a society in which as many people as possible are able to thrive helps them to thrive in turn. This can be reversed: other people are important to us because of their ability to increase our powers of acting and understanding. Their bodies and minds are similar enough to ours such that their insights about snakes, for example, are useful to us in our attempt to understand our own encounters. This allows us to choose encounters that enrich us and avoid those that diminish us. Some useful encounters will be lost if others are unable to thrive. This ethos sounds selfish but cannot be reduced to a utilitarian position because it is not a framework in which competing individuals' interests are set against each other. What it means to be an individual ('a singular thing') will differ at different times depending upon whether we are acting alone or in concert with others in order to have an effect on the world.

From Spinoza's perspective, there is another two-stage process through which we can understand the dance from the perspective of the viewer. This analysis focuses upon the viewer's response to his or her encounter with the dance. To the extent to which a viewer remains subject to sad passions (such as pity at the image of the struggling disabled body) as a result of seeing the dance, s/he remains at the stage of partial or inadequate knowledge. Similarly, joy at the later achievement within the dance, in that the dancer is able to get up, remains at this level. It is only when the viewer is capable of understanding the causes of these emotions and images that s/he associates with a disabled body dancing that s/he moves to an understanding of her encounter with Turinsky. Recall that this adequate knowledge is important because Spinoza's analysis of knowledge is not merely an epistemological claim but one that is ontological. We are able to thrive and enrich our lives when we have a greater understanding of our encounters with others. It is part of an ethos that increases our freedom.

What would constitute such an understanding of Turinsky's dance? Such an understanding would consider the encounter between our minds (our existing ideas of disability) with the mind (ideas) of the dancer. These ideas are ideas of our bodily encounter with the dancer's body. These ideas challenge our emotional reactions of pity and focus our attention on the fact that the body of the dancer challenges the usual image of his body as always passive. In other words, the encounter challenges conventional ideas about disability, while moving beyond an idea of an individualised struggle against nature. It demonstrates our abilities to increase our powers of acting and understanding *as parts of nature*. We are able to do so by understanding our encounters with others rather than through the use of reason to remove us from the world, as envisaged by Kant.

Turinsky's dance specifically acts as a demonstration of a disabled person's successful struggle and so the subject matter itself appears as a comment and a challenge regarding our perception of the dancer's disability. As discussed in the Introduction, there are increasing numbers of disabled dancers for whom this is not the focus of the dance and – like any art form – the meaning of dance is open-ended. It may well be that it is only at this point in time that we can be shocked by disabled dance, a sad reflection of an oppressive history, and yet also a reminder of the ability of oppressed groups to challenge the way in which others understand their encounters with them. This challenge arises from aesthetic practices that emphasise that there is no exemplar of the body; that Spinoza's famous quotation: 'nobody knows what a body can do' (*Ethics:* III.P2S) also applies to the severely disabled. We cannot predict our ability to form into 'singular things' with both others and technology and, as part of nature, there is nothing artificial about such connections.

Conclusion

What is ultimately at stake in a work of art differs for Kant and Spinoza, or rather from a Kantian as opposed to a Spinozan perspective. For Kant, the experience of the sublime reminds us of our super-sensible vocation; of ideas of reason that do not appear in the world, such as God and freedom. For Spinoza, art is associated with the art of living; what is important is to develop an *ethos* of thriving that increases an individual's freedom. This can be contrasted with Kant's image of autonomy as the obeying the (self-imposed) moral law. There is no external God outside of nature for Spinoza. He simply defines God and nature as the same thing, thereby losing the idea that someone on high could be dictating rules of morality as natural laws. Instead, we discover the laws of nature – such as those of gravity, cruelly demonstrated at the start of Turinsky's dance – as part of our understanding of ourselves, others and the world. It opens us up to a greater understanding of the meaning of disability. At this point in history, disabled dance, for some, challenges deeply held ideas associated with disability derived from a history of discrimination and exclusion, which has operated to make the disabled body capable of inspiring shock. Art can help us to live well by communicating a greater understanding of ourselves. As Spinoza argues, the way to joy is not to withdraw from those encounters that may make us sad or uncomfortable, but to enrich our lives by being exposed to as many experiences as possible, thereby increasing our understanding of the world (James 2014).

Kant envisages us as unfree in the empirical world, as creatures of nature, and only free when considered in the intellectual world in which we employ reason. Similarly, Kant's analysis of the sublime in art shares this image of someone who is able to use reason in order to oppose nature. The experience of the sublime involves drawing a boundary around oneself; excluding the external threat imposed by nature or from the 'outside'. In contrast, for Spinoza, we have greater freedom the more we are able to understand our encounters with the world, of which we are a part. We enrich our lives by increasing the variety of our joyful experiences. In his performance of *Heteronomous Male*, Turinsky is – like all of us – heteronomous in Kantian terms – while also, from a Spinozist position, able to increase both his freedom and ours.

References

Balibar, É. (1997), *Spinoza: From Individuality to Transindividuality*, Delft: Eburon.

—— (1998), *Spinoza and Politics* (trans. P. Snowdon), London: Verso.

Battersby, C. (1998), *The Phenomenal Woman: Feminist Metaphysics and the Patterns of Identity*, London: Routledge.

—— (2007), *The Sublime, Terror and Human Difference*, London: Routledge.

Deleuze, G. (1988), *Spinoza, Practical Philosophy* (trans. R. Hurley), San Francisco: City Lights Books.

—— (1990), *Expressionism in Philosophy: Spinoza* (trans. M. Joughin), New York: Zone Books.

Gatens, M. (2015), 'Mark Sacks Lecture 2013: Spinoza on goodness and beauty and the prophet and the artist: Spinoza on goodness and beauty', *European Journal of Philosophy*, 23:1, pp. 1–16.

Held, V. (1987), 'Non-contractual society: A feminist view', *Canadian Journal of Philosophy*, 17 (Suppl), pp. 111–37.

James, S. (2014), 'Spinoza, the body, and the good life', in M. J. Kisner and A. Youpa (eds), *Essays on Spinoza's Ethical Theory*, Oxford: Oxford University Press, pp. 143–59.

Kant, I. (1987), *Critique of Judgment* (trans. W. S. Pluhar), Indianapolis: Hackett Publishing Co, Inc.

—— (1991), *Observations on the Feeling of the Beautiful and the Sublime* (trans. J. T. Goldthwait), Berkeley: University of California Press.

Morrison, J. C. (1989), 'Why Spinoza had no aesthetics', *The Journal of Aesthetics and Art Criticism*, 47:4, p. 359.

Nead, L. (1990), 'The female nude: Pornography, art, and sexuality', *Signs*, 15:2, pp. 323–35.

Nedelsky, J. (2011), *Law's Relations a Relational Theory of Self, Autonomy, and Law*, New York: Oxford University Press.

Osucha, E. (2009), 'The whiteness of privacy: Race, media, law', *Camera Obscura*, 24:70, pp. 66–107.

Shildrick, M. (1997), *Leaky Bodies and Boundaries: Feminism, Postmodernism and (Bio) ethics*, Oxon: Routledge.

Spinoza, B. de (1985), *The Collected Works of Spinoza, Volume I* (ed. E. M. Curley), Princeton: Princeton University Press.

Stoljar, N. and Mackenzi, C. (eds) (2000), *Relational Autonomy: Feminist Essays on Autonomy, Agency, and the Social Self*, Oxford: Oxford University Press.

Turinsky, M. (2012), *Heteronomous Male,* ARGE Kultur, Salzburg, premiere 5 April.

Warren, S. D. and Brandeis, L. D. (1890), 'The right to privacy', *Harvard Law Review,* 4:5, pp. 193–220.

Wheatley, T. (2015), 'Discussion: "Dance and normality" Integrart Symposium 2015', *Disability Arts Online,* 23 June, http://www.disabilityartsonline.org.uk/dance-and-normality-integrart-symposium-2015. Accessed 16 April 2016.

Notes

1 Integrart Symposium 2015 'Dance' and 'Normality', 2 June 2015, http://www.dance-tech.net/profiles/blogs/dance-and-normality-integrart-symposium-2015-geneva-switzerland; see also: https://vimeo.com/97516408.

2 Kant envisaged these viewers as only white men, as discussed in the next section.

3 Kant's view of reason and its intimate link with morality raises issues for anyone with intellectual disabilities that I will not deal with here.

4 For feminist analyses of traditional views of autonomy compared with relational autonomy see Nedelsky (2011) and Stoljar and Mackenzie (2000).

5 For analyses of Spinoza and aesthetics see Gatens (2015).

6 This is the Elwes and Shirley translation. Curley translates it as 'dominion within a dominion'.

7 *Ethics:* II.D7.

Chapter 9

Moving Towards a New Aesthetic: Dance and Disability

Shawn Harmon, Kate Marsh, Sarah Whatley and Karen Wood

Introduction

At base, an 'aesthetic' is a theory or set of principles – a conception or an expression – of beauty at a given time and place, and within a specific context,[1] and its definition will often comprise multiple elements, including, for example, line, surface, texture, space, sensation, sound, colour, movement and more. The notion of an 'aesthetic' is central to many art-forms, and dance is no exception. In this chapter, we first briefly articulate the dominant aesthetic in dance and we consider what it has meant for disabled dancers. We then explore the idea of a dance aesthetic with Dan Daw, an Australian-born, UK-based dance artist who has been an ally to the InVisible Difference project since its beginning, even performing at the project's Symposium at Siobhan Davies Studios.[2] Finally, we explore what a new, more inclusive, diverse and exciting aesthetic might comprise and what it could do for the profession generally and for disabled dancers more specifically.

The Dominant Dance Aesthetic

Obviously, dance has many objectives, including to entertain, to inform and to provoke (Preston-Dunlop 1997). But whatever its objective, at its core is an aesthetic grounded in the body, in expression, movement and interaction. Other elements that shape the dance aesthetic – and the emotional experience of dance – include form, pace, space, costume and props. While the philosophy of aesthetics in relation to dance has raised questions about dance ontology, identity, notationality and its performable nature (McFee 2011)[3] and has therefore explored meanings beyond the external (i.e. including the internal, and the embodied route to expressivity),[4] the dance aesthetic is often associated with the external viewing process and the quantification or evaluation of the body *towards an ideal*. This is perhaps the result of long and often deeply held negative social attitudes towards different or divergent bodies, which have been constructed as weaker, uglier, broken and therefore disabled dance has long been viewed as victim art and freak show (Garland Thomson 2009).[5] Here one must acknowledge that the aesthetic of a context – like dance – is often heavily influenced by the way it is appreciated, and the aesthetic imposed does not necessarily, though often does, coincide with that valued and advanced by the art-form itself.

Ultimately, then, western classical dance has historically been driven by the *ideal* body shape, and not by the creativity and expressivity that *different* body shapes offer. This begs the question:

What has this external perspective constructed as the ideal body shape?

While it has perhaps evolved, we contend that the so-called ideal body shape has consistently been that of the classical balletic body, and, of course, we are not alone in this contention. Such has been noted by Briginshaw (2001), and by McGrath who states:

> From the nineteenth century onwards, the emergence of Romantic ballet led to the prevailing aesthetic considerations which required that all dancers should share a physique based on the construct of the sylph. The sylph represented the perfectly formed, highly trained corporeal presence that, in its transcendence of everyday movement, was the representation of all that was considered superior in both the embodied and in the ideological sense. Slim, long limbed, rigidly trained to achieve virtuosity, aiming to rise above the pedestrian movement of everyday life and offering an ideal based on ethereality, this body was the epitome of artistry.
>
> (2012: 144)

And Thomas notes that this body has become the normalised dance body, informing many western contemporary dance forms:

> [...] the overwhelming majority of professional performers in western theatrical dance are young, predominately female and thin, with bodies that have to be able to master the every-increasing technical challenges that specific dance training regimes, choreographers and performance practices require of them and which are predicated on the idea of an abstract body without 'impairment' and/or 'disability'.
>
> (Thomas 2013: 3)

The thin, vertical, supple balletic body has been associated with the 'cult of slenderness', and, perhaps ironically, has been found to have lower fitness levels and a greater proclivity to injury in comparison to athletes with similar workloads (Twitchett et al. 2011). Despite the fact that the socialisation of ballet dancers has been linked to body image issues, eating disorders, disempowerment and a disregard for wellness (Benn and Walters 2001; Heiland et al. 2008), balletic training and choreographic practice and ideals have proven very influential, and have frequently shaped (and curtailed) our view of beauty in the body and virtuosity in the body's movement, both in dance and society more generally. In this way, the balletic aesthetic has shaped the wider dance aesthetic. As Aalten offers:

Openness, verticality and stylization are the basic aesthetic principles of ballet. The beauty of ballet is created by the straight lines of the extended human body going outward and upward and by the artificiality of the movements.

(2004: 267)

So this aesthetic has affected an enduring and strongly normalizing influence, with the result that the general dance aesthetic has remained surprisingly narrow (and balletic).

Significance for Disabled Dance

The above narrowing of the dance aesthetic has had several negative consequences, two of which are particularly important for present purposes. First, as noted, it prioritises and so values above others a specific physique and style of movement, which means not only that innovations, but also the acceptance of variations in dance and movement are under-appreciated and have sometimes been actively stifled (Albright 1998). Thus, not only have disabled people struggled to attain meaningful citizenship generally (Barston 1993), they have also struggled mightily to secure opportunities for training and routes into professional dance (Aujla and Redding 2013). And when disabled dancers did, historically, break into the scene, they were often untrained, the works produced often lacked artistic rigour and there was little critical response (McGrath 2012). This has created powerful barriers to viewing the disabled body in performance as a body 'in its own right' equally valid and 'correct'. On this point, the following has been noted:

Whilst many contemporary dance pioneers have sought to move away from the exclusivity and homogeneity synonymous with ballet, there remains to a great extent a fixed and 'able-ist' understanding of what meets the contemporary dance aesthetic. Almost inadvertently, then, disabled dancers are excluded from the field of professional dance within its currently defined parameters.

(Charnley 2011: 25)

And this has persisted despite repeated calls for the construction of a more accessible dance culture through the provision not only of accessible techniques, work spaces, training facilities and stages, but also wider education around dance literacy and the reading of dance and the manipulation of bodies, spaces and time (Kuppers 2000).

This latter point ties into the second major consequence of the above narrowing; it limits the vocabulary by which dance is discussed and evaluated and so acknowledged and given value. Again, this means that form and movement that fall out-with the 'norm' struggle to find superlative, or even positive, descriptors. With a limited lexicon with which to talk about a body, it is not surprising that bodies which do not conform to the traditional dancer's body, or 'dancerly body' (Kuppers 2000), are constructed as strange or cautionary (i.e. things to be wondered at), or worse, as uncanny or grotesque (i.e. things to be repelled by).

By way of example, one might consider the (often questionable) contributions of dance critics to the development of the dance aesthetic. Criticism (as undertaken by the critic) is a:

> [...] gesture that carries the dance beyond its curtain time, extending it to readers near and far, present and future. Criticism transfigures dance into a much larger, discursive existence.
>
> (Daly 2002: xv)

Thus, the role of the dance critic and the natural or inevitable consequences of her observations is not only to advance the careers of choreographers and dancers,[6] to stimulate debate amongst and develop, audiences,[7] but to reaffirm (or, alternatively, to move) the dance aesthetic. Moreover, critics hold a privileged place in relation to audiences and the evolution of the dance aesthetic, but they have done little to encourage appreciation of the capabilities of the differently abled body; they have had little tolerance for divergence from the norm and very little by way of positive language to engage with disabled dance. David Toole, a man with no legs who dances on his hands, has been subject to excoriating criticism:

> There is a horrific, Satyricon quality to Candoco that heaves up in the chest – nausea at the moral rudderlessness of a world where we would pay money to watch a man whose body terminates at his ribcage, moving about the stage on his hands.
>
> (Scott 1999 in Smith 2005: 80)[8]

The responses of critic Arlene Croce, who characterised a range of dances as 'victim art' and as 'undiscussable' are in a similar vein.[9] Similarly, in a critique of Candoco's *I Hastened through My Death Scene to Catch Your Last Act* (de Frutos 2000), the reviewer based his judgement of beauty on and compared the dancers to, a classical aesthetic, characterising the disabled state as one of abject negativity (Tay 2000).[10] Even when critics have been more open-minded in their approach to disabled dance, they have exhibited a high level of capture by the balletic aesthetic despite the fact that the disabled dancer may not be striving to recreate that aesthetic. For disabled dancers who are working within a classical vocabulary, there is a tendency towards equating the disabled body with the illusionary properties of the classical aesthetic. For example, the balletic aesthetic is clear in Minns' review of *Conversations with Dystonia* (2014), choreographed and performed by wheelchair dancer Suzie Birchwood:

> There is a moment in *Conversations with Dystonia* – when Birchwood is supported on the equipment and slowly descends in a classical plié as she looks out with those lucid eyes – that is pure magic. The powerful metaphor of support is contrasted with the fragility of the body and force of mind; it is perhaps in itself a pure form of integration.
>
> (Minns 2014)

Regardless of whether they impose the balletic aesthetic on disabled dancers, critics tend to focus on the physiological differences (or divergence from the balletic norm). Caroline Bowditch, choreographer and performer, and Luke Pell, creator and facilitator, examined newspaper articles and online reviews of dance companies featuring disabled dancers from the early 1990s to 2011 (Bowditch and Pell 2012).[11] They note:

> Critics predominantly discussed the morphological differences between disabled dancers and their non-disabled peers (or indeed peers whose disabilities are less visible). With disabled dancers observed as specimens and alluded to as victims, medical model perceptions of disability were embedded throughout.
>
> (Bowditch and Pell 2012: 148)

In other words, there was an absence of focus on the dance; instead, attention was most often placed on the 'otherness' of the differently abled body by comparison with the able bodied. Cooper Albright, who studied reviews of David Toole, concluded:

> Toole's abilities as a dancer are remarkable and are often the subject of extended discussions within reviews and preview articles about Candoco. Adjectives such as 'amazing', 'incredible', 'stupefying', are liberally sprinkled throughout descriptions of his dancing. This language of astonishment reflects both an evangelistic awakening (yes, a disabled man can swagger!) and traces of freak show voyeurism (see the amazing feats of the man with no legs!).
>
> (Albright 1997: 79)

This strain is further exemplified in de Marigny's (1993) observations of another Toole performance:

> David Toole is a man with no legs who possesses more grace and presence than most dancers can even dream of [...]. Toole commands the stage with an athleticism that borders on the miraculous.
>
> (De Marigny 1993 cited in Albright 1998)

Despite this exclusionary context, there are examples of interesting work whereby dance artists are challenging the dominant aesthetic, perhaps by thinking about how they present the body, and how that is different from traditionally valued presentations. For example, a collaboration between Luke Pell and creator and producer Jo Verrent, resulted in an installation called *Take Me to Bed* (2014).[12] By adopting an overhead, ground-viewing approach, it challenges traditional, front-viewing perspectives that uphold the vertical[13] – a view that is dominant in ballet and commented on by Aalten (2004), as previously mentioned. Pell and Verrent invited, indeed challenged, the viewer to explore intimate relationships with different bodies, and thereby exemplified the ways in which a new aesthetic, which firmly locates differently abled bodies within cultural and artistic landscapes, could be realised.

A View on Aesthetics from the Coalface

And of course, Pell and Verrent are not alone in their challenge. Kate Marsh, a disabled dancer herself, spoke with Dan Daw, a UK-based dance artist with cerebral palsy, in an effort to explore his perspective on the dance aesthetic. He has performed with Restless Dance Company (Australia 2002–05), No Strings Attached – Theatre of Disability (Australia; 2004), Frontline Dance (UK 2005) and Candoco (UK 2010–14), for whom he also served as an assistant producer, and has been a guest dancer at Skånes Dansteater (Sweden 2013–14). In 2014, Daw established Dan Daw Creative Projects, and his most recent work is *BEAST*, a solo made in collaboration with Martin Forsberg and Jenny Norberg.[14] This conversation informs and foregrounds our argument that a new dance aesthetic is needed – one that takes into account a greater diversity of bodies, experiences and habitats (or habitus). Numerous stakeholders must come together to construct the new aesthetic and the voices of professional dancers like Daw are very important, not least because they have traditionally been silenced within contemporary dance discourses. This conversation was undertaken in 2015 as Daw promoted his solo work, *BEAST*, which explores the concept of aesthetic from a personal perspective:[15]

KM: How do you see a 'ballet aesthetic' in relation to a 'contemporary dance' aesthetic? Are they on a continuum? And where would you put a 'disabled aesthetic' on that scale?

DD: I actually see them as different scales entirely, because they are completely different aesthetics and completely different ways of working. They are related in that they are both forms of dance, but it stops there. I reject the traditional aesthetic because I really think that dance has improperly attempted to build itself on attaining perfection. I think that there is an aesthetic in contemporary dance that has shifted slightly, but not significantly, and the dominant position of the prevailing aesthetic has marginalised the disabled body in dance. The disabled body is not a part of the main aesthetic; it is still something separate. And that is a weakness of the prevailing aesthetic. How is a form meant to progress if it is still exploring the same body type?

I think that the 'acceptability' of an aesthetic is a possibility determined by audience. As an audience member, I make assumptions about what I like, or might like. I do not think audiences want to see perfection; that's the assumption made by the industry, and it is made without any empirical evidence. It is supported by the fact that it has made money in the past. Major dance venues, particularly in London, know that when they programme high profile mainstream artists at Christmas, they will sell every seat for six weeks. This is obviously a strength, but it is also a weakness because it means that the 'normative' aesthetic is not being challenged. Why aren't theatres and programmers working throughout the year to create a community project that is performed over this period? Because it doesn't bring in the same money. But money is not equivalent to value.

KM: How do you see that (traditional) aesthetic changing?

DD: I'd like to think it is changing, but I don't think it is. I think we've developed a culture where aesthetics in dance are sub-categorised: traditional; balletic; disabled; elder dancers; etc. Sub-categories are created because the subject offers an aesthetic that mainstream dance cannot place, so instead of accepting them as an expansion of the dance aesthetic, sub-categories are created, and they are kept out of the mainstream. At the moment, we are still holding onto the 'aesthetic of perfection', which derives from the ballet aesthetic. But, of course, this perfection doesn't exist. And this is really detrimental to the progress of dance more generally because we are, in essence, holding onto a non-aesthetic.

KM: Where do you see this idea of perfection manifested in dance?

DD: In all areas. For example, contemporary dance companies still have a cut (in audition) after the ballet class, so they're sending dancers away after the ballet barre. Because they're not 'good' ballet dancers. My response is, 'They knew that. That's why they're not auditioning for a ballet company. They're contemporary dancers, not ballet dancers. So why are they excluding people based on this aesthetic that they don't even use?'

KM: Are we premature in talking about a new aesthetic in dance?

DD: We may like to think there is a new aesthetic, but the aesthetic hasn't really changed all that much. If you look at Dance Umbrella or Trisha Brown, one could question whether they are indicators that notions of aesthetic in dance haven't really progressed. Are we bringing them back because they're history or because they're still our dominant aesthetic? One could argue that *Set and Reset/Reset* was in Candoco's repertory for three years because it is an aesthetic that people can place; an aesthetic audiences could recognise and for which they had a coded reference.

KM: Where do you see your own body in relation to the current aesthetic?

DD: Because I am of this world, I am already a part of a universal aesthetic. I do not place myself as a sub-category because that limits the prospect for change. Does what I do always have to be 'disabled dance'? As an artist, I'm not giving into those sub-genres. Disabled dance is not a sub-genre. The disabled body is seen as a different aesthetic, but it shouldn't be. As a dancer with a disability, I do feel the need to challenge the dominant aesthetic. We can start by examining choices relating to programming. It's not the preferences of audiences so much that marginalises; no matter what's on at the theatre, if you love theatre, you go. Programmers have a responsibility to challenge the existing aesthetic; they dictate what is seen, and therefore they, to a large extent, dictate the aesthetic. On the professional stage, there is a pressure to dictate the aesthetic.

KM: Does the desire to challenge a normative aesthetic drive your practice?

DD: It informs my practice, but doesn't drive it. (Laughs.) I really think it's about my aesthetic, informed by my disability, but not driven by my disability. It is more about a somatic inquiry rather than an exploration of impairment.

KM: How does the language used to talk about dance reflect the current population of dance artists?

DD: I'm not so worried about language, because language is based on perception, so we see something and we then create a language from our perception. In order to address language, we first need to address perception. So if we know how we want to be talked about, how do we shift perception to allow for this?

KM: How important is the theme of identity for you in your work?

DD: Identity is extremely important. When we developed *BEAST*, it was all about my relationship to the photography of Joel-Peter Witkin and Diane Arbus, and my relationship to my disability, to sex, to perception, to expectation, so it was very much rooted in identity. We needed the foundation of identity (mine) as it was a solo. We needed to know this in order to fully explore. I am exploring where my own sense of identity meets the audience's senses of identities. Where do they match and mismatch?

I think the choreography – aside from the fact that I'm nearly naked and a disabled dancer – really does start to challenge the dominant aesthetic, and in challenging that aesthetic I am giving the audience a huge role to play. Everything they've ever known about an assumed aesthetic or the reference points they thought they would use when they come and see the work just disappear. It's almost like the audience are being stripped of their securities. So the work is forcing a readjustment of our pre-conceived ideas.

KM: What have been the responses to your body and aesthetic in relation to *BEAST*?

DD: The main feedback has been, 'This sits under visual arts. Maybe you should apply there for funding'. Or people have commented that it feels like live art. I feel like saying, 'Who are you to tell me where it sits!' I've just presented something that makes you, the audience, feel uncomfortable, and you can't place it, so it scares you. You wouldn't even begin to know how to sell this aesthetic, so you say it's not dance. So the responses are less about my body and more about the way that an audience categorises the work.

I would like audiences to see it as dance, and to comment on it as dance, to say, 'I don't understand it, but it was dance', rather than, 'I don't understand it because its performance art'. To help audiences towards a richer understanding of dance, audiences need to see more. They need to be given the opportunity to see diversity. This connects back to the promoters and producers: they need to start bringing diversity into their programming so that this filters to audiences.

KM: If you had to describe your ideal dance aesthetic what would it look like?

DD: I would like the dance aesthetic to be such that it does not subscribe to a sole aesthetic that we all aspire to, but one which acknowledges the aesthetic of each individual. There is something really exciting in that diversity. Dance has the space for a multitude of aesthetics, wherein we are all valid and can all inform the picture of 21st century dance.

What is apparent from this conversation is that Daw is seeking liberation within a landscape of 'normative' aesthetics and that his creativity speaks to his own sense of integrity, the very existence of which is a challenge to assumptions and perhaps even values. The conversation also reiterates a point repeated throughout this book that there is an absence of critical vocabulary to discuss dance in terms other than the traditional aesthetic and this lacunae impedes our ability to perceive work by disabled artists as part of our 'mainstream' experience of dance. And it is non-conforming bodies like Daw's that are most valuable in challenging the prevailing narrow aesthetic; they invite audiences to re-evaluate preconceptions around the dancing body (and bodies more generally).

Towards a New Aesthetic?

Despite Daw's rejection of sub-genres of aesthetics, the idea of a 'disability aesthetic' has arisen as a challenge to the traditional, balletic, aesthetic. According to Siebers, it:

[...] prizes physical and mental difference as a significant value in itself. It does not embrace an aesthetic taste that defines harmony, bodily integrity, and health as standards of beauty. Nor does it support the aversion to disability required by traditional conceptions of human or social perfection. [...] The idea of disability aesthetics affirms that disability operates both as a critical framework for questioning aesthetic presuppositions in the history of art and as a value in its own right important to future conceptions of what art is.

(Siebers 2010: 20)

Very generally, it is a sensual aesthetic that refocuses one's attention onto movement, its quality and diversity, as opposed to physical compliance with an idealised norm and the ability to reproduce certain forms. It is conscious of gaze (which is not accepted as benign) and seeks to widen the scope of meaning-making through the physical. And, perhaps like Disability Arts more generally, it has something of a political element (Abrams 2014). Not only does it object to aesthetic standards and tastes that exclude disability from dance (and art) (Siebers 2010), it resists the socially powerful but blinkered views of sociology and medicine, which define, problematize and manage the 'stranger' or 'other' and which place the disabled person squarely in that category (Hughes 1999, 2000).

Our aim is not to further develop the disability aesthetic (or the disability critique of the dominant aesthetic), but to articulate and advocate a broader aesthetic for dance, one that is more progressive and more diverse, and so more readily accepting of the differently formed and differently abled. We suggest that this ought to be a 'principles-based aesthetic'; this principles-based aesthetic should rest on and be informed by four foundational principles or concepts, namely inclusion, interpretation, rigour and integrity.

The principle of inclusion signals that dance is a mosaic and can hold and value multiple conceptions of beauty and virtuosity. It encourages practitioners to embrace difference and to construct the (professional) dance space as one where diversity can be accepted and where uniqueness of body and ability are welcomed, as opposed to merely tolerated (Purcell 2015).[16] The virtue of this principle is readily demonstrated when one takes notice of certain undeniable truths. First, the variety of (human) bodies that exist in society are manifold; while one might be able to identify a 'traditional' body, non-traditional bodies proliferate, and they embody many forms, capacities and ideals. Indeed, physiological divergence from the 'norm' has been described as 'ubiquitous' and 'mundane' (Sandahl and Auslander 2005:2). Second, almost all bodies, traditional or non-traditional, can hold or characterise beauty; beauty of form, line, surface, movement or interaction, all of which are important to dance to varying degrees. A wheelchair dancer, for example, might move her chair in challenging, evocative and beautiful ways, demonstrating a unique virtuosity that is worthy of value and praise. Third, and importantly, no bodies are static; we are all unique and all in transition, gaining and losing functions, capabilities, movement, etc., as we move through time and nature.

In short, all human bodies occupy a complex, fascinating and transitory reality not often acknowledged and much less within the traditional dance aesthetic. Even bodies chosen and trained to be interchangeable (i.e. such as those within a corps de ballet), are a composite of diverse bodies, each with their own capacities and experiences of living in the world, but again, this is not readily acknowledged. An aesthetic grounded in inclusion would better reflect this reality and would additionally facilitate the shift that has been called for in the 'discourses of legitimacy' (that still marginalise the bodies and artistic contributions of disabled dancers) (Irving and Giles 2011: 371).

The principle of interpretation again emphasises the personal and the unique over the ritualistic reproduction of forms. It is the interpretation of emotion and movement that matters. Artists might be said to be primarily concerned with her or his own 'standard of correctness' (Stern 2004: 110) when making and performing a work and this will necessarily derive from the artist's own direct and singular experience of being in the world, which will thereby privilege variation rather than sameness, opening up new and innovative responses. A central role for the principle of interpretation would encourage performances that exemplify the 'interactive gaze' and the formation of 'empathetic attunement'. The interactive gaze is one whereby the audience is engaged; it is empowering, not asymmetrical (Garland Thomson 2009). Linked to kinaesthetic experience (Sheets-Johnstone 2010), empathetic attunement is the psychological and physiological resonance (or imprinting) that can be achieved during close observance of movement (McGrath 2012). The result will be to broaden the dance pallet, making space for critical appropriations like Daw's *BEAST*, or the autobiographical work of Duffy (in *Venus de Milo* [1996]) and Sandahl (in *The Reciprocal Gaze* [1999]).[17]

The principle of rigour relates to the depth of investigation and creative enquiry, which develops through immersion in a practice and is evident in how dance works take shape but which resists hierarchies of knowledge and techniques in dance. Rigour is what drives the artist and engages the audience. Rigour is ensured through the mechanism of critical judgment applied in the creative process (Tomas 1970). Daw employed rigour in creating *BEAST* as he offered open studios for audiences to see the work in development and contribute to the project's progression.[18] This application of rigour, where audiences critically engage with the work, affords rigour to the creative process and empowers the artist to produce work of artistic quality. Rigour, then, is a key element in engaging with ideas and interrogating one's own biases, furthering our corporeal knowledge. If we remember that rigour is not limited to particular bodies or practices, we will rethink the relationship between ability and disability, echoing Jonathan Burrows' observation that 'artists with so-called disability have shown us exactly how limited our idea of ability is' (Burrows 2015).

The principle of integrity is closely associated with dignity, well-being, truthfulness and unity of the person. It signals, through its concern with the relationship to self, that completeness can be achieved in the absence of conformity to the social or medical norm (i.e. that physiological 'difference' does not necessarily equate to 'compromised' and that truth, beauty and unity can be achieved regardless of form or capability). So whatever the configuration of the dancer's body and whether or not the dancer performs with a prosthetic or some other technical aid, the dancer performs her own individual identity and exemplifies her own unique and valuable physical integrity, exercising, as she does, her agency. If we accept this understanding of physical integrity, we then see the disabled body as an opportunity to explore new forms without the need to orient the dance on the individual's perceived deficits or limitations: an orientation that has been resisted for a long time (Blandy 1991). It parallels the affirmative model of disability insofar as it challenges presumptions of personal tragedy and loss and affirms the disabled dancer as a valid individual, determining her own lifestyles, culture and identity.[19]

If we construct our training, our observation and our critique of dance on these four principles, or rather on an aesthetic that exemplifies and celebrates these four principles, then we will have a dance aesthetic within which disabled dance can better flourish and take its place within our cultural heritage. It has been claimed that:

When a [...] dancer takes the stage, he or she stakes a claim to a radical space, an unruly location where disparate assumptions about representation, subjectivity, and visual pleasure collide.

(Albright 2001: 58)

Our principles-based aesthetic, we contend, could go far to preserving the unruliness and radicalness of the stage. This is important because it is this unruliness that makes the stage so valuable and powerful:

The microcosm of the performance space, this 'unruly location', can be used to bring about the disruption of exclusionary societal perceptions of disability, reframing the notion of difference by providing an experience, through the medium of dance, that is inclusive of different corporealities. This experience can be transformative rather than transgressive.

(McGrath 2012: 143)

Conclusion

The dance stage is a privileged, or rather a privileging and potentially empowering space, where the dancer is encouraged not only to entertain, but also to challenge and to awe. Or it should be. However, the gatekeepers of the performance space have erected barriers to that space becoming genuinely and widely unruly. The balletic form remains central in the construction of what passes as the ideal, or even the acceptable, dancing body. The visibility of dancers with disabilities remains limited, in part as a result of an aesthetic of linearity, weightlessness and erectness and a normative push towards 'sameness', as measured against the balletic body. Despite evolving discourses around alternative aesthetics, including a disability aesthetic, the dance sector tends towards labelling the differently abled body as a separate genre, marginalised and sitting apart from the 'mainstream'. Thinking about a 'new' aesthetic informed in part by disabled dancers allows us to finally see the body in dance for what it is: a unique and almost infinitely shaped and capable form which exhibits physical integrity despite its reluctance to comply with the 'norm' and despite its march towards ultimate dissolution. Not a heroic body, nor a broken body. Just a body. Dancing.

Acknowledgement

We would like to thank Dan Daw for participating in this research.

References

Aalten, A. (2004), 'The moment when it all comes together', *European Journal of Women's Studies*, 11, pp. 263–276.
Abrams, T. (2014), 'Boon or bust? Heidegger, disability aesthetics and the thalidomide memorial', *Disability & Society*, 29, pp. 751–62.
Albright, A. C. (1997), *Choreographing Difference: The Body and Identity in Contemporary Dance*, Hanover: Wesleyan University Press.

——— (1998), 'Strategic Abilities: Negotiating the Disabled Body in Dance', *Disability, Art and Culture*, 37:3, pp. 475–501.

——— (2001), 'Strategic abilities: Negotiating the disabled body in dance', in A. Dils and A. C. Albright (eds), *Moving History/Dancing Cultures*, Connecticut: Wesleyan University Press, pp. 56–66.

Aujla, I. and Redding, E. (2013), 'Barriers to dance training for young people with disabilities', *British Journal of Special Education*, 40, pp. 80–85.

Barston, L. (1993), 'The struggle for citizenship: The case of disabled people', *Disability, Handicap & Society*, 8, pp. 235–48.

Benn, T. and Walters, D. (2001), 'Between Scylla and Charybdis. Nutritional education versus body culture and the ballet aesthetic: The effects on the lives of female dancers', *Research in Dance Education*, 2, pp. 139–54.

Birchwood, S. (2014), *Conversations with Dystonia*, The Place, London, premiere 13 February.

Blandy, D. (1991), 'Conceptions of disability: Toward a sociopolitical orientation to disability for art education', *Studies in Art Education*, 32, pp. 131–44.

Bowditch, C. and Pell, L. (2012), 'Below the waterline', in L. Keidan and C. J. Mitchell (eds), *Access All Areas: Live Art and Disability*, London: Live Art Development Agency, pp. 148–51.

Briginshaw, V. A. (2001), *Dance, Space and Subjectivity*, Basingstoke: Palgrave.

Brown, T. and Yager, A. (2016), *Set and Reset/Reset*, Auditorium Fausto Melotti, Rovereto, premiere 9 September.

Burrows, J. (2015), 'Keynote address', *Postdance Conference*, Stockholm, Sweden, 14 October, http://www.jonathanburrows.info/#/text/?id=183&t=content. Accessed 15 January 2016.

Charnley, E. (2011), 'Towards a new vision of dance', *Animated*, winter, pp. 25–27.

Daly, A. (2002), *Critical Gestures: Writings on Dance and Culture*, Hanover: Wesleyan University Press.

Daw, D. (2015), *Beast*, The Borough Hall, London, premiere 6 November.

Duffy, M. (1996), *D. Vital Signs: Crip Culture Talks Back* (eds S. Snyder and D. Mitchell), Marquettwe, MI: Brace Yourselves Productions.

de Frutos, J. (2000), *I Hastened through My Death Scene to Catch Your Last Act*, Candoco.

Garland Thomson, R. (2009), *Staring: How We Look*, New York: Oxford University Press.

Heiland, T., Murray, D. S. and Edley, P. P. (2008), 'Body image of dancers in Los Angeles: The cult of slenderness and media influence among dance students', *Research in Dance Education*, 9, pp. 257–75.

Hughes, B. (1999), 'The constitution of impairment: Modernity and the aesthetic of oppression', *Disability & Society*, 14, pp. 155–72.

——— (2000), 'Medicine and the aesthetic invalidation of disabled people', *Disability & Society*, 15, pp. 555–68.

Irving, H. and Giles, A. (2011), 'A dance revolution? Responding to dominant discourses in contemporary integrated dance', *Loisir (Leisure)*, 35, pp. 371–89.

Kuppers, P. (2000), 'Accessible education: Aesthetics, bodies and disability', *Research in Dance Education*, 1:2, pp. 119–31.

de Marigny, C. (1993), 'A little world of its own', *Ballet International*, 16, p. 45.

McFee, G. (2011), *The Philosophical Aesthetics of Dance: Identity, Performance and Understanding*, Binsted, Hampshire: Dance Books.

McGrath, E. (2012), 'Dancing with disability: An intersubjective approach', in D. Goodley, B. Hughes and L. David (eds), *Disability and Social Theory: New Developments and Directions*, New York: Springer Publishing, 143–158.

Minns, N. (2014), 'Review by Nick Minns: The integrated dance summit', http://www.pdsw.org.uk/news/news-and-opportunities/review-by-nick-minns-the-integrated-dance-summit/. Accessed 14 December 2014.

Pell, L. and Verrent, J. (2014), *Take Me to Bed*, University of Bedford, Bedford, premiere 25 April.

Pickard, A. (2013), 'Ballet body belief: Perceptions of an ideal ballet body from young ballet dancers', *Research in Dance Education*, 14, pp. 3–19.

Preston-Dunlop, V. (1997), *Dance Words*, Abingdon: Routledge.

Purcell Cone, T. (2015), 'Teaching dance for access, inclusion and equity', *Journal of Dance Education*, 15, pp. 85–86.

Sandahl, C. (1999), *Reciprocal Gaze*.

Sandahl, C. and Auslander, P. (eds) (2005), *Bodies in Commotion: Disability and Performance*, Ann Arbor: University of Michigan Press.

Sheets-Johnstone, M. (2010), 'Kinesthetic experience: Understanding movement inside and out', *Body Movement & Dance in Psychotherapy*, 5, pp. 111–27.

Siebers, T. (2006), 'Disability aesthetics', *Journal for Cultural and Religious Theory*, 7:2, pp. 71–72.

——— (2010), *Disability Aesthetics*, Michigan: University of Michigan Press.

Smith, O. (2005), 'Shifting Apollo's frame – Challenging the body aesthetic in theater dance', in C. Sandahl and P. Auslander (eds) (2005), *Bodies in Commotion: Disability and Performance*, Ann Arbor: University of Michigan Press, 73–85.

Stern, L. (2004), 'Interpretation in aesthetics', in P. Kivy (ed.), *The Blackwell Guide to Aesthetics*, Oxford: Blackwell Publishing, 109–125.

Thomas, H. (2013), *The Body and Everyday Life*, Abingdon: Routledge, pp. 3–4.

Tomas, V. (1970) 'Creativity in art', in M. Weitz (ed.), *Problems in Aesthetics: An Introductory Book of Readings*, London: Macmillan. Rpt. from V. Tomas (1958), 'Creativity in art', *The Philosophical Review*, 67, pp. 1–15.

Twitchett, E., Angioi, M., Koutedakis, Y. and Wyon, M. (2011), 'Do increases in selected fitness parameters affect the aesthetic aspects of classical ballet performance?', *Medical Problems of Performing Artists*, 26, pp. 35–38.

Notes

1   See Dictionary.com at http://www.dictionary.com/browse/aesthetic.

2   The Symposium took place on 26 November 2014 at Siobhan Davies studios, London. See here for videos of the day: https://www.youtube.com/channel/UCLJG38WRvwO9WNgAaYU50Ig.

3   See Bunker, J., Pakes, A. and Rowell, B. (eds) (2013), *Thinking Through Dance: The Philosophy of Dance Performance and Practices*, Binsted: Dance Books.

4   This is particularly so in contemporary dance. For more, see Carr, J. (2013), 'Embodiment and dance: puzzles of consciousness and agency', in J. Bunker, A. Pakes and B. Rowell (eds)

Thinking Through Dance: The Philosophy of Dance Performance and Practices, Binsted: Dance Books.

5 For more, see Sandahl, C. and Auslander, P. (eds) (2005), *Bodies in Commotion: Disability and Performance*, Ann Arbor: University of Michigan Press.

6 For example, John Martin, considered a great dance critic, greatly influenced the career of Martha Graham through his writings.

7 With respect to the former, it has been said that, Phil Chan: 'A good review should promote discussion and persuade the reader to engage in the art, good or bad. A strong criticism should cause the reader to think for themselves': Chan, P. (2013), 'The role of the contemporary critic', *Huffpost Arts and Culture*, http://www.huffingtonpost.com/phil-chan/the-role-of-the-contempor_b_2610965.html. Accessed 27 April 2015. With respect to the latter, some critics explicitly acknowledge that the one of the purposes of their work is to develop an audience: 'Once I became intrigued by the modern dance I was all for it [...]. I thought it was a great art manifestation, and I felt that it was my business [...] to build an audience for this art': Martin, J. (1967), *Reflections of John Joseph Martin*, Berkeley: Oral History Collection, University of California, p. 86.

8 Candoco's work has also been called 'victim art': Macaulay, A. (1996), 'Victim art put through its paces', *Financial Times*, 24 June.

9 As discussed in Jays, D. (2015), 'No pity party: Moving beyond victim art', *The Guardian*, 8 January, who, in interviewing Stine Nilson, of Candoco Dance Company, reported that critiques will still list the dancers' disabilities.

10 See Tay, M. (2000), 'In the company of able(d) dancers', *The Flying Inkpot Theatre Reviews*, http://www.inkpot.com/theatre/00reviews/00revcanddanccomp.html, and the discussion in Briggs H., Kolb, A. and Miyahara, M. (2012) 'Able as anything', *Brolga 37*, http://ausdance.org.au/articles/details/able-as-anything-integrated-dance-in-new-zealand. Both Accessed 27 April 2015.

11 In April 2015, we updated that work, looking at reviews from 2012 to 2015 in *The Times*, *The Guardian*, *The Telegraph*, *The Daily Telegraph*, *The Sunday Telegraph*, *The Daily Mail*, *The Scotsman*, *The Herald Glasgow*, *The Gloucestershire Echo*, *The Penarth Times*, and Google (for blog reviews), identifying 14 examples.

12 It was exhibited on 6–9 November 2014 at Dance Limerick, Limerick, Ireland.

13 See here for Luke's blog about the piece: http://www.lukepell.org/archives/1576.

14 Martin Forsberg is a dance-maker and director of *Forsworks* based in Copenhagen, and Jenny Nordberg is a set designer and regular collaborator with Forsberg.

15 *BEAST* is described by Daw as an intimate, hyper-theatrical, yet low-budget attempt to conjoin the unseen with the familiar. Drawing on the work of photographer Joel-Peter Witkin, it looks at notions of 'normality' and 'abnormality' through the lens of perception and expectation. It is thus an exploration of the gap that exists between intention and effect. See Daw, D. (2014) 'Dan Daw – Open studio', http://www.metalculture.com/event/dan-daw-open-studio-4/.

16 For strategies in developing inclusive programmes, see Morris, M. (2015), 'Developing and sustaining an inclusive dance program', *Journal of Dance Education*, 15, pp. 122–29.

17 For more on which, see Eisenhauer, J. (2007), 'Just looking and staring back: Challenging ableism through disability performance art', *Studies in Art Education*, 49, pp. 7–22.
18 See note 15.
19 For more on which, see Swain, J. and French, S. (2000), 'Towards an affirmation model of disability', *Disability & Society*, 15, pp. 569–82.

Chapter 10

What We Can Do with Choreography, and What Choreography Can Do with Us

A conversation between Catherine Long and Nicola Conibere

S uperflo: I've been thinking about this chapter and how we might introduce ourselves.

Pleonasta: Okay.

Superflo: I always have the question, when I read discursive texts about disability, of whether the author is disabled. I'm curious about whether they have direct experience of the issues they are discussing.

Pleonasta: Right. And in this case, one of us is considered disabled, and the other non-disabled.

Superflo: Yes. So I'd like to propose that we shouldn't say who has which status. I'm also thinking about the questions of visibility, invisibility and disability that are discussed throughout this collection. As it stands, we are invisible to the readers who are reading these words. I wonder if we should retain some degree of that invisibility to enhance our discussion. Let us not include our names in this transcript.

Pleonasta: I see. By not naming ourselves, we choose not to state which social labels our bodies are usually given. This might unsettle the qualities of the claims our individual words will make on the subject of disability.

Actually, I think it's a gesture that hits the crux of issues around visibility and disability: some social situations require that impairment be recognised, whilst others are impeded by the scrutiny of visible disability. In reading these words, readers might see their author as disabled or non-disabled.

Superflo: One of us has direct experience of what you describe. Perhaps the most useful way of retaining our anonymity whilst sharing that experience is to present it as a story in the third person. Here it is: My friend Radicalia is often stared at in public spaces because her body is visibly, structurally quite different from most bodies. She has three limbs and a distinctive way of walking. Additionally, she experiences chronic pain, which is not visible. Sometimes, people ask her about what they perceive to be her missing limb, addressing what they consider her body to be lacking. For her, having one 'less' limb than most people is not particularly problematic compared to her pain. She finds it complicated to navigate this experience of feeling on display and unseen at the same time, and feels she has little influence over these situations. She doesn't want to hide her body or deny who she is, but she doesn't want to be defined by other people's projections of loss and diminished capacity.

Pleonasta: It's important to state that we will be discussing disabilities that are visible in bodies' shapes, structures and movements, as opposed to intellectual disability. And your story demonstrates how the question of visibility in relation to those types of disability can be complex in daily life. This underpins our conversation that is going to focus on bodies in choreographed performances – events that are somewhat bracketed from the everyday. The complicated subject of visibility and disability is made even more complex by the appearances of bodies on stages, in theatres, which are places dedicated to messing around with how people can appear to each other.

You and I have each choreographed and performed in dance works on different types of stages, and will sometimes refer to these experiences. It will be challenging to do so without revealing ourselves – I like your strategy of telling personal experience as the story of another, as it entails a degree of theatricality and fictionalising that is inherent to performance-making. Shall we use this strategy of storytelling throughout?

Superflo: Okay. We will only discuss works that we have seen, made or performed in, and we won't always reveal our specific relationship with a given work, but will, to a degree, fictionalise those affiliations. In fact, this entire conversation is a form of staging. Whilst we did speak with each other about these subjects, the words on these pages have been edited and re-arranged – we have never had this specific conversation. In turn, we invite readers to join us in this unsettling of types of authorial and social claim. Ultimately, by not stating which of us is labelled as disabled, and which is not, we might make more visible some of the implications terms of disability carry, whilst embracing the potentials of unsettling the categorisation of bodies.

Fluidity, Standardised Bodies and Integrative Dance

Pleonasta: This fictionalising and unsettling makes me think of the mutability that comes from refusing to adhere to aspects of social categorisation, whether that refusal is voluntary or not. Alison Kafer writes about the relationship between Disability Studies and queer theory, particularly their shared interest in 'fluidity, ever-changing horizons, and paradoxical treatments of identity' (2013: 16). I think this is interesting ground on which to talk about integrative dance.

Superflo: Kafer also talks about 'crip time' (2013) in relation to ideas of queer temporalities, drawing on Judith Halberstam's writing about queerness as partly defined by doing too much of the wrong thing at the wrong time. In relation to disability specifically, there's a standard expectation about time, about how long bodies take to do things, and what concepts propel our understanding of the future. Often people with physical impairments don't fit those models of time.

Figure 1: Superflo and Pleonasta theatrically retain their anonymity whilst discussing dance and disability. Photo by Karen Robinson.

Pleonasta: Yes, Kafer talks about a time frame for the future 'that casts disabled people [as] out of time' because they 'are not part of the dominant narratives of progress' (2013: 28). When your friend Radicalia walks down the street and people ask her if she was born that way, this is indicative of what Kafer calls 'curative time' (2013: 27) which only figures disabled people as bodies that need to be fixed in order to enter a temporal narrative of progress.

Superflo: Disabled people have to navigate these characteristics of temporal structure in addition to physical environments that privilege non-disabled bodies and social categorisations that classify them as 'other'. Each of these forms of structural organisation depends on a normative standard that denies the experience of many disabled people. In turn, it also refuses the potential insights, and socially valuable re-thinking, that disabled experience can bring to these projects of social arrangement.

I want to follow through this idea of a standard, and consider it in relation to practices of integrative dance. Globally there are numerous companies committed to integrative dance. In the United Kingdom this includes Candoco Dance Company, which describes itself as 'the company of disabled and non-disabled dancers' (Candoco 2015), Amici Dance Theatre Company and Stopgap. International companies include Roda Viva Cia de Dança in Brazil and AXIS Dance Company in the United States. We are both based in the United Kingdom, and will largely speak from our experience of UK-based practices.

Speaking generally, I think a lot of integrative dance still works with a standard of normative bodies trained in techniques from dance's historical canon; that the works they present often engage forms of movement and performance qualities that draw on skills conventional to a trained dancer with a non-disabled body. As Kate Marsh has discussed recently, when 'dancers with disabilities are required to "fit into" existing frameworks of [...] contemporary dance [...] [t]hey are instantly disadvantaged', precisely because those frameworks are based on normative bodies (Marsh 2015). So, you might have a wheelchair user engaging their torso, arms and head with a kind of grace and elegance that is stylistically associated with contemporary dance, but they will only fulfil part of what the standard body that usually enacts those physical languages would present. Works that employ these existing frameworks therefore retain an aspiration towards a standard that holds normative bodies as ideal. The wheelchair user performs this recognisable style of dancing instead of, say, exploring what types of movement might be generated by her body and its capacities. Whilst numerous integrative dance projects might show that disabled dancers can share qualities of expression with normative bodied dancers, they rarely critique choreographic frameworks that engage standardised training.

Pleonasta: It seems you're discussing choreographic choices rather than something fundamental to integrative dance. When you speak about a formal style of grace and elegance, to which I add athleticism, this sounds like a reference to mainstream notions of dance and trained dancers. On the other hand, there exists contemporary choreography driven by experiments with the reaches of the choreographic, or the possibilities of bodies, that will not necessarily contain dancers performing elegance and athleticism. Instead, it might include approaches of inhabiting what movements a given performing body can discover. When you refer to a standard, are you suggesting that most integrative projects work with a more mainstream notion of dance?

Superflo: Not every integrative project works with a standard of recognisable dance techniques, but several do. Perhaps this is motivated by a desire to reach mainstream audiences, to attract as many spectators as possible. In theory this would bring more people into contact with disabled dancers and widely challenge ideas of disabled people as incapable. But, when companies make a decision to stage choreography that privileges techniques to which the normative-bodied trained dancer is central, there is a politics inherent to that choice, and they are making a decision to perpetuate that politics. It is the politics of a society that designates disabled people as worth less than non-disabled people.

Pleonasta: Okay. Let's define that politics in more detail, but first, do you think we need an example to ground this idea of mainstream contemporary dance?

Superflo: Um… anything presented by Rambert or Richard Alston Dance Company in the last twenty years?

Pleonasta: Yep, that's clear enough!

Superflo: And as we're talking about integrative dance, I'd like to briefly discuss two very different works.

In 2011, Candoco Dance Company introduced *Set and Reset/Reset* to its repertoire. The piece is a recreation of American choreographer Trisha Brown's *Set and Reset* (1983). Candoco did not present a literal reconstruction of the piece, rather, dancers learned original phrase material which they then developed according to the five choreographic rules that inform the piece. (The five rules are: Line up; Play the edge; Play with visibility and invisibility; Act on instinct; Keep it simple.) Rehearsal director Abby Yager, from Brown's company, said that the work 'functions like the original piece but the particulars are different' (Yager 2012).

Whilst the five instructions don't refer to physical technique, when watching the piece I saw clear alignment, flow, controlled swinging, flexibility and turn out. Dancers moved with soft precision, some eased into deep pliés in second position and others released loose grand battements. Whilst the choreography asked that dancers realise their actions by giving to gravity, they also clearly drew on training in forms of contemporary dance technique. It is these techniques and their historical delivery that privileges normative bodies. For me, there were several moments in this work in which the dancing of disabled performers expanded my knowledge of how flow might be expressed, or clean lines unfolded, but they did so in relation to the presence of non-disabled dancers who fulfilled the normative-bodied, standard realisation for each recognisable aspect of form.

In contrast, Radicalia performs a solo work called *Impasse* (2014). This piece is also a recreation of choreographer and dancer Doran George's solo *Stalemate* (2009). In *Stalemate*, George's body and its actions do not express common characteristics of formal technique but enact a wider exploration of bodied expression. *Stalemate* was reformulated through a process committed to discovering Radicalia's version of George's movements given the many differences in their bodies. It was a process of translation that did not seek to replicate George's actions, but her expression of the energies originally conjured. Consequently, the two pieces look very different from each other, and Radicalia's version was renamed *Impasse*. The vocabularies of both *Stalemate* and *Impasse* are purposefully awkward and truncated. Radicalia's work with Doran George is an example of choreographic process driven by mining the potentials of her body's possible actions, as a tool for interpreting what his body had created and performed in *Stalemate*. Neither *Impasse* nor *Stalemate* involved fulfilling an ideal image (existing technique), but discovered movement through enquiry without concern for recognisable technical heritage.

Perhaps it's not appropriate to compare *Set and Reset/Reset* with *Impasse* because the former is a group work and the latter is a solo. (Further, given the construction of this writing, it is feasible that one of us is Radicalia, and therefore has privileged knowledge of her experience.) Part of the difficulties I consider inherent to *Set and Reset/Reset* is that it includes both disabled and non-disabled dancers together on stage, all seeking to fulfil aspects of the standard dancer. Any ensemble piece that involves an enactment of recognisable technique, which holds normative bodies as ideal, is sure to highlight substantial physical differences between its performers. It increases the likelihood that disabled dancers will appear as having less capacity (they perform a version of the correct form) and also as being depersonalised sources of inspiration. So, we see the disabled bodies as different from the norm. We see them partly fulfilling the standard. We see them attempting with sincerity to be that standard in spite of the impossibility of their bodies fulfilling that form. We see that they are not fully capable, so might be inspired by their attempts in the face of adversity. Gestures of inclusivity are undone when the choreographic form compounds the appearances of disabled people as sources for incapacity and inspiration – attributes that deny the full scope of possibilities those bodies carry. The politics that place disabled people in a constant condition of lack remains intact.

A brief note to say that the very notion of inclusivity only makes sense according to existing political terms: it seeks to remedy discrimination against disabled people by finding ways for them to join existing structures, even though it is those structures that, having been developed with the non-disabled body as their standard, excluded disabled bodies in the first place. More responsive choreographic practices carry a different type of politics, undoing the need for inclusivity because everybody will already be included.

Pleonasta: Okay. I want to review this, but also to elaborate a little in relation to wider social politics. Your claim is that mainstream dance and dominant social structures both privilege normative bodies. Whilst they might each make gestures for inclusion – integrative dance projects invite disabled dancers to join formal choreography, and the government installs wheelchair ramps on the bus – the invitation is to join a structure primarily intended for non-disabled bodies, and in which that standard is known. Therefore, when an integrative dance project chooses to work with choreographic approaches that are built on the standard dancer, and that don't question that standard, they perpetuate dominant political attitudes that designate disabled bodies as, in Kafer's terms, outside of acceptable notions of progress and futurity (2013: 28).

What would it mean, then, to begin with a structure committed to equal regard for all bodies? Any choreography could begin from a presumption of equal capacity on the part of its dancers. As stated, a number of contemporary choreographers already create frameworks that respond to critical enquiry, and explore performers' potentials for being and relating, rather than asking them to fit a prescribed form. Different experiences of bodied capacity and expression will move equally inside such structures (which is not to say they will be seen equally). *Impasse* is an example of this and we'll talk about others later.

Essentially, we are discussing a procedural difference between response (responding to what bodies can do) and prescription (seeking to have bodies fit an existing form), and these are also political imperatives. The promise of responding to what people can do is to begin with uncertainty about outcome. It is the rejection of a single standard. It is to embrace the qualities of unsettling with which we opened this chapter as well as Kafer's expressions of fluidity, and it necessarily leaves space for what disabled experience can create. The implications for reconsidering societal structure through such a process of response are radical. The canons of Western political thought are full of prescriptions for what an ideal society should look like (from Jean-Jacques Rousseau to the UK Conservative Party 2010 drive for the 'Big Society'), as well as declarations that people should strive to fulfil these ideals, with few voices advocating a commitment to building frameworks for social organisation that respond to what people are capable of doing and making (French philosopher Jacques Rancière is one example). Whilst the latter would require an unlikely overhaul of the fundamental tenets of social contract and governmental procedures, choreographic and dance practices are only

Figure 2: Candoco Dance Company. Photography by Hugo Glendinning 2011.

Figure 3: *Impasse* by Doran George and Catherine Long. Photo by Christian Kipp.

art! They have freedom to explore these possibilities, if not an obligation to do so. Why make art if you're just going to extend the thinking at work in the everyday? It is on this basis that integrative projects are in danger of perpetuating a politics that discriminates against disabled people when they choose to work with mainstream choreographic approaches without interrogating their inherent politics. Essentially, choreographic practices have the potential to challenge, destabilise and restructure the terms and dynamics of conversations about bodies and bodied capacities, precisely because choreography explores procedures through which we might exist with each other.

Superflo: We have spoken about Candoco here, and they are a company who regularly invite more experimental choreographers into their repertoire. Let's chat about one of those works.

The Macarena and Different Differences

Pleonasta: In April 2015, we both saw Candoco Dance Company's production of *The Show Must Go On* by French choreographer Jérôme Bel. The piece was originally created in 2001 and toured internationally for several years, performed by a company of non-disabled dancers. Bel's choreography is known for its absence of athletically virtuosic dance, even though he has regularly worked with trained dancers. *The Show Must Go On* has a cast of twenty dancers, and Candoco recruited a number of performers in addition to their core company members in order to stage it. The cast featured people of a range of ages and body shapes, including what would be considered a range of forms of disability. The choreographic motivation for this piece is one of critical enquiry, rather than a desire to represent metaphor or technique. It includes a section in which the song *The Macarena* by Los del Río is played, and the entire cast performs its corresponding line dance, a social dance that typically occurs in bars, clubs and concerts. We both found this section complicated and rich.

Superflo: Right, and it's the fact that the piece is essentially quoting a social dance that makes this subject complicated when we consider the ways in which it exposes disabled difference. Much like the formal techniques involved in dance training, there is a correct and accepted way of dancing 'The Macarena'; one moves one's two arms, two legs and hips at certain moments in the song's rhythm. (The dance sees each movement correspond to a specific beat, and those movements include stepping your feet whilst stretching your arms out in front of you, turning your palms over, placing your hands behind your head and jumping forwards and backwards.)

In every production of *The Show Must Go On*, 'The Macarena' has included group synchrony as well as the differences that individual dancers bring to the style and energy of its movements. The high energy and buoyant nature of one performer might contrast the more contained expression of another. These differences in performance quality are predetermined, which is to say they are choreographed, yet they communicate the notion of individual differences within a collective whole. So, the choreography of *The Show Must Go On* quotes a social dance, and each dancer's expression of that dance is choreographed in turn, allowing for a range of movement qualities to exist within 'The Macarena's' established form. We encounter the choreography as language and the dancing as translation, but this is translation that has been staged. Indeed, as a whole, *The Show Must Go On* deals in rules and language and experiences of interpretations, including those of its spectators.

In Candoco's production of the piece, the presence of several visibly, physically disabled bodies introduced another layer of difference and translation to 'The Macarena'. Some performers were not able to fulfil particular movements from the dance because their bodies realise different kinds of movements. They performed alongside non-disabled dancers who fulfilled the actions of the established dance.

Again, then, we have a situation of inclusivity. 'The Macarena' was created with non-disabled bodies in mind, and when disabled people perform it alongside non-disabled people, they bring differences to the choreography that might be read as not achieving the correct form. The reductive characteristics we identified above – lack (of a normative body) and inspiration (for having a go anyway) – are called into action once more.

In Candoco's production of the piece, Bel's choreographic choice of quoting 'The Macarena' revealed that, as spectators, we respond to different types of difference, differently.

I responded to differences in energy with a certain set of terms and associations, which are qualitatively different to the terms and associations with which I responded to differences in bodied capacity within the frame of a social dance. When I notice the dancer with high energy as different from the dancer with lower energy, I might read assumptions about personality. I might (unimaginatively) read buoyant as happy and low energy as serious. But when I see the difference of disability, my reading is more overtly political. When a performer on crutches with one leg is positioned at the centre and front of the stage in a scene in which the entire cast is performing, I question whether this is a political gesture of inclusivity. That's to say, I am forced to notice how readily I see the appearance of a disabled person as a symbolic act, as well as the fact that disabled bodies *are* sometimes utilised as political symbols.

Pleonasta: Are you talking about 'political correctness gone mad'?!

Superflo: No! That's very different. I think the person who responds to the appearance of people from minority groups as *only* fulfilling behaviour prescribed for the sake of political correctness believes those minorities only function as symbols and are not fully human. When I watched this section of the piece, I couldn't help wondering if it had been a deliberate choice to place this particular performer front and centre stage, because she would be prominent amidst the whole cast. Her presence amidst this collection of bodies encapsulates a gesture of inclusivity that is essential to Candoco as an integrative dance company, but again, I'm afraid that gesture has not been critiqued.

Pleonasta: I don't know if I agree, and I'm a little troubled by some of the implications of what you've said. I recognise the problem of disabled bodies appearing in a framework in which they are reduced to political symbols, rather than participating through any one of their many capacities. However, your response to 'The Macarena' would seem to suggest that you would only have been comfortable with the presence of visibly disabled performers if they were not prominently placed on stage, as that's the only way you could be sure they weren't being reduced to one-dimensional symbols. If we follow that logic through, it suggests that in performance situations such as this, visibly disabled performers must always take a step back. We should make them slightly less visible as the only way to ensure they are not being exploited.

Superflo: Well, I think it's a no-win situation. Even if they take a step back, they are often deployed as symbols.

Pleonasta: I'm also thinking about a conversation between the artist and activist Sunaura Taylor and philosopher Judith Butler in the documentary film *Examined Life* (2008) by Astra Taylor. The two are taking a walk through San Francisco whilst having a conversation. Taylor describes the city as being the most accessible place in the world, and therefore that more disabled people live there, so one sees quite a number of visibly disabled people out and about, meaning non-disabled people have become more attuned to their presence. She says that 'physical access leads to social access' (Taylor 2008). Essentially she's describing an experience of transition in which disabled people become more visible until their presence is normalised. It's a transition towards a time in which Radicalia can walk down the street and not be asked about her body. In order to reach that point of 'social access' there will presumably be a period in which the appearances of disabled people will straddle two dominant attitudes – they might appear as symbols of political inclusivity and simultaneously participate in social structures more embracing of bodied differences. In this period, they are sowing the seeds for a time in which they will appear as equal participants in the range of bodied experiences on a street. The appearance of the person on crutches in 'The Macarena', the focus she provided for discussing categories of difference onstage, as well as the invocation of bodies reduced to symbols, could be read as part of that journey.

Additionally, you associate high energy with a happy person, and low energy with a more serious person. These are symbolic associations as reductive as reading the disabled performer's presence as only indicative of inclusivity. Bel's choreographic choice to quote 'The Macarena' exposes how all bodies can operate as symbols in this regard. It is Candoco's choice to stage this piece with disabled and non-disabled dancers that enabled us to encounter the different social and political implications produced by these different types of symbolism. If we encounter challenging qualitative differences between these forms of signification, it is because the choreography brought them to us to discuss. It exposed the dominant social matrices that reduce disability to lack, inspiration or inclusivity, as well as the frameworks that say high energy means happy and low energy is serious. I would say that this act of exposure is a form of critique, and one that Candoco has embraced through its decision to stage the piece.

Superflo: I see. This is an example of choreography that is not built on the idea of the standard dancer's training, but deploys a normative framework – 'The Macarena' – as an exercise of critique. One of the outcomes of Candoco's production is to encounter how disability can function as symbol.

As we talk about this it's making me think about how visibly disabled bodies carry the potential to refuse images of synchrony or consensus, which are often attached to ideas of ideal community. This is politically quite exciting because those kinds of images can be terrifying in their lack of deviation and difference. A collection of people designated as physically disabled, living and moving together would not perform physical concord. They could force a reconsideration of how such imagistic concepts are generated.

Okay... what about projects that reject the framework of integration altogether?

Other Frameworks

Most of the works we have considered were presented within a frame of disability. Candoco and other companies announce their work with disabled and non-disabled artists through their branding. There also exist festivals committed to showing work by disabled artists, such as Unlimited or DaDaFest in the United Kingdom. These frameworks ensure spectators will encounter the works through terms of disability and integration. Back in 2002, Adam

Benjamin questioned whether such labels essentially serve to warn viewers that they will encounter a disabled person, fundamentally compounding terms of difference (Benjamin 2002: 15).

What might be offered by the presentation of a choreographic performance that does not announce itself in such terms?

Pleonasta: This is a good moment to talk about an event at Tate Modern in May 2015, which was an incarnation of a project by French choreographer Boris Charmatz. Named *If Tate Modern was Musée de la Danse?* it included a range of live works including several versions of Charmatz' piece *Levée des conflits* (2010). Amongst the different renditions of this choreography was one that included twenty-four dancers and was presented for ninety minutes. The choreography consists of 25 basic movements that are passed across performers' bodies, each always excluding one gesture. Movements travelled across the dancers like incidents of contagion. Whilst the dancers often reached states that were frenetic and generated compelling forms and energies, the piece did not appear to cite formal dance techniques. At times I encountered states of elegance and athleticism but these were not defined by clean alignment, flow or other characteristics already identified in relation to formal technique. Instead, I seemed to be watching dancers receive, embody and deliver the dance's gestures through their particular capacities. The clear structural framework and procedural practice of the choreography left space to respond to what the performers' bodies generated. To that degree it is a piece that works with the potentials of organisational structures as well as the potentials of bodies.

The collection of dancers encompassed a range of signifying categories, so there were people of different ages, genders, ethnicities and other classifications. It's possible some of them had not experienced formal dance training, although the nature of the movement made that difficult to discern. I had watched the work for about 45 minutes when I noticed that one of its performers had a prosthetic arm. It's possible that many people watched the piece and didn't notice this, just as it is possible there were other visibly disabled performers whose status as disabled I did not see. Whilst I may not have looked at her with detail before that moment, I had experienced her volume, her presence as part of the crowd, and the energy of her dance, but it was not until I noticed her arm that I experienced her social designation as disabled.

Superflo: So what did that do? Did it change how you watched the piece?

Pleonasta: No. I don't think so. I forgot about it very quickly because she moved out of view and the energy of the piece absorbed my attention. I mention this moment because I could not have had this experience if I were watching her perform in a company, festival or project that declared itself as integrative from the outset. In relation to our discussion so far there are two main things at work here: firstly, a choreographic approach that does not ask its dancers to fulfil a commonly recognisable and formal dance technique; secondly, the framing of the event which did not refer to dancers as disabled or non-disabled.

Superflo: But we still live in a world in which the presumption will be that most people are non-disabled, and I wonder if that's what your response shows – you assumed they were non-disabled until you saw a prosthesis that declared that performer's disability status.

Pleonasta: Well, I don't know how to tell whether that's true. What I recall is that the performers were moving in ways that did not clearly cite formal dance techniques (although anyone immersed in contemporary practices will recognise qualities of structure and expression), and therefore were not declaring a proximity to normative bodies. I noticed a range of details in the performers, from hair colour to age and, as Jérôme Bel's work revealed, these details all have currency as signifying certain cultural associations, as well as being more or less typical in situations of normative dance. I cannot escape noticing such attributes and their corresponding social associations. However, the piece did not trade on how those physical details signify in the everyday (which is different to denying their existence). Rather, it created a situation in which collectively those bodies generated states of swarm, contagion and reverberating forms. It was impossible to detect a correct version of a given physical action that the dancers might seek to fulfil, and so the idea of technically achieving a prescribed image was not present.

Importantly, this is not the same as a claim for inclusivity, or that all bodies will be perceived equally within this event. As we've already discussed, to engage claims of inclusiveness would be to perpetuate the framework in which that term functions. Instead, I think the piece offered an encounter with some other ways we can be together, an experience of how bodies relate beyond those matrices that dominate the everyday. On a very basic level what was present in *Levée des conflits* was the *possibility* that we can create structures and formulate procedures that will host body shapes, bodily details and bodied expressions and actions, without affirming existing terms of discourse about bodies. As I've already said, this is not a claim that experiences of bodied identity didn't exist within the piece, or that it offers an absolute escape from them. However, it temporarily foregrounded other ways in which bodies can communicate and relate, in a gesture that points to the potentials of the choreographic.

On Motives and Towards an Ending

Superflo: Reflecting back on the kinds of political imperatives we've been discussing in relation to the choreographic, it's also worth saying that disabled dancers don't have an obligation to only perform in works that will challenge normative frameworks for dance.

Pleonasta: I think they should!

Superflo: Okay! Well, what I was moving towards was that different dancers have different motivations. A great many disabled dancers find their roles in more mainstream integrative dance projects fulfilling. They are not motivated by politics but find value in their dancing.

Also, there aren't a huge number of jobs out there, so if there's pleasure in the dancing, then why not satisfy that desire?

Pleonasta: Well, yes and no. I acknowledge that if you're in a body that figures as marginalised in some way, and that you perform in work that is non-mainstream, and whose content might be challenging or estranging for its audience, that it carries the danger of distancing you even further from the public who are those spectators. It could compound experiences of isolation experienced in day-to-day life. On the flipside, I think performing in work that might accentuate feelings of alienation created by social structures, is an opportunity to take ownership of that condition. I'm going to draw on Radicalia's experience again. She speaks about her sense of lack of control over how her body is perceived in the world, specifically in relation to her physical structure. She finds it impossible to think of performing, of using her body as material of display, without considering how it speaks to the politics of disability. Since her body so often figures as wrong, or missing something, when she chooses to perform choreography that claims difficulty, she feels she owns that experience of alienation.

Figure 4: Superflo and Pleonasta, when all is said and done. Photo by Karen Robinson.

But, I do see the appeal of appearing in mainstream dance works. I understand that these pieces are more readily accessible for spectators, and therefore make your appearance as a disabled person more accessible in turn. Part of that accessibility is appearing through terms of inclusivity that are well established and therefore not challenging for most audiences. As you say, if you are a disabled dancer who derives real pleasure from dancing, and there are few jobs, perhaps you will dance at all costs because dancing is what you love to do.

Superflo: Hmmm. Your particular phrasing there makes me think about some wider cultural issues that underlie these abstract aspects of social structure to which we have referred. There seems to be a deep belief in some areas of our society, by which I mean in the United Kingdom, which says if you really want something you will find a way to achieve it, and you should do so without assistance. It's the kind of thinking that Conservatives use to justify persecuting poor and sick people. In fact this takes me back to Sunaura Taylor who, in *The Examined Life* (2008), says that when she asks for help it is a political act. She is choosing to create a public statement of inter-dependency. In the United Kingdom, many right-wing discussions about welfare support define asking for help as an event of shame.

Pleonasta: Right. And this is why I think facing up to the politics of putting your body on stage, whatever type of body you have, is so important. Think about the value of life, especially disabled people's lives, and how they have been thrown into question with the recent wave of cuts to disability support in the United Kingdom. And then there's the Assisted Suicide Bill that was reviewed in 2015,[1] which carries deeply troubling implications for disabled people. When Radicalia puts her body on stage, encouraging people to look at it, showing them what her body can do, and that this is what *she* wants to show her body doing – and that this is just a fraction of her capacities, a tiny gesture towards her value in the world – that is a vital response to cultural attitudes and state policies that declare the lives of disabled people have reduced social worth.

Superflo: And this returns us to the potentials of the choreographic. Choreography can offer a range of structures and procedures through which people can appear to each other and be together. This isn't about representing an alternative way of living, but of revealing how incredibly limited and limiting our social structures tend to be. And these structures are constructed. If our experiences of some people's bodies are limited within our current modes of living, it's not because of those bodies; it's because of the structures in which they are required to exist.

Pleonasta: Looking forward, I'm excited about research that will explore different ways in which choreographic procedures and structures might exercise responsiveness, from a starting point of understanding equal capacity across bodies. And if we like we can throw some non-human bodies into the mix as well.

Superflo: Sounds good to me.

References

Benjamin, A. (2002), *Making an Entrance: Theory and Practice for Disabled and Non-Disabled Dancers*, London and New York: Routledge.

Bel, J. (2004), *The Show Must Go On*, Kaaitheater, Brussels, premiere 14 October.

Brown, T. (1983), *Set and Reset*, Brooklyn Academy of Music, New York, premiere October.

Brown, T. and Yager, A. (2016), *Set and Reset/Reset*, Auditorium Fausto Melotti, Rovereto, premiere 9 September.

Charmatz, B. (2010), *Levée des Conflits*, Théâtre National de Bretagne, Rennes, premiere 4 November.

Candoco Dance Company (2015), 'About us', http://www.candoco.co.uk. Accessed 6 August 2015.

George, D. (2009), *Stalemate*, The Herbert Art Gallery and Museum, Coventry, premiere 24 June.

——— (2014) *Impasse*, Kaufman Hall, UCLA, Los Angeles, premiere 28 April, performed by C. Long.

Kafer, A. (2013), *Feminist Queer Crip*, Indiana: Indiana University Press.

Marsh, K. (2015), 'Do you "do" disabled dancing?', http://southeastdance.org.uk/blog/do-you-do-disabled-dancing/. Accessed 15 August 2015.

Taylor, A. (2008), *Examined Life*, London: ICA Films.

Yager, A. (2012), 'Insight: Trisha Brown *Set and Reset/Reset*', Candoco Dance Company, https://youtu.be/nDXTYHyY0Rc. Accessed 20 August 2015.

Note

1 https://www.publications.parliament.uk/pa/bills/cbill/2015-2016/0007/cbill_2015-20160007_en_1.htm. Accessed 8 June 8 2017.

Chapter 11

Dancing Identity: The Journey from Freak to Hero and Beyond

Eimir McGrath

It is an accepted view that dance provides a window into the very heart of any culture, highlighting the beliefs and perceptions that shape the everyday lives of people. Yet dance also provides a means of critically evaluating and exploring the possibilities for change within that same culture (Dale et al. 2007: 107). These apparently contradictory roles of reinforcement and subversion make dance an intriguing site for exploring the placement of physically disabled bodies in contemporary society, and for considering how existing perceptions of this identity as transgressive can be disrupted through dance performance. Physical disability identity in this context can be defined as embodied presence, which encompasses all forms of corporeal diversity.

This chapter starts with the premise that viewing a dance performance that includes dancers with disabilities may possibly be a transformative experience, nurturing an understanding and acceptance of disability as corporeal diversity[1] rather than transgressive other. Unfortunately, very many dance performances espouse disability identities that inherently uphold existing prejudices, implicitly reinforcing negatively biased received notions of difference. The notion of the 'dancerly' body (Kuppers 2000), which requires specific physicalities as necessary for specific choreographic and aesthetic requirements, needs to be interrogated and redefined. The predominance of the balletic body as the underpinning physicality required for dance performance has dominated western dance and continues to uphold a false dichotomy between those who can and those who can't dance, creating subordinate identities based on perceived imperfection. If these identities can be redefined in a way that would provide a framework for reading a dance performance, a deeper understanding of the dynamics of performing and viewing disability might unfold, which could potentially inform future inclusive dance practice.

In order to explore what might influence the reactions of the viewer when looking at differently abled dancers, a framework for theorising perceptions of disability is proposed, which will encompass the act of viewing dance and the potential impact of choreographic intent on viewers' perceptions of physical difference. Firstly, disability studies, particularly the works of Snyder and Mitchell (2006), Garland Thomson (1997, 2000, 2009), Linton (2007) and Hughes (2005, 2007, 2012), provide the underpinning for a brief analysis of the positioning of physical disability in western society. Secondly, the intersection of dance and disability needs to be considered in order to contextualise the placing of differently abled bodies as dancers in performance. The foundation for this is provided by Kuppers (2003, 2011), Foster (1986, 1997) and Albright (1997, 2001). Thirdly, the contemporary neurobiological approach to the building of relationships, as based on the works of neuroscientists such as Siegel (2012), Schore (2012), Cozolino (2006), Gallese (2003), Trevarthen (2003) and Bråten and Trevarthen (2007), can be explored in relation to the interpersonal connection between dancer and viewer. This understanding of human interaction provides the evolutionary hierarchy contained within the framework, recognising the wide variation in perceptions of disability and offering an explanation of how choreographic intent and dance performance can influence either reinforcement of or change in those perceptions. All these strands are interwoven in order to create a unified approach for viewing any dance performance that is fully inclusive of all corporealities, whether the participant is a viewer or a dancer.

Disability: Whose Construction?

Embodied presence is an integral part of each person's humanity and is a fundamental expression of 'being in the world'. However, contemporary western societal constructions of disability are based on the historic notion of deficit, and consequently people with disabilities have been stigmatised and placed at the margins of society (Wendell 1996), often requiring containment and isolation through institutionalisation. Modern medical sociology continues to emphasise the exclusionary view, whereby disability is generally understood in terms of the biological presence of impairment as pathology (Williams 2006).

Pioneering work in the 1970s by activists such as Vic Finkelstein brought attention to the oppression of those with disabilities caused by environmental and social factors and his insights contributed to the rise of the social model of disability. This social constructionist approach was successful in placing disability in the context of social enquiry rather than in the field of medical specialisation and rehabilitation (Finkelstein 1993). However, this view subsumed the reality of living with a disability beneath a discourse of cultural representation, and embodied experience became secondary to theoretical issues regarding the disabling environment (Linton 2007).

The ongoing debate between the medical sociology understanding of disability and the social model's understanding remains entrenched in a dualistic approach, despite the rise of the unifying biopsychosocial model[2] of disability. None adequately deals with the complex relationship between subjectivity, impairment and the disabling social and environmental factors that are all intertwined. The affirmative model of disability (Swain and French 2000) has suggested an interpretation of disability that recognises positive social identities, a non-tragic view of disability and impairment. This model particularly references the Disability Arts Movement as being an expression of these identities and offers a further step forward. A social relational approach (Thomas 2004; Hughes 2007) would allow for the inclusion of intersubjectivity, which would provide a new route into how the marginalisation of disability can be redressed, and western theatre dance may contribute to providing that route. In order to develop this notion, it is necessary to now look at the placing of disabled bodies in dance performance.

In the Shadow of the Sylph

Up until the beginning of the twentieth century, the balletic body dominated as the prime expression of 'high art' within western theatre dance, the predominant 'dancerly' body as described by Kuppers (2000). Slim, long-limbed, rigidly trained to achieve virtuosity, aiming to rise above the pedestrian movement of everyday life and offering an ideal based on ethereality, this 'sylph' body was the epitome of artistry and represented the cultural hierarchical milieux, which gave rise to the ascendance of this ideal (Kealiinohmoku 2001).

As new genres began to emerge in the earlier part of the twentieth century, the rigidity of the ballet canon was questioned and new ways of dancing were created, which emphasised the expression of inner feeling through movement, a very different experience for the audience as Foster points out:

> Psychological subject matter found authentic realization in the movement vocabularies of each choreographer. And the audiences, for the first time, were asked to identify with dancer and dance and to feel rather than see their own life experience on stage.
>
> (Foster 1986: 145)

This radical shift was a pivotal moment in creating the possibility for the inclusion of corporeal diversity, expanding the accepted notion of what constituted a legitimate dancing body. With the development of new movement vocabularies based on pedestrian movement and contact improvisation,[3] an entry point into professional dance became available for dancers with disabilities.

From the 1970s, inclusive dance performances primarily focusing on disability issues emerged, both within arts practice as well as subject matter for academic research. Consequently, critical reviews and academic analyses tended to remain within the confines of the disability notions of 'freak performance', the performance of 'heroic victim' or an exegesis of societal issues surrounding disability. This largely continues to be the case. By considering the interpersonal connection between dancers and viewers, the intersubjective space, it may be possible to create an understanding of how these particular dynamics are created and maintained, and what exactly might bring about positive change. The neurobiology of social relationships can provide some clues.

Embodiment and the Brain

Recent discoveries in neurobiology offer the possibility for a new theoretical approach to be applied when examining how the disabled dancer is seen and experienced by the viewer; what influences that view; and how positive change in perceptions of disability might come about. By applying neurobiological knowledge and theory to dance performance, a framework that is grounded in intersubjectivity can be conceived. This framework serves two purposes: firstly, to understand existing perceptions of disability and how change might be facilitated, and secondly, to provide a lens through which dance performance can be viewed in terms of inclusivity. As such, it recognises the fluidity of perceptions of disability, as each individual's interpretation of the concept is formed by an accumulation of personal experience filtered through cultural value systems. Consequently, viewers cannot be considered as one unified corpus, but rather as contained within a spectrum that allows for a multiplicity of responses to viewing disability in performance. However, the one unifying element that is present within an audience is the innately social nature of the human brain. This is the underlying precept that is the basis for this exploration of intersubjectivity.

Following the Path of Interpersonal Neurobiology

Neurobiological research is shedding light on to how the human brain is designed to form attachments and to be social. It is impossible to think of individual development without considering it in terms of social interconnectivity, as neuroscientist Louis Cozolino states 'we now recognize that individuals are inseparable from the group, that groups themselves process information and that we live in a field of mutual interpersonal regulation' (2006: 300). This drive for relationship is inbuilt, even prenatally as the brain is developing (Trevarthen 2001; Maiello 2001).

From an evolutionary point of view, research is uncovering how the brain is initially 'hard-wired' to act and react from primitive, emotional states when relating to others, and how subsequent experience can literally change existing neuronal connections leading to the potential for adaptation of this hardwiring (Panksepp and Biven 2012; Trevarthen 2003). As these emotional responses were originally intended to ensure survival, they are generally instinctual and are activated in social situations before conscious awareness is triggered (Schore 1994, 2012). The human experience of recognising difference in another will automatically trigger primitive emotional responses that activate caution and possibly alarm (Perry 2006; Gallese et al. 2007). Repeated experiences of safety in such situations build new neural pathways that suppress the alarm response and awaken the positive responses that foster social connection and acceptance. Viewing dance performance could provide such experiences of familiarisation and the creation of new neural connections, this is the framework within which to consider performance by dancers with different corporealities.

Neurobiological processes can inform a way of perceiving dance performance that is not contained within symbol and language, but rather within a pre-verbal state of being that is fundamental to all human existence. This state provides a direct route to connectedness with the other that can be most easily accessed through embodied communication such as dance. This is confirmed by research into the mirror neuron system of the brain and the mechanisms for creating attachment to other humans (Gallese 2003; Gallese et al. 2007; Trevarthen 2003;

Siegel 2012). Formulating this framework is partially based on recognising the fact that negative reactions to physical difference are part of the human primitive response system. Garland Thomson theorised this when she identified the baroque stare, the stare of wonder that is used by very small children when faced with an unfamiliar sight. She states: 'Because staring strives towards knowing by reducing unfamiliarity, if it is not short-circuited, it can be coaxed toward transformative interaction' (Garland Thomson 2009: 195).

Neurobiology now offers a scientific basis to Garland Thomson's explanation of this phenomenon. In the baroque stare, the immediate startle response is quickly replaced by the wondering stare that is part of the process of making familiar the unfamiliar, recognising similarities, noting differences and assessing the level of danger inherent in the encounter. Caution and curiosity go hand in hand in this sequence, which can last from seconds to minutes (Panksepp and Biven 2012; Trevarthen 2003). Where there is no threat, the new sight is assimilated as a safe one and the process of positive social response becomes activated. The need to stare is biologically based; however, it becomes over-ridden by the social stigma attached to disability. From early childhood in western society, it is culturally ingrained to suppress this automatic stare reaction, and the suppressing reactions of others around them often triggers the shame mechanism in children, the 'visceral experience of being shunned and expelled from social connectedness' (Cozolino 2006: 234). This social referencing mechanism becomes active at the time when very young children are absorbing the cultural coding of their particular environment (Trevarthen 2003; Cozolino 2006) and, when disability is stigmatised in this way, shame becomes an inherent part of looking at differently abled bodies. In order to reverse this stigmatisation and shame, it is necessary to find ways of providing reparative experiences.

The plasticity of the human brain is such that patterns of behaviour and responses can be reshaped through experience, and this is possible throughout the lifespan (Siegel 2012; Panksepp 2012). Those viewers of dance, whose experience of corporeal diversity has not extended beyond this basic level of interaction, will thus experience an engagement with the baroque stare which in turn allows such a neuronal reshaping to take place. Dance performance provides a means of giving permission to stare in order to allow a change process to occur. When this permission is given, the viewer can go through the process that leads to integration of difference, from a position of startle and potential threat, through curiosity and familiarisation, to acceptance and openness of social connection.

As a premise, this appears to provide a solid basis upon which to build a revised understanding that could be developed to encompass the growth of an intersubjectivity grounded in relationship, fostered through viewing dance performance. However, neurobiology alone is not enough to create this new understanding and potential change; other variables also have to be considered. A formulation of dance performance needs to be provided. One which not only recognises the diversity of approaches contained within different choreographies, but also considers how the viewer's experience of disability can be influenced through watching these choreographies in action.

Choreographing Diversity

There is no neat, linear development along the path towards societal integration of bodily diversity, but rather an accumulation of differing attitudes that continue to exist in varying degrees, depending upon each individual's experience of disability within a biopsychosocial context. Understandings of disability can be loosely divided into three historiologically evolving schemata of perceptions: disabled bodies as freaks, as heroic victims, and as an expression of corporeal diversity (McGrath 2013).

Three performances will be used to illustrate these schemata, to consider not only the impact of the choreographic intent upon the viewer, but also the widely varying attitudes towards different physicalities that can be present within an audience at any one performance. This critical examination also facilitates an insight into the efficacy, or otherwise, of dance performance in its potential to achieve a position of equality and integration regardless of the variations in the physicalities of the dancers. Throughout this exploration, the focus will continue to be on the interpersonal relationships that are created within each performance, rather than a purely aesthetic evaluation of each work.

GIMP: 'I Think You're Really Beautiful'. Bodies and Performance as Freak Show

The most primitive reactions to disability are contained in the belief systems that consider physical difference as monstrous, and those who embody such difference as freaks. Such bodies have been given marginalised roles in society, with organised occasions for display providing some of the contexts in which negative beliefs and stereotypes have been reinforced and developed (Garland Thomson 1996). The freak show in its original form has been defined as 'the formally organized exhibition of people with alleged physical, mental or behavioural difference at circuses, fairs carnivals or other amusement venues' (Bogdan 1996: 25).[4]

In recent decades, there has been a transformation in the intent of freak show performance where the emphasis has shifted from degrading display to an interrogation of social and political stances regarding disability and non-normative bodies. Feminist philosopher Elizabeth Grosz offers a very useful definition of 'freak', stating that the person who is labelled freak is 'not an object of simple admiration or pity, but is a being who is considered simultaneously and compulsively fascinating and repulsive, enticing and sickening' (Garland Thomson 1996: 56). This ambiguous response to bodily difference has been identified by Grosz as a threat to accepted ways of being that depend upon the binary oppositions of normal/abnormal.

It is this threat to the perceived integrity of the 'normal' body that gives rise to the objectification of any body that does not conform, and in this objectification, the body becomes a site for exhibition (1996: 57). This is an underlying premise that causes modern day freak show performance to have questionable value. Even though the aim of this type of performance is to confront and deconstruct prejudice by re-imagining the notion of exhibiting different physicalities, the reality is somewhat different because of the primitive neurobiological responses that are inevitably awakened in the viewer by such an approach. The intent to highlight physical difference in order to remove the voyeuristic gaze paradoxically depends on that gaze being engaged in the first place. Consequently, subversion unwittingly remains within the parameters of the original meaning.

Choreographer and dancer Heidi Latsky's *GIMP Project* (2008)[5] provides a useful vehicle to interrogate the processes that have led to contemporary subversive freak show performance and also to examine the emergence of a spectatorship that has its roots in this genre, uncovering inherent limitations.

GIMP is a dance performance, which premiered in Albuquerque, New Mexico, in November 2008 and has since toured internationally with a varying cast of dancers with and without disabilities. Theatre scholar, practitioner and disability theorist Colette Conroy states that 'freaks are made in performance through the establishment of freak and spectator, and there is a process of cultural consensus involved in their creation' (2008: 342). Despite intending the opposite, *GIMP* supports this view of disability through the inability of a freak show approach to fully transcend the objectifying stare which is laden with cultural undertones. As Conroy states, '[t]he freak is a confluence of cultural significations and is formed by spectatorial response' (2008: 345). *GIMP* is very much driven by a confrontational style and this permeates the work. It forces the spectator to watch the performance in terms of physicality, and specifically the physicalities of the dancers with disabilities.

One of the dancers, Lawrence Carter Long, is a disability activist with cerebral palsy whose distinctive gait is used as the basis for sequences that juxtapose his movement style with that of other non-disabled dancers. He repeatedly walks in an angular floor pattern, sometimes alone, sometimes joined by other cast members. It is a leitmotif that recurs throughout the work and is woven into the choreography in a way that accentuates his movement style. Yet, it does not appear to take the opportunity for exploration and development, but rather becomes a statement of difference in comparison to other walking styles contained within the choreography. These sequences tend only to unconsciously emphasise the ascendancy of the idealised dancing body rather than an unfolding of a movement script where the dancer's embodied presence is the fundamental starting point. This is both representative and symptomatic of much of the work's choreographic intent.

In the *GIMP* Project mission statement presented by Latsky,[6] she states that she aims to create an experience for dancers that allows participants to be 'expressive and truthful in ways that are empowering', for them to 'learn to "live in" their own skin' and to be 'encouraged to "own" one's own body through being involved in this project' (2010). These phrases could be interpreted as being contained within the parameters of ableist facilitation, where disabled dancers may achieve agency through performance. This inherent acceptance of these disabling views of corporeality will inevitably curtail the potential for this work to move beyond the confrontational, despite Latsky's very well meaning intentions. This is reflected in a sequence where Carter Long enters into a monologue that is provocatively constructed of comments made by audience members following earlier performances (information shared by Latsky in private conversation, 19 November 2010).[7] Among the comments are statements such as 'I don't know about them, but I think you're beautiful, I think you're really beautiful', 'it's been an honour and a privilege', 'I thought you were going to be weird, but you're not'. Each statement is an inversion of prevailing constructs that provide a negative view of disability; ugliness, powerlessness, invisibility/hypervisibility and condescension. In addressing the audience, Carter Long is giving himself the opportunity to stare back and to engage in a role reversal that aims to highlight stereotypical views of disability. The monologue addresses audience prejudice by acknowledging their need to deny innate reactions brought about by the freak show format of *GIMP*, replacing these reactions with statements that fall into the category of disability as tragedy to be overcome by the heroic victim. 'The way you do it, it's like you're standing at the edge of a cliff' is a very telling quote, projecting a spectatorial response onto the dancers and their performance, of imminent danger before a leap into the unknown. There is recognition of fear and the potential for shame at being involved in the voyeuristic gaze.

In this type of confrontational performance, the neurobiological reactions of shame and disgust as related to prejudice and exclusion can be explored and deconstructed. Schore points out that in normal situations of disgust, the experience 'provokes immediate suppression of visual attention and sensory rejection' (2012: 100). For those viewers who are unfamiliar with diversity, interaction at this level invites the rejecting stare to persevere and engage with the presence of the differently abled dancer, and for rejection to be transformed into the baroque stare. Consequently, there is an opportunity to accommodate the neural changes from the potential for the primordial fear and disgust pattern being activated, to a position of increased familiarity and openness. *GIMP* is a brave attempt to choreograph physical difference in a provocative and challenging manner, but because of the confrontational nature of the work, spectators are placed in a position of having to stare through a filter that awakens all inherent pre-existing notions of disability as aberration. There are other options within dance that can act as effective agents of change without referencing freak show and marginalization.

Diagnosis of a Faun: The Medicalisation of Disability

Continuing on the evolutionary path, the next performance analysed encapsulates the medical model of disability, which emphasises the ascendancy of the 'average' (Kuppers 2003; Snyder and Mitchell 2000; Davidson 2008) and the pathologising of disability. Choreographer and dancer Tamar Rogoff's work *Diagnosis of a Faun* (2009) could be thought of as a progressive step in the evolution of diversity and dance in that it moves beyond the notion of contemporary performance as a vehicle for the deconstruction of the disabled body as monstrous freak, which was clearly the intent of *GIMP*. However, it does bring into question the continuing influence of the medical model of disability in western society, and the negative implications inherent in this model, which tends to valorise the disabled dancer as heroic victim, transcending adversity.

The work was conceived after Rogoff was intrigued by performer Gregg Mozgala and his atypical physical abilities (he was born with cerebral palsy), and she consequently wanted to create a work that would allow her to explore his movement vocabulary. Mozgala and Rogoff began working together and the collaboration ultimately led to the devising of *Diagnosis of a Faun*. The work in itself is interesting because of the narrative chosen by Rogoff. Set in a hospital, it focuses on two parallel occurrences, the rehabilitation and transformation of a young ballet dancer with a ruptured Achilles tendon, and the simultaneous discovery of a 5000-year-old faun at the same hospital who is to undergo the same surgery, which in turn provides a counter-narrative of scientific exploration of the exotic and unknown.

The theme of medical intervention in this work is an extremely useful vehicle with which to explore the divergent approaches to two different physicalities. It makes it possible to deal with the topic both in a metaphorical way as contained within the narratives of the actual performance of the work (although this appears to be completely unintentional on Rogoff's part) and in real life because of the media interest that was sparked as a consequence of the training techniques devised for Mozgala by Rogoff. These were given a transformative and rehabilitative significance by the press where Mozgala could be seen as heroic victim because of the training regime devised for Mozgala by Rogoff. This coverage of the perceived rescue and transformation of a disabled man by a kind-hearted and inspired choreographer did an injustice to both Mozgala and Rogoff, as Mozgala's dance performance was very accomplished and the training regime did in fact bring about physiological changes that resulted in a broader movement range for Mozgala. However, his artistry received practically no attention in the media, but the perceived transformation of his disability became central to any coverage both in the press and online.[8]

The confluence of metaphor and reality in the work gives rise to an apt combination of the complex elements present in a medicalised view of differing corporealities. The ballet dancer's performance of acquired disability with the possibility of reparation, juxtaposed with the exploration of a 'deviant' body in the shape of a faun, is reflective of the inherent ambiguities in this model of disability. The faun represents an otherness that embraces all the unruly and unknowable aspects of a corporeality that is outside the norm, whereas the ballet dancer epitomises an embodiment of the ideal, the sylph. Her temporary state of disability could be understood as representative of the innate societal fear of bodily dysfunction that gives rise to the objectification and rejection of disabled bodies. Where Latsky was very overt in her desire to confront and deconstruct the notion of freak in *GIMP*, Rogoff had not stated an agenda regarding any political intent behind her choreographic decisions in the creation of *Diagnosis of a Faun*. In Rogoff's own words: 'I didn't know what I was going to do for him but I just knew he was inspiring to me' (Genzlinger 2009). 'Inspiring' is an extremely emotive word when used in the context of disability studies, as it often refers to the perceived struggle to surmount physical limitations, creating an expectation of stoic suffering and transcendence from a position of deficit on the part of the disabled person (Kuppers 2003). This perception of the differently abled body as victim is a familiar interpretation to most people and probably the most intrinsic in contemporary society. Dance viewed at this level of intersubjectivity is guaranteed to be viewed sympathetically and favourably, but unfortunately, this places it outside the remit of critical analysis (the position most famously taken by Arlene Croce in her non-review of Bill T Jones' work *Still/Here* in 1994). In Kuppers' words, this underlines the cultural assumption that 'people who are defined by their bodies are trapped by them' (2003: 53). Defining the body in this way is one of the primary effects of medicalisation of disability. However, the emotional response of pity and consequent sympathy creates a level of intersubjectivity that potentially eradicates any primitive fear or alarm response. This again has limitations in terms of fostering inclusivity, and reflects the anomalies and contradictions often contained in perceptions of disability. Garland Thomson states:

> Pity is an emotional cul-de-sac that ultimately distances starer and alienates staree. A block to mutuality, pity is repugnance refined into genteel condescension. Empathy, in contrast, bonds in a mutual recognition of shared humanity.
>
> (Garland Thomson 2009: 93)

The possibility of empathy opens the way for an intersubjectivity that goes beyond mere curiosity, as in disability framed as 'monstrous freak', or condescending pity, as in 'heroic victim'.

water burns sun: Corporeal Diversity and Embodied Practice

The final, most evolved level of viewing dance to be explored is where there is an acceptance of corporeal difference, and the intention of the choreographer is not subsumed or obscured by questionable narratives or other agendas. In this position of interpersonal interaction, the viewer potentially sees diversity rather than freak or victim. A form of equality is achieved that frees the viewer to see the dance and the dancer, in a way that does not reference disability as a prime element of the performance. Kuppers' filmdance work, *water burns sun* (2010) is such a performance. Created as part of a larger project, *Burning* (Berkeley, California, and other sites, 2008–10), it explores 'movement as a tracker of difference, but not to work with ideas of deficit or negativity, struggle or fight', but rather to 'host the multiplicity of movements we hold inside' (Kuppers 2009b). This performance has an immediacy to it that makes it accessible to the viewer by using butoh,[9] a genre that breaks with cultural aesthetics and consequently removes any constraining boundaries that could potentially interfere with the interpersonal connection between the performer and the viewer. Kuppers asks the question: 'Can we think outside the structure of the story, outside the habits of thought that make us sense and position ourselves in time and space, in power and knowledge?' (2009b).

A dance performance that can allow this to happen frees the viewer to be fully present to the dancer, regardless of that dancer's physicality. This creates a level of intersubjectivity that allows the potential for empathic attunement through the action of the mirror neuron system, in conjunction with the social engagement system of the brain.[10] The previous two stages of interaction that have been discussed do not reach this intensity of interpersonal connection. In theorising this difference, Kuppers offers an alternative position for dancers with differing physicalities, one of un-knowing. This is the position that contains an openness to the being of the other. In Kuppers' own choreography, she aims for, 'a form of un-knowing that unfixes certainty about otherness, but that still remains able to act as a dialogue ground with our social and cultural reality' (Kuppers 2003: 11). Un-knowability is the evolved state developing from an acceptance of difference, recognising the centrality of the need to maintain a non-verbal dialogic connection between dancer and viewer, which is the basis of an understanding of dance performance grounded in intersubjectivity.

Figure 1: *water burns sun*. The Olimpias (chor. Petra Kuppers). Image by kind permission Yannis Adoniou (2009).

water burns sun encapsulates this position of un-knowing. Performer Neil Marcus, who has a spastic movement vocabulary, performs this work along with three female dancers without disabilities. In one section, the act of lifting a glass and drinking water provides the narrative framework. Watching a person with a disability negotiate everyday tasks, such as the lifting and drinking of a glass of water can be excruciating, when perceived through the social construction of an incomplete and flawed movement pattern within a damaged, non-normate body. When looked at as a dance however, the movement no longer has to contain the perceptions of disability that otherwise might dominate if considered from such an ableist viewpoint. Butoh delves into the essence of the movement as it is performed by a body that contains the accumulated elements of disability, but is not merely a reference point for that disability. Drinking water becomes a study in the power of movement to bring about an awareness of the humanity of the dancer and his embodied presence within the dance. The use of this pedestrian act, within a butoh idiom, provides Marcus with the possibility of communicating agency and empowerment through movement. This is not the pathologised movement pattern signifying dysfunction in a normalised world; this is an authentic exploration of a valid way of being in the world, using artistic expression as the vehicle.

Looking Beyond

Having explored the three evolutionary stages of intersubjectivity, a framework has been created that recognises the various elements that can potentially influence the viewer in developing positive perceptions of physical disability. From the primitive emotional state where difference is perceived as potential threat, dance performance can lead the viewer towards the social engagement of the baroque stare, to a position where difference no longer defines either the dancer or the performance. This is the position where it is possible to fully experience what Siegel describes as the 'transitional moment of intersubjectivity, the "we-ness" of being' (personal communication, April 2013). Through viewing dance performance, these transitional moments can occur where a synchrony is created that is not shaped by perceived incapacity.

Exposure to dance experiences that embrace physical diversity has the potential to allow an acceptance of embodied difference to evolve. Neurobiological change can come about as culturally acquired responses to disability are undone, through the rewiring of neural connections responsible for acceptance of difference at a primitive level of being, bringing about a state of empathic attunement. There are constant difficulties in considering disability. Politically correct stances create artificial barriers and divides. When dance reaches a position of not having to declare the specific physicality of the dancer as an intrinsic element of performance, then intersubjectivity can occur in its full strength. The greater the opportunity to experience corporeal difference through the non-verbal, embodied communication of dance, the more the culturally acquired perceptions of disability can be undone.

References

Albright, A. C. (2001), 'Strategic abilities: Negotiating the disabled body in dance', in A. Dils and A. C. Albright (eds), *Moving History/Dancing Cultures*, Middletown: Wesleyan University Press.

—— (1997), *Choreographing Difference*, Middletown: Wesleyan University Press.

Barnes, C., Mercer, G. and Shakespeare, T. (2010), *Exploring Disability*, 2nd ed., Cambridge: Polity Press.

Bogdan, R. (1996), 'The social construction of freaks', in R. Garland Thomson (ed.), *Freakery: Cultural Spectacles of the Extraordinary Body*, New York: New York University Press.

Bråten, S. and Trevarthen, C. (2007), 'From infant intersubjectivity and participant movements to simulation and conversation in cultural common sense', in S. Bråten (ed.), *On Being Moved: From Mirror Neurons to Empathy*, Amsterdam: John Benjamins.

Conroy, C. (2008), 'Active differences: Disability and identity beyond postmodernism', *Contemporary Theatre Review*, 18:3, pp. 341–35.

Cozolino, L. (2006), *The Neuroscience of Human Relationships: Attachment and the Developing Social Brain*, Norton Series on Interpersonal Neurobiology, New York: Norton.

Croce, A. (1994–5), 'A critic at bay: Discussing the undiscussable', *The New Yorker*, 26 December/ 2 January.

Dale, A., Hyatt, J. and Hollerman, J. (2007), 'The neuroscience of dance and the dance of neuroscience', *Journal of Aesthetic Education*, 41:3, pp. 89–110.

Davidson, M. (2008), *Concerto for the Left Hand. Disability and the Defamiliar Body*, Ann Arbor: Michigan University Press.

Finkelstein, V. (1993), 'The commonality of disability', in J. Swain, V. Finkelstei, S. French and M. Oliver (eds), *Disabling Barriers, Enabling Environments*, London: Sage.

Foster, S. L. (1986), *Reading Dancing: Bodies and Subjects in Contemporary American Dance*, California: University of California Press.

—— (1997), 'The ballerina's phallic pointe', in S. L. Foster (ed.), *Corporealities: Dancing Knowledge, Culture and Power*, Oxford: Routledge.

Fraleigh, S. (2010), *Butoh. Metamorphic Dance and Global Alchemy*, Chicago: University of Illinois Press.

Gallese, V. (2003), 'The roots of empathy: The shared manifold hypothesis and the neural basis of intersubjectivity', *Psychopathology*, 36, pp. 171–80.

Gallese, V., Eagle, M. N. and Migone, P. (2007), 'Intentional attunement: Mirror neurons and the neural underpinnings of interpersonal relations', *Journal of American Psychoanalytic Association*, 55, pp. 131–75.

Garland Thomson, R. (1996), *Freakery: Cultural Spectacles of the Extraordinary Body*, New York: New York University Press.

—— (1997), *Extraordinary Bodies: Figuring Physical Disability in American Culture and Literature*, New York: Columbia University Press.

—— (2000), 'The beauty and the freak', in S. Crutchfield and M. Epstein (eds), *Points of Contact: Disability, Art and Culture*, Ann Arbor: University of Michigan Press, p. 191.

—— (2009), *Staring: How We Look*, New York: Oxford University Press.

Genzlinger, N. (2009), 'Learning his body, learning to dance', *New York Times*, 24 November, http://www.nytimes.com/2009/11/25/arts/dance/25palsy.html?pagewanted=all&_r=0. Accessed 2 October 2015.

Hughes, B. (2005), 'What can a Foucauldian analysis contribute to disability theory?', in S. Tremain (ed.), *Foucault and the Government of Disability*, Michigan: University of Michigan Press.

—— (2007), 'Being disabled: Towards a critical social ontology for disability studies', *Disability and Society*, 22:7, pp. 673–84.

—— (2012), 'Civilising modernity and the ontological invalidation of disabled people', in D. Goodley, B. Hughes and L. Davis (eds), *Disability and Social Theory: New Developments and Directions*, Basingstoke: Palgrave Macmillan.

Kealiinohmoku, J. (2001), 'An anthropologist looks at ballet as a form of ethnic dance', in A. Dils and A. C. Albright (eds), *Moving History/Dancing Cultures*, Middletown: Wesleyan Press.

Kuppers, P. (2000), 'Accessible education: Aesthetics, bodies and disability', *Research in Dance Education*, 1:2, pp. 119–31.

—— (2003), *Disability and Contemporary Performance: Bodies on Edge*, New York: Routledge.

—— (2009a), '"Your darkness also/rich beyond fear": Community performance, somatic poetics and the vessels of self and other', *M/C Journal*, 12:5, http://www.journal.media-culture.org.au/index.php/mcjournal/article/viewArticle/203/0. Accessed 26 September 2015.

—— (2009b), 'Programme notes for *Burning: An Olimpias Participatory Performance Installation*', Berkeley, 31 July, http://www-personal.umich.edu/~petra/alchemy.htm. Accessed 26 September 2015.

—— (2010), *water burns sun*, Burning, The Olimpias Project, Berkeley, Eugene, Fort Worden, http://www.youtube.com/watch?v=sMvaf6I_A4U, Accessed 2 October 2015.

—— (2011), 'Butoh rhizome: Choreography of a moving, writing self', *Choreographic Practices*, 1:1, pp. 79–96.

Latsky, H. (2011), *GIMP: Alverno College – Milwaukee, WI (January 2011)*, Alverno College, Milwaukee, premiere January, http://vimeo.com/52696690. Accessed 2 August 2012.

Linton, S. (2007), *My Body Politic*, Ann Arbor: University of Michigan Press.

Maiello, S. (2001), 'On temporal shapes: The relation between primary rhythmical experience and the quality of mental links', in J. Edwards (ed.), *Being Alive: Building on the Work of Anne Alvarez*, Hove: Brunner Routledge.

McGrath, E. (2013), 'Beyond integration: Reformulating physical disability in dance', Ph.D. thesis, Bedford: University of Bedfordshire.

Panksepp, J. and Biven, L. (2012), *The Archeology of the Mind*, New York: Norton.

Perry, B. D. (2006), 'The neurosequential model of therapeutics: Applying principles of neuroscience to clinical work with traumatized and maltreated children', in N. B. Webb (ed.), *Working with Traumatized Youth in Child Welfare*, New York: Guilford Press, pp. 27–52.

Rogoff, T. (2009), *Diagnosis of a Faun*, New York: LaMaMa E.T.C., recorded 5 December.

Schore, A. N. (1994), *Affect Regulation and the Origin of the Self: The Neurobiology of Emotional Development*, Hillsdale: Erlbaum.

—— (2012), *The Science of the Art of Psychotherapy*, New York: Norton.

Siegel, D. J. (2012), *The Developing Mind: How Relationships and the Brain Interact to Shape Who We Are*, 2nd ed., New York: Guilford Press.

Sinason, V. (2010), *Mental Handicap and the Human Condition*, 2nd ed., London: Free Association Press.

Snyder, S. L. and Mitchell, D. T. (2006), *Cultural Locations of Disability*, Chicago: University of Chicago Press.

Swain, J. and French, S. (2000), 'Towards an affirmation model of disability', *Disability and Society*, 15:4, pp. 569–82.

Thomas, C. (2004), 'How is disability understood? An examination of sociological approaches', *Disability and Society*, 19:6, pp. 569–83.

Trevarthen, C. (2003), 'Neuroscience and Intrinsic Dynamics: Current knowledge and potential for therapy', in J. Corrigall and H. Wilkinson (eds), *Revolutionary Connections: Psychotherapy and Neuroscience*, London: Karnac.

Trevarthen, C. and Aitken, K.J. (2001), 'Infant Intersubjectivity: Research, theory and clinical applications', *Journal of Child Psychology and Psychiatry and Allied Disciplines*, 42:1, pp. 3–48.

Wendell, S. (1996), *The Rejected Body*, New York: Routledge.

Williams, S. J. (2006), 'Medical sociology and the biological body: Where are we now and where do we go from here?', *Health: An Interdisciplinary Journal for the Social Study of Health, Illness and Medicine*, 10:1, pp. 5–30.

Notes

1 The use of terminology in relation to disability is fraught with difficulties. Underlying meanings are fluid, depending on specific cultural interpretations that can vary widely.

What is an acceptable descriptor in one cultural setting can be deeply offensive in another. As terms become subsumed into everyday usage, there is a tendency for evolving connotations to transform from the neutral to the derogatory, and stereotypical perceptions and discrimination consequently are reinforced by the language in use (Barnes and Mercer 2010: 11). The choice of specific terminology can also identify a particular theoretical perspective that in itself may become a limitation. In order to avoid these pitfalls, and to reflect the inherent imprecision that is contained within a constantly evolving lexicon, a range of terms will be used interchangeably throughout this essay. The most common words for describing embodied presence, 'disabled' and 'non-disabled' will be used, along with descriptors of corporeality and physicality such as 'diverse', 'different', and 'normate and non-normate'. The latter terms were created by disability scholar Rosemarie Garland Thomson. She defined the normate as those bodies without the stigmatising identifiers of disability, 'the constructed identity of those who, by way of bodily configurations and cultural capital they assume, can step into a position of authority and wield the power it grants them' (1997: 8).

2 The World Health Organization (WHO) has tried in recent years to address this fluctuation between the medical model of disability and the social model of disability through the creation of a new approach within their document, *The International Classification of*

Functioning, Disability and Health (2001). This approach is based on the biopsychosocial model of medical intervention within western society, which has been in existence for over 30 years now, and was initially developed by psychiatrist George Engel (1977) in order to recognise all the elements that play a part in illness and its treatment. The 'bio' aspect recognises the organic/somatic element of illness, the 'psycho' aspect recognises the importance of the individual's psychological responses to illness, and the 'social' aspect recognises the importance of the social system in which the individual is placed and how that can influence illness.

3   Pedestrian movement describes dance originating from everyday gestures and movements, performed in a non-stylised way. It emerged in the 1960s, in the works of choreographers associated with the Judson Dance Theater, New York, and heralded the beginning of the post modern dance movement. Contact improvisation, a form of dance based on collaborative, improvised interaction between dancers using weight and momentum, was developed by Steve Paxton, one of the foremost choreographers of the Judson Dance Theater.

4   This describes the familiar understanding of the freak show of the nineteenth and early twentieth centuries, where people with physical anomalies provided entertainment through being displayed, often with a pseudo-scientific intent that allowed for voyeurism in the name of education.

5   The use of the word 'gimp' in the title of the performance is a subversion of the contemporary use of the word, which has very definite derogatory overtones when applied to someone with a physical disability. Disability theorists Sharon Snyder and David Mitchell speak of the 'transgressive reappropriation' of offensive terms such as 'gimp', stating that:

> […] ironic embrace of derogatory terminology has provided the leverage that belongs to openly transgressive displays. The power of transgression always originates at the moment when the derided object embraces its deviance as value.

(2000: 35)

6   *GIMP*, Programme Notes, DaDaFest International, Liverpool Playhouse, 18 November 2010.

7   The complete monologue, as performed by Carter Long at Alverno College, 2011, is as follows:

> I've just gotta tell you I've been watching you, we've been watching you for the last twenty to twenty five minutes or so. I don't know about them, but I think you're beautiful. I think you're really beautiful. Absolutely stunning. I was told this was going to be an incredible experience but never in my wildest dreams did I imagine this. This has moved me. This has really changed me. It has been an honour and a privilege to have the time and space to stop and really look at you. To really see you. I've got to rethink this whole thing. This is not what I expected. I expected this to be weird, I thought you were going to be weird. But you're not. The way you do it, it's like you're standing at the edge of a cliff, it's like you're at the edge of the diving board and you just jump right off! It's so full on, I've never seen anything like that before, I mean wow! What I first thought was a risk is really an opportunity.

8   The media coverage of this aspect of *Diagnosis of a Faun* exposes the inherent assumptions made by journalists when writing about the relationship between dancer and choreographer in the making of the work, giving Rogoff a medicalised authoritative position in relation to Mozgala as research specimen. Genzlinger, when writing in the *New York Times* (2009), astoundingly refers to this relationship in the context of artistic creation, saying 'the more important work of art may be what Ms. Rogoff has done to transform Mr. Mozgala's body'. The incredible elimination of any vestige of agency on Mozgala's part is reflected throughout this review, which barely mentions the actual creation and performance of the work, but reifies Rogoff's perceived rescue and transformation of a man so that now 'he doesn't feel so enslaved' (Genzlinger 2009) by his cerebral palsy. See also Roslyn Sulcas' review (also in the *New York Times*, December 2009). Taking a slightly different stance in her opening paragraphs, Sulcas follows the inspirational path towards the disempowerment of Mozgala as brave, disabled dancer, stating that Mozgala and Rogoff deserve 'both praise and admiration for their collective grit and courage' (Sulcas 2009). She also feels the need to first highlight the changes in Mozgala's physical capacities due to the work done in rehearsals, rather than focusing on a critical review of the performance per se, labelling the achievement as an inspiring story. Another journalist, Mitch Montgomery, writing for the online magazine *Backstage* (December 2009) states 'the rehabilitator stands to gain as much from the act of healing as the one rehabilitated'. This serves to reinforce the notion of charitable giving where superiority and condescension can lurk under the guise of a caring demeanour, unfortunately only too frequently experienced by people with disabilities as an experience of humiliation and disempowerment (Wendell 1996; Linton 2007).

9   The word *butoh* means 'ancient dance' or 'dance step' and is used to describe a form of dance that almost defies any prescriptive definition. It is not easily encapsulated into a neat explanation as it is based in experience and empathy, it is not stylised or symbolic, it depends on what is felt. Butoh focuses on 'the body that becomes', with the emphasis on the transitional phase, known as *ma,* that exists between each moment of movement, each moment of intention and each moment of experience within the dance. This inherent transience contained in butoh performance fits well with the exploration of dance movement that is not circumscribed by body type or codified movement (Fraleigh 2010). Like contact improvisation, butoh focuses on the body in the process of dancing rather than the virtuosity of prescribed movement within a specific technique.

10 Physiologically, there are several areas that form the core of the social brain: the anterior cingulate, the orbito-frontal areas of the pre-frontal cortex, the frontal portions of the temporal lobes, and the amygdala. The anterior cingulate plays a role in social bonding and attachment, and is also an association area for motor, tactile, autonomic, visceral and emotional input. The orbito-frontal areas of the pre-frontal cortex are considered the apex of the limbic system as they connect both with the limbic system and the cortex, acting as a zone of convergence for both sensory and emotional information, mediating information regarding the individual's internal and external world. This is the part of the brain where like and dislike of others is mediated (Cozolino 2006: 255). The frontal portions of the temporal lobes link all areas of the brain to integrate senses, primitive drives and emotional material, enabling rapid responses to take place in conjunction with complex environmental inputs.

Chapter 12

Dance Disability and Aesthetics: A Changing Discourse

Margaret Ames

Introduction

This chapter argues for an expanded aesthetics in theatre and dance that includes people who do not conform to the standard bodies and techniques of crafted performance work. The argument is for a widening aesthetic drawn from and including the work of dance and theatre artists with learning disabilities. Tobin Siebers contends that such an expanded aesthetics has existed over centuries and continues to evolve. His argument specifically tackles disability as 'an aesthetic value' (Siebers 2010: 20) and he makes the case for: 'the presence of disability in the tradition of aesthetic representation' (2010: 2). However, his focus is on the visual arts rather than on theatre, dance and live performance. Siebers positions the disabled body as central to art history and to aesthetics and ends his work by optimistically stating: 'The figure of disability checks out of the asylum, the sick house, and the hospital to take up residence in the art gallery, the museum and the public square' (2010: 139). I am not so sure, and contend that live performances by people with disabilities, and in particular people with learning disabilities, continues as a proscribed and often prescribed activity that remains un- integrated into mainstream performance aesthetics.

The argument is not based on the discourse of community arts, or social welfare but deliberately outside of that context. The conclusion of this chapter is a proposal that calls for an expanded aesthetic encounter with work that might trouble existing discourses, which conceptualise art as therapy and/or a pastime. This writing attempts a tentative response to. Sandra Umathum and Benjamin Wihstutz's provocation to discuss:

> Under what circumstances, for example, can we speak of a *good* performance, of *skilled* acting, of *virtuosic* dancing? How can we escape the ideology of ability? And to what extent does the discussion of aesthetic judgements and the disclosure of their criteria imply a political dimension?
>
> (Umathum and Wihstutz 2015: 7–9, original emphasis)

Context

Governments in the United Kingdom have increasingly positioned artists with learning disabilities as beneficiaries of art rather than as possibly, having something to contribute to aesthetic fields of practice. Liz Tomlin explains the political trajectory of funding the arts in

Britain and in particular states that New Labour from 1997 onwards brought increased funding to companies as a result of the ideology of social inclusion that drove Arts Council agendas (Tomlin 2015). Dave Calvert (2015) makes the point that the medical model of disability had contextualised art work with and by people with learning disabilities as therapeutic and that despite the Conservative Government's policy of care in the community, which saw the closure of institutions that had been the homes of people with learning disabilities, the medical model held sway and imposed a therapeutic agenda on any creative activity in a context where increasingly we are defined by our usefulness, as units of economic capital. Those of us who cannot earn money in full-time work and those of us who need social and state support to survive are increasingly demonised as fraudulent, whilst others are categorised as needy; both categories are unproductive. Writing for the Joseph Rowntree Foundation Jenny Morris states:

> Welfare paternalism – a 'state knows what's best' approach, against which the disabled people's movement campaigned so effectively during the 1980s and 1990s – meant that disabled people were identified as objects of pity and charity. It has now been replaced by liberal paternalism – where the state aims to 'help people to help themselves' – which applies more malicious stereotypes to people who are not economically productive.
>
> (Morris 2011)

An example of the results of such malicious stereotypes can be found in the BBC documentary by Rosa Monckton *Tormented Lives*, which examines the reality of daily life in the community across England in 2010. This programme is an account of daily psychological and physical abuse endured by people with learning disabilities. Monckton herself a mother of a daughter with Down's Syndrome called Domenica, comments:

> We live in a society which is based on youthfulness, efficiency and power and when you look at someone like Domenica, she's not youthful, she's not powerful, but, what she is is something which you can't really put a value on. It's humanity stripped to the bone.
>
> (Monckton 2010)

Briant et al. coin the phrase 'new folk devils' (2013)[1] to describe the way media in the United Kingdom are characterising people with disabilities. This programme makes clear the shocking results of such demonisation of those who are not economically independent. Another participant, Christopher, reveals that he applied for many jobs and was told that there were positions available, 'but not for you' (*Tormented Lives* 2010).

In this chapter, work by people with learning or intellectual disability is considered. By using the paradigm of all disability as constructed I do not however underestimate the concrete effects of learning disability on real lives, of those assigned that label, and those who support them. The concept that disability is constructed lies at the heart of the social model of disability. This model counters the medical model that views disability as an individual's problem characterised as lack, deficiency and deviation from a biological and social norm. Mairian Corker and Tom Shakespeare argue that 'subjects are embedded in a complex network of social relations. These relations in turn determine which subjects can appear and in what capacity' (Corker and Shakespeare 2006: 3). Ideological structures maintained by state apparatus such as the educational system, the media, and importantly in this context, the cultural ISA involving arts and literature (Althusser 2000) enable and produce categorisations such as artist, beneficiary, producer, customer and product. These social designations are temporary and shifting. More permanent designations of role and function are inscribed via medical and social apparatus that produce diagnoses and determine the individual's capacity for independence and deservedness of state support via the Personal Independence Payment. The market paradigm assigns more or less value to individuals and categories of people in relation to economic value within a market economy. Randy Martin speaking at a roundtable discussion refers to the notion of capital as a living entity: 'So that question now of capital being its own form of embodiment nonetheless makes us have to ask, "What does it want?" And part of what it wants is a world of risk' (Martin 2010 80).[2] A person with a learning disability runs the risk of being publicly interpellated as being (whose existence is) of negative use value. That is to say, the deficit of such people's existence serves only the capital of beneficence on the part of the state and the work force. These people are without a market value and are perceived as a drain on resources rather than marketable commodity. The notion of the human as commodity is being tackled by artist Jennifer Lyn Morone who, according to Guardian critic Nell Frizzell (2015), has turned herself into a registered company. Frizzell describes how:

> There are adverts for diamonds made from her hair, her own signature perfume and a manual called How to Become a Corporation in 10 Steps, on sale in hardback.
>
> (2015)

Franco "Bifo" Berardi discusses his notion of semiocapital, the definition of the contemporary worker who produces and consumes information. This constant production of information via language and signs overwhelms us and he states: 'But today it is the social brain that is assaulted by an overwhelming supply of attention-demanding goods' (Berardi 2010). He goes on to situate the human being as information worker who literally has become a unit of production as: 'Their nervous systems act as active receiving terminals' (2010). The cognitarian then, processes 'information in order to give birth to goods and services' (2010). But many people with learning disabilities cannot partake in this electronic, semiotic flow of information. Access to the information superhighway is either limited or simply not possible, and how are Berardi's cognitive workers commensurate with those whose cognitive and intellectual faculties are under question and doubt? How can such people contribute to the economy, unless they/we[3] can be commodified as beneficiary, as a triumph over impossible odds, or as an example of exceptionality. Margrit Shildrick (2015) offers compelling accounts of such precarity, which as Adrian Kear (forthcoming) explains is experienced as anxiety, which is so readily felt as a condition of life in western developed contexts under the neoliberal regime; precarity is our ontological condition. He states that the encounter with the other is a traumatic experience as it produces this anxiety as a disruption of our political normality. Shildrick expands this discussion on anxiety in her work on the anxiety produced by visible disability and difference, which becomes an unconscious expression of negation. The effects that such anxiety may have are dangerous for people with disabilities and she comments that the economic crisis presents new perils for people with disabilities and people who are marginalised:

> These Others are being categorised as scroungers who selfishly use up precious social resources. In politics and the popular media, there is strikingly little sympathy for others less fortunate than the mainstream but rather a feeling that we would all be better off without them.
>
> (Shildrick 2015: 157)

A recent online petition asking for the current Secretary of State for Work and Pensions Ian Duncan Smith to release information about the numbers of people who have died after their welfare benefits were stopped, evidences growing awareness about the perilous positions that many people find themselves in within the social order of austerity in the United Kingdom.[4] This extreme danger is of particular importance to people with disabilities as some lives depend on the vital benefits that are now strictly rationed. Those in receipt of benefits are interpellated as non-productive. Here the connection between market, value and personhood is particularly marked for money is exchanged in recognition of either dependency or money is refused as the person is deemed to be fit to work.

Radical Aesthetics

How do these issues connect with the field of aesthetic production? The stakes are perhaps higher than ever now in the appearance and representation of people with disabilities in the aesthetic realm of live theatre. Siebers contends that: 'the more we enter the modern age, the stronger the equation between art and disability – and to the point where it is difficult to recognize art in itself without summoning the notion of disability' (2010: 135). The demonisation of people with disabilities, and the appalling incidents of hate crime documented by Monckton might require the live and visible appearances of disability within theatre and dance so that these disciplines might summon the notion of disability as integral to the performing arts as well as the visual arts. Michael Shapiro considers the aesthetic subject in cinema and offers: 'Their characters' movements and dispositions are less significant in terms of what they reveal about their inner lives than what they tell us about the world in which they are inserted' (2013: 70). Shapiro thinks of this kind of subjectivity which, in his writing, is considered in terms of cinematic space and not in terms of individual psychology, as having effects on the world, rather than a more passive psychological position.

The action of the characters creates effects in the world and informs the audience about the world they inhabit. Kear, following Shapiro, states that the aesthetic subject is one who forges agency: the status of the aesthetic subject is a means towards agency.[5] People with disabilities are especially reified into a limited set of possible social identities, and it is the possibility of resistance to such reifications, opening up new avenues for subjecthood through aesthetic appearances that lies at the heart of this enquiry. People with learning disabilities interpellated as needy, and of no market value might actually be productive as aesthetic agents whose works sometimes appear as contributions to a dissenting field of aesthetics that critiques reifications of the subject in relation to a living capital condition. Morone examines live capital via her own body and the personal data she produces. She offers this data for sale. Her intervention as an artist draws attention to this condition of personhood, of subjectivity as producing capital. Perhaps people with learning disabilities performing in live dance and theatre might inform the audience about the worlds they inhabit as such performances produce agency. Instead of the production of body as capital, critiqued by Morone, people with learning disabilities might inform audiences of alternative values. Such values might also contribute to Berardi's call for 'an awareness with regard to an erotic, social body of the general intellect' (2010). I am suggesting a recruitment of the apparently intellectually deficient into the intellectual resistance to commodification and as Berardi asserts:

> The political organizer of cognitarians must be able to do away with panic and depression, to speak in a way that sensibly enacts a paradigm shift, a resemiotization of the social field, a change in social expectations and self perception. We are forced to acknowledge that we do have a body, a social and physical body, a socioeconomic body.
>
> (Berardi 2010)

Furthermore, he states that one of the tools for this paradigm shift is the language of poetry. This to my mind is the ground of the artist with learning disabilities.

Watching Back to Back Theatre's *Food Court* (2008), I sat in the dark of a large and grand proscenium arched theatre. I remember the feeling of expectation, heralded by the conventions of lighting, music and the quieting of the audience. The first moments of the performance demanded care and attention and were engrossing; it was delicate, strange material that intrigued. Then, two large, very large, women appeared down stage right. Their demeanour, coupled with their size conveyed menace. Shockingly to me, (and this shock at what I saw is not something I am at ease with) they wore gold lame leotards with tights, revealing every curve of their sumptuous overweight bodies. I experienced a moment of shock at such excessive bodies. Appearing on a major European stage amongst an audience of privileged theatre goers, this moment of unruly excess of body, without the tropes of comedy or stock dramatic character changed and challenged normative order. I was not the only one in the audience to be surprised as I heard small gasps and mutterings scattered throughout the audience. Theron Schmidt states that:

The reality of who they are is on display: their unusual body shapes in all their imperfections, their unique physiognomy, their blank stares. These people are really disabled. This is what disabled people really look like. And yet, these stage entrances emphasise that disability is a matter of appearance: it is a matter if how we see these people. Here, they are revealed, and also masked, by their sparkling golden tops, by their illumination in the stage lights, and in their moment of representing themselves.

(Schmidt 2013: 199)

These women wore clothes that drew focus to their material bodies. Their appearance demanded that we look at them and make an assessment. Kear suggests: 'It happens, sometimes. Sometimes an aesthetic encounter occurs unexpectedly, creating the unanticipated feeling of time suddenly stopping and opening up an experience of another kind of temporality' (2013: 8). He goes on to explain how such moments position the contemporary within historical contexts that produce both performer and audience and that demand co-presence from both groups of performers and spectators. This connection between history and contemporary theatrical manifestations produces, he argues, 'an aesthetic-political apparatus' (Kear 2013: 9), which is the frame of theatre.

Recognising that aesthetic forms are products made by both artists and audiences and that the theatrical frame holds within it the potential to make explicit our political condition within a historical and ideological project, is an essential aspect of how resistance might be articulated within the prevailing political context. Defiant appearances: those by individuals who appear through the means of theatrical apparatus who do not conform to audiences' expectations of who is fit to appear, come in this case, as people with learning disabilities. In terms of a changing discourse of such appearances, both social and aesthetic, Shildrick asserts that there is no clear line of history where changing attitudes and conditions can be neatly tracked. Instead, she considers that:

In relation to extant historical material, what emerges in terms of socio-personal responses to disability is best understood as an oscillation between the processes of integration and invalidation or exclusion, threaded through in each case by a persistent and often unacknowledged anxiety.

(Shilidrick 2009: 44)

Shildrick discusses this anxiety in terms of a social/psychic condition in which the appearance of disability as otherness disrupts the psychic imaginary of a unified and 'proper' body. A theatricalisation and framing of differently abled and differently appearing bodies was exemplified by the late nineteenth and early twentieth-century phenomenon of the Freak Show. Rosemarie Garland Thomson, discussing artist Cheryl Marie Wade's work makes reference to this history: 'She appropriates the allure of the tawdry sideshow' (Garland Thomson 2005: 34) and again with reference to Mary Duffy's performances: 'By making herself into an art object, she shifts the visual display of her body from the medical or freak-show context to the discourse of aesthetics' (2005: 36). Shildrick delves into the complex significations of the phenomenon. She argues that public fascination with 'the anomalous body' (2002: 22) is an essential aspect of our 'morphological imaginary' (2002: 3). She contextualises the notion of the freak as emerging in the eighteenth century as a category of physical difference. Freak Shows became part of social and cultural life during the nineteenth and in to the early twentieth century. She points out that there are however, much earlier examples of this kind of exhibition of the self which offered a means of survival: 'For individual children and adults who survived a monstrous birth, there is plentiful evidence from all periods that self-display was a common strategy of subsistence. (Shildrick 2002: 23).

This is the historical context within which contemporary aesthetic endeavours made by people with disabilities in the west emerge from. Performers and audiences alike are constructed within this historical context as we co-produce the event within the theatrical frame.

Shildrick's thesis is that despite projects of integration in education, work and the arts, we are still beset by a psycho-social anxiety that such difference is aberrant. Even as we integrate we risk contamination and disability is therefore dangerous: 'Disability remains remarked, and therefore set aside' (Shildrick 2009: 53). Moving forward, and reflecting the activist agenda that artists with disabilities have established and continually developed and refined, in 1999, Carrie Sandahl defiantly stated: 'No longer compliant objects of the stare, people with disabilities are staring back, claiming the body as a legitimate part of identity, a body whose metaphors and physicality belong to us' (1999: 13). So, the stare returned is an assertion of agency produced by the performer who demands to be seen. It announces that the performer does have a socioeconomic body that informs us of her world through the aesthetics of her discipline.

Sandahl further comments that 'the disabilities of dramatic characters always signify beyond the conditions themselves' (1999: 15). Yet in *Food Court* materiality of body and action were presented seemingly without metaphor. The theme of the work was bullying and violence, exposure, humiliation and vulnerability. Rather than finding the presence of the performer with disability as a distancing metaphor for particular states of a general human condition as Sandahl observes, the artists demanded that the audience become somehow complicit in the acts of violence represented by virtue of being onlookers. Instead of distancing through metaphor these performers appeared as actors with disabilities, performing scenes of human violence, common to all, a potential within all, dismantling the trope of the smiling and sweet natured person with a learning disability. Howard Loxton reviewing the work comments that: 'this was one of the most disturbing experiences I have had in the theatre, its impact reinforced by the disability of the performers' (2010). Such a comment opens the particular issue of disability causing disturbance. The disavowal of (dis)ability is the final line of his review.

This work is an example of a contemporary aesthetic frontier that moves beyond the nineteenth-century circus freak show and perhaps realises something beyond metaphor, to suggest new practices and readings of art. Within the frame of theatrical representation is a postmodern problematic; that of representation and of appearance. Schmidt takes up this challenge of appearance as essentially political, stating: 'I am interested in the political relevance of artistic practices that invest in and explore theatre as an apparatus of appearances' (2013: 190). Schmidt discusses *Food Court* and offers:

> Rather than denigrating theatre as merely second-hand experience, of value only when it punctures its representational frame, I see in Food Court a sustained engagement with the dynamics of theatrical spectacle as a political realm in its own right. In my reading, the production does not aim to get at some 'real' politics behind these representational surfaces, but instead stages the idea that disability is precisely a matter of appearance as such; it is a problem of appearance […].
>
> (2013: 195)

In an ideological context of neoliberal market driven politics, how can such art be assessed in terms of aesthetic judgement? What appears and how might such appearances resist the negative forces of capitalism that categorize people with disabilities as unproductive beneficiaries or as economic drains on the economy? How can such appearances contribute to the development of dance and theatre and open new understandings of human existence and action? Such work might contribute to the development of an alternative aesthetic imperative that requires a new literacy in dance and theatre. Such a literacy would require Loxton to re-frame his disturbing experience.

Kear argues a complex theory that aesthetics is not simply a means by which the political is enhanced. He considers:

> […] that politics and performance thought in relation as practices of 'dissensus' and agentic creation, reveal the fundamental interconnection yet ultimate separation of the aesthetics of politics and the politics of aesthetics in terms of form and effect, elaborating and demonstrating at every turn their inter-animation by aesthetic subjects in the practice of aesthetic politics.
>
> (Kear 2013a: 8)

Prompted by this analysis I propose that aesthetic appearances or acts by artists with disabilities engaging with the spectator might be acts of aesthetic politics. Such acts are contemporary manifestations of historical conditions as they have been inherited, reproduced, challenged, resisted and reformed in the prevailing ideologies of each era. I propose that the changing discourse that is historically contingent, now might suggest a way that neoliberal conditions of precarity and anxiety about all who appear as Other, might be contested. Material performed by bodies and intellects of difference may originate in entirely different fields of experience and concern to those of us without disabilities. The manifestation of such aesthetic material requires an expanded literacy in aesthetic practices beyond what normative standards of theatrical presentation currently offers or accepts. Anna Catherine Hickey-Moody offers a philosophical analysis of bodies and minds, moving from Descartes towards Spinoza, Deleuze and Guattari. Her project is an advocacy for performance by people with and without learning disabilities, working in integrated contexts. Dispensing with the construct of defective intellect she refers to the 'thinking body' (Hickey-Moody 2009: 6). Understanding the body as a thinking entity means understanding embodied expression and an expanded literacy in aesthetic practices. The appearance of performers with disabilities is a political act as the aesthetic subject insists on agency and the theatrical frame and the performer are interdependent. In Hickey-Moody's argument such aesthetic appearances are 'political in the respect that they inform *the possible* in social imaginings' (2009: 8, original emphasis). All theatrical appearance necessarily makes the performer Other. Audiences both spectate and create this condition of separation, of objectification. The stakes are high then when the performers are people with disabilities, given historical and current socio-political conditions. Alternative embodied ideas are revealed for audiences and non-disabled performers learn a new order of form and material that acknowledges different experiences and understandings via thinking bodies.

Dancer and choreographer Jérôme Bel's collaboration with Swiss-based company Theater HORA, in order to create the piece *Disabled Theater* (2012), further demonstrates dense complications that concern perceptions of theatre as objectifying and therefore abusive and also as a frame for the appearance of the subject as agent. Yvonne Schmidt writes about Theater HORA after they had made *Disabled Theater* and were working on their 'long term performance experiment' (Schmidt 2015: 227), *Freie Republik HORA*. This project commenced after the project with Bel. She explains that this experiment removes anyone without a learning[6] disability from the rehearsal room and that: 'According to Michael Elber, the director of Theater HORA, the aim of *Freie Republik HORA* is to let the ensemble direct itself in order to abolish the hierarchy between a non-disabled director and the disabled performers' (Schmidt 2015: 228). Schmidt conducts a vital argument that troubles my own work and that, in the context of the frame of theatre and its aesthetic political work, must be addressed. The argument has direct implications for the aesthetic political and agentic frame of theatre as a mechanism of and for appearance:

'The appearance of disabled performers on stage is usually determined by non-disabled directors, and this is especially the case for performers with intellectual disabilities, "who are incapable of finding a stage by themselves"' (Schmidt 2015: 229). She quotes Michael Elber here and it is unclear in what tone Elber makes the comment - one of irony, or opinion. She elaborates in her discussion of Bel's *Disabled Theater*:

> Although no roles are attributed to the actors and they are allowed, within specific tasks, to perform their own authority, the freedom to do so remains Bel's own projection on to them. It is this fundamental problem of theatre-making with disabled performers that becomes visible in Disabled Theater.
>
> (Schmidt 2013: 234)

Cyrff Ystwyth based in Wales has worked with different colleagues with learning disabilities leading the process who have not produced material that we found accessible. The notion of a 'good' piece of performance and of the conventions of dramaturgy that produce legible performance have been held in balance. With less experienced colleagues, and indeed colleagues whose disability seemed to bar access to the long-term creative development and organisation of materials has prompted me to take a much more authorial role and to project my own authority onto these performers. Developing her thinking through the experience of *Freie Republik HORA*, Schmidt concludes her essay with the comments:

> How can the work of disabled performers be described and criticized in the context of aesthetic categories? To what extent are disabled performers a projection onto the surface for non-disabled directors, and can this relationship be turned around?
>
> (Schmidt 2015: 240)

She returns to the issue of tension between the social and aesthetic paradigms that for her are present whether it is an internationally acclaimed artist or the members of the company creating the work, because of the mark of difference that contours the being of people with disabilities.

Contextualising performers with learning disabilities as in receipt of education or benefit is the tricky work of animated capital that refuses the possibility of aesthetic encounters. The refusal arises because of the social construction of people with disabilities as needing education or therapy and not as producers of aesthetic experiences. I have been educated to understand certain forms of dance-theatre. I will direct and attempt to create a dramaturgy with the material my colleagues offer, that is legible within this already given context.[7] The frame of theatre is historically produced and transformed over time but always reproducing certain features that define it as theatre. Kear, thinking about how theatre might respond to and articulate this history, comments:

> The co-presence and co-constitutive relational interdependence of the spectator and the work is explicated as being central to both the construction of the theatre event and the identification of its specifically performative historiographic operation […]
>
> (Kear 2013: 16)

He refers to the relationship between the spectator and the work, rather than the spectators and performers. Kear positions the *work* of theatre as actual labour, the labour of the artefact or event. The labour therefore is the production of the performance. So, in this case, the performers might be literally any body. It matters not if such bodies display the signs of disability. The work is the frame for the aesthetic appearance of bodies in theatre. What we understand as spectators is the value of this labour within the aesthetic codes and materials of the theatrical frame and our own labour in co-constructing the work in relation with it. Kear's comments suggest a form of liberation from the constraints of trained dance or actor techniques. Aesthetic value is assigned in respect of how well the materials are managed, within the relevant genre not necessarily by the visual appearance and virtuosic capacity of the bodies that perform. *Kontakthof* (1978) by Pina Bausch with Dance Theater Wuppertal is an example of such work that foregrounds the material rather than the virtuosic individual performer as the piece is performed by many kinds of bodies. The lineage of the work comes directly from the trained performers of the company to a cast of performers aged 65 and over and then to another cast of teenagers, all of whom became experts in the reproduction of the choreography although they had no institutionalised training. The labour of presenting the work is how the integrity and accuracy of the original piece is maintained.[8] I argue here that presenting a theatrical art work that has aesthetic value within the terms of the specific genre requires a level of dramaturgical skill. The final piece is created from material the performers bring to the work and how this material is articulated through the machinery of theatrical presentation rather than historically established training and institutionalised training methods.

To illustrate this I offer a description of a moment in work by Cyrff Ystwyth authored by Lucy Smith and directed by myself. Smith has performed for some years with Cyrff Ystwyth; however, this was her first attempt at creating her own work. *The Old Days* (2014) began with her reminiscing on her early childhood, the house that her family had renovated and the garden full of flowers. Smith's articulation of material, through verbal description and choreography, romanticised events and couched everything in terms of a fantasy or fairy tale. She asked her colleagues to reproduce a mimesis of ballet with extended limbs and elegant postures, balancing on tiptoe. When confronted with the reality that her colleagues could not, and indeed, would not perform these movements she turned to her role as soloist. This self-absorption signalled by her demands to be the sole focus of attention within the ensemble is easily understood as the author crafted her autobiography. It was an assertion of her artistic vision despite her colleague's collective unease and failure. It left the company with a dilemma as to how we might engage with this work and this in turn, questioned Smith's awareness and sense of responsibility to the ensemble she is a part of. Linked with the romantic memories of an idyllic childhood were strange and disturbing scenes of violence that she told us were drawn from her interest in historical accounts of the courts of Henry VIII and Elizabeth I – Tudor England. She produced a lengthy scene in which she chose colleagues without disabilities to walk solo through the performing arena and to prostrate themselves on the ground in front of the audience, whilst she spoke quietly and steadily: 'Look at her, she is disgusting, she is deceitful, she is ugly, off with her head'. It seemed to me to be no accident that she chose female colleagues without disabilities, and I venture the interpretation that this was a projection about her perception of her socially constructed self, worked within the theatrical frame. As the director it seemed important to find a distance between Smith and her material drawn undiluted from her inner world, and the function of the work within the theatrical frame in order to communicate with the audience beyond the solipsistic nature of the performer appearing before her public. Yet, this is part of the rationale for wishing to perform, to make public, embodied existence and for people with learning disabilities this is crucial. People with learning disabilities experience denigration and are not unaware of the larger social/political desire for them to vanish. Appearance is politically weighted. How exactly a person appears then depends on the aesthetic frame. Not the freak show, the talent show, the entertaining charity appearance; not the appearance of heroic human transcendence, not the narrative appearance of equal rights, the appeal of the ever-smiling and sweet nature of the person with Down's Syndrome; not the appearance of the highly trained professional virtuoso either. Smith appeared as Benjamin Wihstutz argues:

> Rather, being an actor also implies exposing oneself in front of an audience, making oneself an aesthetic object, being artist and exhibit at the same time. Voyeurism and showmanship are therefore not exclusive to freak shows or ethnological exhibitions, but constitutive elements of theatre as a social space and a place of aesthetic appearance.
>
> (2015: 36)

The aesthetic frame then is particular and crafted in order to draw attention to itself and in order to make available this particular space of appearance through the poetics of dance-theatre. Smith and Cyrff Ystwyth required a director for no performer completely understands how they appear, how they are seen, nor how they communicate in the context of the labour they perform.[9] This is the case regardless of intellectual, physical or cognitive condition as the gaze and interpretations of the audience dialogues with the artist's beliefs and intentions. No matter how useful a vehicle dance-theatre may be for those who have no social political or aesthetic representations in the world, the aesthetic frame and labour of theatrical appearance is only a partially effective tool; it will always take over from the agency of the individual and is according to Kear yet another closed system of power whereby the performer has far less power than she understands.[10] However, that a person makes the decision to appear and attempt a representation of self just as Smith did is not futile. It is of the highest importance that people with learning disabilities make public appearances and use the potential of the aesthetic-political subject for agency. As people with disabilities as having no use value, then aesthetic discourse might be the vehicle for a strategy of resistance.

Briant et al. comment that 'mass media images are still the foundation for wider understandings of disabled people's lives' (2013: 887). Therefore, the representational frame of the theatre has potential to offer a direct if limited, address to this problem. Earlier I mentioned that people with disabilities might produce work that emerges from contexts that require audiences to think differently and to perhaps learn a new literacy within the frame of theatre. Such a literacy in simple terms may be learning how to see and learning a new grammar of the body and of choreography. For example, Cyrff Ystwyth performers were unhappy at being asked to mimic classical ballet movements. My directorial response was to use Smith's idea of classical port de bras but ask the performers to hold their positions for a long time. Few people could do this taxing task. Instead, the choreography became a strange stuttering mixture of slowly dropping arms, sudden glances to right and left as performers checked in with each other, sighs and adjustments that signalled tension, frustration and perhaps pain, sudden re-engagements with positions that had been let go, yet all produced by remaining true to Smith's intention and original choreography. Mike Pearson[11] has referred to Cyrff Ystwyth's ensemble work as analogous to the Portsmouth Synfonia - a classical orchestra formed by art students in the early 1970s that was comprised of musicians who could not play their instruments. They performed anarchic classical concerts. The listener learns a different relationship with the sounds, the instruments, rhythms and, of particular relevance here, the labour of producing the score and its performance. Former member and scholar Michael Parsons connects the formation and output of the orchestra to art and performance histories such as Dada and the Fluxus events, challenging and demanding a more open definition of, in this case, music, and comments that:

> Technical shortcomings were here turned to positive advantage as an agent of transformation, and process of deviation and decontrol long regarded as legitimate in the visual arts (in the works of Pollock, deKooning, Johns and Rauschenberg, for example) – were transposed into a musical context [...].

(Parsons 2001: 9)

Parsons specifically uses the word decontrol as opposed to out of control or lack of control. Deviation is here taken seriously as creative phenomenon and as technique. In much the same way the ensemble work of Cyrff Ystwyth takes particular, given movements from whoever is authoring work, and whilst remaining an ensemble, produces deviation and decontrol, thereby transforming the initial choreographic proposition. Such propositions themselves emerge from emplaced and embodied experience and example my proposed alternative choreographic grammar.

The Politics of Integration/Inclusion

It may be that as people with learning disabilities often have little opportunity to engage with most theatre and art as audience members and yet are very often targeted to be the recipients of art, dance, drama and music workshops as beneficial, that new work is not necessarily drawn from within the technical or stylistic cannons of those forms. Instead, the work may be drawn from personal experience or perhaps more interestingly, particular views or understandings of life. If such work might emerge from different concerns and experiences of life and suggest alternative ways of being in the world, then it might also be understood as contribution to the ethos of inclusion. However, inclusion as a concept is fraught as Simplican and Leader discuss with their mobilisation of Chantal Mouffe's radical democratic theorisation (Simplican and Leader 2015). Edward Hall comments that the problem of inclusion is that it requires us to:

[…] exercise caution in our interpretation of the apparent connection to and inclusion of the 'other' into majority social and creative spaces and networks. What is possible – indeed what is afforded 'special status' – within dominant sociocultural norms is perhaps limited to particular forms of art and performance, ones that chime with understandings of 'outsider art' (Rhodes 2000) and traditional expectations of 'disability crafts', mixed with feelings of sympathy and charity.

(Hall 2013: 257)

No matter how important the discourse of inclusion may be it is equally important to remember its ideological function. Simplican and Leader (2015) argue that inclusion means joining the mainstream and that this is part of the normalisation agenda. Mobilising Michael Warner's idea of counterpublics, Simplican and Leader consider how artists with disabilities engage publics with disability issues; issues of exclusion, prejudice, anxiety, disgust and abjection. Such work demands, in more or less direct ways, that prevailing conditions be challenged and become acts of dissensus rather than inclusion. In contrast to their understanding of Warner's theme of the counterpublic that defines them as 'not inferior substitutes for mainstream society, but flourishing communities that embrace alternative identities' (Simplican and Leader, 2015: 724), I am interested in how Warner emphasises a split between the public identified as a reading public where the necessary conditions for its existence as a public is brought about through: '[…] direct transposition from acts of private reading to the figuration of sovereign opinion' (Warner 2002: 89). He also argues that: 'Counterpublics tend to be to those in which this ideology of reading does not have the same privilege' (2002: 89). He asks: 'How then, will they imagine their agency?' (2002: 89). Might the counterpublics of artists with disabilities (many of whom cannot read) imagine their agency by committing to public appearance in aesthetic acts? Offering verbs that describe the actions of a queer public for his example, he lists words that conjure poetics in action and indeed his notion of public discourse is exactly the poetic. He concludes: 'To take such attributions of public agency seriously, however, we would need to inhabit a culture with a different language ideology, a different social imaginary' (2002: 89). Further, Hickey-Moody contends that: 'performance texts afford opportunities for working with people with intellectual disability that are not constrained by the pre-established value systems which can accompany language' (2009: 44). I suggest that artistic practice, particularly dance by people with learning disabilities, can take some direction from Warner's proposal. Recognising the need for public agency I find that such dance and dance-theatre work needs to be rooted within its aesthetic origins in order for it to resonate beyond the world of social welfare, therapy and social inclusion agendas. However, this is precisely not to say that mainstream forms should be the mode of engagement. At this juncture, I propose that different embodied grammars might be employed. In attending performances by people with disabilities that have been created within, for example, the category of dance, I have seen work that offered mimicry of existent styles. Such work placed the dancers firmly within the category of social beneficiary within the agenda of normalisation that sees access to dance and theatre and inclusion in performance as participating in the normal leisure activities of interested citizens. Matt Hargrave comments on the specialist activity of theatre and in his discussion on the tensions between the professional and amateur performer advises: 'Be able to work within and against dominant cultural norms in order to influence mainstream practices' (2015: 228).

In the work I have seen where performers did not seem to have Hargrave's advice performers risk reification as beneficiaries not as Warner's actors with the state but as commodities for the state to trade with. In fact, people with different bodies and intellects who desire to be 'dancers', to dance like dancers dance, are not being included. Depressing versions of standard dance movements undermine the value of potential radical otherness that might perform a dance of difference. Hargrave argues that: 'Recognition of a performer as a theatre labourer provides a necessary corrective to a socially harmful perception of learning disabled citizens as economically or culturally unproductive' (2015: 228). This reinforces Kear's consideration of the labour of making theatre referred to earlier. Hargrave continues: 'Philosophically, it corrects a view of the intellectually impaired as "less than" full human beings. It also corrects the imperative to produce a "proper" kind of theatre' (2015: 228). Hickey-Moody comments regarding her work with Restless dance company '[...] one of the most significant static constructions of self and disability that I experienced, was dancers with intellectual disabilities assuming I was more of an "expert" than them' (2009: 53). She recalls how her colleagues would watch those without disabilities and understand that these moments:

[...] were predominantly a performance of parts of the 'history' of the dancer's life: a history of being told to watch people 'without disabilities'. For example, most settings that bring together people with and without intellectual disability involve people 'without' disability role-modelling the 'right' thing to do.

(Hickey-Moody 2009: 53–54)

How might people with learning disabilities be understood as productive and as contributors to the aesthetics of dance production if their work is only reproduction of the existing lexicon of dancing bodies? If, rather than mimic existing tropes of the dancer, dancers with learning disabilities might 'suggest alternative mastery of movement and write with their bodies, choreographic signs and codes that hold information about alternative value systems within specific cultural contexts' (Ames 2015: 177), then our current dance world might reflect Simplican and Leaders' proposition for a 'non-normative understanding of social inclusion' (2015: 727).[12] Returning to Warner's play of words to describe his notion of a queer public, I borrow his idea and offer a list of verbs that might describe such a new turn in the aesthetic of dance and dance – theatre by people with disabilities and in particular learning disabilities. Such a dancing public might be one that: stumbles, twitches, stutters, lurches, shouts, mutters, laughs, stares, forgets; is marked by difference – for example. This vocabulary of apparent dance defects is however not a license for poor performance. Such dances performed within the aesthetic frame and performers understanding their performances as aesthetic, produces agentic aesthetic subjects appearing as such within the theatrical frame. To emphasise the point further, Hargrave asks: 'what if gaps and erasures, verbal inconsistencies and semi decipherable registers of speech are not "authored" but "naturally" embedded in the aesthetic? What if they were not performative games but real presentational states?' (2015: 51).

Conclusion

The problem of how any performer might be able to understand how exactly they appear before others, how exactly is their performance manipulated, articulated and what is their function within the frame of the overall dramaturgy remains open.

Understanding how the frame represents and yields up meanings to the spectator is not something owned solely by the performer but as Maaike Bleeker argues is: 'a shifting set of relationships' (2015: 76). The task then is to maintain the strength of the aesthetic frame of theatre, in order for the dance of difference to manifest as aesthetic contribution as opposed to one of defective or poorly executed therapy, for as Bree Hadley comments it is 'not just the thematic or therapeutic agendas of disability performance, but also its aesthetic strategies, structure and style' (2014: 17). Within the theatrical conventions keeping the aesthetic frame demands that the performer be skilled within their chosen context. Martin Seel's philosophical work can extend Kear's assertion of 'spectatorship as an active and constitutive mode of creative and critical *co-compostion*' (2013: 218, original emphasis). Kear affirms that the aesthetic subject is created by the performer in relation with her audience. Seel develops the notion of the aesthetic and offers that: 'in contrast to the resonating of nature or of the city, the resonating of art is an arranged resonating and its perception an arranged encounter with a resonating' (2005: 147).

And he goes on: 'Artistic resonating *reveals itself* as resonating, and it transpires *within* a play of shapes' (2005: 147). He offers a definition of an art work, which I recruit as a means of differentiating between therapeutic and community based work:

The work of art is, in other words, an appearing of a special kind. It does not simply appear; it reveals itself in its appearing. It presents its appearing. It directs its beholder to explore and discover, understand and interpret, marvel and follow the construction of its appearance. The beholder who wants to have something from the art work has to take it in one previously unspecified way or another.

(Seel 2005: 151)

This is the labour of the spectator and the performer. The changing aesthetic discourse of dance and disability is a move from a passive mode of appearance. Instead such labour makes possible the effects of resonation, which in Seel's terms is that which is perceived and causes interest in its appearance: 'the work presents itself as something forming, not as something formed' (2005: 153). Seel argues that the work of perceiving art, perceiving its resonances, we become lost within it: 'we are one not with the work but with the movement of the work. All perception of resonating in art has the form of a dance, however motionlessly we perform it' (2005: 153).

This chapter offers an argument for an expanded and challenging turn in aesthetic manifestation; an understanding and appreciation that turns away from the mainstream, that challenges the already given models of appearance and yet does not dispense with skill, rigour, attention and intention to the aesthetic act. Performers with learning or intellectual disabilities might contribute a radical aesthetics that does not seek approval and is not justified by the political agenda of usefulness and market worth. A changing aesthetic discourse created by performers with disabilities might resonate with the patterns and rhythms of misfires and pause, stutters and lurches. Such an aesthetic, produced through a certain kind of labour from artists and audiences might suggest that the aesthetic is a function of the political and that we can learn new ways of understanding what appears before us. Shapiro and Kear's aesthetic subject, here with a learning disability, contributes to authoring the world, produces effects and contributes visions of life alternative to an existence of commodification.

References

Althusser, L. (2000), 'Ideology interpellates individuals as subjects', in P. du Gay, J. Evans and P. Redman (eds), *Identity: A Reader*, London, Thousand Oaks and New Delhi: Sage Publications.

Ames, M. (2015), 'Dancing place/disability', *Theatre Research International*, 40:2, pp. 170–85.

Back to Back Theatre (2008), *Food Court*, Malthouse Theatre, Melbourne, premiere 9 October.

Bausch, P. (1978), *Kontakthof*, Opera House, Wuppertal, premiere 9 December.

Bel, J. (2012), *Disabled Theater*, Halles de Schaerbeek, Brussels, premiere 10 May.

Berardi-Bifo, F. (2010), 'Cognitarian subjectification', *eflux Journal*, 20, http://www.e-flux.com/journal/20/67633/cognitarian-subjectivation//. Accessed 10 October 2017.

Bleeker, M. (2015), 'Thinking no-one's thought', in P. Hansen and D. Callison (eds), *Dance Dramaturgy: Modes of Agency, Awareness and Engagement*, Basingstoke: Palgrave Macmillan, pp. 67–86.

Briant, E., Watson, N. and Gregory, P. (2013), 'Reporting disability in the age of austerity: the changing face of media representation of disability and disabled people in the United Kingdom and the creation of new "folk devils"', *Disability and Society*, 28:6, pp. 874–89.

Browning, B. (2010), 'Rethinking technique and the body proper', *Dance Research Journal*, 42:1 pp. 75–88.

Calvert, D. (2015), 'Mind the gap', in L. Tomlin (ed.), *British Theatre Companies 1995–2014*, London: Bloomsbury, pp. 127–154.

Corker, M. and Shakespeare, T. (2006a), 'Mapping the terrain', in M. Corker and T. Shakespeare (eds), *Disability/Postmodernity: Embodying Disability Theory*, London, New York: Continuum, pp. 1–17.

Corker, M. and Shakespeare, T. (eds) (2006b), *Disability/Postmodernism: Embodying Disability Theory*, London and New York: Continuum.

Frizzell, N. (2015), 'Human for sale: The artist who turned herself into a corporation', *The Guardian*, http://www.theguardian.com/artanddesign/2016/feb/09/jennifer-lyn-morone-neoliberal-lulz-data-surveillance. Accessed 16 February 2016.

Garland Thomson, R. (2005), 'Dares to stares: Disabled women performance artists and the dynamics of staring', in C. Sandahl and P. Auslander (eds), *Bodies in Commotion: Disability and Performance*, Ann Arbor: University of Michigan Press, pp. 30–41.

Hadley, B. (2014), *Disability, Public Space and Performance Spectatorship: Unconscious Performers*, Basingstoke: Palgrave Macmillan.

Hall, E. (2013), 'Making and gifting belonging: Creative arts and people with learning disabilities', *Environment and Planning A*, 45:2, pp. 244–62.

Hansen, P. and Callinson, D. (eds) (2015), *Dance Dramaturgy: Modes of Agency, Awareness and Engagement*, Basingstoke: Palgrave Macmillan.

Hargrave, M. (2015), *Theatres of Learning Disability: Good, Bad, or Plain Ugly?*, Basingstoke: Palgrave Macmillan.

Hickey-Moody, A. C. (2009), *Unimaginable Bodies: Intellectual Disability, Performance and Becomings*, Rotterdam, Boston and Taipei: Sense Publishers.

Kear, A. (2013a), *Theatre and Event: Staging the European Century*, Basingstoke: Palgrave Macmillan.

—— (2013b), 'Introduction; Interlude: Inhumanities', in J. Edkins and A. Kear (eds), *International Politics and Performance: Critical Aesthetics and Creative Practice*, London and New York: Routledge, pp. 1–16.

—— (2015 forthcoming), 'Re-staging the anxiety of the image', *Performance Research*, 20:5, pp. 51–62.

Loxton, H. (2010), http://www.britishtheatreguide.info/reviews/foodcourt-rev Accessed 10 October 2017.

Martin, R. (2010), 'Toward a Decentered Social Kinesthetic', *Dance Research Journal*, 42:1, pp. 77–80.

Morris, J. (2011), 'Rethinking disability policy', http://www.jrf.org.uk/sites/default/files/jrf/migrated/files/disability-policy-equality-summary.pdf. Accessed 15 February 2016.

Parsons, M. (2001), 'The scratch orchestra and visual arts', *Leonardo Music Journal*, 11, pp. 5–11.

Sandahl, C. (1999), 'Ahhhh freak out! Metaphors of disability and femaleness in performance', *Theatre Topics*, 9:1, pp. 11–30.

Schmidt, T. (2013), 'Acting disabled: Back to back theatre and the politics of appearance', in K. Jurs Munby, J. Carroll and S. Giles (eds), *Postdramatic Theatre and the Political: International Perspectives on Contemporary Performance*, London, New Delhi, New York and Sydney: Bloomsbury, pp. 189–208.

Schmidt, Y. (2015), 'After disabled theater: Authorship, creative responsibility, and autonomy in Freie Republik HORA', in S. Umathum and B. Wihstuz (eds), *Disabled Theater*, Zurich and Berlin: Diaphanes, pp. 227–40.

Seel, M. (2005), *Aesthetics of Appearing* (trans. J. Farrell), Stanford: Stanford University Press.

Shapiro, M. J. (2013), 'Justice and the archives: "The method of dramatization"', in J. Edkins and A. Kear (eds), *International Politics and Performance: Critical Aesthetics and Creative Practice*, London and New York: Routledge.

Shildrick, M. (2002), *Embodying the Monster: Encounters with the Vulnerable Self*, London, Thousand Oaks and New Delhi: Sage Publications.

——— (2009), *Dangerous Discourses of Disability, Subjectivity and Sexuality*, Basingstoke: Palgrave Macmillan.

——— (2015), 'XI death, debility and disability', *Feminism and Psychology*, 25:1, pp. 155–60.

Siebers, T. (2010), *Disability Aesthetics*, Ann Arbor: University of Michigan.

Simplican, S. C. and Leader, G. (2015), 'Counting inclusion with Chantal Mouffe: A radical democratic approach to intellectual disability research', *Disability and Society*, 30:5, pp. 717–30.

Sivier, M. (2015), 'Known number of deaths while claiming incapacity benefits nears 100,000', http://voxpoliticalonline.com/2015/08/27/known-number-of-deaths-while-claiming-incapacity-benefits-nears-100000/. Accessed 10 October 2017.

Smith, L. (2014), *The Old Days*, Aberystwyth University, Aberystwyth, premiere 12 June.

Tomlin, L. (2015), *British Theatre Companies 1995–2014*, London: Bloomsbury.

'Tormented Lives' (2010), R. Monckton, 19 October (UK: BBC One).

Umathum, S. and Wihstutz, B. (2015), 'Prologue: Disabling the theater', in S. Umathum and B. Wihstutz (eds), *Disabled Theater*, Zurich and Berlin: Diaphanes.

Warner, M. (2002), 'Publics and counterpublics', *Public Culture*, 14:1, pp. 49–90.

Wihstutz, B. (2015), '…And I am an actor', in S. Umathum and B. Wihstuz (eds), *Disabled Theater*, Zurich and Berlin: Diaphanes.

Notes

1 The authors make explicit how the current austerity agenda in the United Kingdom and the accompanying benefit cuts appears to be causing increased use of derogatory remarks, reporting and negative perceptions of people with disabilities.

2 Browning (2010).

3 There are two reasons for doubling the person here; the first is that disability scholars and activist recognise that we are Temporarily Able Bodied (TAB) and even without any accident or disease our bodies change with age, and the second is a marker of my own identification as ally with people with disabilities.

4 The DWP released information on 27 August 2015. The relevance of the figures to the exact question is unclear as is the interpretation. Online activist Mike Sivier (2015) offers a digest of the information and states that: 'The DWP has strenuously asserted that "any causal effect between benefits and mortality cannot be assumed from these statistics". It is correct to make

this point'. Nevertheless the headlines statistics are astonishing: 'The Department for Work and Pensions has admitted defeat in its attempt to hide the number of people who have died while claiming incapacity benefits since November 2011 – and has announced that the number who died between January that year and February 2014 is a shocking 91,740. This represents an increase to an average of 99 deaths per day or 692 per week, between the start of December 2011 and the end of February 2014 compared with 32 deaths per day/222 per week between January and November 2011' (Sivier 2015).

5 This comment comes from informal conversation with Professor Adrian Kear and I am grateful to him for constant lively interrogation on themes of representation and appearance that are common to both our research interests.

6 Schmidt uses the term intellectual disability in common with most other European nations, North America and Australia.

7 With regards to dramaturgy as a practice I take my current understanding from Pil Hansen who explains that the challenge of dramaturgy is 'drawing out potential connections while working in process, of engaging with continuously changing materials, and of working without a specific target or conceptual frame' (Hansen and Callison 2015: 6).

8 In conversation with Adrian Kear.

9 I consider this complex notion of the performer not being fully in control of their appearance before an audience in the terms Maaike Bleeker sets out: 'A performance is not a thing but exists only as a dynamic set of relationships. It is from these relationships that what is usually considered the performance emerges' (2015: 76). And then: 'Performances are dynamic sets of relations that transform over time: relations between performers, performers and space, performers and the audience, performers and their costumes, and so on. One might even argue that this set of transforming dynamic relationships extends to include the relationships between performers and themselves' (2015: 76.). Therefore, the performer is only ever in relationship and bound to audience's perceptions.

10 In conversation with Adrian Kear.

11 In conversation with Mike Pearson Emeritus Professor of Performance Studies at Aberystwyth University and founder member of Brith Gof.

12 Simplican and Leader (2015).

Interruption 4

Difference

1 April 2014

Kate Marsh

*I*t is difficult to explore the concept of difference without including an examination of 'normal'. In straightforward terms one cannot exist without the other. Difference exists outside our perception of the 'norm'. It is the unexpected or the unfamiliar. In specific relation to bodies, difference is a manifestation of 'otherness' or blurring of normality. One hand where there should be two, sitting instead of standing, signing instead of speaking.

The image of the 'normative' body is ingrained in our understanding of being human. It is an image that is presented to us through many channels throughout of lives; education, employment, the media – representations of difference in these contexts are largely from a position of segregation. We live in a world where the 'normal' body rules. We are 'accepting' of difference, charitable even, but there is still an underlying narrative of curiosity and freakishness relating to the 'different' body.

On the subject of the narrative of different bodies Garland Thomson suggests that 'Conservative shapes make conservative stories. Extraordinary shapes require extraordinary stories' (Garland Thomson 2009: 167). There seems to be a fascination with difference, we question how difference occurs, captivated by stories of difference, whether through 'tragedy' or 'fate' we want to know the story behind the difference.

It is possible that this interest in difference originates from our socialisation into a culture of normality, when we see difference we want to protect ourselves from it, to hold on to our sense of being 'normal'. By staring and asking questions the different body becomes spectacle and somehow unreal. Being confronted with difference highlights the fragility of 'normality'. In a desire to conform and 'fit in' we disassociate our 'normal' selves from the differentness of others.

We all develop our own understanding of 'normal' through our individual experience of being in the world. By getting up each day and doing the mundane daily tasks I am 'being normal' in my 'bubble' of existence I am my own definition of normal. From the outside, however, I appear different, my shape is 'different' from the 'norm'. My body is unfamiliar to the normative gaze.

Difference is a marker of impairment, it is a characteristic of the disabled person – in medical terms impairment is often referred to as an anomaly, something to be fixed or normalised. This legacy of being perceived or labelled as different has informed the experience of impairment. Being different makes us who we are.

Difference as a currency can be empowering for those with impairment, there is a kudos attached to being away from the 'norm'. We are edgy, exciting, unique, part of an exclusive set, flying in the face of conformity. Of course this is a flawed observation, any examination of *this idea reveals that we are all 'different' having the same 'outline' as another person does not make us the same.*

For me personally, I wear my difference with pride, not necessarily because I feel different, but because my 'difference' is part of my whole being – in my experience of 'normal' life my 'difference' is always there. So I reject the cliché that there is no such thing as difference, I think the difference in all of us is to be embraced and acknowledged. Of course in doing this, the 'difference' becomes 'normal.' In our embodied experience of life we are both of these opposing terms at any time and in any context. Constantly shifting definitions of our selves, our bodies and the world around us.

Reference

Garland Thomson, R. (2009), *Staring – How We Look,* Oxford: Oxford University Press.

Interruption 5

Disability Dance and Philosophy: Liminal Spaces

29 July 2015

Charlotte Waelde

*D*isability Arts is a movement that has been around since the mid-1970s although the exact starting date seems unclear. When it comes to describing what the movement is, Allan Sutherland opines that Disability Art is 'art made by disabled people which reflects the experience of disability'. Sutherland also suggests that without disability politics, Disability Art may not be what it is now:

> I don't think Disability Arts would have happened without disability politics coming first... Our politics teach us that we are oppressed, not inferior... Our politics have given us self-esteem. They have taught us, not simply to value ourselves, but to value ourselves as disabled people.
>
> (Sutherland 1989: 159)

Something of the political flavour of the movement can be gleaned from a blog post that Melvyn Bragg wrote in 2007. In narrating the outcomes of a debate held at the Tate with the motion that 'Disability and deaf arts ought to be dead and buried, i.e. that we are all in the mainstream now', Bragg noted the passion elicited in favour of Disability Arts, going so far as to quote the view of one of the speakers that Disability Arts could be seen as 'the last remaining avant-garde movement' comparable to the early days of feminism and the black arts. More recently, Dadafest, as part of its Congress in 2014, held a debate with the motion 'This congress proposes that Disability Arts is a form of human rights activism and as such only disabled people should be its leaders' (see http://www.dadafest.co.uk/initiatives-projects/current-projects/congress/). The motion was ultimately carried by 31 votes to 26 – a surprisingly close result perhaps.

Where, then, do our dance collaborators stand in relationship to Disability Arts and the Disability Arts movement: does their work sit within this philosophical tradition? Their work is certainly about disability: Falling in Love with Frida (2014) by Caroline Bowditch and Guide Gods (2014) by Claire Cunningham are excellent examples. But we have asked our dance collaborators questions around Disability Arts and the response has been muted. The central focus of their efforts is the same: it is that they all want to make great dance and to be considered great dancers. In other words, they wish to be viewed and evaluated as dance artists equal to other professional dance artists. Their approach is, in essence, apolitical.

Such a response would seem at odds with the philosophy of the Disability Arts movement. In keeping with the politicised nature of the movement, Paul Darke argues that,

> *Disability art philosophy is based upon legitimising the experience of disabled people as equal within art and all other cultural practices' [...] it is 'part of a process of re-presenting a more accurate picture of society, life, disability and impairment and art itself. Disability Art is a challenge to, an undermining of (as a minimum), traditional aesthetic and social values.*
>
> *(Darke [2003] 2014: 132)*

While, as we have argued extensively elsewhere, disabled dance certainly challenges traditional aesthetic values, it is difficult to claim that it also seeks to undermine them in the sense of making traditional aesthetics less powerful or less likely to succeed on their own terms. But if then the philosophy underlying Disability Arts is found wanting when it comes disabled dance, what should we replace it with, and indeed, why should we be concerned with finding philosophical foundations for the work that our collaborators do?

Thinking about the 'why' question first. This goes to the heart of what philosophy is about: it is a quest to find rational arguments to help us to deepen our understanding and knowledge of the world around us and to give us a way of making sense of the world. When we sit within a particular philosophical tradition, it can act both as a guiding principle for our actions, and enable outsiders to better understand what drives and shapes our actions. The brief discussion on the philosophy underpinning the Disability Arts noted above illustrates this point: an artist working within the movement follows an established tradition while at the same time her audience has an intellectual framework to better understand the work.

A quest for a philosophy should not, however, be a sop for an intellectual inferiority complex, reminiscent of the fears of Duchamp who, Copeland reports,

> *[...] seemed to suffer from an intellectual inferiority complex – or at least a fear that the visual arts were perceived as less 'mentally demanding' than the verbal arts. In a remarkable burst of candor, he once admitted, 'the painter was considered stupid, but the poet and writer were intelligent. I wanted to be intelligent.*
>
> *(Copeland 2004: 226)*

Neither should a quest for a philosophy be used to shield a work against aesthetic judgment. As Boyce has noted, there is a mutual dependence between the artistic and philosophical attainment of a work:

> *[...] it is in virtue of what the work achieves as art that it achieves something philosophically important. It is in virtue of what it achieves philosophically that the work succeeds as art.*
>
> *(Boyce 2013: 265)*

A philosophy of disabled dance then can help us to deepen our understanding and knowledge both of the dance and of the philosophy of the dance. A starting point in thinking about what shape that might take, may be to consider the advice offered in the introduction to the collection, 'Thinking through dance: the philosophy of dance performance and practices', edited by Jenny Bunker, Anna Pakes and Bonnie Rowell (2013). In it they tell us that dance as an art form poses unique philosophical questions. These include issues and observations relating to the importance of the human body in dance; of the need to understand the dynamics of agency, the dancer experience and audience understanding; of the collaborative nature of the dance and the individuality of the body; and of the meaning generated in different dance activities – among others. These questions, we are told, become particularly acute as dance enters the academy and starts to test 'traditional assumptions about knowledge' and institutional conventions.

These are all pertinent to disabled dance. But disabled dance raises much deeper enquiries. It also requires us to interrogate ideas around disablism, essentialism, exclusion, voyeurism, otherness, invisibility – among others – and challenges us to find insightful meaning around which the dance, dancers and audiences can coalesce.

We will be exploring these questions in the edited collection as part of our In Visible Difference project and through which we aim to make significant advances in our understanding of the philosophy of disabled dance. Having deepened and broadened our knowledge about the legal frameworks that support the disabled dancer in her efforts, this philosophical enquiry will form yet another part of the mosaic of our understanding about disabled dance and which, cumulatively, will contribute to moving 'Beyond the Tipping Point'.

References

Bowditch, C. (2014), *Falling in Love with Frida*, Dance 4, Nottingham, premiere 29 May.

Boyce, K. (2013), 'The thinking body: Philosophy, dance and modernism', in J. Bunker, A. Pakes and B. Rowell, *Thinking Through Dance: The Philosophy of Dance Through Performance and Practice*, Hampshire: Dance Books, pp. 256–272.

Bragg, M. (2007), 'The last remaining avant-garde movement', *The Guardian*, https://www.theguardian.com/society/2007/dec/11/disability.arts. Accessed 20 October 2017.

Bunker, J., Pakes, A. and Rowell, B. (2013), *Thinking Through Dance: The Philosophy of Dance Through Performance and Practice*, Hampshire: Dance Books.

Copeland, R. (2004), *Merce Cunningham: The Modernizing of Modern Dance*, London and New York: Routledge.

Darke, P. A. (2014), 'Now I know why disability arts is drowning in the River Lethe (with thanks to Pierre Bourdieu)', in S. Ridell and N. Watson (eds), *Disability, Culture and Identity*, 2nd ed., London and New York: Routledge, pp. 131–42.

Sutherland, A. (1989), *Disability Arts, Disability Politics*, http://pf7d7vi404s1dxh27mla5569.wpengine.netdna-cdn.com/files/library/Sutherland-Disability-Arts-Disability-Politics.pdf. Accessed 20 October 2017.

Interruption 6

A Wider Significance for a Philosophy of Disabled Dance?
14 September 2015

Shawn Harmon

*A*s noted by Charlotte in last month's blog, Bunker et al. (2013) argue that dance raises unique opportunities to question: the importance of the human body (in dance); the dynamics of agency and individuality; and the performer/observer relationship. If this is true – and surely it is – it is perhaps more acutely true for disabled dance, which greatly diversifies the bodies and aesthetics on view and the experiences and stories offered for interpretation. That being so, disabled dance might have a surprisingly wide significance – indeed wider than so-called 'mainstream' dance – for these are questions that are directly relevant to much wider concerns around:

- the notions of normality and social acceptance of difference;
- language and dynamism in relation to the human form; and
- the characterisation, availability and mode of (legitimate) interventions into the human body.

And these, in turn, are – or should be – of great interest to medical ethics, and to the larger, though too often blinkered, medical/ethical community.

It has long been assumed that the role of the humanities in medicine is to provide critical reflection on assumptions and predominant metaphors in medicine and the healthcare professions. However, the reality is that the medical humanities have shied away from this role (MacNeill 2011). In fact, Bishop has accused the medical humanities of acting as a 'compensatory mechanism for the mechanical thinking that has dominated and continues to dominate medicine' (Bishop 2008), while Davis and Morris note that the humanities have too readily accepted a boundary between 'biology' and 'culture' (Davis and Morris 2007).

The result has been that medicine, with the connivance of bioethics, has assumed a dubious distinction between fact and value as if medicine (aligned with science) is about fact, and ethics and the humanities are about value. MacNeill, at 87, has reported:

Anyone engaged (as I am each year) in interviewing incoming medical students will know that the 'body-as-machine' and a 'story of restitution' are dominant narratives of students even before entry into a medical course. [...] these are inaccurate and misleading portrayals of medical practice, yet the metaphors have been remarkably resilient.

(MacNeill 2011: 85)

The effect of this acquiescence has been to marginalise the humanities, and the arts, in the healthy evolution of medical and life science development and education practices.

Ultimately, science and the humanities are incomplete without each other (MacNeill 2011). Neither can adequately answer the questions we ask of them without admittance of the insights and interpretations offered by the arts and cultural practices. On this, it has been argued that, 'the biological without the cultural, or the cultural without the biological, is doomed to be reductionist at best and inaccurate at worst' (Davis and Morris 2007: 411).

In short, the arts, in addition to a more critical humanities, are important. Avant-garde art like disabled dance – and some view disabled dance as one of the last avant-garde movements (Bragg 2011) – can only help. But to do so, it must trigger discussions about embodiment and aesthetics that go beyond dance; its questions, its interpretations, its framework of evaluation must bleed into medical and ethical debates and, importantly, medical education.

If it hopes to do this, a sound philosophy of disabled dance – an agreed framework for talking critically about a much wider range of embodiments, creative processes and aesthetics, and lived experiences (on the margins) – is critical not only for improving debates around, and undertsandings of, disabled dance and dance more broadly, but also of the 'divergent' body in society, and indeed the diversity and dynamism of the human body itself. Given this, our efforts within the InVisible Difference project to ensure that a broad range of disciplines contribute to that framework are surely not wasted; indeed Albright and Brandstetter acknowledge that, whilst critical scholarship about dance and disability has expanded, it still remains too narrow, with too little attention paid to how physical difference can radically transform the transmission of embodied knowledge, and to debates about how to dance (Albright and Brandstetter 2015).

And in our pursuit for a philosophy of disabled dance, let us always remain keenly aware of its potential usefulness in expanding our social-shaping medical narratives and our medicine-shaping (bio)ethical assessments.

References

Albright, A. C. and Brandstetter, G. (2015), 'The politics of a prefix', *Choreographic Practices*, 6:1, pp. 3–8.

Bishop, J. (2008), 'Rejecting medical humanism: Medical humanities and the metaphysics of medicine', *Journal of Medical Humanities*, 29:1, pp. 15–25.

Bragg, M. (2011), 'The last remaining avant-garde movement', *The Guardian*, 11 December.

Bunker, J., Pakes, A. and Rowell, B. (2013), *Thinking Through Dance: The Philosophy of Dance Performance and Practices*, Hampshire: Dance Books.

Davis, L. and Morris, D. (2007), 'Biocultures manifesto', *New Literary History*, 38:3, pp. 411–18.

MacNeill, P. (2011), 'The arts and medicine: A challenging relationship', *Journal of Medical Humanities*, 37:2, pp. 85–90.

Section III

Disability, Dance and Audience Engagement

Chapter 13

The (Disabled) Artist Is Present

Claire Cunningham

I have to try to keep my head up, and it's really hard. I spend all my life looking down at the ground. Watching the ground. I'm an expert in surfaces – gravel, slate, tarmac, mossy paths, marble floors in a shopping centre… and the difference it makes when they're wet [...] and cobblestones – exactly where to put the crutch. Always in the joins. I used to set myself goals, like – walk to the next lamppost without looking at the ground. It's really hard. It's… it's unnatural. To look up, and to move. To not see exactly what's under my feet, or more importantly, what's under my crutches. That's just terrifying.

(Cunningham 2008)

Introduction

In the early days of my performing career, initially as a singer, and then later as I began to work in dance, I would often hear the following from audience members after the show: 'You have such amazing presence!', 'Such a powerful presence!'. I hear it phrased this way less often now, and I do not intend in this writing to get into an analysis of the concept of presence (there are far smarter people than me articulating those ideas) but the same sentiment seems to manifest itself still in my hearing from people that they find me an incredibly strong, engaging performer onstage. In my typically cynical way I used to view these remarks, undeniably meant as compliments, as being simply related to voyeurism, to people being drawn to watch me because of my impairment, because I was moving in a way (in a dance context especially) that they had not seen before, or because I was giving them time and permission to look at my body. Or indeed that the spectacle of my movement – the way I danced on my crutches – that I presented new vocabulary to a contemporary dance world in my more 'tricksy' moves (suspensions etc.) was what was engaging to people. I knew myself there was an interesting illusion at times in relation to where my weight was, to gravity. That I was, in fact, a bit like a circus act.

As my work has moved on (I made my first solo, *evolution* in 2007, and my most recent and sixth work *Guide Gods* in 2014b), I have become less interested myself in that more 'virtuosic' movement vocabulary – the moves very much created by the potential of the crutches to suspend the body – (see Figure 1) – and have stripped my work down more and more, and yet I understand that the level of engagement I create in my audiences (at the risk of sounding egotistical) remains. It took a long time to gain the confidence to understand

Figure 1: *Evolution.* 2007, Claire Cunningham.
Photo: Colin Hattersley.

that, to a degree, I do simply have a number of skills necessary for creating reasonably strong performance. I trust now in the originality of my ideas, my sense of timing and dramaturgy, my comfort in being watched, among other things. But I feel there is something else going on for my audiences, in my performances, in my *performative state*, that is the root of this engagement. And that this state is present not only in my own work, but is inherently fused within the performative work of many disabled artists, and it is this that I am curious in this chapter to try to cast light on. I think there are things – both tangible and intangible – within the lived experience of disability itself that many disabled performers through their process, material and live work bring to performance that distinctly shifts the experience of an audience and which is perhaps not present within the work of non-disabled artists, or indeed is partly that which is being perpetually sought by non-disabled artists in their work.

In the last year, I have become more fascinated by the subtlety of my lived experience as a disabled person, the small things, the realisation that my perception of the world is intrinsically shaped by my impairment, as well as the emotional and psychological aspects of growing up with an impairment. From the fact that I spend most of my time negotiating the surface of the world with my head down – looking for hazards my feet might trip on or my crutches slip on, to the understanding that 'my time' is different from the time of someone who walks in a more 'normative' way in relation to distance (e.g. 'a 5-minute walk'). I have only recently become aware of the fact that these understandings are already out in the world – in disability studies circles, in the form of 'crip time' (McDonald n.d.),[1] or in the realisation that what I have been trying to articulate is actually the phenomenology of disability. These things are out there and known among more academic and philosophical circles, but this is not a world I have engaged with beyond my original undergraduate music degree (also significantly a time before I embraced my identity as a disabled person), and is a world I have always found quite alienating and intimidating… so I write here, purely as an artist and not an academic.

The Lived Experience of Disability

I don't remember when I first heard the term 'the lived experience of disability', but it is a concept that has had a profound effect on me, akin to first learning of the idea of the Social Model of Disability (of course still problematic) but making me understand that neither I, nor my body, was inherently 'wrong', but rather that circumstances, attitudes or environments disabled me at times. The concept of 'the lived experience of disability' however began to make sense to me in accounting for all the subtlety of my life as a disabled person. Not only then noticing the difficulties or problems but also the beauty of the observations it created, such as my strange 'geeklike' knowledge of different pavements/terrains from different countries (I know I'm back home in Glasgow as there is unfortunately more spit on the pavements than anywhere else I have been in the Western world!). (See Figure 2.)

I began to recognise all qualities, not simply skills, that my impairment has created in my body and mind, and how this shapes how I negotiate the world.

My medical condition (predominantly Osteoporosis), means my bones are slightly weaker than average. I had a high risk of fracturing as a teenager, and indeed did fracture bones often when I was younger. This instilled a sense of fragility, and a heightened awareness of potential risk – of impact to my legs (the most sensitive area for me), of falling, or being bumped into, of hazardous environments, or indeed people. My spatial awareness therefore grew quite heightened, and when I began to use crutches from the age of 14 my attentiveness for risk/trip/slip hazards became even more refined, as did my spatial awareness in now negotiating 4 'legs', and thus my relationship to the ground began to really develop. This acuity for monitoring for risk meant that my vision became intrinsically linked to my movement – I don't move, or place my crutches, without literally looking where they go. I am very aware of what, and who, is around me at all times – including behind me. I don't 'bump into' people. I read quite well where people are walking, and if they are distracted, in order that they don't bump into me or trip over my crutches (that being more a concern about me than them!), I spot – from a long way off – the drunk person that might fall on me or into me. I read space, I read terrain. I scan constantly for things that might affect where I walk – rain, moss, etc. the hazard of some kids playing football (I am a magnet for being hit with footballs).

Figure 2: Ground studies. Photos: Claire Cunningham.

The need to organise is often part of many disabled people's lives – whether that be the intricate planning required to get from A to B by public transport, using accessible routes, or the need to sequentially organise your possessions in order to prepare to move. For example, I can't put my jacket on and stuff things into my bag *as* I leave a café. I have to put everything away into my bag, put all my clothing layers on, then my bag, then my keys in the correct pocket for later access, etc. *before* putting my crutches on my arms to then walk away. Often the helpful colleague that retrieves my crutches for me as we first move to leave is left waiting – somewhat awkwardly – for quite a while as this whole routine takes place. And it takes time. It takes the time it takes. And I have learned to be comfortable in that, to not feel intimidated or uncomfortable by the queue of people behind me at the checkout waiting for the money to go in the purse, the purse to go in the bag, the bag to go on my back and then to put on my crutches… it's crip time. It's my time. It's deliberate, it's functional, it's efficient. There's no wasted movement – except perhaps when people try to help. It's lived understanding of exactly how something needs to happen. There is problem-solving, efficiency, organisation and experience all in this act – and often this is an act being observed in public.

I spent a lot of my childhood being examined by doctors. Regular visits every couple of months from my earliest years until I was 17 when I refused to go anymore. Countless visits of being questioned, stripped of layers of clothes, introduced to the group of new student doctors every time, being asked to parade up and down corridors while they looked at and discussed my gait, being physically examined, manipulated and demonstrated and photographed. Now this is not that unusual for many disabled children and adults, and not as invasive as many other people have had to experience. But growing up with the constant examination, of being very specifically observed – of 'performing' for the doctors, as well as being watched out in the world by people because of looking a bit 'different', I think potentially has a huge effect on some disabled performers and their way of 'being' onstage. This is also a vital part of the lived experience of disability. The sense of being watched, often perpetually, whenever you leave your own home, and the paradoxical comfort that creates with the act of being observed and the desire to potentially challenge or control that, I think, is a vital part not only of my choice to perform, but also the way in which I am accustomed to it offstage as well as onstage. I have recently begun to speculate as to whether this upbringing might partly have even conditioned me to perform, which startled me as an idea as I had always thought it was about me taking back control, but perhaps not.

If the lived experience of disability potentially requires individuals – often from childhood – to develop a finely tuned understanding of their physicality or sensory abilities, to necessitate a questioning relationship with their body and their surroundings, and then their engagement with it more so than those who are able to engage in a more 'normative' manner, then perhaps the skills that many non-disabled performers seek to learn through drama or dance training are (to my mind) already present within many disabled individuals. And these skills, this embodied knowledge, is present both on AND offstage, and does not simply switch off when the performer is offstage. In fact the disabled artist brings this consciousness to the stage with them, and if as Alva Noë, Professor of Philosophy (and collaborator on my upcoming project with US artist Jess Curtis) suggests our embodiment, our skills and knowledge is how the world 'shows up' for us (2008), then disabled artists bring this world with them into performance. In their very way of being, of being observed. Perhaps it is *this* that an audience becomes engaged by? By that unspoken shift in time, in risk, in awareness, etc. that the disabled artist enacts for them.

Lived Experience – How Does It Manifest?

How then does this lived experience of disability manifest itself in my life? As I stated, I am an artist and not engaged in academic work, so my observations here are based on conversations with other artists and reflections on my own work, but is not 'empirical research' by any means. It is simply the start of my curiosity and triggered by desire to start a dialogue. I began to consider what were some of the observations I could make of how my 'own lived experience of disability' manifests itself:

Being observed

- A self-questioning and examining from a very young age of 'why' I was not 'normal'? Why I looked different? A struggling to accept my physical difference.
- My short stature – due to my impairment – that meant I constantly looked up at the majority of people, even when I reached my full height. A sense of often not being treated as an adult, of being protected by people, and of my own perpetuation of that relationship. Of struggling to feel empowered among people who are literally looking down on you.
- An awareness of being observed often in public, of being a spectacle on arrival into a new space.
- Problem solving – ability to work out ways to carry objects/variety of objects in different ways. Need to plan travel that will not require large amounts of walking or standing.

Risk

- A tuning-in to my own body, in particular to certain parts of my body that were fragile or painful, a recognition of identifying when problems were arising in those places.
- Highly tuned spatial awareness (as mentioned above).
- Dislike of crowds – due to my height, trip/risk potential of other people, dislike of spaces where I cannot place myself somewhere that people will not bump into me, again related to personal perceptions of risk.
- Ability to 'read' surfaces/terrain for walking on with crutches and specific hazards.
- Tendency to orient visual observation specifically to movement of crutches on the ground (i.e. walk with head down).
- Extreme precision in movement, crutches and feet placed very carefully and specifically, degree of 'testing' of surfaces in unfamiliar or risky terrains. Very little 'purposeless' movement, or wasting of energy.

Energy/Time

- Understanding of specific time required for me to travel/walk distances.
- Opportunities to rest when walking are used for observation – looking up and around – enjoying architecture, etc. taking the time to rest/stop.

- Tendency to not talk when walking due to energy it requires, or any other activity when walking (e.g. using phone as hands not free).
- An attentiveness to rationing of energy.

Lived Experience to Artistic Practice

How then might these 'qualities' or aspects manifest themselves in my artistic process, material and performance and that of other disabled artists? First I began to look at what *my* physicality was, what constituted my movement vocabulary? And then with the other artists that I spoke to, what were the lived experiences of their disability/their ways of being in the world?

For the purposes of this chapter I interviewed three other artists:

Caroline Bowditch is a performing artist and choreographer making work with disabled and non-disabled dancers, identifies as a disabled artist with a physical impairment relating to Osteogenesis Imperfecta, and using an electric wheelchair.

Jo Bannon is an artist often working in field of Live Art (so not working within the field of Dance as such but whose work I perceive as highly choreographic). She talks here about the relationship her Albanism has to her work.

Dan Daw is a dance artist and producer, who identifies as a disabled artist with a physical impairment relating to Cerebral Palsy. He was previously a company dancer with Restless Dance Theatre in Australia, then Candoco Dance Company (UK) now creating solo work.

All of these artists make and perform in their own work (although not exclusively).

Environment and Space

One of the main aspects of my way of being/living in the world is my relationship to the ground. The ground is something that is always very present to me, rarely if ever, ignored. I am consistently making an examination of floor/terrain, with a heightened awareness of hazards, an understanding of the specificity of hazard unique to me, and the qualities of different terrain and the effects of environment – such as water on terrain. I exercise a direct visual correlation with the placement of crutches and feet. I asked the other artists about their relationship to the environment around them:

> Like you, I'm very aware of surfaces and constantly looking for kerb cuts, points of access and hazards (having fallen in a pothole and done serious damage to myself). And then there's the whole other thing -about people who have very little spatial awareness, and who don't always see me. There is a real difference between being incredibly visible and completely invisible sometimes.
>
> (Bowditch 2015)

Because of my lack of pigment there's literally not enough filter between light and my retina so light is also a really dangerous thing to me. It's blinding and too much, yet there's this… allure. Like some kind of Icarus fetish. Like wanting to get close to the light and being very light (in appearance) but also that light being the thing that, if I lived in a very different climate, might be the thing that would kill me.

(Bannon 2015)

So how does this then manifest itself through our work and practice?

Relationship to Environment

This concept appears throughout my work in a number of ways – in particular my relationship with the ground. In my work *Mobile* (2008) there is a conscious creation of a space that is hazardous to traverse – that of a space strewn with crutches – that requires care to negotiate, to the description of my observations of terrain, as demonstrated by the text at the start of the chapter.

Pink Mist (2013) – a project looking at the subject of landmines – grew from these being seen by me as objects that created other crutch users, but also constituted a fascinating danger to me as someone so skilled in spotting hazards on the ground, but presented a danger even I could not spot, and the reality that being a crutch user made me more susceptible to damage (four points of contact with the ground, not just two). The research resulted in a work in progress performance in which landscapes were created and crutch ferrules (the stoppers at the ends of crutches) became 'mines'. (See Figure 3).

The work was entirely about the ground – the laying and clearing of mines, a space in which the audience were pushed to consider their own relationship to it, and to have to remove their shoes and therefore lose the 'protection' of shoes in the theatre space. *Guide Gods* (2014b) – took advantage of my need to/habit of focusing on the floor, and creating again a space dangerous to traverse quickly – by placing china teacups across the floor.

The negotiating of the space is made possible by my specific awareness of space and the coordination and precision required for moving four points of contact through and around these objects without damage. It also created a unique environment for me to traverse by walking across the upturned cups (due to my ability to disperse my weight through the crutches and feet and the 'testing' quality I have alluded to earlier). (See Figure 4).

The relationship to environment for me is intrinsically linked to the issue of risk. I asked Bannon about how this might relate to her work:

My materials, the things that I continue to be obsessed with, are things that emit light – lightboxes, pen torches, all different kinds of torches, little home darkroom kits, things

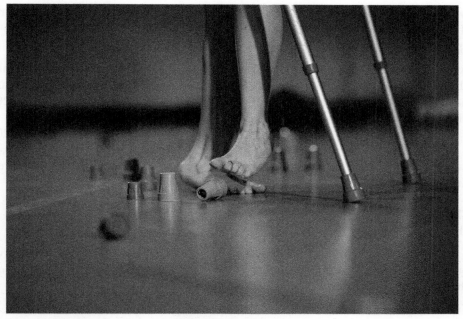

Figure 3: *Pink Mist*. 2013, Claire Cunningham. Photo: Eoin Carey.

Figure 4: *Guide Gods*. 2014, Claire Cunningham. Photo: Colin Mearns Sunday Herald.

where light and dark affects and changes something. I think there's a clear link for me that light is a lifegiver and a beautiful thing, something I want to work with, but it's also ephemeral. You can't hold it. You can't squash it. You can't shape it.

A lot of my works have extreme contrast, black and white, light or dark, and that is absolutely how I think about my eyes. It's easier for me to see in contrast [...] than to navigate subtlety. My eyes cannot embrace the level of subtlety that the level of 20/20 vision can have.

(Bannon 2015)

We are creating environments that are intrinsically suited to us, but that also push directly against our limitations.

The things that are specific to your body and your lived experience are also where I find challenges within my work, to challenge my limits.

I think that there are things you lean into because of your body or because it suits your body, but there are also the things that are pushing *against* how your body functions in the world and that, for me, is a way of provoking yourself.

I've realised recently that I'm often in company, in my personal life, I'm often with someone. I don't do many things alone, and I think that is about feeling fragile in the world, feeling like you might fall or you might not see or you might not visually remember the way home. But then I was thinking , ah yeah Jo but you go onstage alone where there are people just sitting there watching you deal with the hazards of whatever's happening in that space. And I think that relates to when you have to learn to practice to do something really, really well and if you don't learn how to you might burn yourself or whatever. And it's a challenge to be in that space.

My work is really choreographic even though I'm not from a dance background at all, but I think –if I have to go up there and do this thing in front of you – then I will know exactly, and my body needs to know exactly, what to do. Even in *Exposure* (2010), which is set in total darkness, I can find exactly the set, props, action, in one move.

Author: the choreography of your environment is part of it?

Jo: Always.

The senses for me are very heightened, but the visual one for me less so. [...] In my work *Exposure*, the visual sense is taken out for most of it, so it's really about proximity, and the sound and the idea of blackness. What that feels like. Not what it looks like but what it feels like.

So, with how my eyes function in the world I'm much more sensory [...] 'this is the exact dimension I want this to be', and I can count how many steps I take. I use touch a lot, but I've also learned how to hide doing that touch, and how it might just look like I'm just leaning on that wall but really I'm testing 'Are there steps down there? Yeah there's steps', and I do the same on stage. I have to have my obstacles around me.

(Bannon 2015)

I asked Bowditch about how her relationship with her environment might shape her choices in her work (see Figure 5):

I've become interested in what are the other platforms that we can use – rather than just the floor. Hence the box that we've used over and over again in previous pieces, now being up on a table in *Frida*², and all those sorts of things like creating different platforms to work on rather than just thinking about the floor, and that absolutely comes from my physicality and it opens up other options.

(Bowditch 2015)

I discussed with Daw the possibility that perhaps having a heightened sense of spatial awareness might affect our ways of being onstage, or our process, or our awareness of our own physicalities:

I really relate to what you said in relation to having increased spatial awareness. And the specificity of knowing where my body is in place, space and time. Not moving fast

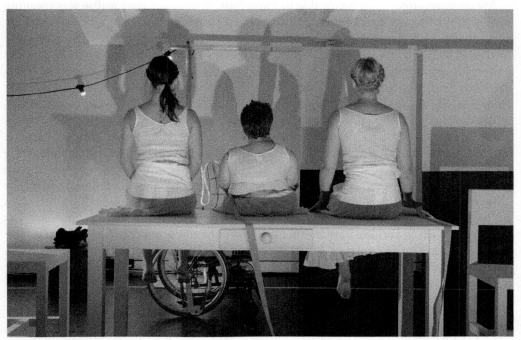

Figure 5: *Falling in Love with Frida*. 2014, Caroline Bowditch (performed by Nicole Guarino, Caroline Bowditch and Welly O'Brien). Photo: Anthony Hopwood.

because that's something that's harder to control. If I'm tired its even harder to control. And also thinking when I create now; 'okay so could I perform this after sitting 3 hours on a train? Okay probably not. Better look at this again tomorrow'. So there's the really practical perspective as well.

(Daw 2015)

Energy

Having been unable to do activities that offered a cardiovascular workout my body is unaccustomed to fast, sustained activity. Such activities require impact on the legs (walking, running, etc.), and this combined with the need – for safety – to visually check where my crutches will land, means it is incredibly rare for me to move very fast. Instead – following the advice of one of my mentors, Bill Shannon – a fellow crutch dancer and choreographer – I learned that moving more slowly meant I widened the frame of reference for my range of speeds (e.g. my fastest then appeared very fast in relation to moving very slow). The energy required to travel using crutches is greater than that of 'normative' walking. Consequently, I always ration my energy quite carefully, it is never 'thrown away' in wild movement, in order that I have sufficient energy to perform through to the end of the work, this is always being carefully monitored and is changeable day to day.

My concern around not being able to move 'fast', of course I now realise was meaning fast in comparison to non-disabled dancers. I had imagined that virtuosity and dynamic performance was intrinsically linked to being able to move quickly. As I have become more interested over the years in the movement vocabulary that is specific to my body, and my body with my crutches, rather than in trying to make my body move like another (non-disabled) body, this has also inevitably meant an understanding of the time that my body takes to do things, and also an enjoyment of that. I have progressively in my works slowed things down, fought the compulsion in 'mainstream theatre' to 'keep it moving', to 'entertain', but rather to start to value giving an audience time to look at an image, time to absorb it and negotiate their thoughts in relation to it. At the same time the processes of investigating my own movement have then meant a desire to work slower – in process too- in order to genuinely feel the movement I am doing, rather than simply progressing through a sequence of moves. The maturing of my relationship to my impairment- to accepting the time it takes for me to do things, to organize myself, and to not force myself to 'other people pace' has manifested itself in various ways in my work; from the unhurried undressing in *evolution* and in *Give Me a Reason to Live* (2014a), the careful building of the mobile made of crutches, the carrying and laying out of the teacups in *Guide Gods*, and the 'standing' scene of *Give Me a Reason to Live*, in which I lay down my crutches and simply stand for as long as I am able to – usually between five and seven minutes. Daw speaks to this theme:

I would say encouraging myself to allow that more time be spent on each task or each body of practice in a sense. So that I've got time to reconnect with my physicality because it does differ slightly every time I go into the studio, so it's as if I'm asking 'so... where am I at today? Okay this is where I'm at today'. When I'm creating I like to have time to gauge those places. I'm really interested now in my performance becoming practice and developing those clear practices, so that in performance I really take my time, like in the studio, to find what it is in there. It's no longer about stringing a sequence of phrases together, that comes later. When I've done the research and the practice on my body then I layer the phrase or the choreography, the form of the sensation... so that I can set in place a score that is totally on my terms and on my timings and timed by me. It's not about aiming to finish by the time the music does. It's about finding other ways.

In *Beast* (2015) for example, all the tracks can be played on a loop or cut short if necessary. The world isn't going to suddenly cave in if I either take too long, or I'm not fast enough.

I really enjoy 'sensing time', I feel a bit that if it is 'to the music' or to counts then I almost feel a bit 'ripped off', because I'm no longer in the present moment, I'm worrying about the counts. That's the thing [...] I'm worried and I shouldn't be worried because it's a work I've chosen to make, and why am I worrying about my own practice?

I think it's really down to time. It's really about the time, the flexibility of the time in performance.

(Daw 2015)

I asked Daw how working independently was different for him in relation to his way of working with his body as opposed to having been in a repertory company (see Figure 6):

To not be in a rush and have that space to breathe and to relax, because my body's a different animal when it's relaxed and that's really interesting for me, as opposed to say the structure in Candoco where it was very prescribed, because I was sharing the space with 6 or 11 other people. Which is also really interesting for me, but sometimes it felt like I was 'keeping up' rather than performing or creating. It was just about keeping up with the choices in the studio and just doing the same thing at the same time.

(Daw 2015)

I asked him, 'does this relaxed body feel like a new exploration? Does this feel like something you haven't really had opportunity to explore before?'

He responded, '[i]t does and it gives me a new access point. It's new but it's familiar as well in an odd way' (Daw 2015).

Turning to the experience of energy, I proposed the idea that perhaps having to monitor or ration our energy in relation to our impairments might also affect or appear within our work to Bowditch:

Rationing is really interesting as a thought. Maybe I do ration energy in a way that I'm completely unaware of because I do just keep going. I just go. And actually I have very little downtime, and I'm not suggesting that that's healthy in any way shape or form, but

Figure 6: *Beast*. 2015, Dan Daw. Photo: Graham Adey.

… it makes me wonder. Perhaps because my every move is measured and every move is considered and that's always been what I've done, how hardwired that is in me actually? I don't know but I wonder if it's been a learned behavior and so, I don't throw myself around, but I do potentially have lots of energy to just continue….

And perhaps that energy isn't physical but it's more brain energy or focusing on things. That's where the energy is being expended more than the physicality. It's spent in keeping that focus.

(Bowditch 2015)

Functional and Precise Movement

My movement is largely generated through my interaction with the crutches, the movement they instigate from my body – this creates very functional vocabulary, there is no 'superfluous'

Figure 7: *Give Me A Reason To Live. 2014*, Claire Cunningham. Photo: Hugo Glendinning.

or simply 'expressive' movement. Crutches are rarely – if ever – taken off the ground. The inability to truly 'feel' through the crutches means that correct placement is not always known until weight is committed, so there is a quality often of 'testing', but to a certain degree I *can* feel through the crutches and there is a degree of testing that comes also from that act (e.g. using the crutches at extreme angles).

My arms are not free to gesture when travelling, placing emphasis on the act of travelling. Activity is largely in crutches and legs. A precision of movement is linked to a sense of protection, to the need to not fall. Additionally the act of falling while on crutches carries the additional danger of not having hands free to cushion the fall. Falling is not a desirable act, but the potential of falling, is engaging to an audience, especially those who are not understanding the mechanics of my movement. The crutches also demand a lot of precision and care in controlling their movement because even 1cm of difference in where the point lands has a huge knock-on affect in terms of the possibilities of movement generated at what is essentially at times a meter-long pivot point. (See Figure 7.)

The relationship with time for myself and the other artists that I spoke to seemed also irrefutably linked to the need or desire for precision and care, which in itself I feel creates a quality in the material it produces (or as Bannon states is actually the material itself), and the effect on an audience's engagement. There is a shift - not only focusing an audience's attention onto detail but also into a different timeframe. Our timeframe. 'Crip time' as McDonald (n.d.) might say.

> There's definitely a carefulness in my work -which is frustrating, 'cause like you say it takes a long time. I spend a long time on stuff, and I think that's to do with feeling like I'm not going on that stage until everything is in my control and decided by me, so a lot of my work is quite meticulous and precise and careful and considered. I'm not saying that those things are qualities or good things about the work. I'm saying that they're almost the material of the work.

> Do you think there's something also there about having a messy body? Like an imperfect sprawling body that falls over and bangs into things, that has fairly ugly equipment attached to it that is like a counter [to the clean space] almost?

> (Bannon 2015)

Autobiography/Self-Questioning

The tendency to put myself at the centre of my work – while to some may appear egotistical – came originally from the fact that when thinking to make my first work I did not feel confident to comment on anything outside my own experience. The natural course for me was autobiography, the tendency to question myself, to have had my body questioned and examined throughout my childhood was ingrained in me. To be contemplated as a problem (literally) by doctors and society perhaps meant that I felt accustomed to that sort of display. I know many artists are horrified by that degree of revelation of themselves. To me I felt I knew no other option.

I have heard disabled artists criticized for their work being too auto-biographical, or predominantly personal. However, I think there is a general reality that partly these are stories that have not been told and therefore have a place on the stages of a diverse society. But again, I think the subtlety of the lived experience that is inherent in these works – beyond what is being literally told or displayed – is something that has a great deal of engagement.

Being Observed

I asked Bannon about the impact being observed throughout her life might have on her work (see Figure 8):

> I think, 'well... if you're gonna have a good look, then you'll have a good look on my terms!', you know to be honest! In *Exposure* that's very evident. I control the light. You literally only look at what you are allowed to look at and when.

Figure 8: *ALBA*. 2015, Jo Bannon. Photo: Paul Blakemore.

A lot of my work is also about hiding. It's about hiding but of course it's also about revealing because it's happening with an audience, so there's something there again that is like the opposite of what my body wants to do and my lived experience and how I want to be in the world.

I think it's also about control. We or I have the experience of living in a world where I often feel different, visually (visibly?) different, and so there's like an opportunity in theatre to literally control the conditions of the world. Literally everything! And create a world that you fit into, both emotionally and meaning-wise but also physically.

(Bannon 2015)

I think there is something in always being observed and there is always an element of performance, all the time. In *Frida* I have a line that says 'you and I are always performing whether they've bought a ticket or not', because we are. People are always watching me and I think there then becomes this internal/external situation. Actually there is a difference between the way I am outside of my home and how I am inside.

I think I become aware of other people's observation of me mainly when I am with someone who is non-disabled who notices how much other people look at me. I think they notice more than I do, and it frustrates the shit out of them. It really disturbs them and I think that I've now got to a stage where I just don't even notice, because it happens so often.

(Bowditch 2015)

The conditioning we may have been subjected to means this may be a quite natural form for our work to take. That, along with the desire to take control of our stories, as individuals constantly being the subject of projected narratives out in the world, the stage gives us the opportunity to take control of that view.

> Having grown up in that way, being watched by doctors and technicians, there's something ingrained in me still about being seen and getting a reward. For having done it well, or having done it right. That goes back to the hospital, to my mum saying 'If you're good at the hospital today you can get that T-shirt I've been promising you' and that kind of thing. Maybe it is tantamount to my practice now! The reward is a good review from the teacher.
> (Daw 2015)

Conclusion

Of course I am not saying that all disabled artists or performers bring these ideas I have tried to articulate here into their work – not all will have a different sense of timing, need for detail or precision, awareness of energy or heightened spatial awareness etc, but I think that some do. And I think some will bring qualities other than those that I am equipped with or that I have touched on here. I think there is often a higher level of attentiveness going on for individuals who are negotiating a different physical or sensory relationship with the world (as so with gender, sexuality, race etc.), but I think that this level of attentiveness brings with it into performance something very nuanced, that is often not being recognised beyond the more obvious and sensational easily perceived aspects of disability. I think this higher attentiveness disabled people engage in order to daily negotiate the world is partly what drama and dance schools the world over are trying to teach their students – being 'present': through developing their spatial awareness, their reading of space and people, being in control, being precise, understanding your body and your energy, being observed and being comfortable being observed. These 'skills' are all inherent to the lived experience of disability, and they don't stop at the wings of the stage, they are not 'switched on' for enacting a role, we bring our world with us to the stage, and I think audiences are seeing/sensing far more than they realize. I try to articulate these ideas because I would like to see the work of disabled artists recognized for more than the superficial, first layer of 'difference' that they might be perceived to be bringing to art, and rather for the nuance and subtlety of the worlds that they bring to and share with audiences.

> There's a brilliant Tim Etchells quote[3] about investment. I see you obsessed in the thing you are doing so I become obsessed with you – that's a misquote but it's about the level of attention that the thing you are doing takes, and of course you can train yourself to do that but if in real life it actually takes a lot more attention from you then you are kind of … well I mean its great to have some cheats in life! Some shortcuts!
> (Bannon 2015)

References

Bannon, J. (2010), *Exposure*, South Hill Park, Bracknell.

——— (2015), interview with author, Edinburgh, 27 August.

Bowditch, C. (2014), *Falling in Love with Frida*, Dance 4, Nottingham, premiere 29 May.

——— (2015), interview with author, Glasgow, 20 September.

Cunningham, C. (2008), *Mobile*, The Furnace, DaDa Fest International, Liverpool, premiere 6 September.

——— (2013), *Pink Mist*, The Arches, Glasgow, premiere 25 April.

——— (2014a), *Give Me A Reason To Live*, CEMENT Festival, 's-Hertogenbosch, Netherlands, premiere March.

——— (2014b), *Guide Gods*, Greater Easterhouse Supporting Hands, Glasgow, premiere 12 June.

Daw, D. (2015), *Beast,* The Borough Hall, Greenwich, premiere 6 November.

——— (2015), interview with author, via Skype, 27 August.

Etchells, T. (1999), *Certain Fragments*, London and New York: Routledge.

Fischer, J., Nüesch, C., Göpfert, B., Mündermann, V., Valderrabano, A. and Hügle, T. (2014), 'Forearm pressure distribution during ambulation with elbow crutches: A cross-sectional study', https://jneuroengrehab.biomedcentral.com/articles/10.1186/1743-0003-11-61. Accessed 15 April 2016.

McDonald, A. (n.d.), 'Crip time', http://www.annemcdonaldcentre.org.au/crip-time. Accessed 16 April 2016.

Noë, A. (2008), 'Life is the way the animal is in the world', https://edge.org/conversation/alva_no-life-is-the-way-the-animal-is-in-the-world. Accessed 15 Februry 2016.

Sandahl, C. (2015), 'Watch & talk group', *Wildwuchs Festival*, Basel, Switzerland, 7 June.

Notes

1 I first encountered this idea during a workshop run by Carrie Sandahl.
2 *Falling in Love with Frida* (Bowditch 2014).
3 (Etchells 1999: 48).

Chapter 14

Disability, Disabled Dance Audiences and the Dilemma of
Neuroaesthetic Approaches to Perception and Interpretation

Bree Hadley

In twenty-first century studies of dance, drama, theatre and performance investigation of the interpretative processes of spectators has become a critical facet of the field. Following the success of Susan Bennett's *Theatre Audiences* (1997), a number of scholars have focused attention on this area – including Bruce McConachie in *Engaging Audiences: A Cognitive Approach to Spectating* (2008), Helena Grehan in *Performance Ethics and Spectatorship in a Global Age* (2009), Helen Freshwater in *Theatre & Audience* (2009) and Caroline Heim in *Audience as Performer: The Changing Role of Theatre Audiences in the Twenty-First Century* (2016), amongst others. Throughout these texts, there is acknowledgement that the spectators who come together to constitute an audience are a collection of individuals, rather than a cohesive whole. Although this represents an advance over prior scholarly practice, in which the perspective of the white, heterosexual, able male spectator was taken as the norm (Butsch 2008), studies of the ways in which specific spectator groups perceive, interpret and make meaning have been slower to emerge. In particular, there has been little analysis of the 'distinctive spectatorial processes, modalities and preferences' (Hadley 2015: 154) of people with disabilities as audiences. Though the presumed spectator in most of these studies may no longer be male, or heterosexual, or white, they are still typically assumed to be able.

In this chapter, I want to consider one emerging approach to spectatorship – the neuroaesthetic approach – through the lens of disability spectatorship. In the twenty-first century, neuroaesthetics is gaining traction amongst scholars looking to provide accounts of spectatorship in less story-based performing arts such as classical and contemporary dance, as well as in more story-based practices in drama, theatre and performance. 'It would be fair to say that neuroaesthetics has become a hot field', as Alva Noë puts it (2011). To date, though, the assumptions that underpin neuroaesthetic approaches to spectatorship have not been brought together with the assumptions that underpin the equally emergent field of disability spectatorship studies. As Carrie Sandahl (2002: 18) has noted, different cognitive, sensory and corporeal abilities result in a range of different phenomenologies, perceptual processes and perceptual preferences that can in turn produce different styles of engagement with experiences, events and objects. These differences impact on how people with disabilities produce and perceive aesthetic performances – somatically, syntactically, symbolically and socially, as disabled people hear with their eyes, see with their fingers, or perceive phenomena vicariously via the intervention of technologies or translators. Accordingly, disability spectatorship, and more detailed attention to the presence of distinctive cognitive, sensory and corporeal processes amongst disabled spectators, has the potential to complicate, extend and challenge assumptions embedded in emerging neuroaesthetic approaches to spectating. In bringing neuroaesthetics together with accounts of disabled people's approaches to audiencing – an awkward neologism for the practices, processes, and relationships that underpin acting as an audience – I want to initiate a conversation about the place of diversity in this emerging field. In doing so, I hope to contribute to equally nascent conversations about the place of diversity in spectatorship and audience studies as a whole.

Spectatorship and Audience Studies

In studies of spectatorship, as Helen Freshwater (2009: 56) says, there is an 'orthodoxy' that holds that the live, physical, co-present relationship between performers and spectators gives live performance special power to prompt spectators to think, feel, and reflect on what they feel. The longstanding tendency to position spectators as co-creators of live performance notwithstanding, it is not until the last decade that a tendency to talk about spectators as individuals within an audience has started to dominate the field. This, Richard Butsch (2008) argues, is a legacy of Western cultural, production and critical practices which sought to control the power of live performance to produce changes of perception amongst spectators by positioning white, heterosexual, able male critics as 'ideal' spectators, articulating 'ideal' interpretations, to help educate an ignorant public. It is a legacy that is problematic philosophically, because it precludes alternative perspectives on the experiences presented onstage. It is legacy that is also problematic practically, because in less story-focused forms – such as virtuosic classical and contemporary Western dance – it alienates spectators who fear they do not have the sophisticated literacy required to perceive and interpret what they see.

In the past few years, the desire to develop more nuanced approaches to audiences and audiencing has led to calls to acknowledge different interpretative practices amongst spectators as collections of individuals – a call answered in some recent philosophically oriented texts on spectating, such as Helena Grehan's *Performance Ethics and Spectatorship in a Global Age* (2009), or my own *Disability, Spectatorship and Public Space Performance: Unconscious Performers* (2014). Though historically, politically and ethically different in approach, what such texts share is an interest in the way individual and cultural histories, memories and habits impact on spectatorship, and the meanings spectators make, in performances that are not complete until the moment of encounter with spectators.

It has also led to calls to develop more empirical, evidenced-based approaches to spectatorship, which, though long seen in film, television and media studies of reception, have not historically been prominent in live performance studies of reception. Again, this call is being answered in empirically oriented audience response research, for example in Caroline Heim's *Audience as Performer: The Changing Role of Theatre Audiences in the Twenty-First Century* (2016), and in many publicly funded research reports that evaluate the effect, value, and value-for-money of spectators' participation in dance, theatre or performance (Hadley 2015).

Finally, it has led to an interest in approaches to audiences and audiencing that take advantage of advances in science to understand the physical, neurological and psychological processes that underpin perception and interpretation – which, of course, is where the questions about neuroaesthetic approaches to audiences in focus in this chapter come from.

Where the field of spectator studies across these various sub-disciplines may be in most need of development, as I have argued elsewhere (Hadley 2015), is in development of approaches that are able to go beyond acknowledging individuality, and start discussing diversity. Although development in this direction is difficult – ethically, politically, as well as practically – it also holds rich potential to add to studies of spectatorship by identifying, unpacking and exploring challenges to seemingly logical theorisations that come from perceptual or cultural differences in response to performance practices. This potential is clear in the few works that have attempted to address the spectatorship of specific groups to date – for example, Matthew Reason's *The Young Audience* (2010), or Jill Dolan's *The Feminist Spectator as Critic* (1988), along with my own recent attempts to start a debate about the spectatorial practices of people with disabilities (Hadley 2015) to add to the strong body of scholarship on the performance practices of people with disabilities that has emerged in the past decade (Kuppers 2004, 2011; Auslander and Sandahl 2004; Kochhar-Lindgren 2006; Davidson 2008; Hickey-Moody 2009; Henderson and Ostrander 2010; Johnson 2012; Hadley 2014). To date, there has been little study of the spectatorial practices of people with disabilities, and no study of the newest neuroaesthetic approaches to audience as applied to the practices of people with disabilities. Though applying a neuroaesthetic approach to people with disabilities may prove the most ethically, politically and practically challenging step in audience studies to date, it may also, in the attempt, shed light on issues critical to the further development of this approach.

Neuroaesthetic Spectatorship and Audience Studies

A largely twenty-first-century lens for analysis of the arts, neuroaesthetics attempts to deploy insights from neuroscience to explain the way spectators perceive, interpret and make meaning of an artwork, including the experiential and emotional dimensions of perceiving and interpreting an artwork. It is, as Susan Broadhurst says, based on 'neurological research directed towards the analysis, in brain-functional terms, of our experiences of objects and events which are culturally deemed to be of artistic significance' (Broadhurst 2012: 225). Taking neuroscientific studies of the link between stimuli and spectatorial response to an object, event or experience as its point of departure (Cross et al. 2011), neuroaesthetics applies these studies to the arts. In recent years, there have been a number of articles on the pros and cons of a neuroaesthetic approach to the arts in general (Chatterjee 2011; Di Dio and Gallese 2009; Brown and Dissanyake 2009; Nalbantian 2008). There have also been articles on neuroaesthetic approaches to visual arts (Kawabata and Zeki 2004; Zeki 1999), and to music (Corness 2008; Juslin and Västfjäll 2008; Provine 2008; Simpson et al. 2008; Molnar-Szakacs and Overy 2006; Brown et al. 2004; Blood and Zatorre 2001; Blood et al. 1999). Most recently, neuroaesthetics has produced what Emily Cross and her collaborators call a 'rich subfield' (Cross et al. 2011) in the performing arts. Several scholars of dance, drama, theatre, performance and other live arts have offered theoretical or empirical studies in this area. In dance, the main contributors include Beatriz Calvo-Merino (e.g. Calvo-Merino et al. 2005, 2006, 2008, 2010), Emily Cross (e.g. Cross et al. 2006, 2009, 2011, 2012), Corrine Jola (e.g. Jola et al. 2008, 2012), Sarah Rubidge (e.g 2008, 2010), Catherine Stevens (e.g. 2005), Ivar Hagendoorn (e.g. 2004, 2010) and Bettina Blasing (e.g. Blasing et al. 2010, 2012), all of whom approach the field from a sports psychology perspective. In drama, theatre, performance and technologically mediated performance, the main contributors include Bruce McConachie (McConachie 2008), who focuses on conventional plays, and Josephine Machon and Susan Broadhurst (e.g. Machon 2009, 2013, 2014; Machon and Broadhurst 2006, 2012) who focus on technologically mediated performance, performance art, live art and installation. Though acknowledging the emergent nature of neuroaesthetics as a field of study, these scholars all signal its potential as a means of analysing how audiences perceive and interpret art works.

Underpinning each of these scholars' work is a desire to examine the way audiences engage with artistic stimuli. This engagement can, as David Freedberg and Vittorio Gallese (2007) say, be quite multifaceted – it can include engagement with the effort it takes a performer to produce a work, with the artistry a performer uses to present particular speech, sound, movement or emotion within the work, or with the socially or symbolically recognisable events a performer depicts within a work. Neuroaesthetic analyses of spectatorship focus attention on the way engagement with these stimuli results in activation of sensorimotor areas or networks in the brain – what Cross and collaborators call the 'Action Observation Network (AON)', combining premotor, parietal and occipitotemporal cortices of the brain (Cross et al. 2011, following Rizzolatti and Sinigaglia 2010; Gazzola and Keysers 2009; Grezes and Decety 2001, amongst other neuroscientists). In neuroaesthetics, the activation of this 'AON' is thought to help spectators perceive and interpret other bodies in action, and, therefore, to be 'a critical element of the [a]esthetic response' (Cross et al. 2011: 1).

Most neuroaesthetic studies of dance, drama and theatre spectatorship to date concentrate on what neuroscientists – in particular, Giacomo Rizzolatti (Rizzolatti and Craighero 2005) and Christian Keysers (Keysers 2009; Keysers and Gazzola 2010) – call 'mirror neurons'. At its most basic, the theory of mirror neurons suggests that when spectators and performers come together in the moment of performance 'th[e] perceptual representations of the observed action are mapped to motor representations of the observer's own action repertoire' (Sebo et al. 2011: 607). In lay terms, a dance performance stimulates sensorimotor areas of a spectator's brain, activating the neural connections the spectator might use to embody the movement they see, at the moment they see the dancer doing it – and thus, the theory goes, allowing the spectator to imagine themselves embodying the same speech, sound or movement, a phenomenon integral to appreciation of the aesthetics of dance. The general theory emerges, James Kilner and Chris Frith (2008: 32) explain, from theories of perception that go as far back as pragmatist philosopher William James, who argued that 'every mental representation of a movement awakes to some degree the actual movement which is its object (James 1890)' (Kilner and Frith 2008: 32). Those who study mirror neurons are interested in the way this aspect of brain architecture 'may constitute a neural bridge between action and perception' (Hagendoorn 2004a: 80). A bridge which, if proven to exist in humans, may be responsible not just for perception, and interpretation, but for phenomena like empathy, shared emotion, and shared enjoyment of speech, sound and movement sequences – including the ability 'to anticipate others' intentions "intuitively"' (Rubidge 2010: 9) – which arise when performers and spectators meet. The potential of this hypothesis leads scholars to make a range of claims about its power in dance spectatorship. These range from the relatively cautious suggestion that '[i]f this hypothesis is correct when watching dance the observer is in a sense virtually dancing along' (Hagendoorn 2004a: 95), and this 'dancing along' is at least partly responsible for their appreciation and pleasure. To the rather more cavalier suggestion that 'mirror neurons make dance appreciation possible' (Blakesee and Blakesee 2007:170), and, therefore, that 'dance demands an agility of perception equal to the agility of the dancers[, i]t requires good mirror neurons' (Blakesee and Blakesee 2007: 170).

In dance, the first evidenced-based neuroscientific studies of the mirror neuron hypothesis emerged in the early 2000s. Beatriz Calvo-Merino studied professional dancers, who were asked to watch dance movements in their own style – classical Western ballet or Capoeira – and also in another style (Calvo-Merino 2008: 4). A functional magnetic resonance imagining (fMRI) scan was used to monitor brain activity. The study, according to Calvo-Merino, showed that a 'dancer's expertise in movement execution (motor domain) corresponds to movement perception (visual domain)' (2008: 8). Calvo-Merino was quickly joined by colleagues and occasional collaborators Cross, Jola, Rubidge and Stevens, conducting similar studies separately or together. Over the years, their studies, both empirical and philosophical, have often focused on similarities and non-similarities in movement perception in dancers (e.g. Cross et Al. 2006; Calvo-Merino et al. 2005, 2006), male and female dancers (Calvo-Merino et al. 2006), non- or novice dancers (Cross et al. 2009a, 2009b, 2011; Calvo-Merino 2008), and people who regularly watch but rarely take part in a particular dance practice (Jola et al. 2012), differences between the groups (Jan 2011; Cross et al. 2011; Blasing et al. 2010), and what happens when people are taught to do a movement then watch others do what they have been trained to do (Kirsch et al. 2015). About five years into evidence-based study in the field a number of the biggest players – Calvo-Merino, Cross, Jola, Stevens, and Blasing amongst others – collaborated on a 'state of the field' style review on the application of cognitive science to dance in light of these studies (Blasing et al. 2012).

In each of these studies, the neuroaesthetic approach leads researchers to look for positive or negative correlations between what Steve Brown and Ellen Dissanyake (2009: 51) call 'exteroceptive' or external perception of the speech, sound and movement of the performer and the 'interoceptive' or internal perceptions felt by a spectator. In the evidence-based studies, these correlations are examined via fMRI images of activation of the 'AON'. The presence of dancers and non-dancers as participants enables the researchers to examine the way in which prior experience with particular movements, and personal ability to perform particular movements – that is, 'perceived physical ability to reproduce the movements they watch' (Cross et al. 201: 1) – impacts on a spectator's engagement with, enjoyment of, and thus overall perception and interpretation of dance movements. The studies report that the fMRIs show a bigger, better brain response from dancers who have the ability to perform the movement they are watching (e.g. Cross et al. 2006, 2009a, 2009b, 2011; Rubidge 2010; Calvo-Merino 2005, 2006). For example, female dancers respond strongly to the movements they usually perform, male dancers respond strongly to the movements they usually perform, and classical dancers respond strongly to the movements they usually perform, at least in terms of level of reported preference for, pleasure in, and intensity of engagement with the experience. The studies also report that the fMRIs show a bigger, better brain response from regular spectators of the specific dance form in focus, compared to novices, suggesting that prior experience of seeing a movement also heightens empathy, emotional resonance and 'tendency to imaginatively transpose oneself into fictional characters' (Jola et al. 2012: 1). Some, such as Seon Hee Jan, read this as evidence that activation of 'autobiographical memory' (Jan 2011: 275) acquired during prior experiences of watching, reflecting and reporting to family, friends and colleagues on the dance form is activated when regular spectators watch dance movements they have seen before. Others, such as Cross (Cross et al. 2011: 1), read this as evidence that understanding the energy, effort and training required to produce a prized movement pattern is activated, and contributes to appreciation, when spectators watch dance movements they have done or at least seen done before, so they have direct understanding of how difficult they are to produce, and thus of how powerful or virtuosic the performers producing them are.

Most recently, scholars have started to examine spectatorial perception of non-human movement, or at least non-naturalistic movement – for instance the movement of robots (Cross et al. 2012; Miura et al. 2010). Naoki Miura and collaborators, for example, found that normal, able people's perception of awkwardness, as might occur when watching a pre-programmed robot – or, though they do not attend to it, a disabled person – makes movement 'strange' (Miura et al. 2010: 41), hard to understand, and thus impacts on transmission of 'aesthetic qualities in dance performances' (Miura et al. 2010: 40).

While Calvo-Merino, Cross, and other first-adopters of neuroaesthetics come from sport psychology, their studies have informed the work of arts scholars more interested in how physical, social, and cultural processes come together in spectatorship. As Andrea Brassard notes, Westerners have long favoured the notion that astute acting comes from 'astute observation and understanding of others as well as oneself' (Brassard 2008: iii). It is, therefore, theoretically possible that mirror neurons play a role in the way actors use observation to guide their speech and gestures, as well as the way spectators use observation to perceive and interpret the actors' speech and gestures. This, Amy Cook agrees, means mirror neurons may be 'responsible for action understanding, intention, emotional attunement, communication, joint action, and imitation' (Cook 2007: 590) in performance. For example, mirror neurons may help explain why '[w]hen we witness an actor picking up a telephone and moving it upward, it is the MNS that tells us whether she/he does so in order to answer the phone or swing it' (Cook 2007: 588). Indeed, Cook argues that mirror neurons 'might even help to explain the pleasure for spectators of laughing, clapping, and standing together' (Cook 2007: 590). It is this territory Bruce McConachie approaches in *Engaging Audiences*, where he applies a neurocognitive approach to audience appreciation of story, plot and character in theatre, bringing it together with cultural aspects of audiencing. According to McConachie, there is 'strong evidence that it is audiences who mirror the actions of those they watch onstage' (2008: 72), so neurocognitive studies are a necessary step forward in the audience studies field. McConachie's study takes Gestalt psychology ideas about the brain's ability to cohere complex stimuli into a meaningful whole, and make differentiations between patterns, foregrounds, backgrounds and different areas of focus, as his point of departure. However, he then moves from physiology, and psychology, to more philosophical argument about how neuropsychological precepts and cultural precepts come together in spectating. For McConachie, both play a part in spectators' perception and interpretation of what they see onstage. The Gestalt precepts the brain projects onto stimuli are joined by the cultural precepts that 'helps people learn what to pay attention to' (McConachie 2008: 122). This means past, present and anticipated future encounters with similar stimuli in dance, in drama, or in daily life play a part in the way spectators perceive and appreciate patterns in speech, sound and movement onstage – the way they interpret the inflection of speech or the intensity of gesture, and the way they interpret the formal systematisation of speech, sound and gesture into a 'choreography' or 'dramaturgy' informed by cultural rules for representing events, experiences and emotions on stage. McConachie uses the term 'conceptual blending' (McConachie 2008: 43) to describe the way past, present and future precepts come together when spectating. He positions this blending as particularly important when interpreting contemporary performance, where patterns emerging from the fictional relationships between characters are frequently interrupted by patterns emerging from the factual relationships between the performers, and by meta-reflections on the links between the two (McConachie 2008: 47). Though McConachie mainly analyses traditional theatre, other scholars, most notably Josephine Machon and Susan Broadhurst (2006, 2009, 2012, 2013, 2014), have looked at how neuroaesthetics might help understand spectators' engagement with performance art, live art, installation and technically mediated performance practices, where linear narratives to lead meaning-making are less likely to be available.

These neuroaesthetic studies all point to a positive correlation between performance and perception, which plays a part in the way a performance provokes a reaction in a spectator's brain. 'Evidence is accumulating to support the hypothesis that *observing* an action involves the same repertoire of motor representations that are used to *produce* the action' (Stevens and McKechnie 2005: 247, original emphasis) as Catherine Stevens and

Shirley McKechnie say. The finding, clearly, is that the experience of dance is enhanced by being able to do dance. Spectators prefer and take more pleasure in movements they have done before, what Louise Kirsch calls 'motor familiarity' (Kirsch et al. 2015: 130), or from movements they have seen before, what Kirsch calls 'general familiarity' (Kirsch et al. 2015). Both contribute to a viewer's liking of a movement, and, as a result, 'to a viewer's aesthetic appraisal' (Kirsch et al. 2015: 130). The phenomenon is akin to what other dance scholars call 'kinaesthetic empathy' – that is, the feeling of empathy that comes from watching or otherwise vicariously engaging with another person while they move (Reynolds and Reason 2012; Strukus 2011; Warburton 2011; Reason and Reynolds 2010). Scholars suggest that the more a spectator can feel 'kinaesthetic empathy' with the dancer, the more they can feel pleasure and enjoyment (Jola et al. 2012: 33). At this stage, though, the spectators comments about the activation in their brain in the fMRIs in scientifically based studies of mirror neurons relate only to appreciation, or pleasure, not to more nuanced accounts of aesthetic quality, entertainment, enjoyment, catharsis, ability to provoke a change of perception, or other more complex aspects of meaning-making. The connection between these studies, and the broader implications of these studies considered by the more theatrically oriented scholars, remain the subject of conjecture. Nevertheless, the studies to date provide evidence enough for scholars such as Rubidge to assert that mirror neurons are 'an element of aesthetic response' (2008: 6) to both figurative and non-figurative artworks, because, as Stevens and McKechnie argue, they can 'activate a semantic network associated with the meaning of particular gestures and actions' (Stevens and McKechnie 2005: 247).

Neuroaesthetic Spectatorship and Audience Studies – Potentials, Assumptions, and Problems

With the assumptions outlined here at its core, the neuroeaesthetic approach to spectatorship hinges on the notion that an audience member's ability to imagine themselves embodying the same movement, sound or speech they see on stage, and, in doing so, fire off the same synapses and neural connections they would use to embody those movements in their brain, is integral to appreciation of the aesthetics of dance performance.

The appeal of this approach lies in its ability to offer a new angle to address thorny questions of aesthetics, and is strong amongst scholars interested in less story-based performance forms, where experiential engagement with bodies in motion in space in sometimes highly stylised ways – as opposed to narrative exposition – is central. The neuroaesthetic approach allows for empirically-based studies of reception that have historically been lacking in dance, drama and theatre, as compared to film and television. It allows for STEAM (Science, Technology, Engineering, Arts and Mathematics) collaborations, where artists and scientists come together (Cross et al. 2014). It also opens paths to new and potentially more rigorous justifications of the value of engaging with the arts, including the therapeutic benefits of engaging with the arts (Tortora 2011; Overy and Molnar-Szakacs 2009; Berrol 2006).

The approach has, though, also been criticised for 'achiev[ing] critical recognition without much antecedent theoretical support' (Broadhurst 2012:225). In the sciences, the existence of 'mirror neurons' in human beings remains an area of debate, with some recent reviews suggesting the evidence is 'weak' (Turella et al. 2009; Dinstein et al. 2008). Some say that while 'research based on single-cell recordings allows for unlimited content attribution to mirror neurons' (Sebo et al. 2011: 607), their role in more complex action, interaction and perceptual correlations remains understudied. Indeed, some studies have failed to find correlation between acts a person executes themselves then observes executed in others (Lingnau et al. 2009: 9925), or failed to find it when the action is new or complex (Kilner and Frith 2008: 32). This leads some to suggest that the actual, real-life processes may be too complex – physiologically, psychologically and culturally – to account for in terms of sensorimotor activation of similar areas in performer and spectator brains. Accordingly, Remy Debes and others have issued 'a call to revise the mirrored understanding claim, whether in neuroscience, psychology, or philosophy' (Debes 2010: 219), until the 'myth of mirror neurons' (Hickok 2014) has been subject to more rigorous research (Hickok 2008, 2014; Vivona 2009). 'Unfortunately', Gregory Hickok says, 'more than 10 years after their discovery, little progress has been made in understanding the function of mirror neurons' (Hickok 2008: 1241). Accordingly, Jeanine Vivona agrees, '[t]he present state of mirror neuron research may offer us new hypotheses or metaphors, but does not provide empirical validation of the proposed models' (Vivona 2009: 525).

While assessment of the scientific claims of this research is best left to scientists, it is interesting that discussion about the limitations of the mirror neuron hypothesis often occurs in the context of disability science, and, in particular, autism spectrum disorder science (Rizzolatti et al. 2010; Keysers 2009; Dinstein et al. 2008). The presumption in mirror neuron studies is that 'children with autism process the actions done by others in a manner different from that of TD [typically developing] children' (Rizzolatti et al. 2010: 231). The mirror neuron hypothesis is, as Maxine Sheets-Johnstone says, 'contingent on morphology' (2012: 385) – on morphological sameness between performers' and spectators brains' – and people with disabilities present challenges to this, whether through atypical brain patterns, atypical perceptions, or atypical correlations between the two. A problem which, though broached in the scientific literature, is not broached in the dance literature to date.

Although arts scholars have broached the 'pitfalls' as much as the potentials of neuroaesthetics (Nadal and Pearce 2011), the subjectivity of responses tends to be located in the cultural rather than the physical aspects of perception. In the evidenced-based studies of Calvo-Merino, Cross, and others, for instance, this difference is linked to the degree to which audience have been culturally educated to understand the dance form they watch. As Calvo-Merino puts it, '[a]n audience is essentially a number of independent observers. Each observer may process the dance performance in their own, highly subjective way. However, *humans share a basic common neural mechanism comparable among individuals*' (Calvo-Merino 2008: 8, added emphasis). Calvo-Merino therefore concedes, '[m]uch more work is needed before we can start to fully combine in an experimental setting all the elements that ultimately form a dance performance' (Calvo-Merino 2008: 9). Hagendoorn agrees, conceding that so many parts of the brain 'light up' (Hagendoorn 2004a: 96) when watching a dance performance, based on so many complex stimuli, perceptual systems, and social experiences, that testing assertions in an experimental setting is near impossible. In this sense, though evidence-based experiments to date do engage with difference: it is the difference between dancers and non-dancers, or between non-dancers who have been educated in dance and non-dancers who have not. There is still a presumption that all 'share a basic common neural mechanism'. The studies pick 'physically and neurologically healthy young adults' (Cross et al. 2011: 1) to ensure this. There is no account of the difference between, for instance, the neurotypical spectator who has education in ballet, and the neuroatypical spectator who has equal education in ballet, and how that complicates the matter. In McConachie's study, there is acknowledgement of potential gender and racial differences, but, as Machon (2014) says, there is room for criticism about lack of detail. Others, like Brown and Dissanyake (2009), are more forceful in their criticism of lack of attention to a range of different differences in neuroaesthetic studies of audiences. For them, understanding of 'the tremendous ambiguities inherent in the terms "aesthetics" and "art"' (Brown and Dissanyake 2009: 43) is so lacking in neuroscientific studies, they become 'inappropriate and misleading' when considering the differences in aesthetics across times, cultures and communities. Neuroaesthetics fails to tell us how perceiving the symbolism embodied in art objects, events and experiences is different to perceiving other events, fails to acknowledge the instrumental as well as intrinsic qualities of arts events, and turns on understandings of empathy and emotion that are unproven (Brown and Dissanyake 2009: 44–45). Other scholars, like Katarzna Kaczmarcsyk (2014), and Noë (2011), are suspicious of neuroaesthetics for similar reasons, suggesting they are based on presumptions about human consciousness that science has never been able to prove, and can at best tell us something about preferences, not about aesthetic perceptions. 'What is striking about neuroaesthetics is not so much the fact that it has failed to produce interesting or surprising results about art', Noë says, 'but rather the fact that no one – not the scientists, and not the artists and art historians – seems to have minded, or even noticed' (Noë 2011).

The criticism hinges on the fact that although many neuroaestheticisans do acknowledge the physical and cultural aspects of cognition, and the part cultural memory plays in cognition – what I, following Pierre Bourdieu (1997, 1998) have often called the spectator's habitus (Hadley 2014, 2015) – they do not attend to differences on either front enough.

Assumptions of Neuroaesthetic Audience Studies

The assumption that spectators share a standard neural system clearly poses dilemmas when it comes to the question of how spectators with cognitive, sensory and corporeal differences – who are more present in spectator populations than mainstream scholars tend to acknowledge – perceive and interpret dance. It risks suggesting that if a dancer, choreographer, dance theorist or long-time dance lover becomes disabled, so their brain synapses can no longer fire in a supposed standard way, their ability to perceive, interpret and offer analysis of the aesthetics of a dance performance by abled bodied dancers is somehow diminished. Plus, equally problematically, that if a dance audience member is able, their ability to perceive, interpret and analyse the aesthetics of a dance performance by a disabled dancer with different neurosensory processes is somehow diminished. That the experience will always be strange, or difficult to understand, or somehow less powerful, pleasurable or kinaesthetically engaging, because the performer and the spectator cannot activate the same aural, visual, kinaesthetic, haptic or proprioceptive senses in the brain when they perceive each other. A set of dilemmas that, if not further unpacked, risks again excluding people with disabilities from mainstream dance production, reception and criticism.

Participating in dance, drama, theatre or performance in any capacity – as a creator, performer, critic or audience member – remains challenging for disabled people (Hadley 2014, 2015). Partly because disabled people rarely see themselves depicted onstage, or, if they do see themselves depicted onstage, it is an able-bodied dancer's stereotyped portray of disability. Partly because the buildings in which dance traditionally takes place are inaccessible. Plus, of course, partly because the buildings in which dance takes place demand modes of spectatorship that are problematic – the ability to sit in the dark, still, quiet, for a set period of time, and see, hear and sense the dancers' performances from a distance, without noise from translators whispering, or light from surtitles shining, or stops and starts while specific audience members catch up on the action, 'disrupting' the show too much.

In the past three decades, the work of activists calling for intuitional and legislative change in this area have certainly led many powerholders – in the arts, and beyond – to acknowledge the need to provide better access to disabled people. At this stage, though, as Margrit Shildrick (2012) argues, these policies, protocols and laws only prompt institutions to offer reasonable accommodation within current institutional structures – a special entrance, a special seat, a special session with interpreters – not to change institutional, social, or ideological norms to be more inclusive of different modes of spectating as par for the course rather than as a special case. With the exception of emergent work in 'relaxed theatre' for disabled audiences (Kempe 2015), the spectatorial modes and preferences of disabled people remain a problem to be dealt with, rather than a potentiality to be developed, explored and experimented with in most approaches to spectatorship, including neuroaesthetic approaches.

Which is a shame, given what consideration of – as opposed to pathologisation of – a wider range of perceptual practices could offer to studies of spectating in general, and neuroaesthetic studies of spectating in particular. While the term disability covers a range of different differences, most disabled people do spectate differently – they 'need to be closer to things, further from things, see things, touch things, translate things into different formats, to perceive and interpret their worlds' (Hadley 2015). Expanding neuroaesthetic approaches to examine these differences would encourage attention to a number of new areas. It would encourage scholars to attend more to multi-channel, multi-discursive and multi-disciplinary communication as part of the aesthetics of dance performance. Because, in disability spectatorship, multi-modal communication to suit different perceptual systems is the norm. It would encourage scholars to attend more to cross-sensory translations – the question of synesthetics as well as the question of kineasthetics – because, in disability spectatorship, seeing with ears or finger-tips, hearing with eyes, sensing through the technological mediation of a screen, a sensory augmentation device, or simply another language, is the norm. It would encourage scholars to attend more to the 'blurring' of boundaries between reality, representation and meta-level reflection on representation within a performance. Because, in disability spectatorship, meta-level reflection on the pros, cons and confusions of different stimuli, symbolic systems and communication systems, along with gaps, delays, commentary and sometimes conflicted debate about the rhythms and relationships that subtend different communication systems, is the norm. The range of different differences involved in disability spectatorship come together to create a type of performance, and a type of spectatorship, where meta-reflection on spectatorship, including both our own and our fellow spectators spectatorship – the very thing many scholars of spectatorship appreciate most in the postmodern, participatory practices they study (Hadley 2014, 2015; Bennett 1997) – is the norm. Finally, attention to difference would encourage scholars to attend more to relationships not just between stage and spectators, but also between one spectator and another spectator. Because, in disability spectatorship, the real-time negotiation of the rhythms, continuities and discontinuities of different perceptual systems makes spectators more aware of other people's ways of perceiving, interpreting and making meaning and whether these ways do or do not match up with their own ways.

The implications of attention to disability in audience studies – including neuroaesthetic audience studies – come out, for instance, in Tony McCaffrey's descriptions of the way spectators respond to disabled performers. In many of his articles, McCaffrey (2011, 2012, 2014, 2015) eloquently conveys spectators' feelings when watching disabled performers. For example, the bullying of a small, shaky, mostly non-verbal character played by a seemingly palsied Sarah Mainwaring by two other characters in Back to Back Theatre's *Food Court* (2008) (McCaffrey 2011, 2015), a still shaky Mainwaring attempting to insert a microphone into a stand in Back to Back Theatre's *Super Discount* (2013) (McCaffrey 2015), or Julia Hausermann from Theatre Hora introducing herself at the beginning of Jerome Bel's *Disabled Theater* (2012) with downcast eyes and disruptive but strangely beautiful hand gestures he could not himself repeat (McCaffrey 2014), amongst others. For McCaffrey, 'performance' is 'an activity which, even in its most resistant and postdramatic forms, generally presupposes a virtuosity dependent on cognitive abilities' (McCaffrey 2012: 9). Our field presupposes that it is difficult for disabled people to play a choreography, persona or character other than their own, because their body will not disappear smoothly into that choreography – and, of course, that it is easy for able people to play other than themselves because their body will. The power of the encounter between able and disabled in performance lies, McCaffrey contends, in the fact that it reminds us that this preference for performers with supreme physical, neurological and psychological abilities, who succeed in doing difficult movements spectacularly well, instead of struggling to do daily movements – the preference for movements 'both [a]esthetically pleasing and difficult to reproduce' (Cross et al. 2011: 1) neuroaestheticians note – is just that, a cultural preference, rather than an acultural perceptual phenomenon. The encounter forces spectators to reflect on perceptions and misperceptions that can happen when able and disabled encounter each other – whether it is a disabled spectator misperceiving shakes, shuffles, shimming or stutters as a fact of physical life when the performer wanted it to stand as a sign of 'nerves,' or an able spectator misperceiving shakes as a sign of anxiety, nerves, stress, deceit, weakness or vulnerability when it is simply a physical fact of life. McCaffrey describes how movements a spectator finds strange can be both discomforting and captivating at the same time. How they can acquire an aesthetic quality that keeps a spectator on the edge of their seat, caught up in a palpable tension created by uncertainty about whether an attempted gesture, act, or interaction will or will not come to completion in the way they expect it to. For McCaffrey this tension, uncertainty, or 'precarity' (2012: 3) forces spectators contemplate the feeling of 'a strong *affective force* experienced in the encounter between able and disabled' (McCaffrey 2012: 18–19), between neurotypical and neuroatypical, and, as a result, contemplate the personal, political and ethical implications of their readings of those they cannot not mirror. A tension that can often be equally clear, and equally viscerally compelling to able spectators, to disabled spectators, and to long-time disability performance spectators with experience of the disjunctions that characterise these encounters, albeit likely in different ways.

These spectating experiences draw attention to the power of mismatches, and negative correlations between performer and perceiver, not just to the power of matches, and the positive correlations between performer and perceiver, that neuroaesthetic scholars have emphasised to date. They show that mismatches may be as powerful as matches in activating the 'action observation network' neuroaestheticians seek to study. They speak to the complexities of the somatic, intersubjective relationships that subtend human communication – in dance and in daily life – as reality, representation and access requirements collide.

The power of mismatches is shown not just in studies like McCaffrey's, but in the practice of choreographers who have found themselves fascinated by the prospect of asking their able-bodied dancers to don a disabled body, and a set of disabled movement patterns, to try to generate something of the palpable tension, attention and activation of the 'AON' the encounter between able and disabled can produce. For example, choreographer Marie Chouinard's *bODY rEMIX / gOLDBERG vARIATIONS* (2005). In *bODY rEMIX* Chouinard has able-bodied dancers moving with crutches, canes, walkers and other contraptions to produce a highly aestheticized portrayal of the human body gone awry, not because these prosthetics are part of able dancers own movement reality – as they are the case of well-known disabled dancers like Bill Shannon in the United States or Claire Cunningham in the United Kingdom – but to make a metaphor for what dancers feel when their body changes or becomes mutant during dance training (Hadley 2014). To confront spectators with a set of corporeal mismatches and miscorrelations, which are awkward, but, at the same time, productive, and aesthetically pleasurable, both for the dancer, and for the spectator. The question of whether Chouinard's construction of an encounter between able spectators and pretending-to-be-disabled dancers achieves anything approximating the palpable tension McCaffrey identifies encounters between able and disabled aside (Hadley 2014), the very fact of the Chouinard's fascination with these phenomena points to their potentialities. To the fact that, while the neurons of disabled people may be wiring and firing 'in different configurations' (McCaffrey 2014: 6), meaning the perceptual agility of the spectator does not match the dancers, the lack of neural mirroring or matching may not always diminish appreciation or aesthetic pleasure.

Conclusion

Addressing disability, difference, and non-mirroring as an affective force in neuroaesthetic approaches to spectatorship is, as I have noted throughout this chapter, a possibility scholars working in this field have not discussed to date. Yet, as these preliminary thoughts demonstrate, drawing on research into the different modes of spectating of disabled spectators, to initiate conversation about these critical questions of diversity, has rich potential to contribute to the emergent field of neuroaesthetics. It has the potential to help scholars start to consider the question of whether the mismatches as well as the matches that come about in the complex, intercorporeal encounter between performer and perceiver could be part of the power of live performance. To consider whether uncertainties about when, whether and how mismatches or matches will come about in a dance performance – a live performance that cannot be complete until the moment the performer and the spectator meet – might in fact contribute to activation of spectatorial interest in or appreciation of a dance performance. If not to the thornier questions of aesthetics. In this sense, considering disability, difference and non-mirroring could in fact help neuroaestheticians move beyond current findings in the field, where the complexity of spectators' identity positions and perceptions are still rather reductively conceptualised in terms of experts versus novices, dancers versus non-dancers, males versus females, or other binary terms, rather than in terms of wider range of individual intersectionalities of gender, sexuality, race, class and (dis)ability present in each of us as we watch a dance performance. Plus, of course, it could also help neuroaestheticians begin to consider how both relationships between stage and spectator, and relationships between one spectator and another spectator, contribute to appreciation, pleasure, provocation or enjoyment in a live performance encounter. At this stage, in a chapter designed to initiate a conversation rather than come to a conclusion, it is hard to predict what sort of impact this might have on the field of neuroaesthetics – for instance, while most of the studies tell us that they recruited 'healthy' spectators, to watch a dance live or via a video, they do not tell us whether they watched together or separately, whether they had any awareness of the way their perceptions matched or mismatched others perceptions, and what impact this had on appreciation or activation of perceptual networks. As neuroaesthetic approaches gain traction, though, attention to these issues has clear potential to provide new impetus to study, in a field where there is such a clear desire to understand spectators as collections of individuals rather than as undifferentiated masses whose perception, interpretation, and meaning making can be spoken for by single, dominant, and to date mostly able spectators.

Acknowledgements

I would like to acknowledge the work of Morgan Batch, the research assistant who helped identify the scope of literature in mirror neuron studies discussed in this chapter.

References

Auslander, P. and Sandahl, C. (eds) (2004), *Bodies in Commotion: Disability and Performance*, Ann Arbor: University of Michigan Press.

Back to Back Theatre (2008), *Food Court*, Malthouse Theatre, Melbourne, premiere 9 October.

——— (2013), *Super Discount*, Wharf 1 Theater, Sydney.

Bel, J. (2012), *Disabled Theater*, Halles de Schaerbeek, Brussels, premiere 10 May.

Bennett, S. (1997), *Theatre Audiences: A Theory of Production and Reception*, 2nd ed., London: Routledge.

Berrol, C. F. (2006), 'Neuroscience meets dance/movement therapy: Mirror neurons, the therapeutic process and empathy', *The Arts in Psychotherapy*, 33:4, pp. 302–15.

Bishop, C. (2006), *Participation*, Cambridge: MIT Press.

Blakeslee, S. and Blakeslee, M. (2007), *The Body Has a Mind of Its Own: How Body Maps in Your Brain Help You Do (Almost) Everything Better*, New York: Random House.

Blasing, B., Calvo-Merino, B., Cross, E. S., Jola, C., Honisch, J. and Stevens, C. J. (2012), 'Neurocognitive control in dance perception and performance', *Acta Psychologica*, 139:2, pp. 300–08.

Blasing, B., Puttke, M. and Schack, T. (eds) (2010), *The Neurocognition of Dance*, London: Psychology Press.

Blood, A. J. and Zatorre, R. J. (2001), 'Intensely pleasurable responses to music correlate with activity in brain regions implicated in reward and emotion', *National Academy of Science*, 98, pp. 11818–23.

Blood, A. J., Zatorre, R. J., Bermudez, P. and Evans, A. C. (1999), 'Emotional responses to pleasant and unpleasant music correlate with activity in paralimbic brain regions', *Nature Neuroscience*, 2, pp. 382–87.

Brassard, A. (2008), 'Mirror neurons and the art of acting', Masters thesis, Montreal: Concordia University, http://search.proquest.com.ezp01.library.qut.edu.au/docview/578483449?pq-origsite=summon. Accessed 6 June 2016.

Broadhurst, Susan (2012) 'Merleau-Ponty and neuroaesthetics: two approaches to performance and technology', *Digital Creativity*, 23.3–4, pp. 225–38.

Brooks, A. (2013), 'Neuroaesthetic resonance', in G. de Michels, F. Isato, A. Bene and D. Bernini (eds), *Arts & Technology: Third International Conference*, Milan, Italy, 2012.

Brown, S. and Dissanyake, E. (2009), 'The arts are more than aesthetics: Neuroaesthetics as narrow aesthetics', in M. Skov and O. Vartanian (eds), *Neuroaesthetics*, Amityville: Baywood, pp. 43–57.

Brown, S., Martinez, M. J. and Parsons, L. M. (2004), 'Passive music listening spontaneously engages limbic and paralimbic systems', *NeuroReport*, 15, pp. 2033–37.

Butsch, R. (2008), *The Citizen Audience: Crowds, Publics and Individuals*, London and New York: Routledge.

Calvo-Merino, B. (2008), 'The neural signatures of the aesthetics of dance', in C. Stock (ed.), *Dance Dialogues: Conversations Across Cultures, Artforms and Practices*, refereed *Proceedings of The World Dance Alliance Global Summit*, Brisbane, Australia, July.

Calvo-Merino, B., Glaser, D. E., Grèzes, J., Passingham, R. E. and Haggard, P. (2005), 'Action observation and acquired motor skills: An FMRI study with expert dancers', *Cerebral Cortex*, 15, pp. 1243–49.

Calvo-Merino, B., Grèzes, J., Glaser, D. E., Passingham, R. E. and Haggard, P. (2006), 'Seeing or doing? Influence of visual and motor familiarity in action observation', *Current Biology*, 16:19, pp. 1905–10.

Calvo-Merino, B., Jola, C., Glaser, D. E. and Haggard, P. (2008), 'Towards a sensorimotor aesthetics of performing art', *Consciousness and Cognition*, 17:3, pp. 911–22.

Calvo-Merino, B., Urgesi, C., Orgs, G., Aglioti, S. M. and Haggard, P. (2010), 'Extrastriate body area underlies aesthetic evaluation of body stimuli', *Experimental Brain Research*, 204, pp. 447–56.

Chatterjee, A. (2011), 'Neuroaesthetics: a coming of age story', *Journal of Cognitive Neuroscience*, 23, 53–62.

Chouinard, M. (2005), *bODY rEMIX / gOLDBERG vARIATIONS*, Venice Biennale's International Festival of Contemporary Dance, Venice, premiere 18 June.

Cinzia, D. D. and Gallese, V. (2009), 'Neuroaesthetics: A review', *Current Opinion in Neurobiology*, 19, pp. 682–87.

Cook, A. (2007), 'Interplay: The method and potential of a cognitive scientific approach to theatre', *Theatre Journal*, 59:4, pp. 579–94.

Corness, G. (2008), 'The musical experience through the lens of embodiment', *Leonardo Music Journal*, 18, pp. 21–24.

Cross, E. S. (2011), 'From dancing robots to action aesthetics: Re- examining mirror system activity as a function of the observer's experience', *Neuroscience Research*, 71, p. e44.

Cross, E. S., Acquah, D. and Ramsey, R. (2014), 'A review and critical analysis of how cognitive neuroscientific investigations using dance can contribute to sport psychology', *International Review of Sport and Exercise Psychology*, 7:1, pp. 42–71.

Cross, E. S., Hamilton, A. F. and Grafton, S. T. (2006), 'Building a motor simulation de novo: observation of dance by dancers', *Neuroimage*, 31, pp. 1257–67.

Cross, E. S., Hamilton, A. F., Kraemer, D. J., Kelley, W. M. and Grafton, S. T. (2009a), 'Dissociable substrates for body motion and physical experience in the human action observation network', *European Journal of Neuroscience*, 30, pp. 1383–1392.

——— (2009b), 'Sensitivity of the action observation network to physical and observational learning', *Cerebral Cortex*, 19, pp. 315–326.

Cross, E. S., Kirsch, L., Ticini, L. F. and Schultz-Bosbach, S. (2011), 'The impact of aesthetic evaluation and physical ability on dance perception', *Frontiers in Human Neuroscience*, 5:102, https://www.ncbi.nlm.nih.gov/pmc/articles/PMC3177045/.

Cross, E. S., Liepelt, R., Hamilton, A. F., Parkinson, J., Ramsey, R., Stadler, W. and Prinz, W. (2012), 'Robotic actions preferentially engage the action observation network', *Human Brain Mapping*, 33:9, pp. 2238–54.

Cross, E. S., Mackie, E. C., Wolford, G. and Hamilton, A. F. (2010), 'Contorted and ordinary body postures in the human brain', *Experimental Brain Research*, 204, pp. 397–407.

Cross, E. S., Stadler, W., Parkinson, J., Schütz-Bosbach, S. and Prinz, W. (2011), 'The influence of perceptual training on the prediction of complex biological and non-biological action sequences', *Human Brain Mapping*, 34:2, pp. 467–86.

Cross, E. S. and Ticini, L. F. (2012), 'Neuroaesthetics and beyond: New horizons in applying the science of the brain to the art of dance', *Phenomenology and the Cognitive Sciences*, 11:1, pp. 5–16.

Davidson, M. (2008), *Concerto for the Left Hand: Disability and the Defamiliar Body*, Ann Arbor: University of Michigan Press.

Debes, R. (2010), 'Which empathy? Limitations in the mirrored "understanding" of emotion', *Synthese*, 175:2, pp. 219–39.

Dinstein, I., Thomas, C., Behrmann, M. and Heeger, D. J. (2008), 'A mirror up to nature', *Current Biology*, 18:1, pp. 13–18.

Dolan, J. (1998), *The Feminist Spectator as Critic*, Ann Arbor: University of Michigan Press.

Foster, S. L. (2011), *Choreographing Empathy: Kinesthesia in Performance*, Oxon: Routledge.

Freedberg, D., and Gallese, V. (2007), 'Motion, emotion and empathy in esthetic experience', *Trends in Cognitive Science*, 11, 197–203.

Freshwater, H. (2009), *Theatre & Audience*, London: Palgrave Macmillan.

Gazzola, V., and Keysers, C. (2009), 'The observation and execution of actions share motor and somatosensory voxels in all tested subjects: single-subject analyses of unsmoothed fMRI data', *Cerebral Cortex*, 19, 1239–55.

Grehan, H. (2009), *Performance Ethics and Spectatorship in a Global Age*, London: Palgrave Macmillan.

Grèzes, J. and Decety, J. (2001), 'Functional anatomy of execution, mental simulation, observation, and verb generation of actions: a meta-analysis', *Human Brain Mapping*, 12, pp. 1–19.

Hadley, B. (2014), *Disability, Public Space Performance and Spectatorship: Unconscious Performers*, London: Palgrave Macmillan.

——— (2015), 'Participation, politics and provocations: People with disabilities as non-conciliatory audiences', *Participations*, 2:1, http://www.participations.org/Volume%2012/Issue%201/11.pdf Accessed 6 June 2016.

Hagendoorn, I. (2004a), 'Some speculative hypotheses about the nature and perception of dance and choreography', *Journal of Consciousness Studies*, 11:3–4, pp. 79–110.

——— (2004b), 'Towards a neurocritique of dance', *BalletTanz Yearbook*, pp. 62–67.

Hagendoorn, I. (2010), 'Dance, choreography, and the brain', in D. Melcher and F. Bacci (eds), *Art and the Senses*, Oxford: Oxford University Press, pp. 499–514.

Heim, C. (2016), *Audience as Performer: The Changing Role of Theatre Audiences in the Twenty-First Century*, London: Routledge.

Henderson, B. and Ostrander, N. (eds) (2010), *Understanding Disability Studies and Performance Studies*, London and New York: Routledge.

Hickey-Moody, A. (2008), *Unimaginable Bodies: Intellectual Disability, Performance and Becomings*, Rotterdam: Sense Publishers.

Hickok, G. (2008), 'Eight problems for the mirror neuron theory of action understanding in monkeys and humans', *Journal of Cognitive Neuroscience*, 21:7, pp. 1229–43.

——— (2014), *The Myth of Mirror Neurons: The Real Neuroscience of Communication and Cognition*, New York: W. W. Norton & Company.

Johnston, K. (2012), *Stage Turns: Canadian Disability Theatre*, Montreal: Mcgill Queens University Press.

Kaczmarczyk, K. (2014), 'Art and reality: Towards a neuropsychological theory of aesthetic perception', *Via Panorâmica: Revista Electrónica de Estudos Anglo-Americanos*, 3, pp. 163–78.

Kochhar-Lindgren, K. (2006), *Hearing Difference: The Third Ear in Experimental, Deaf, and Multicultural Theater*, Washington: Gallaudet University Press.

Kuppers, P. (2004), *Disability and Contemporary Performance: Bodies on Edge*, New York and London: Routledge.

——— (2011), *Disability Culture and Community Performance*, London: Palgrave Macmillan.

James, W. (1890), *Principles of Psychology*, New York: Holt.

Jan, S. H. (2011), 'Experience influences brain mechanisms of watching dance', *Dance Research*, 29:2, pp. 376–401.

Jola, C., Abedian-Amiri, A., Kuppuswamy, A., Pollick, F. E. and Grosbras, M.-H. (2012), 'Motor simulation without motor expertise: Enhanced corticospinal excitability in visually experienced dance spectators', *PLoS ONE*, 7:3, p. e33343.

Juslin, P. N. and Västfjäll, D. (2008), 'Emotional responses to music: The need to consider underlying mechanisms', *Behavioral and Brain Sciences*, 31, pp. 559–621.

Kawabata, H. and Zeki, S. (2004), 'Neural correlates of beauty', *Journal of Neurophysiology*, 91, pp. 1699–705.

Kempe, A. (2015), 'Widening Participation in Theatre through 'Relaxed Performances', *New Theatre Quarterly*, 31:1, pp. 59–69.

Keysers, C. (2009), 'Mirror neurons', *Current Biology*, 19:21, pp. 971–73.

Keysers, C. and Gazzola, V. (2010), 'Social neuroscience: Mirror neurons recorded in humans', *Current Biology*, 20:8, pp. 353–54.

Kilner, J. M. and Frith, C. D. (2008), 'Action observation: Inferring intentions without mirror neurons', *Current Biology*, 18:1, pp. 32–33.

Kirsch, L. P., Dawson, K. and Cross, E. S. (2015), 'Dance experience sculpts aesthetic perception and related brain circuits', *Annals of The New York Academy of Sciences*, 1337:1, pp. 130–39.

Lingnau, A., Gesierich, B. and Caramazza, A. (2009), 'Asymmetric fMRI adaptation reveals no evidence for mirror neurons in humans', *Proceedings of the National Academy of Sciences of the United States of America*, 106:24, pp. 9925–30.

Machon, J. (2009a), 'Review: McConachie, Bruce: *Engaging audiences – A cognitative approach to spectating in the theatre*', *Participations*, 6:1, http://www.participations.org/Volume%206/Issue%201/machon.htm Accessed 6 June 2016.

—— (2009b), *(Syn)aesthetics Redefining Visceral Performance*, Basingstoke and New York: Palgrave Macmillan.

—— (2013), *Immersive Theatres: Intimacy and Immediacy in Contemporary Performance*, Basingstoke and New York: Palgrave Macmillan.

Machon, J. and Broadhurst, S. (eds) (2006), *Performance and Technology: Practices of Virtual Embodiment and Interactivity*, Basingstoke and New York: Palgrave Macmillan.

—— (eds) (2012), *Identity, Performance and Technology: Practices of Empowerment, Embodiment and Technicity*, Basingstoke and New York: Palgrave Macmillan.

McCaffrey, T. (2011), 'The mediatization and re-membering of voice: Questioning assistive/aesthetic technology in performance by people with intellectual disability', *PSi 17*, Utrecht, Netherlands, https://www.academia.edu/2399011/The_Mediatization_and_Re-membering_of_Voice_questioning_assistive_aesthetic_technology_in_performance_by_people_with_intellectual_disability_PSi_17_Utrecht_the_Netherlands_2011. Accessed 6 June 2016.

—— (2012), 'Precarious tenure: Precarity and disability performance', unpublished paper, https://www.academia.edu/1468269/Precarity_and_Disability_Performance.

—— (2014), 'How are we supposed to respond? The presence of performers perceived to have intellectual disabilities interrogating ethics and spectatorship in contemporary performance', *Theatre, Performance, Philosophy Conference: Crossings and Transfers in Anglo-American Thought*, University of Paris, Sorbonne, France, 26–28 June, https://www.academia.edu/9663948/How_are_we_supposed_to_respond_The_presence_of_performers_perceived_to_have_intellectual_disabilities_interrogating_ethics_and_spectatorship_in_contemporary_performance._Video_link._Paper_delivered_at_Theatre_Performance_Philosophy_Conference_June_26-28_2014_University_of_Paris-Sorbonne. Accessed 6 June 2016.

—— (2015), 'A dance that draws you to the edge of your seat': Incapacity and Theatricality', *Performance and Disability, Bodies on Stage: Acting Confronted By Technology* Conference, University of Paris, Sorbonne, France, 3–5 June, https://www.academia.edu/12808343/A_dance_that_draws_you_to_the_edge_of_your_seat_Incapacity_and_Theatricality. Accessed 6 June 2016.

McConachie, B. (2008), *Engaging Audiences – A Cognitive Approach to Spectating in the Theatre*, Basingstoke and New York: Palgrave Macmillan.

Miura, N., Sugiura, M., Takahashi, M., Sassa, Y., Miyamoto, A., Sato, S., Horie, K., Nakamura, K. and Kawashima, R. (2010), 'Effect of motion smoothness on brain activity while observing a dance: An fMRI study using a humanoid robot', *Social Neuroscience*, 5:1, pp. 40–58.

Molnar-Szakacs I. and Overy, K. (2006), 'Music and mirror neurons: from motion to 'e'motion', *Social Cognitive and Affective Neuroscience*, 1:3, pp. 235–41.

Nadal, M. and Pearce, M. T. (2011), 'The Copenhagen neuroaesthetics conference: Prospects and pitfalls for an emerging field', *Brain and Cognition*, 76, pp. 172–83, http://www.ini.ch/~alumit/Nadal_2011.pdf Accessed 6 June 2016.

Nalbantian, S. (2008), 'Neuroaesthetics: Neuroscientific theory and illustration from the arts', *Interdisciplinary Science Reviews*, 33:4, pp. 357–68.

Noë, A. (2011), 'Art and the limits of neuroscience', *The Stone*, 4 December, http://opinionator.blogs. nytimes.com/2011/12/04/art-and-the-limits-of-neuroscience/?_r=0 –. Accessed 6 June 2016.

Overy, K. and Molnar-Szakacs, I. (2009), 'Being together in time: Musical experience and the mirror neuron system', *Music Perception*, 26:5, pp. 489–504.

Provine, R. R. (2008), 'Notation and expression of emotion in operatic laughter', *Behavioral and Brain Sciences*, 31, pp. 591–92.

Reason, M. (2010), *The Young Audience: Exploring and Enhancing Children's Experiences of Theatre*, Stoke on Trent: Trentham Books.

Reason, M. and Reynolds, D. (2010), 'Kinesthesia, empathy, and related pleasures: An inquiry into audience experiences of watching dance', *Dance Research Journal*, 42:2, pp. 49–75.

Reynolds, D. and Reason, M. (eds) (2012), *Kinesthetic Empathy in Creative and Cultural Practices*, Bristol and Chicago: Intellect.

Rizzolatti, G. and Craighero, L. (2005), 'Mirror neuron: A neurological approach to empathy', J. P. Changeux, A. Damasio and W. Singer (eds), *Neurobiology of Human Values*, Berlin: Springer, pp. 107–23.

Rizzolatti, G. and Fabbri-Destro, M. (2010) 'Mirror neurons: From discovery to autism', *Experimental Brain Research*, 200:3, pp. 223–37.

Rizzolatti, G., Ferrari, P. F., Rozzi, S. and Fogassi, L. (2006), 'The inferior parietal lobule: Where action becomes perception', *Novartis Foundation Symposium*, 270, pp. 129–69.

Rizzolatti, G. and Sinigaglia, C. (2010), 'The functional role of the parieto-frontal mirror circuit: interpretations and misinterpretations', *National Review of Neuroscience*, 11, pp. 264–74.

Rubidge, S. (2008), 'Towards an understanding of liminal imagery in the digital domain', in C. Stock (ed.), *Dance Dialogues: Conversations Across Cultures, Artforms and Practices, Refereed Proceedings of The World Dance Alliance Global Summit*, Brisbane, Australia, July.

——— (2010), 'Understanding in our bodies: Nonrepresentational imagery and dance', *Degrés*, 38:141, http://www.sensedigital.co.uk/writing/UrbinoDgrsWeb.pdf.

Sandahl, C. (2002), 'Considering disability: Disability phenomenology's role in revolutionizing theatrical space', *Journal of Dramatic Theory & Criticism*, 2:XVI, pp. 17–32.

Sheets-Johnstone, M. (2012), 'Movement and mirror neurons: A challenging and choice conversation', *Phenomenology and the Cognitive Sciences*, 11:3, pp. 385–401.

Shildrick, M. (2012), *Dangerous Discourses of Disability, Subjectivity and Sexuality*, London: Palgrave Macmillan.

Simpson, E. A., Oliver, W. T. and Fragaszy, D. (2008), 'Super-expressive voices: Music to my ears?', *Behavioral and Brain Sciences*, 31, pp. 596–97.

Stevens, C. (2005), 'Trans-disciplinary approaches to research into creation, performance, and appreciation of contemporary dance', in R. Grove, S. McKechnie and C. J. Stevens (eds), *Thinking in Four Dimensions: Creativity and Cognition in Contemporary Dance*, Melbourne: Melbourne University Press, pp. 154–68.

Stevens, C. and McKechnie, S. (2005), 'Thinking in action: Thought made visible in contemporary dance', *Cognitive Processing*, 6:4, pp. 243–52.

Strukus, W. (2011), 'Mining the gap: Physically integrated performance and kinesthetic empathy', *Journal of Dramatic Theory and Criticism*, 25:2, pp. 89–105.

Tortora, S. (2011), '2010 Marian Chace lecture: The need to be seen: From Winnicott to the mirror neuron system, dance/movement therapy comes of age', *American Journal of Dance Therapy*, 33:1, pp. 4–17.

Turella, L., Pierno, A. C., Tubaldi, F. and Castiello, U. (2009), 'Mirror neurons in humans: Consisting or confounding evidence?', *Brain and Language*, 108:1, pp. 10–21.

Uithol, S. van Rooij, I., Bekkering, H. and Haselager, P. (2011), 'What do mirror neurons mirror?', *Philosophical Psychology*, 24:5, pp. 607–23.

Vivona, J. M. (2009), 'Leaping from brain to mind: A critique of mirror neuron explanations of countertransference', *Journal of the American Psychoanalytic Association*, 57:3, pp. 525–50.

Warburton, E. C. (2011), 'Of meanings and movements: Re-languaging embodiment in dance phenomenology and cognition', *Dance Research Journal*, 43:2, pp. 65–83.

Zeki, S. (1999), 'Art and the brain', *Journal of Consciousness Studies*, 6, pp. 76–96.

Chapter 15

Finding It When You Get There

Adam Benjamin

[...] the research evidences the ways in which performative modes of assessing teaching excellence potentially preclude deeper consideration of pedagogical issues, while the absence of meaningful engagement with issues of pedagogy in institutional documentation sidelines core issues of teaching, and detaches pedagogy from issues of equity and inclusion.

(Stephenson et al. 2015: 5)

'Finding it when you get there' was the title of an integrated dance workshop I led in Berlin during the Tanzfabrik summer programme 2014. It was part of an initiative by directors Christa Flaig and Gabriele Reuter, who, despite the access difficulties associated with the school, were determined to open their programme to disabled students. The title was reference both to the uncertainties that awaited me in Germany but also to my own practice of improvisation, a commitment to un-scored work, and a willingness to leave space for the unknown and the unexpected. In *10 Rules for Students and Teachers* (often mis-attributed to John Cage) Sister Mary Corita Kent[1] refers to this as 'leaving plenty of room for "x"'. Her point being that there are always going to be elements in creative processes that come into play only if we allow time and space for them. The implication being that those of us in the arts should therefore avoid being overly prescriptive about what our outcomes might be or, in the case of dance, too 'conscriptive' about what kind of body might qualify for training.

In conversation with Steve Paxton in the mid-1990s I argued that integrated dance would only be assured a sustainable future when we were able to see courses in universities open to disabled students, and that those students would be given the access and opportunity to train alongside their non-disabled peers. Paxton, the founder of Contact Improvisation and one of the first postmodern dancers to explore integrated dance[2] replied that he '100% agreed... and 100% disagreed'. In response to the 100% with which he agreed, I have, since entering the Academy in 2008, pushed ahead with the issue of access, and in November 2014 was able to celebrate with my colleagues at Plymouth University, the opening of a fully accessible theatre and performing arts programme that positively encourages disabled students to apply. What, though of the other 100%, that part of the argument with which Paxton disagreed? Perhaps it was because he was able to see that higher education is conservative by nature, and that radical movements (and I would include integrated dance in this category with its historical links to Contact Improvisation), are more likely to thrive outside of the academy, where exploration and 'unforced' research progress at their own pace. Paxton's concerns might be summarised by educational reformer and Dean of the School of Education at the University of San Francisco, Kevin Kumashiro:

> [...] pedagogy often does what is harmful to itself, such as by privileging rationalism and repressing other ways of knowing and relating, such as 'touching' (which is what Britzman suggests can lead the ego to desire to know, change, and make reparation).
>
> (Kumashiro 2010: 46)

I hope to explore some of these themes in this chapter as I reflect on my Berlin workshop experience, and my position as a non-disabled, Jewish artist traversing the fields of dance and disability. I will make particular reference to the notion of reparation that Kumashiro, (citing Britzman) refers to in the above quote. By including the voices of some of the workshop participants I hope to reveal how an embodied approach to learning prepares us for our lives in the world and indeed has the capacity to repair and renew our connection to the world we live in. It is both educative and regenerative, a model of the arts that seems increasingly usurped by an economic paradigm in which entrepreneurship and industry driven curriculum design, threaten to outweigh and eclipse artistic exploration, and in which increasingly conservative models of dance education prohibit radical departures, leaving precious few openings for 'x'.

Berlin – July 2014

I was, truth be told, feeling the strain of a very full summer schedule on the back of a hectic year's teaching. Luckily I was staying in Kreuzberg, a stone's throw from Viktoriapark and the light summer mornings allowed me solitary re-adjustment time amidst the capital's early morning dog walkers; a welcome space to prepare for and contemplate each day ahead.

I was aware that there might be discussion and questions as to why we were placing the work in a building that was far from wheelchair friendly, and why I should have agreed to teach in an environment that clearly handicapped disabled participants. Such were my thoughts as I practiced Tai Chi in the park, unnoticed other than by the occasional Alsatian and track-suited owner.

As it transpired, although there was conversation (and problem solving) around access, there was also a huge amount of goodwill from both the organisers and participants. I was accompanied to Germany by a graduating student from Plymouth University,[3] Zoë was allocated the role of 'access aid', ensuring wheelchair users were able to use the industrial lifts and make their way via the adjoining building to the Tanzfabrik studio.

First morning and dancers began to arrive, amongst them, lawyer (and dancer) Silke Schöenfleisch accompanied by her helper dog, Jack. Between snoozes, Jack watched our activities with mild curiosity, occasionally meandering amongst the moving bodies before flopping down in his favoured spot by the piano.

Figure 1: Silke Schöenfleisch and Jack. Photo by author.

I became increasingly fascinated by his unencumbered reliance on sensing and by the immediacy of his responses. As the workshop unfolded he began to serve as litmus test to my teaching and my sense of presence. It was under Jack's gaze that I began to monitor and reflect on how forced or faithful my choices and responses felt. I wrote in my diary:

> It is in relation to Jack's responses that I measure my steps, my tone, my playfulness, my resting; not all the time, sometimes I am oblivious to him, but his presence in the space is part of my sensorial world, a part I find myself taking more and more notice of. His senses out reach mine, his ears prick to sounds beyond my range, his nose tastes the air, his body gives way to resting with ease, while mine, full of a teacher's thoughts, resists the floor; Jack, an uncanny, canine referee, seems able to sniff out a lie at forty paces.

Joint Action[4]

On the second day we play with a temporal-spatial score that involves dancers entering the performance space, improvising for an agreed period, and then seeking their most opportune/satisfying/meaningful moment to leave, departing the space across the same line by which they entered. Jack watched the proceedings. Towards the end of one improvisation a dancer becomes stranded alone in the space, temporarily unable to find the moment to leave. As we all watch, attending to her choices, gauging our need to offer assistance against her need to explore this moment of uncertainty, Jack emerges from behind the piano, wanders across to where she stands, gently takes her by the wrist and tenderly (her wrist in his mouth), guides her out across the (imaginary) line to join the rest of the group. It is such a remarkable moment that no one can think of anything very much to say. Silke, Jack's owner, seemed fairly un-phased by it and explained that Jack saw what needed doing and was just trying to help: 'He is a helper dog, Adam, a retriever, that's his job'. And Jack just looked at me, with his doleful eyes as if to say, 'That wasn't too difficult, was it... Adam?'

It is part and parcel of my teaching methodology to encourage students to be aware of everything that is in the space and be cognizant of how the space, and all that is in it, offers itself to the improvisation. Here is Gearóid McCann, one of the workshop participants describing the early work in the studio:

> For the first two days the ground work of the practice; an attention to breath and to the senses was gently introduced and bedded in. This awareness of what is seen, heard, felt, sensed, touched connects us not only to each other but to physical space we move within, our breath connects us to the air that breezes in from the open windows, to the sounds of the city, police sirens sounding, birds singing, a dog barking somewhere down on the street below, our practice brings us into 'being' rather than 'acting' or the dance equivalent; 'throwing shapes'.

McCann's reference to the 'ground work' brings to mind the work of social anthropologist Tim Ingold who talks of the ground comprising 'a domain in which the lives and minds of its human and non-human inhabitants are comprehensively knotted with one another' (Ingold 2015: 49). For many years, the cognitive sciences laboured under the misapprehension that studying isolated individuals in laboratory conditions, through psychological and neurological testing, could give definitive answers about human behaviour and the nature of consciousness. It is an approach that has been referred to as the 'experimental quarantine' approach (Richardson et al. 2008) one that aligns itself to a medical model of the human psyche and neurologically centred explanations of consciousness. The unexpected contribution of Jack, clearly no respecter of 'quarantines', raises myriad questions about social interaction and in particular about joint action; that field of enquiry that explores events where two or more individuals coordinate their actions in space and time to bring about a change in the environment (Sebanz et al. 2006). Whatever 'motive' we might apply to Jack's action, his intervention in our score was a beautiful and unexpected example of Corita's 'x', a moment when something 'other', something outside of our field or frame of enquiry, actively intervened in our research. It was a reminder that we are connected to the world and interact with it in multiple ways some of which transcend individuated action or language. It was also a reminder that the purpose of research and education is to open us to possibilities that we might not have previously considered and to raise questions that we might not previously have imagined.

[I]t can hardly be expected that students will emerge from their higher education imbued with personal flexibility, able to respond deftly to the unexpected, unless they have encountered something of the kind in their educational experience.

(Barnett 2014)

Breathing Space

I was somehow very aware that each morning the workshop participants made their way across the city to the studio, and each evening carried something of the studio research with them back out through the Berlin streets: that each day the studio seemed to breathe us in, and each evening breathe us out again, the boundaries of our workshop experience, increasingly porous and difficult to define. Below, two of the participants record their experiences on different sets of wheels, the first provides an alternative perspective to the issue of 'assistance' raised by Jack's actions, the second touches the idea of 'grounds for play'.

In everyday life it's very seldom that, if I approach someone, he or she will respond to me in the way they did in the workshop. Usually people are scared and back away from me or they worry that I will run them over and hurry their children out of my way.

If I look at someone in everyday life usually they ask 'Do you need help?' So I avoid making eye contact. In the workshop this changed. When I travelled by train after the week and wanted to relocate from my wheelchair to a train seat, and to do so I need to sit on the floor, and this time when someone offered me help there was no accompanying feeling of stress or shame, just a simple understanding between us of what help was needed. I would say that I now move more and in different ways. I don't sit so long in the same position in my chair, I put my legs on a bench or my back on a wall. And I allow myself to move more slowly. I notice impulses more often, and follow them, I am less the object of others' gaze, more the director of my own.

(Denise Kastler)

Today a hitherto unpleasant cycle along a route where cyclists, pedestrians and motorists share limited space became a chance to dance attentively through the crowd. The necessity I often feel to defend my space gave way to playfulness. Tempo, balance, all round vision and especially, consideration for the others sharing the space with me became the elements of an improvisation that I joined in.

(Gearóid McCann)

Kastler reminds us that integrated work is educative in the most profound sense, that it leads the individual out into new understandings, it widens the field of knowledge that we all share, and along with McCann that this new shared knowledge shapes how we perceive and interact with the world around us. The world is no longer 'other' but a field of play that is mutual – a rather wonderful word 'mutual', which denotes not only 'shared', but has its roots in the Latin *mutare* – to change. Perhaps then, change need not always solely be presaged with disruption and dissatisfaction (Kumashiro 2010), perhaps change might arise also through play, which would therefore require the provision of 'playground' and 'play time' within our pedagogic offer.

Watching

On the Wednesday afternoon of the workshop I was scheduled, as part of the summer programme, to perform with Gabi Reuter and another dancer who was teaching in the summer festival, and Sharon Hilleli-Assa, a visiting artist from Israel. That day my workshop session overruns and I find myself hurrying along the corridor to the performance space. Gabi and Sharon greet me and recognize my flustered, less than prepared state of body/mind. They weight me down, with knowing hands that guide me into my muscles and bones. My breathing shifts, my eyes meet theirs, they seem to trust me – I don't know why, as I have not an idea in my head, but I in return, empty, trust them. I am temporarily tethered and held, and for a brief moment I stand willing and expectant but also, a little vacant, waiting to be led. This very uncertain, nascent, one might say 'dog-like' interlude, served as a reminder that some of our most basic emotive states might well be shared by species other than Homo sapiens. Perhaps it is the 'sapient' nature of our species, and the enforced sapience of higher education that at times leads us away from this place of waiting, where what is yet to be 'x'-perienced can be given time to unfold, and perhaps it is the duty of teachers and artists precariously placed within education, to both make the case for, and safeguard this experience. Lacuna or lack as argued by Orozco and Parker-Starbuck (2015) makes us no less human, and may indeed help us understand and respect different kinds of knowing.

Performance

I have performed twice before with Gabi, but never with Sharon, who I had met only that morning. After the performance I discovered each of us had had a moment of crisis about the performance, and each of us had been brought back to this moment of readiness by one or other of our trio. It takes a certain courage to embrace the risk of failure publicly, and improvisation invites us repeatedly to stand by our conviction that 'not knowing' is a valid artistic and educational experience.

Capturing an improvisation in film is an impossible task, the perspectives and responses that inhabit the performance space are ephemeral and often felt rather than seen. Below is a response to the performance written toward the end of the workshop, accompanied by photos taken during the performance by Anna Stein.

Two pillars rise from circular troughs in the wooden floor. Around the base of the pillars are white stones, stranded like memories. In a corner of the studio hangs an anatomical

Figure 2: A calcification of weighting. Photo by Anna Stein.

skeleton. Benches are lain out along the right hand side of the studio behind the pillars, along with cushions for people to sit on.

We shift some benches that seem oddly positioned in the performance space, sweep the floor, and share our thoughts about what, or rather how we will approach the improvisation. It comes down to an agreement that we will start as soon as the audience arrive and end around the forty-minute mark… or whenever we feel like we have found an ending.

The doors open. People begin to drift in and take their seats, the 'them' and the 'us'. I decide not to be divided and begin to play with the broom, over and around the feet of the front row, causing a constant shuffling and reshuffling, laughter and tickles, toes in the water, sons and daughters at the beach brushing, not rushing.

After a while I notice, Gabi and Sharon patiently kneeling by the side of the studio, them and me, should be us. How to keep 'us'? I go obediently and kneeling too, feel our 'threedom', tiny articulations and waves, emanating from breath and shared awareness that grow beyond fragility into motion… The space is soon open, swept clean, awaiting a journey, stories to unfold on the ground shared with those who watch now, resting from their own dancing, their own lives, to witness ours.

In the performance I find Sharon, back outstretched, and picking white pebbles from around the pillars, place them, a calcification of weighting, along her spine.

A feeling of deep sadness and grief settles temporarily, a ghost wave engulfing us to the throat, bedecked in small stones,
and then recedes
as suddenly
stealing words
lifts and flies out through the open windows across the Berlin cityscape...
and we are left
empty and shining as the blue sky.

After the performance, Gabi asks how I knew about Sharon's recent bereavement. I didn't. I hadn't. The dance had allowed a moment of sharing (a moment of healing perhaps). A reminder if one was needed, that the arts constantly offer up new possibilities and space for unexpected voices. 'Every scene of improvisation is haunted by these multiple addressees – is composed of these hauntings' (Fischlin 2015: 289). Thus, without pre-ordaining what will happen, and by respectful listening, what needs to arise is noticed, welcomed and dances with us for a while,

Figure 3: Gabriele Reuter, headless skeleton, Adam Benjamin and Sharon Hilleli-Assa. Photo by Anna Stein.

like an old friend or trusting park bench, patiently waiting our arrival. The creative journey is essentially about other ways of seeing, about how *others* see, it is about framing the world differently and sharing that vision through whatever our medium happens to be.

> Researchers have suggested that the 'knowledge' many students have about the Other is either incomplete because of exclusion, invisibility, and silence, or distorted because of disparagement, denigration, and marginalization. What makes these partial knowledges so problematic is that they are often taught through the informal or 'hidden' curriculum (Jackson 1968), which means that, because they are taught indirectly, pervasively, and often unintentionally, they carry more educational significance than the official curriculum.
>
> (Jackson et al. 1993)

One might therefore argue that it is the absence of disabled bodies within higher education performing arts programmes that re-affirms, on a daily basis, that disabled people exist only outside of formal training cultures. That the disabled body is disruptive to 'normal procedures', and therefore (in the minds of students within the academy), that disabled people continue to be a 'client group' or 'community activity'; someone to help, rather than someone with whom we might be in partnership in joint action[5] and joint learning. To quote Riyad A. Shahjahan, '[t]ime and the use of time mark unruly bodies as out of place in academic institutions, much as they marked colonial difference' (2015: 492).

As universities in the United Kingdom become increasingly wedded to governmental prerogatives of economic growth and graduate employability, and research within higher education increasingly sees dance academics courting and courted by new technology, I am minded that the park bench may be more than a useful analogy for where and when inspiration and insight arises, and indeed might provide a useful metaphor for the student teacher relationship itself; a space that allows us to converse about more than just how to pass assessments; about the links between the imagination and life as it is lived. Ingold (2015) makes the unexpected etymological connection between our word 'school', and the Greek *skholē* a word that incorporates the notion both of leisure and learning and I wonder where this kind of experience and exchange might take place in courses where number of students is increasingly see as the most important index of success.

A Seat of Learning

Claudia Neumayer, another of the Berlin workshop participants, effortlessly and eloquently reminds us of what dance is and what it does.

> After a while I felt less shy and more communicative. While dancing I felt connected somehow with everybody and everything. I experienced that my senses connect me to the environment and to myself at the same time. It was like coming home.
>
> (Claudia Neumayer)

Neumayer also reminds us of another meaning of the word repair, which has its origins in the old French *repatriare* – to return to our own country. In our context, the home referred to here is the body; coming back to our senses is what brings us home or at least sets us on a journey towards a way of knowing that is situated as Maurice Merleau-Ponty suggested, in the body, rather than remotely, through written word or diagram (Howes and Classen 2014). Sensate, we inhabit a terrain that is both immediate and vulnerable. Our everyday filters removed, hidden voices are given parole. I am happy to have been part of a workshop, a festival, a performance, a reparation, a repatriation; and amongst the 'othered' bodies, unexpectedly at home in Berlin. 'Je suis Juif'[6] I say silently to myself on my last day, as the Alsatian and its owner watch my slow dance in the early morning sunshine.

Back in England, working on this chapter, the leitmotif of the park bench seemed apposite, a counter intuitive symbol for learning in an age of digitally driven haste, and I regret not having taken a picture of Viktoriapark. I turn to the Internet for images, entering into my search 'park benches' and then, for more local flavour 'Kreuzberg'. Within seconds, I am furnished with a photo from 1933, in which two elderly Kreuzberg residents sit on a park bench inscribed with the words *Nicht für Juden*. Sitting at my screen, I experience what disability dance artist and scholar Petra Kuppers refers to as 'the collapsing of historical

Figure 4: Park Bench. Kreuzberg, 1933. Photo by Fred Ramage/Getty Images.

distances' (Kuppers 2015: 50) and am reminded of the impossibility of dividing who I am from what I teach (Ashwin 2015: 20).

To paraphrase Paul Stoller (2014) – the personal and the professional are never separate because as teachers within the arts, we are always interacting with and learning from our 'others'. The role of the teacher is not just to instil information or technique but to open up a place of exchange, of enquiry and possibly of wonder.

> [...] pedagogy traditionally attempts to control and to grasp the knowable, leaving no space open for what is really uncontrollable and unknowable in education; and it attempts to do so out of desire for self-affirmation, desire for sameness and repetition.
>
> (Kumashiro 2010: 46)

To Kumashiro's list above we might today add the word 'profit', not in its original sense of advancement or progress, but in terms of monetary value as universities in the United Kingdom compete for the funds that increased numbers bring. I hope that the fledgling integrated dance initiatives within higher education can help resist that desire for 'sameness

Figure 5: Plymouth Dance Theatre graduate Kevin French, outside The House, the new accessible theatre at Plymouth University. Photo by author.

and repetition' and that in the face of endless improvement, efficiency and profitability metrics, universities might allow students, teachers and artists the freedom and importantly, the time to 'find it when they get there'.

Acknowledgements

I would like to thank Gabriele Reuter and Christa Flaig for inviting me to teach at Tanzfabrik, all of the participants of the Berlin workshop and particularly those who contributed their voices to this chapter Claudia Neumayer, Gearóid McCann and Denise Kastler. Zoë Mote for her stalwart assistance during the project. Sharon Hilleli-Assa for 'finding it in performance', Silke Schöenfleisch for looking out for me in Berlin and last-but-not-least, Jack, for whom all of this was just a walk in the park.

In 2018 Adam left Plymouth University to return to working as a freelance dance artist. Perhaps Steve was 100% correct after all.

References

Barnett, R. (2014), 'Conditions of flexibility. Securing a more responsive higher education system', https://www.heacademy.ac.uk/sites/default/files/resources/fp_conditions_of_flexibility.pdf. Accessed 21 December 2015.

Benjamin, A. (2002), *Making an Entrance: Theory and Practice for Disabled and Non-Disabled Dancers*, London and New York: Routledge.

—— (1993), 'In search of integrity', *Dance Theatre Journal*, 10:4, pp. 42–46.

Fischlin, D. (2015), 'Improvised responsibility: Opening statements (call and) responsibility: Improvisation, ethics, co-creation', in R. Caines and A. Heble (eds), *The Improvisation Studies Reader. Spontaneous Acts*, Oxon and New York: Routledge, pp. 7–16.

Howes, D. and Classen, C. (2014), *Ways of Sensing. Understanding the Senses in Society*, Oxon and New York: Routledge.

Ingold, T. (2015), *The Life of Lines*, Oxon and New York: Routledge.

Jackson, P. W., Boostrom, R. E. and Hanson, D. T. (1993), *The Moral Life of Schools*, San Francisco: Jossey-Bass.

Kumashiro, K. (2010), 'Seeing the bigger picture: Troubling movements to end teacher education', *Journal of Teacher Education*, 61:1–2, pp. 56–65.

Kuppers, P. (2015), 'Waltzing Disability Culture: Finding History with Raimund Hoghe', *Choreographic Practices*, 6:1, pp. 41–56.

Merleau-Ponty, M. ([1962] 2002), *Phenomenology of Perception*, Oxon and London: Routledge.

Noë, A. (2004), *Action in Perception*, Cambridge: MIT Press.

—— (2012), *Varieties of Presence*, Cambridge: Harvard University Press.

O'Regan, K. J. and Noë, A. (2001), 'A sensorimotor account of vision and visual consciousness', *Behavioral and Brain Sciences*, 24:5, pp. 883–975.

Orozco, L. and Parker-Starbuck, J. (2015), *Performing Animality*, London: Palgrave Macmillan.

Panagia, D. (2009), *The Political Life of Sensation*, Durham: Duke University Press.

Richardson, D. C., Hoover, M. A. and Ghane, A. (2008), 'Joint perception: gaze and the presence of others', in B. C. Love, K. McRae and V. M. Sloutsky (eds), *Proceedings of the 30th annual conference of the cognitive science society*, Austin: Cognitive Science Society, pp. 309–14.

Sebanz, N., Bekkering, H. and Knoblich, G. (2006), 'Joint action: Bodies and minds moving together', *Trends in Cognitive Sciences*, 10:2, pp. 70–76.

Shahjahan, R. A. (2015), 'Being "lazy" and slowing down: Toward decolonizing time, our body, and pedagogy', *Educational Philosophy and Theory*, 47:5, pp. 488–501.

Stevenson, J., Burke, P. J. and Whelan, P. (2014), 'Pedagogic stratification and the shifting landscape of higher education', https://www.heacademy.ac.uk/sites/default/files/resources/pedstrat_finalreport.pdf. Accessed 21 December 2015.

Stoller, P. (2014), 'Afterword: Restlessness and well-being', *Anthropology and Humanism*, 39:1, pp. 32–35.

Notes

1 http://www.corita.org/coritabio.html.

2 Paxton and Anne Kilcoyne founded Touchdown Dance in 1986, exploring partnership between sighted and blind/visually impaired dancers.

3 Zoë Mote was recipient of a bursary from Plymouth University on completion of her degree.

4 There is an implied reference to the seminal dance company Joint Forces here, and the pioneering work of Alitto Alessi, Karen Nelson and Emery Blackwell in the United States, which led to the Dance Ability Movement.

5 Joint action has been defined as any form of social interaction where two or more individuals coordinate their actions in space and time to bring about a change in the environment (Sebanz et al. 2006).

6 Referencing the 'I am Charlie' slogan adopted by supporters of freedom of expression in the wake of the killing of workers at the offices of the French satirical weekly newspaper *Charlie Hebdo* in Paris on 7 January 2014.

Interruption 7

Understanding and Appreciation

6 October 2015

Hetty Blades

*R*eading 'Let's Dance! – But who owns it?' (Waelde et al. 2014), I was interested by the suggestion that increased audience understanding about the nature and quality of dance works might help with commercial exploitation. On the one hand this suggestion seems straightforward enough, if audiences understand a choreographer's work, they are more likely to appreciate it and therefore buy tickets for future performances. It seems that this perspective is prevalent across the wide array of contemporary dance practices. The wealth of after show discussions, choreographic publications and public articulations by choreographers, imply that highlighting the labour, intention and thinking behind the work will increase audience engagement with it. So is the need for this type of extra-performance information particularly relevant in the case of dance works made and/or performed by people with disabilities? As Shawn points out in his blog post last month, such work, 'greatly diversifies the bodies and aesthetics on view and the experiences and stories offered for interpretation' (Harmon 2015). Does this diversity mean that more explanation is required? If so, what are the repercussions of this claim?

The idea that contemporary dance can be opaque and that novice audiences don't always 'get it' has been around for some time. But what does the suggestion that audience appreciation depends upon education and access to information from outside of performance mean for the nature of the form? Such questions have been thoroughly explored and debated in the philosophy of music and visual art. Conventional theories of art appreciation, dating back to Kant ([1781] 1855), commonly suggest that art should be perceived, appreciated, valued and judged merely on the aesthetic experience that it affords (see Stolnitz 1969), specifically, that knowledge external to the physical experience of the work is not relevant. This view, labelled 'aesthetic empiricism', is defined by David Davies (2004) as the term used for, 'epistemologies of art that minimize the role, in artistic appreciation, of resources not available or derivable from an immediate encounter with an instance of a work' (Davies 2004: 25).

A strictly empiricist opinion, that a work of art should speak entirely for itself, is perhaps a little strong, and arguably counter-intuitive. After all, what does it really mean to have an 'immediate encounter'? No one sees from a neutral position; our appreciative capabilities are constructed and developed through a wide array of experiences and information. However, there is value in thinking through the counterargument, that extra information is always required to truly appreciate and value a work, which implies that a dance performance itself is not enough. This also feels like a problematic outcome.

So where does that lead us? It seems that dance spectatorship, in alignment with other forms of artistic appreciation, requires expertise and therefore training. We might want to argue that *performance is enough, but we need background knowledge that enables us to encounter the work fully in performance.*

In 'Let's Dance!' Charlotte, Sarah and Mathilde suggest that this research project has shown that understanding the artistic intention and artistic skills informs audience appreciation of a work. They consider audience responses to a range of examples by disabled dancers, which demonstrate a set of reactions that are arguably distinct from responses to non-disabled dancers. In response, they suggest that deepening understanding,

> *[…] allows the viewer to go beyond a response of 'Ain't they Marvelous', or a wholly negative response, or no response at all, or a response of 'why bother, what is the point?', to a position where it is possible to learn how to critique and appreciate the dance as a serious art form.*
>
> *(Waelde et al. 2014: 6)*

So whilst questions around understanding, empiricism and appreciation are relevant for many choreographers, these findings suggest that there is further motivation to inform audiences about features of works made and performed by disabled dance artists in order to challenge and confront preconceptions, and allow for dance by disabled and non-disabled dancers to be responded to on the same terms. Perhaps the advocation of an empiricist perspective is the remit of those working in art forms with longstanding traditions of audience education. The appreciation of features of visual art and music are often taught in school, and are aspired to as forms of cultural capital. It seems that if the appreciation of dance, made and performed by all bodies, was integrated into educational and cultural value systems, we may well be able to argue that a work needs no explanation. For now, however it seems that encouraging audiences to see, understand and value dance by disabled dance artists can not only help these artists to develop commercially, but also to shift the cultural landscape.

References

Davies, D. (2004), *Art as Performance*, New Jersey: Blackwell Publishing.

Harmon, S. (2015) 'A wider significance for a philosophy of disabled dance', http://www.invisibledifference.org.uk/blog/62/. Accessed 17 October 2017.

Kant, I. ([1790] 1855), *The Critique of Judgment* (trans. J. M. D. Mieklejohn), London: Henry G. Bohn, http://ebooks.adelaide.edu.au/k/kant/immanuel/k16ju/complete.html. Accessed 1 March 2014.

Stolnitz, J. ([1960] 1969), 'The aesthetic attitude', in J. Hospers (ed.), *Introductory Readings in Aesthetics*, New York: The Free Press, pp. 17–27.

Waelde, C., Whatley, S. and Pavis, M. (2014), 'Let's dance! – But who owns it?', https://ore.exeter.ac.uk/repository/handle/10871/16903. Accessed 29 September 2015.

Interruption 8

Mainstream and Marginal: Have We Progressed in the Last Decade Plus?

10 June 2015

Charlotte Waelde

*I*n 2003, Paul Anthony Darke penned a highly informative chapter about Disability Arts in which he explained the philosophy behind the movement. As elucidated by Darke, 'Disability Art used art to identify and reveal how "cultural forms and practices do not simply reflect an already given social work but, rather, play a constitutive role in the construction of that world"' (Bowler in Darke [2003] 2014: 132). Throughout the chapter Darke argues that Disability Arts has been both mainstreamed and marginalised. It has been mainstreamed through the assimilation of Disability Art into the establishment by way of, for example, traditional training programmes (in which Disability Arts does not feature); and it has been marginalised such that the majority of Disability Artists 'wander from one small commission to another, filling the void with equal opportunities training or audience development initiatives...' (2014: 138).

While the dancers and choreographers who we have worked with during the currency of our project don't necessarily identify with the philosophy underpinning Disability Arts, one of the key messages that has emerged from our symposia in 2013 and 2014, is that there is frustration within the community that questions around exclusion, otherness, difference, invisibility, and disability aesthetics are repeatedly asked (and have been for the past decade) without significant movement. There is a sense now, however, that the community is at a 'tipping point', a point at which these questions can be put in the past and the dance can move into a new phase; validated and embraced within the cultural ecosystem on an equal footing with other dances and dancers. However, there is also a sense that it has been at this tipping point for years. There is, in other words, both a sense of anticipation, that it is possible to move forwards, but also a sense of frustration, that the means for actually doing so remain elusive.

One of our current plans to take the work that we have been doing forwards has been to develop ideas for the filming of a documentary that we hope will respond to this frustration. It is our contention that the absence of disabled dance from our memory institutions is a contributory factor to the repetitive nature of the discourse: there is a need constantly to revisit these same issues precisely because there is no memory of them. The focus of the documentary will be on our dance partners at work: in the studio, in rehearsal and making work together, resulting in an art-documentary rather than a public information film. The intention is to raise awareness of how disabled dancers and choreographers need to think about organising their working day dealing with every day matters such as getting to work, navigating through the rehearsal space, and negotiating with facilitators such as sign language specialists (all of which have been raised by our project participants as issues). Woven into this story will be interviews that will articulate the policy frameworks applicable to, and the practical conditions within, *our memory institutions that support a work becoming part of our 'formal' cultural heritage. Our aim is then to show this film at two venues; one in Scotland and one in England and have an associated round-table high level policy-maker discussion event to debate the policy issues that have been raised in our project.*

Let me, at this point, take the reader back to Darke's chapter. One of the points that Darke makes about both mainstreaming and marginalisation is as follows: 'As a result of existing art hierarchies, Disability Art events, exhibitions and performances are invariably marginalised as art per se or held purely as education-based events' ([2003] 2014: 139). When we asked a Scottish mainstream venue if they would be interested in hosting our event the response was: (a) perhaps you should think of a dance studio (thus inevitably keeping the audience limited to those who are (already) interested in dance); or (b) if that did not work, re-approach the venue but do so through their person responsible for education.

Darke's chapter was written in 2003; we are now in 2015. It is thus for significantly more than a decade that the same barriers have been erected against the penetration of dance made by our colleagues within the 'arts establishment'. It is particularly saddening that this has arisen in Scotland. Our dance collaborators have almost without exception said how welcoming Scotland is to artists with disabilities, to the extent that they consider themselves not as 'disabled dance artists' but as dance artists. Further, it is notable that one of the people who has so far agreed in principle to participate in the round-table debate is Janet Archer, CEO of Creative Scotland.

Reference

Darke, P. A. (2014) 'Now I know why disability art is drowning in the River Lethe (with thanks to Pierre Bourdieu)', in S. Riddell and N. Watson Pearson (eds), *Disability, Culture and Identity*, 2nd ed., Oxon and New York: Routledge, pp. 131–42.

Interruption 9

Mainstream or Marginal? Still on the Edge...

29 June 2015

Sarah Whatley

*C*harlotte's blog post encouraged me to reflect on a number of recent encounters with discussions about dance and disability; some very stimulating and illuminating, but some acknowledging or even inadvertently reinforcing the status quo; disability is still marginalised in dance.

Challenging the status quo is the recent special issue of Choreographic Practices *(Vol. 6:1)* – 'Dis/abilities: The Politics of a Prefix' – a fabulous collection of intelligent and probing articles (including one from us!), guest edited by Ann Cooper Albright and Gabriele Brandstetter. In their editorial they say that whilst critical scholarship about dance and disability has expanded,

> [...] disability remains a marginalised and under-theorized area in dance studies. Many discussions in the dance field remain on the level of single-issue identity politics with the specific goal of improving access to dance for people with disabilities. Whilst we applaud this important focus on inclusion, we also want to acknowledge how physical difference can radically transform the transmission of embodied knowledge as well as the choreographic act.

> *(Albright and Brandstetter 2015: 5)*

They offer that the writing in the issue is 'intended to challenge our thinking not only about who can dance, but also about how to dance' (Albright and Brandstetter 2015: 5). Their emphasis on how to dance feels important – we are often focused on access, equal opportunities and the right to participate (etc.) but as we have discovered through our work on this project, there is not enough attention on the dancing itself. Attending to the 'how' is a timely reminder.

Still on the edge... Ann Cooper Albright also figures for me as convener of the recent SDHS/ CORD conference in Athens – Cut and Paste: Dance Advocacy in the Age of Austerity (2015). Ann brought her usual energy and generosity to pull together a fantastically nourishing conference. One panel focused on inclusion, with presenters offering some fascinating accounts of teaching initiatives and post-graduate research that focuses on dance and disability. But of all of us attending, representing the worldwide dance research community, disability was nowhere visible. We still have some distance to travel.

Marginal to mainstream... Alice Fox and Hannah Macpherson recently launched their beautiful new book, Inclusive Arts Practice and Research *(2015)* at Tate Modern. Apart from a celebration of a book that skilfully weaves together theory with the voices/images and reflections of disabled artists, it showed that Inclusive Arts has absolute right to be featured in *one of our leading cultural institutions that is primarily concerned with promoting the best in contemporary art.*

References

Albright, A. and Brandstetter, G. (eds) (2015), 'Dis/abilities: The Politics of a Prefix', special issue, *Choreographic Practices*, 6:2.
Fox, A. and Macpherson, H. (2015), *Inclusive Arts Practice and Research: A Critical Manifesto*, London: Routledge.

Policy Brief for Venues: Providing Space. Obligations and Approaches to Dancers with Different Bodies

The InVisible Difference: Dance, Disability and Law project is an Arts and Humanities Research Council-funded project that is exploring issues confronted by professional disabled choreographers and ownership and authorship of their work.

Project Overview

Running from January 2013 to December 2015, ours is an interdisciplinary partnership between academics in Higher Education and artists working in the creative industry. Members of the project are: Professor Sarah Whatley, Coventry University; Professor Charlotte Waelde, University of Exeter; Dr Abbe Brown, University of Aberdeen; Dr Shawn Harmon, University of Edinburgh; Dr Karen Wood and Hannah Donaldson, research assistants; Mathilde Pavis and Kate Marsh, doctoral candidates and dance artist Caroline Bowditch. During the course of our research we are conducting qualitative research with disabled choreographers and dancers, including Caroline Bowditch, Claire Cunningham, Marc Brew, Chisato Minamimura and others. We also have strong links with Candoco dance company and other independent disabled dancers.

There are obligations under human rights and disability laws for providers of rehearsal and performance space to make them available to all dancers. One of the key challenges faced by dancers with different bodies, and those who enjoy observing, sharing and analysing their performances, is the limited availability of such space. This brief introduces the laws, and makes practical recommendations for providers of these spaces.

Development and application of human rights and disability laws is a key part of the InVisible Difference project. The results of our research, and proposals for policy change, are being shared as the project progresses, including through other policy briefs.[1]

This policy brief introduces the legal tools of human rights and disability laws, the obligations they impose on providers of dance space, and suggests possible future action. This should ensure that the obligations of providers are met, the rights of dancers and supporters are met, and help providers to move towards new opportunities which can arise from more embracing of accessibility in dance.

Discussion

There are many human rights which are relevant to providers of dance space, to dancers with different bodies and to their supporters. International and European treaties set out rights to expression,[2] to share in cultural life,[3] and against discrimination.[4] The dedicated Convention on the Rights of Persons with Disabilities includes a right against discrimination on the basis of disability,[5] to equal access to the physical environment,[6] to freedom of expression[7] and to participation in cultural life.[8] So all people who wish to dance, or who would like to observe and enjoy the dance of others, should be able to do so. What does this really mean for providers of dance space – particularly in times of financial strain, and when there is also a right to property which would apply to the business of the space provider?[9]

The treaties discussed impose obligations on states (e.g. the UK). This does not mean, however, that providers of dance space can ignore human rights. In the UK, the Human Rights Act 1998 means that arguments based on human rights can be made on a more individual level, if a dispute is before a court on another basis.[10] For providers of dance space, this could arise on the basis of disability legislation.

The Equality Act 2010 requires providers of services to the public to ensure that their services are equally available to all, and reasonable adjustments must be made to ensure that this is the case.[11] For example, a performer who is unable to access performance space because there is no ramp or lift, could raise a court action against the provider. The key question is the meaning of reasonable. The provider might argue that, say, a new ramp is not reasonable. No court has yet considered an issue like this in respect of dance. An interesting argument would be that given previous failure to provide opportunity for people with disabilities, particularly in respect of dance, there should be more support now, even if this imposes a burden on space providers. If the court found in favour of the dancers, space providers could be ordered to pay financial compensation.

This burden might seem unfair. Further, dealing with such an action would be expensive and a distraction from the important activities carried out by space providers. Yet in parallel with this, complaints and court actions might also be being made by dancers and their supporters against the state and funders, including at international monitoring level[12] and at the European Court of Human Rights.[13] So responsibility does not lie only with space providers – but it cannot be ignored.

Viewed more positively, there are important examples of venues embracing dance and accessibility, leading to new opportunities and events. Valuable examples of constructive engagement are the Tramway in Glasgow, where the Gathered Together inclusive dance festival was held in August 2014,[14] the Southbank Centre in London, where the Unlimited Festival was held in September 2014[15] and the Step Forward initiative at City Moves in Aberdeen.[16]

Conclusions

Providers of dance space must have regard to human rights and disability laws. These laws create an environment within which all those who wish to dance and engage with it must be able to do so. Changes might seem costly and unnecessary; but from one perspective, this is likely cheaper than engaging in a court action; and from a more positive perspective, taking this step enables dance spaces to engage with more with a thriving and growing dance community.

Recommendations

1. When making decisions regarding service provision, have regard to human rights and disability laws when considering the appropriate balance to be struck in each case – and be aware of the risks if you do not.
2. When applying for your own funding: refer to human rights and disability laws and seek funding, possibly through new sources, to increase opportunities for dancers with different bodies and for your space.

If you would like further details, do feel free to contact Dr Abbe Brown, University of Aberdeen, abbe.brown@abdn.ac.uk. We should also be delighted to share your experiences of these avenues on our website.

September 2014

Notes

1 See Brief for Royalties v Public Funders on Publications section of project website, http://www.invisibledifference.org.uk/research/publications/.
2 Article 10 European Convention on Human Rights (ECHR), article 11 EU Charter of Fundamental Rights (EU Charter), and article 19 International Convention on Civil and Political Rights (ICCPR).
3 Article 15.1a International Convention on Economic Social and Cultural Rights (ICESCR).
4 Article 14 ECHR, article 21 EU Charter, Article 2.2 ICESCR, and article 2.1 ICCPR.
5 Article 3b, 4, 5 Convention on the Rights of Persons with Disabilities (CRPD).
6 Article 9 CRPD.
7 Article 21 CRPD.
8 Article 30 CRPD.
9 Protocol 1, article 1 ECHR and article 17 EU Charter.
10 Section 3.
11 Section 29 and Part 9 Equality Act 2010.

12 E.g. Committee on Rights of Persons with Disabilities http://www.ohchr.org/en/hrbodies/crpd/pages/crpdindex.aspx.
13 Once national avenues are exhausted. See http://www.echr.coe.int/Pages/home.aspx?p=applicants.
14 http://www.tramway.org/events/Pages/Gathered-Together.aspx.
15 http://www.southbankcentre.co.uk/whatson/festivals-series/unlimited.
16 http://danceaberdeen.com/about/.

Position Brief for Dancers. Policy Brief: Asserting Copyright

The InVisible Difference: Dance, Disability and Law project is an Arts and Humanities Research Council-funded project that is exploring issues confronted by professional disabled choreographers and ownership and authorship of their work.

Project Overview

Running from January 2013 to December 2015, ours is an interdisciplinary partnership between academics in Higher Education and artists working in the creative industry. Members of the project are: Professor Sarah Whatley, Coventry University; Professor Charlotte Waelde, University of Exeter; Dr Abbe Brown, University of Aberdeen; Dr Shawn Harmon, University of Edinburgh; Dr Karen Wood and Hannah Donaldson, research assistants; Mathilde Pavis and Kate Marsh, doctoral candidates and dance artist Caroline Bowditch. During the course of our research we are conducting qualitative research with disabled choreographers and dancers, including Caroline Bowditch, Claire Cunningham, Marc Brew, Chisato Minamimura, and others. We also have strong links with Candoco dance company and other independent disabled dancers.

This paper explores the contribution of copyright laws to the development and funding of disabled dance artists. Are disabled dance artists the authors and owners of the copyright in a dance? Could the resulting rights be a source of revenue?

This brief suggests disabled dance artists can find the key to a better (commercial) dissemination of their work through the proper identification and assertion of copyright, whether their practice is located in the artistic mainstream or not.

This brief describes the legal requirements for copyright authorship and ownership, and how it can be used to help to drive artistic practices towards sustainable business models as recommended by the Arts Council.[1]

Why Copyright?

The government is withdrawing funding from the arts and encouraging artists to consider commercial exploitation of their works as one alternative.[2] Copyright laws are specifically designed to manage and regulate the use by others of one's creative work, including use for commercial purposes.[3]

In this context, legal authorship and ownership of the dance is relevant on two counts. First, copyright management is one of the entrepreneurial skills the Arts Council is advocating as a way forward for the artist to sustain her art. Second, exploitation of copyright can provide a source of income. Royalties could be earned when the work is disseminated through a variety of media including on the television and the Internet. With the creative ways in which works can now be exploited, such as royalties earned when YouTube videos are viewed, the possibilities for diversification of income streams based on copyright are many.

In addition to economic prerogatives, copyright authorship also grants artists a moral control over their work. Moral rights allow them to ensure that the integrity of their pieces is respected, and that they are identified as the author of the dance.[4]

Who is the Author of the Dance?

Dance artists must comply with three conditions to be recognised as legal author of a choreographic piece. First, the work must fit in one of the categories of protectable works (categorisation requirement).[5]

Second, the work has to be fixed in writing or otherwise (fixation requirement).[6] Third, the eligible work must be original (originality requirement).

In the context of dance works, the categorisation requirement is easily satisfied. Choreographic works are listed in the legislation as protectable dramatic works and are, as such, eligible for legal protection.[7]

Similarly, dance artists will have little issue complying with the originality condition. What the law means by 'originality' has nothing to do with 'novelty'. For a work to be considered as 'original' it has not to be the copy or the mere trivial derivation of a protected work.[8] This is a low level of originality that may be changing through the influence of European law to a slightly higher standard. Nonetheless, the works created by dancers with disabilities will have no difficulty in meeting this definition. It should be noted here that dance steps as such will not be protectable; neither will well-known dances such as ballroom dancing and the Tango. What is protectable is the combination of steps in new ways.

Finally, the choreographic work has to fulfil the fixation requirement. To be protected the dance must be fixed, such as via notation or through video recording. The 'fixed' version will be considered by many to be an incomplete account of the work, but the fixation requirement exists to serve a legal purpose rather than to give a true, artistic, account of the work.

It is our contention that a disabled dance artist who interprets the work of a choreographer will expend sufficient originality in the work to be considered an author of the copyright in the arrangement of the dance on her body, while the choreographer will be considered to be the author of the copyright in the choreography.

Because copyright law focuses on the work, and not on the personal attributes of the author, it makes no difference if the dancer is disabled or not.

Who Owns the Copyright in the Dance?

Our legislation states that the author of the copyright in a work is the author. That is unless the work has been created by an employee during employment, or if there is an agreement that a third party should own the copyright. In a dance performed by a dancer with disabilities and choreographed by a choreographer there will therefore be two copyrights: one in the choreography – or composition – belonging to the choreographer; and one in the interpretation – or arrangement – belonging to the dancer with disabilities.

Conclusion

Dance artists should be made aware of their rights and what it means to be a legal author and owner of the copyright in the dance.

Recommendations

1. Dance artists should understand what it means to be the author and owner of copyright in a dance.
2. Dance artists should engage with the management of copyright with a view to securing potential income streams.
3. Dance artists should ensure that their work is fixed (video record for instance) to ensure the subsistence of copyright.

Should you require further information please contact Professor Charlotte Waelde, ac2450@coventry.ac.uk.

August 2014

Notes

1 Waelde, C., Whatley, S. and Pavis M. (2014), 'Let's dance! But who owns it?', *European Intellectual Property Law Review*, 36, p. 217.
2 'In 2010–2011 public grant in aid funding to the Arts Council stood at £450 million. In 2011–2012 it as reduced by 14 per cent to £388 million; in 2012–2013 by 7.5 per cent to £359 million; in 2013–2014 by 3 per cent to £348 million; and in 2014–2015 it will be reduced to £343 million' (Waelde et al. 2014).
3 See Chapter II Sections 16–27, Copyright Designs and Patents Act 1988.
4 See Chapter IV Sections 77–89, Copyright Designs and Patents Act 1988.
5 Section 1, Copyright Designs and Patents Act 1988. Although this requirement has been loosened in 2011 by the European Court of Justice in its *BSA case* (Case C-393/09), a recent

case *Taylor v. Macguire* paper-cutting work insisted on qualifying the work at stake when considering its eligibility to copyright protection. See *Taylor v. Macguire* (2013) EWHC 3804 (IPEC).

6   Section 3.2, Copyright Designs and Patents Act 1988.

7   Copyright Act 1911 s.35.1: '"Dramatic work" includes any piece for recitation, choreographic work or entertainment in dumb show, the scenic arrangement or acting form of which is fixed in writing or otherwise, and any cinematograph production where the arrangement or acting form or the combination of incidents represented give the work an original character'. Now under Section 3.1d, Copyright Designs and Patents Act 1988: 'dramatic work' includes a work of dance or mime' (Waelde et al. 2014: 223, *supra* note 1).

8   Of a protected work or work whose protection has expired.

Policy Brief: For Dancers

The InVisible Difference: Dance, Disability and Law project is an Arts and Humanities Research Council-funded project that is exploring issues confronted by professional disabled choreographers and ownership and authorship of their work.

Project Overview

Running from January 2013 to December 2015, ours is an interdisciplinary partnership between academics in Higher Education and artists working in the creative industry. Members of the project are: Professor Sarah Whatley, Coventry University; Professor Charlotte Waelde, University of Exeter; Dr Abbe Brown, University of Aberdeen; Dr Shawn Harmon, University of Edinburgh; Dr Karen Wood and Hannah Donaldson, research assistants; Mathilde Pavis and Kate Marsh, doctoral candidates and dance artist Caroline Bowditch. During the course of our research we are conducting qualitative research with disabled choreographers and dancers, including Caroline Bowditch, Claire Cunningham, Marc Brew, Chisato Minamimura and others. We also have strong links with Candoco dance company and other independent disabled dancers.

Introduction

The development and application of human rights and disability laws is a key part of the InVisible Difference project. The results of our research, and proposals for policy change, are being shared as the project progresses, including through other policy briefs, including the UN Convention on the Rights of Persons with Disabilities.[1]

The aim of this policy brief is to make the dance community aware of the legal tools of human rights and disability laws, and to suggest how they might be pursued in a range of situations, some of which are being explored by the project: from seeking the availability of performance and rehearsal space to the search for funding, and from the need for more inspirational leaders and peer groups to the application of copyright law when dancers with different bodies recast an established piece of dance.

Discussion

Human rights treaties include rights relevant to dance. International and European treaties have rights to expression[2] and to share in cultural life[3] and rights against discrimination[4] There is also the dedicated international Convention on the Rights of Persons with Disabilities, which includes a right against discrimination on the basis of disability, a right of equal access to the physical environment, and rights to freedom of expression and participation in cultural life.[5] Accordingly, people who wish to dance should be able to do so – irrespective of their bodies. Bringing this about is not, however, straightforward.

The treaties confer rights on individuals (e.g. dancers) against states (e.g. UK). The United Kingdom has taken some useful steps: the Unlimited programme,[6] the Arts Council of England's Disability Equality Scheme[7] and Creative Scotland's Dance Agent for Change.[8] Yet if a dancer considers progress to be inadequate, he/she cannot make a direct application to the local court to require the state to act to ensure that their rights are respected. Rather, international committees monitor a state's respect for its obligations, on the premise that if a state is considered not to have met its obligations, the state will change its practice when this is pointed out, and inquiries can be made into the behaviour of states.[9] Dance and creativity have not yet received significant attention in the monitoring process or in the reports made by states. The InVisible Difference team have criticised the Initial State Report made by the United Kingdom[10] for its lack of reference to dance and disability, or attention to cultural inclusion.[11] Under the specific Disability Convention, a dancer could also make an individual complaint to the international body about the UK's (in)action,[12] but there have not yet been any examples of this.

Given the focus on states, the dancer cannot complain directly to other individuals or companies who are involved (say, choreographer, manager of performance space with no ramp or operator of development programme). In the United Kingdom, however, human rights arguments can be made on a more individual level if a dispute is before a court on another basis, say a different piece of legislation, and human rights can influence the decisions made.[13] Possible bases for the action might be a copyright dispute between a dancer with a different body and the choreographer of the original piece of work,[14] or a complaint based on the Equality Act 2010.

The equality legislation means that providers of services to the public must make reasonable adjustments to ensure that their services are equally available to all.[15] One possibility for dancers could be the argument that accessible performance space must be made available, or spaces on a development programme are to be allocated to people with disabilities, together with appropriate support, for example, an interpreter. If the court route is taken, ultimately this could lead to applications being made by dancers to the European Court of Human Rights in Strasbourg, arguing that the United Kingdom has not met its obligations to them.[16]

Court actions are slow and expensive. Further, the treaties do also include human rights, which might support the position of those the dancer wishes to challenge (say, right to property or copyright of the choreographer of a work which a disabled dancer would like to remake[17] or the right to property of the manager of a dance space who argues that they cannot afford ramps).[18] This, together with likely arguments about what is reasonable adjustment (does it include the provision of interpreters to ensure that dancers without speech can participate fully in a leadership programme?) means that the outcome cannot be predicted. Nonetheless, a well-resourced and robust legal team and a determined litigant could bring about an outcome which could benefit all dancers with different bodies.

There is also another role for human rights. Alongside court proceedings, they can contribute to more collaborative activity, to advocacy and thought leadership. The language of rights, rather than merely the language of desire or fairness, worked effectively in arguments for new exceptions to copyright in respect of some print impairments[19] – though it had less success in the UK objections to the bedroom tax,[20] disability assessments[21] and cuts to the Access to Work scheme.[22] Activist steps could lead to a wider, more engaged approach to dance, culture and creativity for all, without the need for a court to tell people what to do.

Conclusions

Human rights and disability laws provide useful opportunity for dancers, which can be pursued through activism and through the courts. Together, they can contribute to important changes in approach.

Recommendations

The following recommendations can combine to deliver change and create a new environment:

1. When applying for funding, services and leadership opportunities: refer to human rights and disability laws and the rights and responsibilities they create.
2. If you involved in a copyright dispute: make human rights arguments.
3. If you are unhappy about decisions of service providers, and have time and money: raise a court action against a provider or funder on the basis of the UK Equality Act and include human rights arguments.

If you are unhappy about decisions in UK courts and have time and money: consider application to European courts and international bodies.

If you are unhappy about specific instances of the dance and disability landscape in the United Kingdom: consider an individual complaint to the Committee on the Rights of Persons with Disabilities.

Needless to say, only an introduction to these points can be provided here.

If you would like further details, do feel free to contact Dr Abbe Brown, University of Aberdeen, abbe.brown@abdn.ac.uk. We should also be delighted to share your experiences of these (and other) avenues on our website.

Notes

1   See generally briefing papers section on Publications section of project website, http://www.invisibledifference.org.uk/research/publications/.
2   Article 10 European Convention on Human Rights (ECHR) , article 11 EU Charter of Fundamental Rights (EU Charter), and article 19 International Convention on Civil and Political Rights (ICCPR).
3   Article 15.1a International Convention on Economic Social and Cultural Rights (ICESCR).
4   Article 14 ECHR, Article 21 EU Charter, Article 2.2 and Article 2.1 ICCPR.
5   Article 3b, 4, 5, 9, 21, 30, Convention on the Rights of Persons with Disabilities.
6   http://weareunlimited.org.uk/.
7   http://www.artscouncil.org.uk/publication_archive/disability-equality-scheme-2010-13/.
8   http://www.scottishdancetheatre.com/index.php?pid=126.
9   Committee on Rights of Persons with Disabilities, http://www.ohchr.org/en/hrbodies/crpd/pages/crpdindex.aspx. Human Rights Committee re. ICCPR, http://www.ohchr.org/en/hrbodies/ccpr/pages/ccprindex.aspx. Committee on Economic, Social and Cultural Rights, http://www.ohchr.org/EN/HRBodies/CESCR/Pages/CESCRIndex.aspx.
10 Accessible via http://tbinternet.ohchr.org/_layouts/treatybodyexternal/Download.aspx?symbolno=CRPD%2fC%2fGBR%2f1&Lang=en.
11 A submission has been made to the Minister for Disabled People by Charlotte Waelde on behalf of the InVisible Difference Team challenging this and calling for more engagement with and acknowledgement of activities ongoing in dance and disability in the UK. A copy can be found at http://www.invisibledifference.org.uk.
12 See www.ohchr.org/EN/HRBodies/CRPD/Pages/OptionalProtocolRightsPersonsWithDisabilities.aspx.
13 Section 3, Human Rights Act 1998.
14 Waelde, C. Whatley, S. and Pavis, M., (2014) 'Let's Dance! – but who owns it?', *European Intellectual Property Law Review*, 36, p. 217. Whatley, S. Waelde, C. Harmon, S. and Brown, A. (2014), 'Validation and virtuosity: Perspectives on difference and authorship/control in dance', *Dance Research Journal*, http://www.invisibledifference.org.uk/research/publications/.
15 Section 29 and Part 9, Equality Act 2010.
16 Once national avenues are exhausted. See http://www.echr.coe.int/Pages/home.aspx?p=applicants.

17 Protocol 1 article 1 ECHR, article 17.2 EU Charter, article 15.1c ICESCR.

18 Protocol 1 article 1 ECHR.

19 The Marrakech Treaty to Facilitate Access to Published Works for Persons who are Blind, Visually Impaired, or otherwise Print Disabled 2013.

20 See Disability Rights UK webpage, 'The Bedroom Tax', http://www.disabilityrightsuk.org/bedroom-tax.

21 Details of disability assessments at UK Government webpage https://www.gov.uk/government/policies/simplifying-the- welfare-system-and-making-sure-work-pays/supporting-pages/introducing-personal-independence-payment; and comment in *The Independent* (18 February 2014), http://www.independent.co.uk/news/uk/politics/atos-itself-not-fit-for-work-disability-benefit-test-provider-may-finally-have-contract-terminated-9136353.html.

22 See e.g. http://dpac.uk.net/.

Interruption 10

The Need for a Wide Approach

27 March 2017

Abbe Brown

*T*he key goal of this project is to raise awareness, to improve capacity and increase willingness to explore links between dance and disability and different forms of law. When one is within one of these fields (for me, law) and has had the privilege of working with experts in others, it is deceptively easy to think that the importance of this exercise is obvious. For this reason it is always useful to be challenged to move out of one's own comfort zone. I experienced this when attending a presentation at the University of Aberdeen on 24 February organised by the active Elphinstone Institute (itself a strong advocate of public engagement, https://www.abdn.ac.uk/elphinstone/) by Ella Leith (@Leithyface) on 'Storytelling without Sound: Traditional Deaf Motifs and Performance in British Sign Language ("BSL")'. Dr Leith of the University of Edinburgh led discussion on deaf folklore to an audience split fairly equally between the hearing and the non-hearing, with most of the non-hearing communication being in British Sign Language.

As well as being a fascinating intellectual exploration of a new area (including hearing that an important figure in deaf history is the Muta Domina, whose tomb in Dalkeith is next to where my sons used to go to nursery), I gained two things. First, a sobering understanding of the past and present challenges of people who do not hear; of decisions made for these people regarding their education, their communication pathways and their community by the hearing majority. Second, a rich demonstration of the existing parallel culture through sign languages (for example BSL) which are languages like any other, and also of deaf culture – a culture like any other with its rules, users, norms and practices. The culture and language are not adapted versions of the so called mainstream.

As I had attended Ella's event just after attending the Law Schools LGBTQ History event (https://en-gb.facebook.com/events/1842527585996308/), I spent the next few days in reflective mode. It is tempting, not least through lack of time, resource or knowledge, to operate within the area within which one is comfortable. To assume that some things are just the way they have to be. While understandable, there can be a thin line between this and exclusion of others, and the entrenchment of structures which enable this. To avoid this, there is a need for crossing barriers, facilitating discussion, usable education and appreciation of the activity of others. This can build a foundation for respect, analysis and debate – rather than patronising tolerance or looking the other way.

This was my main takeaway from the two events I attended on that Tuesday evening. It is one of the themes emerging in a Wellcome funded project which also has some of its roots in InVisible Difference – Identity and Governance of Bodily Extensions, http://www.pci.leeds.

ac.uk/research/featured-research-projects/identity-and-governance-of-bodily-extensions-the-case-of-prosthetics-and-avatars/, which explores extensions of self in both limb prosthetics and digital avatars. And it is of course the goal of this project notably through its toolkit and documentary, to increase usable, open and critical engagement within and around disabled dance.

Interruption 11

Golden Age?

1 March 17

Sarah Whatley

*A*s we are planning the content for the toolkit and looking forward to the film being finished, much is happening in parallel with this project. For example, two of our Ph.D. students in C-DaRE, Vipavinee Artpradid and Kathryn Stamp, are tracking People Dancing's 11 Million Reasons project. The project, multi-stranded, is rooted in a photographic exhibition of disabled dancers reconstructing images inspired by iconic dance moments in film, photographed by Sean Goldthorpe, including for example, The Red Shoes, The Black Swan and Dirty Dancing. In tandem with the exhibition, which is touring to a number of UK locations, several engagement activities are introducing new audiences to disability in dance through performances aligned with the exhibition by leading dance artists in conjunction with performances by local dancers, and accompanying workshops. The aim of the exhibition is to positively profile deaf and disabled people who dance and the project overall is designed with the aim of challenging and changing audience perceptions of disability in dance. Visitors are invited to respond to the exhibition in a photo booth to capture their experiences and reflections. Kathryn, funded through an AHRC Collaborative Doctoral Award, is involved in evaluating the project as a whole as well as examining how the project sits within People Dancing's wider strategy for supporting inclusion in dance. Two of the artists who feature in the photographs and have been performing as part of the wider aims of the project, Kate Marsh and Welly O'Brien, are beginning a research residency at Critical Path, Australia, and Kate, who is also now a researcher in C-DaRE and involved in our project may well report on their visit on her return http://criticalpath.org.au/program/international-research-residency/. Then there is the National Disability Arts Collection and Archive (NDACA) that has raised some questions about the focus on archiving work from what has been termed the 'golden age' of Disability Arts, identified as being during the 1980s and 1990s, http://www.bbc.co.uk/news/disability-35063050. Disabled artists and commentators have questioned this term. If there was a 'golden age' of the past, what about the present and the future? Does Disability Arts have to accept that the good times are over, that we have to look back and not forwards? The artwork that emerged during that time, named 'protest art', was certainly powerful and the archive project, funded by the Heritage Lottery Fund, is intended to preserve and make visible some of this work that captured the energy of the time and expressed the frustrations of artists. But whilst this was a time of exciting art, the work of today's artists is no less so, if concerned with other themes of protest or simply with making good art. Wider questions about what should be preserved, who preserves, what is included and what is left out, are always raised in the context of archives. But disabled dancers are largely absent from our records of cultural heritage so with the increase in methods and resources to store and make their content available and accessible, we can be optimistic that this *is changing – and maybe the NDACA project will prompt other archive projects that focus on dance. However, as with 11 Million Reasons, but in a different way, the NDACA project might be experienced as a project of nostalgia. And I know that people with disabilities can distrust nostalgia if it creates a sentimental and fictionalised past, which was not a better time. Others have described nostalgia as not always about the past but as a 'projective prologue' whereby motives are projected on the future, producing a different kind of fantasy and fiction. We need to retain a healthy relationship with the past; life was not better for people with disabilities. The future will no doubt be flawed but the work by disabled dance artists today continues to be about human rights – and the creation and promotion of good art.*

Interruption 12

Disabled Dancers: Agents of Change?

14 March 2017

Shawn Harmon

s with those posts preceding it, this blogpost is inspired by my involvement in the AHRC project, 'Resilience and Inclusion: Dancers as Agents of Change', itself a follow-on to the InVisible Difference project. And as Blades notes in her preceding blog (Blades 2016), our belief and ambition in this project is that disabled dancers are and ought to be recognised as leaders and agents of change. However, again as Blades suggests, agency is not at all straightforward; it is tangled up with social frameworks. What are the measures of agency that we might rely on to make judgments about whether the field is moving appropriately forward (and whether the project is achieving its aims)?

Writing in the context of development and social justice, Sen argues that agency is a person's ability to act in support of what she values and has reason to value, and that it (agency) is both intrinsically and instrumentally valuable (1985). People with high levels of agency can more readily pursue actions congruent with their values, and those without it may be alienated from their reality, or be forced to submit to conditions that they decry (Ryan and Deci 2004). So understood, agency clearly has both internal and external elements, but what elements exist and what do we need to attend to in the context of disabled dance to realise the objective of agency for change? Sen offers five measures for analysing agency; according to Sen, agency:

1. *is exercised in relation to one's wellbeing and goals;*
2. *must be supported by 'effective power' (i.e. the power to achieve desired goals); though this may be exercised by a group rather than an individual, the individual must have the ability to influence processes and exercise choice;*
3. *requires 'capability' (i.e. the space within which individuals might exercise 'wellbeing freedom', which itself might be other-regarding);*
4. *is appropriately associated not only with values, but with goals the individual has a reason to value (and so might be differentiated substantively from raw autonomy); and*
5. *is associated with responsibility to understand one's role in the prevailing conditions as well as that in realising alternative (better) conditions (Sen 1985).*

There has been some laudable work in support of raising the profile of disabled dance, and expanding the opportunities for disabled dancers, but what is the current state of the disabled dancer's agency in relation to these measures?

Our findings in the InVisible Difference project offer some grounds to believe that disabled dancers have made significant strides in (1) systematically advancing a reasonably cohesive set of goals; (4) articulating cogent and both culture- and rights-based reasons to value those goals; and (5) appreciating the responsibility that leadership imposes on those (pioneers) who have wedged their way into the conscience of the elite dance scene and the dance-viewing public. However, the InVisible Difference project has also demonstrated that disabled dancers are incredibly under-resourced and under-supported with respect to measures (2) and (3), a reality which continues to undermine the just advancement of their roles as creators of culture and agents of change.

This reality must be viewed as an affront to the human rights that disabled individuals/ dancers hold under the Universal Declaration of Human Rights, the UN Convention on the Rights of Persons with Disabilities, and the European Convention on Human Rights (and so the Human Rights Act 1998). And many actors have been complicit in the deficiencies that exist, from arts funders, to dance organisations, to memory institutions, to dance critics, and more (Whatley et al. 2015). Disabled dancers need to be much more effectively facilitated in exercising their agency if they are ever to adequately perform their desired, demanded and deserving role as 'agents of change' and equal creators of culture.

The Online Toolkit mentioned by Blades, and the associated film described by Brown (2016), both being developed in the Resilience and Inclusion project, are just two small steps in the many that are needed to realise this objective, another being further research to ascertain the state of the shortfalls in the above measures. Let us hope that more funding is made available to help generate the 'effective power' and to open up the 'capability spaces' that are so needed for real change to occur.

References

Blades, H. (2016), 'Narratives and agency', 4 December, https://invisibledifferenceorguk. wordpress.com/2016/12/04/narratives-and-agency/.

Brown, A. (2016), 'Words, bodies and film: The start of a journey', 16 December, https:// invisibledifferenceorguk.wordpress.com/2016/12/04/narratives-and-agency/.

Ryan, R. M. and Deci, E. L. (2004), 'Autonomy is no illusion: Self-determination theory and the empirical study of authenticity, awareness and will', in J. Greenberg, S. Koole and T. Pyszczynski (eds), *Handbook of Experimental Existential Psychology*, New York: Guilford Press, p. 450.

Sen, A. (1985), 'Wellbeing, agency and freedom: The 1984 Dewey lectures', *Journal of Philosophy*, 82, pp. 169–221, 206.

Whatley, S. Waelde, C., Harmon, S. and Brown, A. (2015), 'Validation and virtuosity: Perspectives on difference and authorship/control in dance', *Choreographic Practices*, 6, pp. 59–83.

Annex 1: Blog Postings

11 November 2015: Dance, Medicine and Marginalisation: The Limits of Law and a Shift to Values by Shawn Harmon

9 November 2015: Walk the Walk, Talk the Talk: A Critique of the Medical Model by Michel Foucault by Mathilde Pavis

6 October 2015: Understanding and Appreciation by Hetty Blades

14 September 2015: Digging Deep: Dance and Energy by Abbe Brown

14 September 2015: A Wider Significance for a Philosophy of Disabled Dance? by Shawn Harmon

29 July 2015: Disability Dance and Philosophy: Liminal Spaces by Charlotte Waelde

29 June 2015: Mainstream or Marginal? Still on the Edge… by Sarah Whatley

10 June 2015: Mainstream and Marginal: Have We Progressed in the Last Decade Plus? by Charlotte Waelde

1 June 2015: Dance and Cultural Heritage by Charlotte Waelde

26 May 2015: The UK General Election and the Future of Disabled Artists Part 2 by Kate Marsh

26 May 2015: The UK General Election and the Future of Disabled Artists Part 1 by Abbe Brown

27 April 2015: Recent Dance Activities and the Inclusion/Exclusion of Disabled Dance by Karen Wood

13 April 2015: Bourdieu, Habitus and the Disabled Dancer by Hannah Donaldson

30 March 2015: The Closure of the ILF by Sarah Whatley

10 March 2015: The Miniamura Saga – Part 3 by Mathilde Pavis

10 February 2015: Experiences on InVisible Difference by Kate Marsh

11 December 2013: Thoughts on the Intersections Forum by Hannah Donaldson

5 December 2013: Physically Being Me by Karen Wood

3 December 2013: International Day for Persons with Disabilities by Hannah Donaldson

2 December 2013: The Body in Copyright by Mathilde Pavis

28 November 2013: Project Update by Sarah Whatley

21 November 2013: Difference? by Charlotte Waelde and the InVisible Difference team

14 November 2013: Time to Dance by Kate Marsh

8 November 2013: Project Experiences by Abbe Brown

4 November 2013: Qualitative Health Research Conference, Halifax by Shawn Harmon

14 October 2013: The DEMOS Report – Cultural Olympiad, One Year on… by Karen Wood

30 September 2013: Fieldwork with Caroline Bowditch by Hannah Donaldson

30 September 2013: Discourse Analysis by Hannah Donaldson

23 September 2013: Avoidance in the Academy 11–12 September 2013 by Hannah Donaldson

18 September 2013: Reflections on Hidcote by Sarah Whatley

19 August 2013: I Am Copying You, Can You Tell? by Mathilde Pavis

5 August 2013: Fieldwork by Hannah Donaldson

6 June 2013: Caroline Bowditch 'Love Games' by Hannah Donaldson

http://invisibledifference.org.uk/blog/

Annex 2: Policy Briefs

- **InVisible Difference, Policy Brief for Venues: Providing Space. Obligations and Approaches to Dancers with Different Bodies** Abstract: This policy brief contains guidance for owners and operators and venues.

- **InVisible Difference, Policy Brief Asserting Copyright** Abstract: This policy brief provides guidance on the legal requirements for copyright and ownership.

- **InVisible Difference, Policy Brief for Supporters of Dance** Abstract: This policy brief contains guidance to assist supporters of dance.

- **InVisible Difference, Policy Brief Collaboration and Copyright** Abstract: This policy brief provides guidance to dancers on issues surrounding collaboration and copyright.

- **InVisible Difference, Policy Brief A Bioethics Perspective Through Disabled Dance A Policy Brief for Ethics Educators and Practitioners** Abstract: This policy brief gives a summary of the bioethics perspectives within the InVisible Difference project.

- **InVisible Difference, Policy Brief for Dancers** Abstract: This policy brief provides guidance for disabled dancers on the legal tools available to them under human rights and disability laws.

- **InVisible Difference, Policy Brief: Copyright Royalties vs Public Funding for Dance Made and Performed by Dancers with Disabilities** Abstract: This policy brief contains guidance on royalties v public funding.

- **InVisible Difference, Policy Brief The UN Convention on the Rights of Persons with Disabilities** Abstract: This policy brief contains guidance on the impact of the UN Convention on the Rights of Persons with Disabilities.

- **InVisible Difference, Policy Brief Human Rights and Culture: Human Rights Obligations on States in Respect of Dance Made and Performed by Dancers with Disabilities** Abstract: This policy brief provides guidance on human rights and culture.

Consultation Papers and Responses

- **InVisible Difference, Department of Work and Pensions Response, Consultation Responses** Abstract: This document is a response from the Department of Work and Pensions dated 29 September 2014. It is a response to the briefing paper 'Policy Brief: The UN Disability Convention'.

- **InVisible Difference, Response to Arts Council England Funding Criteria by Members of InVisible Difference 2013–2015, Arts Council Response.**

- **InVisible Difference, Response to Arts Council England – The Value of Arts and Culture to People and Society, Arts Council Response.**

- **Waelde, C. and Brown, A., Submission to Inquiry: Creative Industries Scotland 2015, Inquiry: Creative Industries in Scotland** Abstract: This document was submitted in 2015 and is a response to a parliamentary inquiry on the creative industries in Scotland.

Notes on Contributors

Margaret Ames is senior lecturer in the Department of Theatre, Film and Television at Aberystwyth University where she teaches ensemble, devising and body work on the theatre studies curriculum. Her research is carried out through practice with participants who together form the dance-theatre company Cyrff Ystwyth. This work explores the aesthetic and political implications of theatre work made by people with learning disabilities and contributes to the growing research field of performance and disability. She was previously a contributor to the work of former Wales based theatre company Brith Gof and artistic director of the community dance project for the West of Wales, Dawns Dyfed Dance. She has also worked in adult psychiatry and was a senior registered dance movement therapist. Her writing appears in *Performance Research, Theatre Studies International, Studies in Theatre and Performance* and *The Journal of Arts and Communities*.

Adam Benjamin was joint founder and artistic director of Candoco Dance Company and a pioneer of integrated dance. A long time improviser and a founder member of 'Five Men Dancing', he has performed and taught with Kirstie Simson, Rick Nodine, Kim Itoh, Jordi Cortés and Russell Maliphant. His book *Making an Entrance* (Routledge, 2002) is considered a seminal text and he has written extensively on integrated practice and improvisation. Adam has choreographed for community groups and professional companies around the world. He founded the award winning Tshwaragano Dance Company, the first South African dance company integrated on both racial and disability lines. In Ethiopia he developed the integrated strand for the Adugna Dance Theatre Company. He has received numerous awards in dance (TimeOut, Sainsburys and Prudential with Candoco). He has been an associate artist at The Place, a Wingate Scholar, Rayne Fellow and recipient of an Arts Council International Artist Fellowship. He was awarded a National Teaching Fellowship in 2013 and was named a *Change Maker*, by the South Bank Centre in 2015. As a lecturer at Plymouth University (2008–17) he advised on the design of the new fully accessible theatre The House.

Hetty Blades is research fellow in the Centre for Dance Research (C-DaRE) at Coventry University. Her research considers the philosophical questions posed by dance's circulation on and offline. She was research assistant on Resilience and Inclusion: Dancers as Agents of

Change and is co-investigator on the AHRC-funded project Performing Empowerment: Dance, Disability and Inclusive Development in Post-War Sri Lanka.

David Bolt is associate professor and has a first-class degree, an award for excellence, and an AHRC-funded doctorate from the University of Staffordshire. He has been working at Liverpool Hope University since 2009 where he is director of the Centre for Culture & Disability Studies, and teaches disability studies and special educational needs. David is founding editor-in-chief of the *Journal of Literary & Cultural Disability Studies* (Liverpool University Press), and co-editor of the book series *Literary Disability Studies* (Palgrave Macmillan). He is on the board of *Disability & Society*, the *Journal of Visual Impairment and Blindness* and the *Journal of Language and Discrimination*, and is an executive board member of *Considering Disability*. David is founder of the International Network of Literary & Cultural Disability Scholars and was the first Honorary Research Fellow in the Centre for Disability Research at the University of Lancaster.

David co-edited *The Madwoman and the Blindman: Jane Eyre, Discourse, Disability* (Ohio State University Press, 2012) and *Disability, Avoidance, and the Academy: Challenging Resistance* (Routledge, 2015), and is co-guest editor of the special issue 'Theorising culture and disability: Interdisciplinary dialogues' (*Review of Disability Studies*, University of Hawaii at Manoa). He has published extensively internationally including journal articles, book chapters, special issues and works of creative writing. He is the author of *The Metanarrative of Blindness: A Re-Reading of Twentieth-Century Anglophone Writing* (University of Michigan Press, 2014) and editor of *Changing Social Attitudes Toward Disability: Perspectives from Historical, Cultural, and Educational Studies* (Routledge, 2014).

Abbe Brown is professor of law at the University of Aberdeen Her research and teaching focus on intellectual property, human rights and their intersection with other legal fields. Other key projects include 'Identity, Governance and Bodily Extensions' funded by the Wellcome Trust. Before returning to academia, Abbe practiced as a solicitor specializing in technology litigation in London, Melbourne and Edinburgh.

Nicola Conibere is senior lecturer in dance at Coventry University and Visiting Lecturer at Trinity Laban Conservatoire of Music and Dance. Her practice-based doctoral research explored choreography in relation to the politics of spectatorship, notions of publics and ideas of the social. She is a practising choreographer who shows her work internationally.

Claire Cunningham is a performer, maker and creator of multi-disciplinary performance. Originally a classically trained singer, she began to work in dance in 2005 and is now one of the UK's most acclaimed and internationally renowned self-identifying disabled artists, Cunningham's work is often rooted in the study and use/misuse of her crutches and the exploration of the potential of her own specific physicality with a conscious rejection of traditional dance techniques (developed for non-disabled bodies) or the attempt to move with the pretence of a body or aesthetic other than her own. Claire's work combines multiple artforms and ranges from the intimate auto-biographical solo *ME (Mobile/Evolution)*, to the large-scale *Menage a Trois* made in partnership with Gail Sneddon and National Theatre of Scotland, and includes the large ensemble work *12* made for Candoco Dance Company. In 2014, she created a new solo: *Give Me a Reason to Live*, and the full length show *Guide Gods*. She is former artist-in-residence at the Women of the World Festival at the Southbank Centre and of the Ulster Bank Belfast Festival at Queens. In 2016 she was artist-in-residence at the Perth International Arts Festival in Australia and associate artist at Tramway, Glasgow and is a factory artist with Tanzhaus NRW, Germany, 2017–19.

Catherine Easton is senior lecturer in law at Lancaster University. She researches in the areas of technology law, intellectual property and access for disabled people. Her work examines international law and policy relating to Internet accessibility and universal design. Catherine is co-chair of the Internet Rights and Principles Internet Governance Forum dynamic coalition and is currently chair of the British and Irish Law, Education and Technology Association. She is the general editor of the *European Journal of Current Legal Issues*, Europe's oldest open access online law journal. Catherine teaches and supervises in the areas of intellectual property law and Internet law.

Bree Hadley is associate director of the Creative in the Creative Industries Faculty at Queensland University of Technology, where she is also head of studies for a range of postgraduate courses in design, digital media, arts management, marketing and advertising, entrepreneurship and innovation. Hadley's research has appeared in her most recent book *Disability, Public Space Performance & Spectatorship: Unconscious Performers* (Palgrave), and in many scholarly journals, including *Performance Research, About Performance, Liminalities, Australasian Drama Studies, Brolga: An Australian Journal About Dance, M/C Media and Culture Journal, Scope: An Online Journal of Film and Television Studies, Asia Pacific Journal of Arts and Cultural Management* and *Journal of Further and Higher Education*. She is currently working on two book projects, one on *Theatre, Social Media and the Democratisation of Spectatorship*, and one on *The Performativity of Pranks – Dark Play, Spectatorship and Subversive Social Practice*. Hadley has also written extensively for newspapers and online platforms such as The Australian, ArtsHub and Australia Stage Online. Hadley is immediate past president and now treasurer of the Australasian Association for Drama, Theatre and Performance Studies (ADSA), a Director of Performance Studies international (PSi), and a nationally recognised commentator on all forms of drama, theatre and performance as a result of her role as a critic for The Australian, judge for the Matilda Awards, and committee member and consultant to many arts agencies, organisations and festivals.

Shawn Harmon is reader in law at the Edinburgh University, where he specialises in medical law and ethics, health research regulation and interdisciplinary research around the partnering of the arts and the humanities for discovering new insights into social and legal conditions. He has published in numerous international journals, his research has been funded by the AHRC, the ESRC, the Wellcome Trust, the IMI and various University of Edinburgh funds. He is Joint editor-in-chief of *Medical Law International* and former editor-in-chief of *SCRIPT-ed*.

Catherine Long is London based artist who has been performing since 2002. She was artist-in-residence at the Institute of Cognitive Neuroscience, where she researched into the neurological processes and relays involved in visual, kinesthetic and proprioceptive relationships between bodies, specifically with knowing processes involved with knowing one's own body in and through the body of another. She intervenes into audience/performer relationships, drawing attention to the role of spectatorship in identity. Her recent work critiques the position of Disability Art relative to 'mainstream' art, as well as the training and representation of disabled dancers; Long has spent the last two years exploring and adapting movement vocabularies that prove challenging for her particular skeletal and muscular abilities in order to interrogate foundational suppositions of 'integrated' dance, in which a range of differently abled performers share the stage. She has received funding from organizations to include Arts Council England, Artsadmin, the Wellcome Trust and The Winston Churchill Memorial Trust. Catherine has performed nationally and internationally, including Tate Modern and Tate Liverpool, UCLA, UC Berkeley, The Kennedy Centre Washington DC, ICA Boston and Abrons Arts Centre NYC.

Heidi Mapley is an ESRC-funded student at Manchester Metropolitan University in the first year of a 2+6 Ph.D. programme. Her research will explore how the representation of disability in the early years classroom impacts on interpersonal relationships and identity. She is a core member of the Centre for Culture and Disability Studies at Liverpool Hope University, where she holds a BA in education (special educational needs), an MA in disability studies, and the Faculty of Education Prize for Best Performing MA Student 2017. Heidi has published in *Disability and Society*, *Considering Disability* and the *Journal of Literary and Cultural Disability Studies*.

Kate Marsh is dance-artist and teacher, her practice includes ongoing employment as an associate artist for Candoco Dance Company and visiting artist for Dance4. Performance work has included: *Prometheus Awakens* (Graeae), *Floor of the Forest* and *Set and Reset/Reset* (Candoco) alongside an ongoing performance/research collaboration with dance artist, Welly O'Brien. Kate has maintained a focus on dance pedagogy, teaching in a range of contexts. Alongside continuing aspects of her teaching and choreographic projects, she completed a Ph.D. at Coventry University in 2016. Kate's doctoral research explored the shifting role of the disabled dance artist with a focus on the development of disabled dancers undertaking leading roles in the sector.

Fiona Macmillan is professor of law at Birkbeck, University of London, and visiting professor of law at the University of Roma Tre and the University of Gothenburg. Her areas of research traverse intellectual property, cultural property and international economic law. She has extensive interdisciplinary collaborations in all these research areas, and is the co-director of the International Society for the History of Theory of Intellectual Property (ISHTIP, www.ishtip.org), which provides a forum for interdisciplinary work on intellectual property.

Eimir McGrath is researcher, lecturer and practitioner in several disciplines including dance, critical disability studies, psychotherapy and play therapy. Her current research interests focus on the role of creative arts in psychotherapy, critical analysis of perceptions of disability within society and the theoretical application of interpersonal neurobiology to the psychotherapeutic process. Her doctoral research focused on the intersection of, dance, critical disability studies and psychotherapy. Interpersonal neurobiology and contemporary attachment theory were utilized in order to challenge disablism through the use of dance as a vehicle for societal change. As a psychotherapist and play therapist specializing in attachment issues and complex trauma, she has worked in a wide variety of educational and clinical settings and also has extensive experience in working therapeutically with children and adults with disabilities. Somatic practice informs her therapeutic work. Her recent publications include 'Dancing with disability: An intersubjective approach' in *Disability and Social Theory. New Developments and Directions* (Palgrave McMillan, 2012); 'Group Play Therapy for children with multiple disabilities' in *Play Therapy Today: Contemporary Practice with Individuals, Groups, and Carers* (Routledge, 2014); 'The role of music and rhythm in the development, integration and repair of the self', in *Creative Psychotherapy: Applying the Principles of Neurobiology to Play and Expressive Arts-based Practice* (Routledge, 2016); and 'Creativity and the analytic condition: Art, play, drama and dance within a psychoanalytic frame' in *Being Human: The theories, practice and influence of Valerie Sinason* (Karnac, 2017).

Mathilde Pavis is researcher in law at the University of Exeter and completed her doctoral studies on the legal status of performing artists as part of the InVisible Difference team. Her research and teaching focuses on intellectual property law, more specifically copyright and neighbouring rights, and its interaction with other disciplines such as cultural heritage regulation, creativity research and disability studies. More recently, Mathilde was a John W. Kluge research fellow at the US Library of Congress in Washington, D.C., where she retraced the socio-legal status of artists with intellectual disabilities in the British and American societies from the end of the nineteenth century to present day.

Luke Pell, fascinated by detail, nuances of time, texture, memory and landscape, is an artist living in Scotland. Working in and in between space of dance, theatre and live art. Maker, curator and dramaturg he collaborates with other artists and organisations imagining alternative contexts for performance, participation and discourse that might reveal wisdoms for living. Noticing threads that weave between people and place his work takes form as intimate encounters, poetic objects, installations and designed environments – choreographies – for physical and virtual spaces. Underpinned by ongoing research into finding language for loss. His curatorial projects create spaces for artists and experts across disciplines to gather together to explore relationships between words and movement, periphery and community, arriving at new perspectives, articulations and understandings of what it is to be in the world, through interdisciplinary collaboration. Formerly head of learning and research with Candoco Dance Company, Luke has worked as a collaborator, dramaturg and writer with many of the UK's leading disabled artists including Marc Brew, Caroline Bowditch, Claire Cunningham, Rachel Gadsden, Catherine Long, Janice Parker Projects, Jo Verrent and Birds of Paradise Theatre Company.

Sita Popat is professor of performance and technology and deputy director of the Leeds Humanities Research Institute at the University of Leeds. Her research lies at the intersections between bodies and technologies, with particular interest in digital avatars and medical prosthetics. She is author of *Invisible Connections: Dance, Choreography and Internet Communities* (Routledge, 2006) and co-editor with Nicolas Salazar Sutil of *Digital Movement: Essays in Motion Technology and Performance* (Palgrave, 2015). She is associate editor of the *International Journal of Performance Art and Digital Media* (Taylor & Francis). In her spare time she enjoys playing online multiplayer games including *World of Warcraft* and *Guild Wars 2*.

Janice Richardson is associate professor at Monash University and is author of *Selves, Persons, Individuals: Philosophical Perspectives on Women and Legal Obligations* (Ashgate, 2004), *The Classic Social Contractarians: Critical Perspectives from Feminist Philosophy and Law* (Ashgate, 2009) and *Law and the Philosophy of Privacy* (Routledge, 2015). She is co-editor of Routledge's *Feminist Perspectives on Tort law* and *Feminist Perspectives on Law and Theory*, and has published extensively in journals, including: *Feminist Legal Studies, Law and Critique, Angelaki: Journal of the Theoretical Humanities, Minds and Machines: Journal for Artificial Intelligence,* and *Philosophy and Cognitive Science.*

Charlotte Waelde's focus of work lies at the interface between intellectual property law (particularly copyright) and changing technologies, the changes in the law wrought by those technologies, and the impact that those changes have on the way that the law is both perceived and used by the affected communities. Waelde's work reaches out into other domains including intangible cultural heritage, human rights, competition law, international private law and the regulation and promotion of new technologies more generally as they intersect with my core interests. Waelde has written and spoken widely on these topics both in the United Kingdom and internationally. For more information see http://www.coventry. ac.uk/research/research-directories/researchers/professor-charlotte-waelde/.

Sarah Whatley is director of the Centre for Dance Research (C-DaRE) at Coventry University, UK. Her research interests extend to dance and new technologies, intangible cultural heritage, somatic dance practice and pedagogy, dance documentation, and inclusive dance practice; she has published widely on these themes. Her research is funded by the AHRC, European Commission and Leverhulme Trust. She is also founding editor of the *Journal of Dance and Somatic Practices* and sits on the editorial boards of several other journals.

Karen Wood is a dance practitioner/researcher/educator. Her research has a practical perspective – the training principles of dancers, teaching dance techniques, somatic work – and a theoretical perspective considering embodiment and audiences experiences of dance. She has worked on artistic projects, supported by Arts Council England, collaborating with other art forms, such as fine art, lighting design and music. For the InVisible Difference project, she was the part-time Research Assistant and is interested in how disabled choreographers contribute to our cultural heritage.

Index